WITHDRAWN
UTSA LIBRARIES

THE
DOMESDAY OF INCLOSURES
1517–1518
VOL. II.

KENNIKAT PRESS SCHOLARLY REPRINTS
Dr. Ralph Adams Brown, Senior Editor

Series on
ECONOMIC THOUGHT, HISTORY AND CHALLENGE
Under the General Editorial Supervision of
Dr. Sanford D. Gordon
Professor of Economics, State University of New York

THE
DOMESDAY OF INCLOSURES
1517–1518

BEING THE EXTANT RETURNS TO CHANCERY FOR BERKS
BUCKS, CHESHIRE, ESSEX, LEICESTERSHIRE, LINCOLNSHIRE
NORTHANTS, OXON, AND WARWICKSHIRE
BY THE COMMISSIONERS OF INCLOSURES IN 1517
AND FOR BEDFORDSHIRE IN 1518

TOGETHER WITH

*DUGDALE'S MS. NOTES of the WARWICKSHIRE INQUISITIONS
IN* 1517, 1518, *AND* 1549

EDITED FOR THE ROYAL HISTORICAL SOCIETY
WITH NOTES AND TABLES
BY
I. S. LEADAM, M.A., F.R.Hist.S., F.S.S.
FORMERLY FELLOW OF BRASENOSE COLLEGE, OXFORD

IN TWO VOLUMES——VOL. II.

KENNIKAT PRESS
Port Washington, N. Y./London

THE DOMESDAY OF INCLOSURES

First published in 1897
Reissued in 1971 by Kennikat Press
Library of Congress Catalog Card No: 74-137958
ISBN 0-8046-1460-1

Manufactured by Taylor Publishing Company   Dallas, Texas

KENNIKAT SERIES ON ECONOMIC THOUGHT,
HISTORY AND CHALLENGE

CONTENTS

OF

THE SECOND VOLUME

	PAGE
THE INQUISITION OF 1517 FOR WARWICKSHIRE	389
THE INQUISITION OF 1518 FOR BEDFORDSHIRE	454
APPENDICES I.–IX. :— PARALLEL AND ILLUSTRATIVE MANUSCRIPTS	477
STATISTICAL TABLES — BERKSHIRE	500
STATISTICAL TABLES — BUCKINGHAMSHIRE	570
THE INQUISITION OF 1517 FOR CHESHIRE	640
THE INQUISITIONS 1517, 1518 AND 1549 FOR WARWICKSHIRE FROM THE DUGDALE MSS.	645
INDEX	695

THE
DOMESDAY OF INCLOSURES,
1517

WARWICKSHIRE.

INTRODUCTION

THE Returns for Warwickshire appear to be complete. The total area presented as inclosed is 7,948 acres, besides 5,795½ acres ingrossed. This is a smaller area than any of the counties Berkshire, Buckinghamshire, Northamptonshire, and Oxfordshire, from which we have considerable Returns. From what Rous has told us of inclosures in Warwickshire [1] it may be suspected that this result is due less to a comparatively slow progress of inclosure in this county than to the fact that inclosure had advanced to a great extent at a comparatively early date.[2]

In Warwickshire we find, on the other hand, a larger area inclosed for parks, *i.e.* for sport, than in any of the other counties mentioned above, viz. 722½ acres. This may indicate a soil too poor to be worth careful cultivation or resident landowners sufficiently wealthy to be able to indulge in such luxuries. The wealth of landowners again suggests a developed system of inclosure;[3] which is probably the correct

[1] J. Rossi *Historia Regum Angliæ*, ed. T. Hearne, Oxon. 1745 (2nd ed.), fo. 110 b.

[2] Rous died January 14, 1491, only six years later than the earliest date of inclosure presented before this Commission.

[3] In 1847 it was remarked of this county, 'The extent of uninclosed land is very considerable. The only extensive commons are those of Sutton Coldfield and Sutton Park.'

explanation. The agricultural revolution was, even during the period within the limits of the Commission, being carried through more drastically than in Berkshire, Buckinghamshire, Northamptonshire, and Oxfordshire, the area inclosed to pasture bearing the proportion of 86 to that enclosed as arable, fractions being omitted.

Among the four Hundreds, that of Knightlow, which includes Coventry, on the east of the county, bordering on Northamptonshire, returns the largest area of inclosure, 3,106 acres in all, of which 2,872 are pasture, and only 234 arable, proportions of 92·4 and 7·5 per cent. respectively. The movement towards pasture was thus more pronounced than in the county generally. The same may be said of the Hundred which follows in the extent of area inclosed, that of Kington in the south-east of the county, where it juts out into Gloucestershire and Oxfordshire. Here 2,532½ acres are presented as inclosed, 2,278 to pasture, and 254½ to arable, proportions (fractions omitted) of 90 to 10 per cent. Yet Leland in his 'Itinerary,' which was made during the years 1536–32, twice insists upon this generalisation: 'I learned at Warwike that the most part of the Shire of Warwike that lyeth as Avon River descendeth on the right Hand or Ripe of it is in Arden . . . and the ground in Arden is much enclosed, plentifull of Grasse, but not of Corne. The other Part of Warwikeshire that lyeth on the left Hand or Ripe of Avon River, much to the South, is for the most part Champain, somewhat barren of Wood, but plentiful of Corne.'[1] This last applies particularly to the Hundred of Kington, with its 90 per cent. of inclosure to pasture between 1485 and 1517. What, then, must have been the actual proportion of corn to pasture land in the west of the county? Here, it may be inferred, the agricultural revolution had been mainly carried through before the accession of Henry VII. And this conclusion is strengthened by the Returns of the Inquisition. In the Hundred of Barlich-

---

[1] Ed. by T. Hearne, Oxford, 1744, iv. fo. 166 a. The same statement is made in slightly different language in viii. fo. 74 b, where the first 'lefte' is an evident blunder for 'right.'

way, in which Arden is situate, only 583½ acres are presented as inclosed, and of this 318½ acres only are inclosed to pasture as against 265 inclosed to arable, proportions (fractions omitted) of 54 and 45 per cent. respectively. The movement to inclosure in general and to conversion from arable to pasture in particular, was here clearly at an end.

In the county taken as a whole, the Table 'Yearly Progress of Inclosure' shows it to have been in full vigour in 1491–1500. During those years 170 acres are returned as inclosed to arable, against 2,856 acres inclosed and converted to pasture. Most of this was in the Hundreds 'on the left Hand or Ripe of Avon River,' Knightlow and Kington. The increase over the preceding six years was 142·85 per cent. of arable and 819·8 per cent. of pasture inclosed. But with this decade it is apparent that the movement of inclosure to pasture had spent its force. The following ten years (1501–10) show a decline of 6 per cent. in conversions to pasture only; the inclosure of arable land increased by 107·94 per cent. The septennate of 1511–17 shows a further decline of 54·91 per cent. of inclosed pasture. Considering the high prices of wheat and wool during those seven years, it can scarcely be doubted that the decline must have been connected with the legislation against inclosures, with this Inquisition, and with the subsequent proceedings against inclosers. The decline of 6 per cent. in 1501–10 is synchronous with a much heavier fall in the price of wool, and may be attributed to that cause, for inclosures of arable increased by 107·94 per cent., and this was accompanied by a rise of 7·8 per cent. (5s. 0¾d. to 5s. 5½d.) in the price of the quarter of wheat. In the septennate 1511–17 the only increase in any form of inclosure was of 42·2 in arable or ecclesiastical land. In inclosure to pasture there was a fall of 54·91 per cent.

The part played by inclosing ecclesiastics or their tenants in Warwickshire was not a great one. The total percentage of ecclesiastical to lay land inclosed is 15·72 to 84·27, exceeding by some 5 per cent. the proportion of inclosures upon ecclesiastical land in Buckinghamshire, but considerably below the 25·28 and 35 per cent. of Berks, Northants, and Oxfordshire respectively. The inclosures of ecclesiastical land had a slight tendency to the inclosure of arable rather than of pasture, being 19·04 per cent. of the whole arable inclosed. The same tendency has already been remarked in Bucks. The percentage of evictions and displacements from employment on ecclesiastical land is 18·71, a figure but slightly in excess of the proportionate area of ecclesiastical to lay land, but indicating, so far as it goes, that, as in Berkshire, Northants, and Oxfordshire, ecclesiastics or their tenants did not err on the side of indulgence. The Table 'Status of actual Inclosers' proves, however, that this rigour was due rather to the action of the tenants of ecclesiastical land than to the ecclesiastical landlords themselves. Still even these show a smaller area per person displaced than do the lay proprietors, an evidence that when they did embark upon agricultural improvements they were the more thorough of the two classes in their methods.

The Table of 'Number of Inclosures and Distribution of Areas according to Tenures and Tenancies' shows us that of the land in hand of owners 89·10 per cent. was in the hands of lay and 54·96 of ecclesiastical owners. This is a very large proportion and makes it clear that the ecclesiastics of Warwickshire were amongst the farming clergy of the period. When we come to examine the proportions in the hands of freeholders and manorial lords respectively, we come to the conclusion that the ecclesiastics in question were chiefly the dignified clergy and monastic houses, since these held 65·79 per cent. of the total ecclesiastical land in hand. The large proportion of 80·45 per cent. of the total of lay land which was in hands of the lay lords of manors shows a wealthy resident gentry, even to a greater extent than in Bucks and Leicestershire. While no mention of copyholds occurs, the fixity of tenure indicated by leaseholds appears to have advanced further on ecclesiastical than upon lay land, being 85·78 per cent. of ecclesiastical as contrasted with 62·73 per cent. of lay land let. The average areas inclosed on lay and ecclesiastical land were

38·49 as against 39·06, as nearly as possible equal. The same practical equality appears in the areas attached to messuagia. Minor tenants, the occupants of cottages, were somewhat better off upon lay land, with an average area attached of 8·28 acres, than upon ecclesiastical land, with an average area of 5·25 acres. The population was slightly thinner upon ecclesiastical land, being at the rate of five instead of six inhabitants to a messuage. In this respect Warwickshire is as Berks and Bucks. Judged by the number of persons dependent upon a ploughland, the standard of comfort on the two classes of estate was much the same. A ploughland of 37·5 acres supported 5·6 persons on lay land, one of 44·2 acres 7·3 persons on ecclesiastical land.

The rental values of lay land in Warwickshire are considerably higher than those of ecclesiastical land, being $1s.\ 5\frac{3}{4}d.$, as contrasted with $9\frac{1}{2}d.$ an acre. But it is to be observed that this difference is due, not to a greater indulgence on the part of ecclesiastical landlords to their tenants, but apparently to the inferior quality of the land held in hand by ecclesiastical owners. In fact, for arable the ecclesiastical landlords exacted a rent of $1s.$ an acre as compared with the $5\frac{1}{4}d.$ an acre for arable on lay land. The rent of lay pasture was $1d.$ an acre more than that of ecclesiastical pasture ($1s.\ 1\frac{1}{4}d.$ to $1s.\ 0\frac{1}{4}d.$), and the whole average rent of land let was only $\frac{1}{4}d.$ higher in the lay than in the ecclesiastical schedule.

INQUISITION OF 1517

WARWICKSHIRE

(Membrane 45)
W.irr[ewicus]

INQUISICIO INDENTATA capta apud allesley in predicto Comitatu Warrewici vicesimo secundo die Septembris [1] anno regni Regis henrici Octaui nono coram Iohanne Veysy decano Capelle dicti domini Regis et Rogero Wygston nuper de leicestria Comissionariis predicti domini Regis pretextu literarum patencium ipsius domini Regis eis confectarum et directarum ad inquirendum per sacramentum proborum et legalium hominum de Comitatu predicto tam infra libertates quam extra que et quot ville quot domus et edificia a Festo Sancti Michaelis archangeli anno regni illustrissimi domini henrici nuper Regis anglie septimi patris domini Regis nunc quarto prosternuntur et quot et quante terre que tunc in cultura erant et iam in pasturam conuertuntur necnon quot et quanti parci pro Feris nutriendis citra idem Festum includuntur et que terre aliquibus parcis vel alicui parco qui tunc fuerint aut fuerit pro elargacione huiusmodi parcorum includuntur et per quos vel per quem vbi quando qualiter et quo modo ac de aliis articulis et circumstanciis premissa qualitercumque concernentibus plenius veritatem assignatis per sacramentum henrici Squier Gentilman Nicholai Rugeley Gentilman Ricardi Mountford Gentilman Iohannis lysle Gentilman Roberti Redell de Colshill Ricardi Smyth de Nonneton Willelmi abell de Sheldon Willelmi Morecote de lemyngton Roberti Worsley Gentilman laurencii Eberall de Knoll Iohannis heyes de Wytnasse Thome lee de Solyhull Iohannis Glover de Meryvale Simonis Ryley de Braylys

[1] The 22nd September gave a margin of a month for the returns to Chancery (*Trans. R.H.S.* 1892, p. 265).

WARWICKSHIRE 395

Thome Fels de Kenelworth et Roberti Chariour de eadem proborum et legalium hominum predicti Comitatus Warrici Qui dicunt super sacramentum suum quod ^b Prior Monasterii de Malbourne¹ nuper fuit seisitus in dominico suo vt de feodo in iure Monasterii predicti de Sex Mesuagiis duobus Cotagiis et Centum et quateruiginti acris terre arrabilis cum pertinenciis in Shyttyngton² in Comitatu predicto vt de parcella sui Manerii siue Prioratus de alcote³ celle predicti Monasterii de Malbourne que quidem terra a tempore de quo non exstat memoria annuatim arrari et debitis temporibus vsu seminacionis granorum p[oni]^b solebat et fuit et cum quolibet Mesuagio⁴ Mesuagiorum predictorum de terra illa per totum dictum tempus viginti et quatuor acre terre ad minus arrabilis et culture apte ocupari tradi et dimitti ad Firmam solebant et fuerunt et predictus Prior sic inde seisitus ante sextum diem Marcii anno regni domini Regis nunc sexto tenementa illa cuidem ^c Willelmo Cartwright ad firmam pro termino certorum annorum dimisit per quod idem Willelmus in tenementa illa intrauit et inde fuit possessionatus ipseque sic inde possessionatus et predicto Priore sic inde seisito existente predictus Willelmus Cartwright predicto sexto die Marcii dicto anno sexto assensu et consensu predicti Prioris et per agreamentum et Conuencionem inter ipsum Priorem et dictum Willelmum antea factam predicta [Me]suagia^d Cotagia ad terram proiicire^e et in decasum cadere voluntarie permisit ac predictas terras arrabiles ab vsu Cultus granorum in pasturam pecorum conuertit et ea sic extunc semper

Prior de Malborn f[ac] scr[ibere] Gilez • r[espondeat] bil[le] lxxxiij

Scr[ibe] per Roodes r[espondere] Oct[aua]

^a MS. *f. scr. Giles ꝑ bil*.   ^b MS. partly illegible.   ^c Sic.
^d MS. mutilated : ' et ' omitted.

¹ ' Malbourne,' *i.e.* Great Malvern.
² Shuttenton, Dugdale. Now Shuttington.
³ ' Alcote.' In Dugd. *Monast.* iii. 455 Aucot or Avecote. Now Alcot. This entry is exceptional in stating what must have been the case upon the destruction of houses by leaseholders or by copyholders, that the assent of the immediate manorial lord was explicitly given. See *Trans. R.H.S.* 1893, pp. 128–131. The statement justifies the tables showing the ultimate responsibility attaching for the inclosures.
⁴ Note the cotagia, as in other Returns, without land : ' sine terris . . . tanquam cotagia,' p. 383, *supra*.

hucusque vsus est et custodit   Et dicunt quod tenementa predicta valent per annum vltra reprisas sex libras duos solidos et quatuor denarios et tenentur de domino Rege vt de Comitatu suo Warrewici   Et dicunt quod predictus Prior adhuc in iure Monasterii sui predicti seisitus existit in predictis terris et tenementis in forma predicta et quod racione permissorum sex aratra deponuntur et triginta et tres persone que circa culturam earundem terrarum ocupabantur abinde lamentabiliter recesserunt et minuuntur et [a]

Et Iuratores predicti dicunt quod predictus Prior nuper fuit seisitus in dominico suo vt de feodo in iure Monasterii predicti de quadraginta et duabus acris terre arrabilis cum pertinenciis et Cultui vsitate et [b] apte a[d a]nuum [c] valorem quadraginta solidorum in Shittyngton predicta in Comitatu predicto et sic inde seisitus tercio die Octobris anno regni Regis henrici Regis anglie Spetimi [c] octauo terras illas a priore inde vsu Cultus et iconomie in pasturam ouium et aliorum animalium conuertit et illis sic hucusque vsus est et terre ille tenentur de domino Rege et duo persone vt alias de consimilibus dicitur abinde recesserunt et minuuntur.

Et dicunt quod idem Prior nuper fuit seisitus in dominico suo vt de feodo in iure Monasterii predicti de triginta acris terre arrabilis et Cultui vsitate et [b] apte et valent per annum vltra reprisas quadraginta solidos in Shyttyngton in Comitatu predicto et sic inde seisitus octauo die Octobris anno regni predicti nuper Regis decimo octauo terras illas a priore inde vsu cultus et iconomie in pasturam ouium et aliorum animalium conuertit et illis sic hucusque vsus est et tenet ob quod sex persone minuuntur [1] et ab eorum occupacione in ocium aduertuntur et terre ille tenentur de domino Rege.

[a] Blank in MS.   [b] Thus struck through in MS.   [c] Sic.

[1] It does not follow that a house was destroyed either in this or in the preceding case. Such destruction involved penalties under the Act 4 Henry VII. c. 19 (see General Introduction, p. 6, *supra*).   I interpret 'minuuntur' here, as elsewhere, as indicating a diminution of the population and therefore an eviction. Dugdale's notice of these inclosures in his *Warwickshire* omits all direct mention of the land.   '[It] continued a pretty Village till about the beginning of K.H. VIII. time that the Monks of Aucote depopu-

Et dicunt quod idem Prior[1] nuper fuit seisitus in dominico suo vt de feodo in iure Monasterii predicti de decem acris terre arrabilis vocate le Brache et Cultui vsitate et apte ad anuum valorem xxvj s. viij d. in Shyttyngton in Comitatu predicto et sic inde seisitus quinto die Octobris anno regni predicti nuper Regis quinto terras predictas ab vsu Culture et seminacionis granorum in pasturam animalium conuertit et illas sic modo tenet et duodecim persone ab eorum occupacione[2] detrahuntur et in ocium ducuntur et tenentur de domino Rege.

Et dicunt vlterius quod Ricardus Varneham nuper fuit seisitus in dominico suo vt de feodo de vno Mesuagio et decem acris terre arrabilis et Culture apte in Shyttyngton in Comitatu predicto que quidem decem acre terre cum predicto Mesuagio pro seminacione granorum et arrura in eisdem terris habendis tradi et occupari solebant et predictus Ricardus sic de tenementis illis vt prefertur seisitus existens secundo die Octobris anno regni predicti nuper Regis duodecimo predictum Mesuagium voluntarie permisit ad terram cadere et predictas terras ad pasturam Ouium et aliorum animalium conuertit et illas sic adhuc tenet quam ob causam sex persone ibidem nuper manentes et laborantes abinde penitus in suam desolacionem recesserunt et tenementa illa valent per annum decem solidos   Et tenentur de[a]

[a] Blank in MS.

lated six Messuages and two Cottages therein; which I take to be a third part thereof (Inq. super Depop. 9 H. VIII.)' (*Warw.* p. 801, ed. 1775). Dugdale, however, can hardly fail to have read the whole of these entries, as the numerous citations of this Inquisition show. This carelessness must be borne in mind when differences occur between Dugdale's version and the original Returns.

[1] The list of the Priors of Gr. Malvern is chronologically defective in Dugdale. These four inclosures were not all the work of the same Prior. The sequence, as given by Dugdale, is: 'Richard Frewen, occurs 1480 and 1483. Maculinus Ledbury, 11 Feb. 1503. Thomas Keyworth, Jan. 5, 1506, occurs again in 1516.' To this last the first inclosure can be ascribed with certainty; but all the rest may have been the work of Frewen, though more probably the third, that of 1502, was by Ledbury (*Monast.* iii. 443).

[2] 'Occupacione' is not occupancy, but occupation (but see pp. 120, *n.* 3, 207, *n.* 2, *supra*).

398 THE DOMESDAY OF INCLOSURES, 1517

Dors[ett]

 Et dicunt quod Thomas nuper Marchio Darsett nuper fuit seisitus in dominico suo vt de feodo de decem Mesuagiis trescentis acris terre arrabilis et vsualiter arrate et seminacioni granorum posite in Wedyngton[1] in Comitatu predicto et cum quolibet Mesuagio Mesuagiorum predictorum viginti et sex acre terre de terris illis ad firmam tradi locari et occupari in cultura et iconomia a tempore cuius contrarii memoria hominum non existit solebant et fuerunt et sic seisitus sexto die Octobris anno regni predicti nuper Regis septimo tenementa predicta sepibus inclusit et illis sic in separalitate inclusis predicta Mesuagia voluntarie devastari et in ruinam existere permisit ita quod Mesuagia illa [totaliter deuastata][a]

ij. (Membrane 46) existunt et terras illas ad pasturam ouium et aliorum animalium conuertit per quod [b] aratra[2] deponuntur et sexaginta persone a mansionibus et occupacionibus suis ibidem recesserunt et in ocium perducti sunt Et dicunt quod Thomas nunc Marchio Dorsett modo seisitus existit de tenementis predictis Et quod valent per annum viginti sex libras Et tenentur de[c]

 Et iidem Iuratores dicunt quod Iacobus at holt armiger fuit seisitus in dominico suo vt de feodo de [quinquaginta acris terre arrabilis][d] cum pertinenciis in Manceter[3] in Comitatu predicto et sic inde seisitus septimo die Octobris anno regni predicti nuper Regis vicesimo primo terras illas a priore inde vsu Culture et iconomie ad pasturam Ouium et animalium conuertit et illis sic hucusque vsus est et tenet

---

[a] MS. illegible: text restored from Exch. Q.R. Mem. Roll 300, E.T. 12 H. VIII. (1520), m. 3.
[b] MS. illegible. A restoration of the text is not possible here, the recital in Exchequer Roll 300 ending at 'conuertit.'
[c] Blank in MS.
[d] MS. illegible: supplied from Dugdale's MS.

[1] Wedington, Dugdale. Now Weddington.
'Together with Astley, divolving to Grey, was inclosed, and for the most part depopulated by Thomas Grey, Marquess Dorset in 7 Henry VII., who decayed ten messuages here, whereunto belonged ccc Acres of Land (Inq. super Depop. 9 Henry VIII.)' (Dugdale, *Warwickshire*, p. 775).

[2] In Warwickshire the average number of persons to an aratrum on land in hand of lay lords of manors = 6, and the average area to an aratrum on such land = 36·36 acres. The first of these gives 10, the second 8 aratra. I adopt [9] as a mean number.

[3] Now Mancetter.

per quod vnum aratrum deponitur et tres persone minuuntur et ociosi existunt et terre ille tenentur^a

Et dicunt quod Ricardus Cave[1] fuit seisitus in dominico suo vt de feodo de quinquaginta ^b terre arrabilis Cultui vsitate et apte ad anuum valorem triginta et trium solidorum et quatuor denariorum in Manceter predicta in Comitatu predicto et sic inde seisitus quarto die Nouembris anno regni predicti nuper R[egis]^c vicesimo primo terras illas a Cultura et iconomia ad pasturam ovium et aliorum animalium conuertit et terris illis sic in pastura ad presens vtitur per quod vnum aratrum deponitur et sex persone que i[bidem]^d occupari solebant ea occasione ab occupacionibus suis ibidem recesserunt et ociosi existunt et terre ille tenentur de ^a

ET vlterius dicunt quod Willelmus Rowley nuper de Couentre humfridus [Alablaster]^e et Thomas harper de Meryvale fuerunt seisiti in dominico suo vt de feodo[2] de quinquaginta acris terre arrabilis et vsualiter arrate et seminacioni granorum posite in Manceter in Comitatu predicto ad annuum valorem triginta et trium solidorum et quatuor denariorum et sic inde seisiti tercio die Octobris anno vicesimo secundo predicti nuper Regis terras illas arrabiles ad firmam dimiserunt cuidam Iohanni Barkeby pro termino certorum nondum finitorum ^f virtute cuius dimissionis idem Iohannes de terris predictis fuit possessionatus et sic inde possessionatus existens tercio die Nouembris anno regni nuper Regis vicesimo tercio terras illas sepibus et Fossis inclusit et a priore inde vsu cultus et iconomie ad pasturam ouium et aliorum animalium conuertit et illis sic hucusque vsus est et tenet ob

Rowley Barkeby

lxxxiiij

^a Blank in MS.
^b Sic : 'acris' omitted.
^c MS. illegible.
^d Conjectural : MS. partly illegible.
^e MS. illegible : supplied from Dugdale's MS.
^f Sic : 'annorum' omitted.

[1] Richard Cave had bought a manor (a third part of the original manor) here in 1491 and exchanged it on July 20, 1517, for lands in Stormysworth, Leicestershire (Dugd. *Warw.* p. 762).

[2] William Harper, Nicholas Rowley, both of Manceter, and Thomas Arblaster of Longdon, co. Stafford, were jointly seised of a manor here (a third part of the original manor) in 10 H. VI. (1431-32) (*Ibid.*).

quam Causam vnum aratrum deponitur et sex persone minuuntur et ociosi existunt et terre ille tenentur de [a]

<small>Bonde f[iat] s[ub] p[ena]</small>

Et Iuratores predicti dicunt quod Iohannes Bonde de Couentre Draper fuit et adhuc existit seisitus in dominico suo vt de feodo de triginta acris terre pasture et boscis cum pertinenciis in parua Bromwyche[1] in Comitatu predicto et sic inde seisitus sexto die Marcii anno regni domini Regis nunc sexto terras illas Fossis sepibus et palis circumquaque inclusit et imparcauit et parcum nouum inde fieri fecit pro feris ibidem nutriendis et feras in eodem parco posuit et adhuc habet ac terras illas sic imparcatas adhuc tenet et a priori vsu illas mutauit et terre ille tenentur de [a] et valent per annum quadraginta et sex solidos et octo denarios.

<small>Cokeyn f[iat] s[ub] p[ena]</small>

ET DICUNT quod Thomas Cokayn Miles fuit et adhuc existit seisitus in dominico suo vt de feodo de Centum et quadraginta acris terre et bosci cum pertinenciis in Poley[2] in Comitatu predicto et sic inde seisitus [sexto][b] die Nouembris anno regni predicti nuper Regis vicesimo secundo terras illas Fossis sepibus et palis circumquaque inclusit et imparcauit et parcum nouum inde fieri fecit pro Feris ibidem nutriendis et Feras in eod[em par]co[c] posuit et adhuc habet ac terras

[a] Blank in MS.   [b] MS. illegible: supplied from Dugdale's MS.
[c] MS. mutilated.

[1] 'Parua Bromwyche,' Ward-End, *alias* Little-Bromwich, Dugdale. Now Ward-End.

The incloser, John Bonde, was 'a wealthy clothier in Coventre and merchant of the Staple,' who appears to have bought the manor. It is a noticeable example of that common subject of complaint at this date, the assumption by wealthy manufacturers of the dignity of country squires. Dugdale's notice of this inclosure is: 'Which John Bonde made a small Parke here of xxx Acres in 6 H. VIII. and stored it with Deer (Inq. super Depop. 9 H. VIII.).' (*Warw.* p. 620). This inclosure was not presented again in 1518, but reappears among the Returns of 1549.

[2] Pooley, Dugdale.

'This Sir Thomas built the Manor-House here at Pooley, of Brick (as is yet to be seen) having in 22 H. VII. imparked the Woods lying westwards thereof (Inq. super Depop. 9 H. VIII.)' (*Warw.* p. 794). Dugdale's addition to the facts given in this entry is doubtless from his own observation.

illas sic imparcatas adhuc tenet et a priori vsu illas mutauit et terre ille tenentur de ᵃ et valent per annum tres libras.

ET DICUNT quod Iohannes Wardern armiger fuit seisitus in dominico suo vt de feodo de duobus Croftis vocatis Ladye Croftes¹ continentibus decem acras terre arrabilis et culture vsitate et apte in Castell Bromyche² predicta in Comitatu predicto et sic inde seisitus quarto die Decembris anno regni domini Regis nunc secundo terras illas coniungere et in parco includere fecit et illas imparcauit et cum terris illis parcum suum elargire ᵇ fecit et in pasturam Ferarum Conuertit et feras in eodem parco posuit et adhuc habet ac terras sic imparcatas adhuc tenet et priore inde vsu illas mutauit et terre ille tenentur de ᵃ et valent per annum ᶜ

Et Iidem Iuratores dicunt quod Thomas Massy Gentilman fuit et adhuc existit seisitus in dominico suo vt de feodo de vno Mesuagio et viginti et quatuor acris terre arrabilis et arrari vsitate annuatim cum pertinenciis in Mereden in Comita'u predicto ad anuum valorem viginti solidorum que quidem viginti et iiij^or acre terre cum Mesuagio predicto pro seminacione granorum et arrura in eisdem terris habendis tradi et occupari solebant et predictus Thomas sic inde seisitus decimo die Octobris anno regni domini Regis nunc primo predictum Mesuagium ad terram cadere voluntarie

---

ᵃ Blank in MS.   ᵇ Sic.   ᶜ Sic : 'sum' omitted.

¹ 'Croftes.' 'Croft, Croftum and Crofta, is a little Close or Pightle adjoyning to a House, either for Pasture or Arable, as the owner pleases' (Cowel's *Interpr.* s. v.).

² Castle-Bromwich, Dugdale and modern.

This inclosure appears to be referred to under 'Park Hall' as a 'member of Bromwich.' Dugdale says of this manor : 'When it came to the Ardens, or was by them impark't I have not yet discovered. In 2 H. VIII. I find that the Park was enlarged with cxl acres of Wood and Pasture, as also with x acres of Arable Ground by John Arden, Esquire (Inq. super Depop. 9 H. VIII.)' (*Warw.* p. 621). This quotation appears to be a mistake on Dugdale's part, arising from the eye being caught by the acreage of the Poley entry, which indicates that the two were on the same certificate (see preceding page). 'Wardern' is evidently for Ardern or Arden.

permisit ob quam causam sex persone ibidem nuper manentes et laborantes abinde penitus in suam desolacionem recesserunt et tenementa illa de [a]

Et dicunt quod Cornelius Wyrley et Ricardus Cave nuper fuerunt seisiti in dominico suo vt de feodo de vno Mesuagio et viginti acris terre arrabilis et cultui vsitate et apte cum pertinenciis in Brymycham[1] in Comitatu predicto ad anuum valorem viginti solidorum et que quidem viginti acre terre cum Mesuagio predicto pro seminacione granorum et arrura in eisdem terris tradi et occupari solebant et predicti Cornelius et Ricardus sic de tenementis illis vt prefertur seisiti existit [b] quarto die Nouembris anno regni domini Regis nunc septimo Mesuagium predictum in decasum cadere voluntarie permisit [b] et adhuc permittit [b] per quod vnum aratrum deponitur et sex persone que ibidem manere solebant abinde recesserunt et vagarunt et Willelmus Worsley modo habet statum in tenementis predictis et tenementa predicta tenentur de [c]

Et dicunt quod Willelmus Chetwyne nuper fuit seisitus in dominico suo vt de feodo de vno Mesuagio vocato Mereden hall et centum acris terre arrabilis cum Mesuagio illo occupari locari et tradi consuetis in Meredene predicta in Comitatu predicto et sic inde seisitus quarto die Ianuarii anno regni domini Regis nunc secundo voluntarie Mesuagium illud devastari et in decasum fore permisit et sic adhuc existit per quod decem persone que ibidem manere solebant abinde recesserunt et vagarunt Et predictus Willelmus Chatwen (Membrane 47) modo habet statum predicti in tenementis predictis [2] Et tenementa illa valent per annum viginti marcas Et tenentur de [c]

Et vlterius dicunt quod Iohannes Brereley fuit et adhuc seisitus existit in dominico suo vt de feodo de vno Mesuagio et decem acris terre arrabilis cum Mesuagio illo occupari locari et tradi consuete in Fyllongley in Comitatu predicto et sic inde seisitus duodecimo die Ianuarii anno regni predicti

[a] Sic : blank in MS.   [b] Sic.   [c] Blank in MS.

[1] Now Birmingham.
The putting down of a plough implies conversion to pasture.
[2] In 2 E. VI. this manor was sold by Thomas Chetwyn to John Hales of Coventry, the chairman of Somerset's Inclosure Commission (*Warw.* (p. 696). See p. 5, *supra*.

[nuper]ᵃ Regis decimo octauo voluntarie tenementum illud devastari et in decasum fore permisit et sic adhuc existit per quod quatuor persone que ibidem manere solebant abinde recesserunt et vagarunt Et tenementa [illa]ᵃ valent per annum viginti sex solidos et octo denarios et tenentur de ᵇ

Et dicunt quod   ᵇ   heres Willelmi Spencer nuper fuit et adhuc existit seisitus in dominico suo [vt]ᵃ de feodo de vno Mesuagio et viginti acris terre arrabilis cum Mesuagio illo occupari locari et tradi consuete ad anuum valorem viginti sex solidorum et octo denariorum in Fyllongley predicta in Comitatu predicto et sic inde seisitus sextodecimo die Iulii anno regni predicti nuper Regis vicesimo voluntarie Mesuagium illud devastari et in decasum fore permisit et sic adhuc existit et terras illas a Cultura et iconomia ad pasturam ouium et aliorum animalium conuertit et terris illis sic ad presens vtitur per quod vnum aratrum deponitur et quatuor persone que ibidem manere et occupari solebant ea occasione a tenuris occupacionibus et mansionibus suis ibidem recesserunt et ociosi existunt et terre ille tenentur de Edwardo . . .ᵈ Et tenementa illa valent per annum ᵇ

Et Iuratores predicti dicunt super sacramentum suum quod Willelmus Coope Gentilman nuper fuit seisitus in dominico suo vt de feodo de duodecim Mesuagiis tribus Cotagiis et de ducentis et quadraginta acris terre arrabilis et arrari ᵉ a tempore cuius contrarii memoria hominum non existit consueuerunt in Wormeleighton ¹ in Comitatu predicto et cum quolibet eorum xij Mesuagiorum viginti acre terre arrabilis et

lxxxv h[eres]ᶜ

Wormeleighton Gill[es] r[espondeat] quindenaᶠ pasche

ᵃ Conjectural : MS. illegible.   ᵇ Blank in MS.   ᶜ MS. *h.*   ᵈ MS. illegible.
     ᵉ Sic : 'que' omitted.   ᶠ MS. *xv.*

¹ 'Wormeleighton.' Wormleighton, Dugdale and modern.
This is one of the most instructive entries in the Inquisition. The improved rental value of the lands when inclosed was 50 per cent. higher than before, which sufficiently shows the inducement to inclose on a large scale. It must be remembered that during this decade the average price of wool per tod was 6s. 0½d., a rise from the 4s. 8½d. of the previous decade amounting to 28·3 per cent. The much greater rise of rent points to active competition for land. Compare, however, this rise with the extraordinary rise of 173 per cent. since 1512 at Churchehull, Oxfordshire p. 360, *n.* 1, cf. p. 65, *supra*).

annuatim arrate ad minus occupari et ad firmam dimitti et tradi per totum dictum tempus solebant et vse fuerunt et sic inde seisitus sexto die Octobris anno regni predicti nuper Regis henrici septimi quartodecimo tenementa illa sepis [a] et fossatis vndique inclusit et tenementa illa [sic] [b] inclusa adhuc existunt ac Mesuagia illa et cotagia predicta voluntarie devastari et in decasum et ruinam cadere et sic adhuc existere permisit et predictas terras arrabiles ab vsu culture et arrure inde in pasturam animalium conuertit et terra illa sic in pastura animalium adhuc vsa est et terram illam in seperalitate [a] sic inclusam adhuc operatur et [c] tenet ob quod duodecim aratra que circa agriculturam terrarum illarum occupata fuerunt penitus deponuntur et sexaginta persone que in mansionibus predictis dum manutente fuerunt moram fecerunt et circa culturam in terris predictis occupate fuerunt abinde exire lacrimose et vagare coacte fuerunt et in ocium ducti et sic fame vt supponi potest perierunt et tenementa predicta tempore quo sic inclusa fuerunt inde extenderunt ad anuum valorem quadraginta librarum et modo tempore capcionis huius inquisicionis tenementa illa valent per annum sexaginta libras et tenentur de domino Rege. Et dicunt quod in Wormeleighton predicta adhuc supersunt et edificantur vnum principale Mesuagium situatum in situ Manerii ibidem et eciam sex cotagia Et residua vt supradictum est devastata sunt Et dicunt quod quidam Iohannes Spencer armiger modo habet statum predicti Willelmi Coope [1] in tenementis predictis in Wormeleighton predicta.

Spencer

[a] Sic.   [b] MS. mutilated. Text restored from Exch. Q. R. Mem. Roll 301, H. T. 13 H. VIII. (1522), m 8.   [c] Thus struck through in MS.

[1] The 'Willelmus Coope gentilman' was Cofferer of the Household to Henry VII., founder of the family of Cope of Bramshill. He received a grant of this property from the Crown only the year previous to his inclosures. 'Which Will. Cope in 14 H. VII. depopulated xii messuages and 3 cottages here, as was certified by *one* Inquisition, and inclosed ccxl Acres of Land. And Sir Edw. Raleigh, knight, wasted vj Messuages more : After which viz. 3 Sept. 22 H. VII. the said William Cope sold this Lordship to John Spenser, Esquier, who soon after began the structure of a fair Mannour-House, wherein, when that Inquis. was taken, he had his Residence, with lx Persons of his Family, being a good Benefactor to the Church in Ornaments and other Things (Inq. super Depop. 9 and 10 H. VIII.)' (*Warw.* p. 273).

Et Iuratores dicunt quod Willelmus Gascoigne Miles Gascoign f[iat]ᵃ
nuper fuit seisitus in dominico suo vt de feodo de vno
Mesuagio et triginta acris terre arrabilis et annuatim arrate et
cum Mesuagio illo a diu occupate et ad firmam in cultura
tradite in Grafton¹ in predicto Comitatu Warrewici et sic inde
seisitus sexto die Marcii anno regni domini Regis nunc quinto
voluntarie Mesuagium illud permisit in ruinam cadere et
penitus distruere ᵇ et sic adhuc permanere permittit ac terras
predictas cum alio suo Mesuagio ibidem tradi et occupari²
consuetas ob quod quatuor persone que in Mesuagio illo
manere solebant abinde vagando recesserunt et tenementa
illa valent per annum viginti et vnum solidos et tenentur de
domino Rege vt ducatu suo lancastrie.

Et dicunt quod henricus Smyth nuper de Couentre nuper Smyth
fuit seisitus in dominico suo vt de feodo de vno Mesuagio
et sexaginta acris terre arrabilis cum pertinenciis in Grafton
predicta que terre cum Mesuagio illo a tempore quo non
exstat memoria hominum occupari locari et ad firmam tradi
et ad vsum iconomie et culturam poni consueuerunt idemque
henricus sic de Mesuagio et terris illis seisitus existens

ᵃ MS. f. Qu. *fiat* i.e. *sub pena*.   ᵇ Sic.

This John Spencer, afterwards Sir John Spencer of Wormleighton, was the nephew of John Coope or Cope by the marriage of Cope to Jane, daughter of William Spencer of Rodbourne, co. Warwick, and sister to J. S. (Lipscomb's *Hist. of Buckingham*, i. 565 ; Wotton's *Baronetage*, i. 113, ed. 1741 ; cf. p. 285, *supra*).

Among Earl Spencer's MSS. is a petition from this J. S. undated, but apparently consequent upon an order to restore these inclosures to tillage (see p. 485, *infra*). According to this petition ' The seid William Coope inclosid the same lordship of Wormleighton long tyme byfore the seid John Spencer bought the seid lordship of the seid William Coope.'

¹ Presumably Temple-Grafton, though Dugdale makes no mention either here or at Arden's Grafton of these inclosures nor of the lands held of the Duchy of Lancaster (*Warw*. pp. 503-5). The manor of Temple-Grafton belonged to the Knights Hospitallers ; that of Arden's Grafton to the Abbey of Westminster.

² This implies a holding ingrossed of two farms. The average area to a messuage on the land of lay freeholders in Warwickshire = 32 (32·37) acres, which would give a total held in one hand of [62] acres (30 + 32), which I have accordingly entered in the column of areas ingrossed. Cf p. 268, note 2, *supra*.

decimo nono die Octobris anno regni predicti nuper Regis henrici septimi decimo octauo voluntarie Mesuagium illud vastari et ruina perire et sic ruinosum permanere permisit [1] et sic adhuc existit terrasque illas cum alio suo Mesuagio ibidem tradi [2] et in iconomia occupari fecit terrasque predictas [a] cum predicto Mesuagio devastato nuper dimisse valent per annum quinquaginta et tres solidos et octo denarios et tenentur de [b] Et Walterus Smyth modo habet statum predicti henrici Smyth in terris illis etc.

(Membrane 48)
iiij
Abbas de Kenelworth scr[ibat] G[iles]

ET dicunt quod Radulfus[3] nuper abbas Monasterii de Kenelworth nuper fuit seisitus in dominico suo vt de feodo in Iure Monasterii sui predicti de medietate Manerii de Tachebroke Malory alias dicti Manerii de Tachebroke Malory cum

[a] Sic.   [b] Blank in MS.

[1] (*a*) In Warwickshire the average number of inhabitants to a messuage on land held in hand of lay freeholders = 5. (*b*) The average area to such a messuage = 32·37 acres. Upon these data 9 would be the number of evictions. (*c*) The average area per person evicted from inclosed arable by lay freeholders = 4·07 acres. This gives 14 evictions. (*d*) The average area per person evicted from lay freeholds = 6·37 acres, which again gives 9. I take [11] here as a mean number.

[2] The reasoning of the last note but one gives an area of [92] acres ingrossed.

[3] 'Radulfus' cannot have been Ralph Maxfield, as Dugdale assumes (*Warw.* p. 354), since that Abbot did not receive the temporalities until 2 Feb. 10 H. VIII. 1519 (*Monast.* vi. 220). Cf. also the entry sub Bevyngston, p. 409, *infra.* There is a gap in Dugdale's list of the Abbots after 1458, when John Yardley was elected (*ibid.*). The jurors in this Return appear to have been in doubt as to the ownership of the manor; but according to Dugdale (*Warw.* p. 354) the lord of the manor was William Medley, son and heir of Benedict Medley, Clerk of the Signet to Henry VII. In *Monast.* vi. 225 the Abbey of Kenilworth had here at the Dissolution a 'Firma' (not 'Firma manerii') of the value of 7*l.* 9*s.* 4*d.* It was this doubtless of which W. M. was tenant. Dugdale's account of these inclosures, though professing to be based upon this Inquisition, varies from this text. He says that W. M. and the 'Prior of Kenilworth converted cccx Acres of Land into Pasture, which kept six Plows, so that there is not above 4 Houses left in all the Village (Inq. super Depop. 9 H. VIII.).' The omission of the cottage and the number of ploughs shows this note to have been really taken from the Inquisition of 1518 and not from that of 1517, and points to the restoration of four of the ten ploughs put down according to the former Inquisition, and of 36 of the displaced inhabitants (60 − 24 = 36). The statement as to the number of houses is apparently from his own observation.

medietate octo Mesuagiorum et vnius Cotagii trecentarum et lxxxvj
decem acrarum terre arrabilis et in Cultura et seminacione
granorum apte et sic a tempore cuius memoria hominum non
existit vsitate vt parcella eiusdem Manerii in Tachebroke
Malory predicta in Comitatu predicto Et quod Willelmus
Medley nuper fuit seisitus de alia medietate eiusdem Manerii
cum medietate predictorum tenementorum parcelle eiusdem
Manerii in dominico suo vt de feodo ipsisque abbate et
Willelmo sic inde seisitis existentibus predictus abbas ante
primum diem Iulii anno regni dicti nuper Regis henrici
septimi vicesimo tercio apud Tachebroke Malory predictam
in Comitatu predicto predictam medietatem ipsius abbatis
Manerii et tenementorum predictorum cum pertinenciis dimisit predicto Willelmo Medley habendum sibi pro termino
certorum annorum adhuc non finitorum virtute cuius dimissionis predictus Willelmus ante predictum primum diem
Iulii dicto anno vicesimo tercio dicti nuper Regis in medietate
illa predicti abbatis intrauit et inde possessionatus fuit et sic
inde possessionatus et de alia medietate inde seisitus existens
sexto die Ianuarii anno primo domini Regis nunc Manerium
predictum cum tenementis predictis sepibus et fossatis inclusit
et ea[b] sic inclus[um][c] tenuit et adhuc tenet Mesuagia et
Cotagium predicta voluntarie prosterni proici et devastari
fecit predictasque terras arrabiles ab vsu iconomie arracionis
et seminacionis granorum in pasturam brutorum animalium
conuertit et mutauit Et dicunt quod cum quolibet Mesuagiorum predictorum a tempore quo non exstat memoria
hominum vsque predictum sextum diem Ianuarii dicto anno
primo domini Regis nunc cum quolibet Mesuagio Mesuagiorum predictorum sexaginta acre terre arrabilis ad minus de
terris predictis in vsu iconomie seminacionis granorum et
arrure posite[d] occupari ad firmam dimitti et tradi[d] fuerunt Et
Iuratores predicti dicunt quod occasione premissorum decem
aratra que circa culturam terrarum illarum occupari solebant
deponuntur et sexaginta persone que circa eandem culturam
similiter occupari et in Mesuagiis illis eorum Mansionibus
teneri vtebantur abinde dolorose exire et ociosi fore et coacti

[a] Sic : struck through in MS. [b] Sic. [c] MS. *inclus.* [d] Sic.

fuerunt et existunt   Et d[icu]nt [a] quod Thomas nunc Marchio Dorsett [1] habet statum et terminum predicti Willelmi vt in Iure domine Margarete vxoris sue de et in Manerio et tenementis predictis   Et quod predictus abbas de medietate sua predicta et de reuercione in forma predicta adhuc seisitus existit   Et dicunt quod predicta Mesuagia et terre arrabiles in pasturam conuerse valent per annum vltra reprisas decem et nouem libras   Et tenentur de [b]

Ralegh f[iat] s[ub] p[ena]

Et predicti Iuratores dicunt quod Edwardus Ralegh miles nuper fuit seisitus in dominico suo vt de feodo de vno Mesuagio et viginti et duabus acris et dimidia acra terre arrabilis et annuatim arrate et cum illo Mesuagio occupate et locate in parochia de Dorsett [2] in Comitatu predicto et sic inde seisitus sexto die Marcii anno regni predicti nuper Regis henrici septimi vicesimo quarto voluntarie permisit Mesuagium predictum devastari et in ruinam cadere et sic extunc hucusque permanere et terras illas in vsum culture per alias personas cum aliis Mesuagiis [3] occupari fecit et racione premissorum sex persone mansione sua ~~querenda exspectare potuissent~~ [c] recesserunt   Et tenementa illa valent per annum tresdecim solidos et quatuor denarios cuiusquidem statum predicti Edwardi antonius Raughley modo habet   Et tenementa predicta tenentur de [b]

Kenelworth scr[ibat] Rodes r[espondere] quindena [d] Mich[ael]is †

Et dicunt super sacramentum suum quod Radulfus nuper abbas de Kenelworth [4] in iure eiusdem Monasterii fuit seisitus

[a] MS. mutilated.   [b] Blank in MS.   [c] Sic: struck through in MS.   [d] MS. r. xv[a].

[1] The descent of the manor to Thomas Grey, second Marquis of Dorset, here mentioned, also seems to have escaped Dugdale. This Margaret is Margaret Medley, widow of William Medley and daughter of Sir Robert Wotton of Bocton Malherb, Kent, who became the second wife of the Marquis (Collins's *Peerage*, iii. 349, ed. 1812). The date of this marriage does not appear in the Peerages, but may now be fixed at some time prior to September 1517. On the valuation given by this entry see General Introduction, p. 59.

[2] The manor was in the family of Belknap. See *infra*, pp. 424, 478.

[3] Assuming a minimum of two more ('aliis') holdings ingrossed, the reasoning on p. 405, *n.* 2, *supra*, would give us 64 + 22½ acres, in all = [86½] acres ingrossed.

[4] For 'Radulfus nuper Abbas de Kenelworth' *vid. sub* Tachbroke Malory, p. 406, *n.* 3, *supra*.

in dominico suo vt de feodo de duobus Mesuagiis et vno Cotagio et sexdecem acris terre arrabilis et a tempore cuius contrarii memoria hominum non existit in Cultura et seminacione granorum et arrura vsitate et posite in hameletto vocato Bevyngton[1] in parochia de Salford in Comitatu predicto et cum vnoquoque Mesuagio Mesuagiorum predictorum viginti et quatuor acre terre ad minus de predictis terris arrabilibus per totum dictum tempus occupate et locate et ad firmam tradite fuerunt et idem nuper abbas sic inde seisitus ante sextum diem Marcii anno regni predicti nuper Regis henrici septimi vicesimo primo apud Salford predictam in Comitatu predicto tenementa illa per assensum Conuentus eiusdem factum sub eorum sigillo cuidam Willelmo Grey de Bevyngton ad firmam pro certo redditu eidem abbati et successoribus suis super dimissione illa reseruato pro termino certorum annorum adhuc durancium dimisit virtute cuius dimissionis predictus Willelmus Grey fuit et adhuc existit inde possessionatus et sic possessionatus ac predictus abbas sic inde seisitus existens idem Willelmus predicto sexto die Marcii dicto anno vicesimo primo predicti nuper Regis predicta Mesuagia et Cotagium devastari et in decasum et ruinam cadere voluntarie permisit et adhuc permittit necnon terram predictam arrabilem ab vsu culture et seminacionis granorum in pasturam animalium conuertit et ea sic vsus est Ita quod Mesuagia predicta non manutenentur pro vsu iconomie vt deberent et solent ob quod duo aratra que ibidem occupari solebant deponuntur et quadraginta persone ea de [cau]sa[a] de suis Mansionibus et laboribus destituti sunt et vagantur[2] et Willelmus nunc

[a] MS. mutilated.

[1] Wood-Bevinton, Dugdale. Now Bevington.

[2] Dugdale's version of these inclosures is taken from the Inquisition of 3 E. VI. It runs as follows : 'Of which Wood-Bevinton the said Canons [of Kenilworth] did make a Lease to Will. Grey the elder in H. VII.'s time ; who in 21 of that King's reign depopulated here 6 messuages and one cottage xxx Acres of Arable land belonging to each Messuage, which he converted into pasture (Inq. super Depop. 3 E. VI.)' (*Warw.* p. 606). Assuming that the date was merely borrowed from this older Inquisition, we have here a measure of the progress of the inclosing

abbas Monasterii predicti in iure eiusdem Monasterii modo
seisitus existit et exitus et proficua vt de redd[itu]^a . . .
prefato reseruato inde percipit et habet Et tenementa illa
tenentur de domino Rege vt de Comitatu suo Warrewici Et
valent per annum vltra reprisas decem marcas etc.

 Et dicunt quod I^a . . . priorissa Monasterii de Roxall¹
in iure eiusdem Monasterii nuper fuit seisita in dominico suo
ut de feodo de triginta acris terre arrabilis et annuatim arrate^b
consuete i[n Hig]hershukburgh^a in Comitatu predicto et sic
inde seisitus^b sexto die Decembris anno regni predicti nuper
Regis henrici septimi octauo terras illas sepibus inclusit **Et** in
separalitate sibi custodiri fecit et in pasturam animalium
conuertit et illas sic hucusque tenet et valent terre ille per
annum quadraginta solidos Et terre ille tenentur de^c

 Et dicunt quod quidam [Thomas]^d Catesby nuper fuit
seisitus in dominico suo vt de feodo de vno Mesuagio et de
viginti acris terre arrabilis cum Mesuagio illo occupari locari
et tradi consuete in Nethershukburgh predicta in Comitatu
predicto et sic inde seisitus sep[timo]^f die Nouembris anno

(Membrane 49)
v

Catesby
Nethershuk-
burgh
[respondeat]^d
quindena pasche^e

^a MS. mutilated.   ^b Sic.   ^c Blank in MS.   ^d Conjectural: MS. illegible.
    ^e MS. *xv pasche*.   ^f MS. partly illegible.

movement between 1517 and 1547, viz. from 64 to 180 acres, and three
more houses; an increase of inclosed land amounting to 181·2 per cent.
and of houses to 100 per cent. Dugdale proceeds, speaking of William,
son and heir to William Grey the elder, the lessee in this text, 'who,
surrendring that Lease, purchased the inheritance thereof from those
Canons, for a Fee Farm Rent of 13*l*. 13*s*. 4*d*. per An. And in 10
H. VIII., when the statute of Inclosures was lookt into, re-edifyed four
of the said Messuages (Inq. super Depop. 3 E. VI.)' (*Ibid.*). This is a
side-light upon the effects of this inquiry. The rent of the 'feodi firma'
of Wodebevyngton is given as stated by Dugdale in the *Monast.* vi. 225.

 ¹ 'I . . . priorissa Monasterii de Roxall.' Possibly Isabella Aste-
ley, elected in 1431. Between this date and that of Jocosa Brome, who
resigned in 1524, there is a gap in Dugdale's list (*Monast.* iv. 89), but an
Isabella appears as prioress in 16 H. VII. 1500-01 (*Id.* p. 90). At the
Dissolution the priory (a Benedictine house at Wroxhall) held the church
and glebe at Shuckborough-Superior (*Warw.* p. 219), but no land at
Nether Shuckborough. This confirms the conjecture, the MS. being
injured, '[Hig]her Shukburgh,' and it is to be observed that in his Tables
Dugdale gives this entry under Shukburgh, distinguishing it from the
entry following *sub* Nether Shuckborough.

regni predicti nuper Regis henrici septimi octauo voluntarie Mesuagium illud devastari et in decasum fore permisit et sic adhuc existit per quod sex persone que ibidem manere solebant [abinde][a] recesserunt et vagarunt Et Thomas Shuk- borough modo habet statum predicti Thome Catesby in tenementis predictis Et tenementa illa valent per annum viginti solidos Et tenentur de domino Rege vt de Comitatu suo Warrewici.[1]

xxxvij

Et dicunt quod Thomas Shukborough nuper fuit seisitus de vno Mesuagio et quatuordecim acris terre arrabilis et annuatim arrari consuete et cum Mesuagio illo locate in Nethershukborugh predicta in dominico suo vt de feodo et sic inde seisitus [Mesuagium][a] illud sexto die Iunii anno regni domini Regis nunc primo in ruinam cadere et sic adhuc existere permisit Et quod sex persone que ibidem morare[b] solebant abinde exire cohortebantur[c] et tenementa illa valent per annum . . . .[d] et octo solidos Et tenentur de de[e] domino Rege vt de Comitatu Warrewici et idem Thomas adhuc inde seisitus est in forma predicta.

[a] Conjectural : MS. illegible.　[b] Sic.　[c] Sic : apparently for *cohertebantur*—the form used elsewhere.　[d] MS. illegible.　[e] Sic : *de* repeated.

[1] This entry fills a gap in Dugdale's *Warw.* p. 373, he having been unable to trace the lordship of the manor between 47 E. III. (1373-74) when it belonged to the family of Catesby and 3 Eliz. (1560-61), when it had already passed to the Shukboroughs. In 1516 this Thomas Shukborough or Shukborow was sued in the Court of Requests for an inclosure of common lands at Shuckborough. Sir Edward Grevyle, Sir Edward Herres and John Spenser, Esquire, were appointed commissioners to take evidence. Their 'certificate' of the evidence is among Earl Spencer's MSS. It does not appear that the inclosures complained of were any of those returned in 1517, from which it may be concluded that the case had been decided previously to the Inquisition. Two appearances of Thomas Sughborowe or Shukburgh in this suit are entered in the appearance books of the Ct. of Requests (MS. R. O.) in May 1516 and Trinity Term, 1517. As no further entries occur, the inference is confirmed that the suit had terminated prior to these Returns (MS. R. O. Ct. of Requests ; Mr. Hunt's *Cal.* Bdle. 8, no. 339 ; *Decrees and Appearances*, vols. vii.-xi. Earl Spencer's MSS.). Dugdale MSS. fo. 562 gives under the reference '|King's Remembrancer' (Hill. Rec. 38 H. VIII.) 'Thomas Shukbrogh ten. in capite terr. in Shukburgh per lic. Rot. 19,' but I have failed to verify this from the Rolls in the R. O.

Edward[us]
Raughley
Mil[es]
Vpton
scr[ibat] Gill[es]
r[espondere]
quindena^a pasche

ET DICUNT quod Edwardus Raughley Miles nuper fuit seisitus in dominico suo vt de feodo de vno Mesuagio et vna carucata terre arrabilis et arrari consuete annuatim in Vpton[1] in Comitatu predicto Et carucata illa continet in se quadraginta acras terre arrabilis ad minus que cum Mesuagio predicto a tempore de quo non [exstat][b] memoria locari et occupari in iconomia solebant et sic seisitus sexto die Marcii anno regni predicti nuper Regis henrici septimi quartodecimo Mesuagium predictum devastari et ad terram proici fecit et predictam Carucatam t[erre][c] arrabilis in pasturam animalium conuertit et terre ille sic in pasturam et non in vsu culture adhuc ponuntur Et valent per annum quadraginta sex solidos et octo denarios Et tenentur de domino Rege vt [d] Et racione premissorum vnum aratrum ibidem deponitur et sex persone abinde recesserunt et in ocium ducebantur Et dicunt quod Georgius Raughley modo habet statum predicti Edwardi Raughley in tenementis illis.

Et dicunt quod Iohannes Waryner nuper fuit seisitus in dominico suo vt de feodo de vno Mesuagio et vna Carucata terre et dimidia arrabilis et seminacioni granorum apte et arrari consuete in Vpton[2] predicta cum pertinenciis Et Carucata illa et dimidia continet sexaginta acras terre arrabilis que cum Mesuagio illo a tempore de quo non exstat memoria locari et occupari in iconomiam solebant et sic seisitus sexto die Marcii anno regni predicti nuper Regis henrici septimi quartodecimo Mesuagium predictum devastari et ad terram proici fecit et predictam Carucatam terre et dimidiam arrabilis in pasturam animalium conuertit et terre ille sic in pasturam et non in vsu Culture adhuc ponuntur Et valent per annum quatuor libras Et tenentur de domino Rege Et racione premissorum vnum aratrum ibidem deponitur et octo persone

---

[a] MS. *xv^a*. [b] Conjectural : MS. illegible. [c] MS. partly illegible. [d] Blank in MS.

[1] Upton iuxta Ratley, Dugdale. This is Upton, near Edge Hill. Sir Edw. Raughley or Ralegh inherited land here from his mother, Margaret Verney (cf. Dugdale, *Warw.* pp. 383 and 390).

[2] According to Dugdale, the manor belonged to the family of Danvers (*ibid.* 390). See next entry.

abinde recesserunt et in ocium ducebantur Et dicunt quod predictus Iohannes Waryner adhuc seisitus existit de tenementis illis in forma predicta.

Et dicunt quod Willelmus Davers Miles nuper fuit seisitus in dominico suo vt de feodo de tribus Mesuagiis et Centum et viginti acris terre arrabilibus [b] et seminacioni granorum apte et arrari consuete in Vpton in Comitatu predicto et cum quolibet Mesuagio Mesuagiorum predictorum quadraginta acre terre arrabilis de quo non exstat memoria locari et occupari in iconomia solebant et sic seisitus sexto die Marcii anno regni predicti nuper Regis henrici septimi quartodecimo Mesuagia predicta devastari et ad terram proici fecit et predictas terras arrabiles in pasturam animalium conuertit et terras illas sic in pastura custodit et in vsu Culture adhuc non ponuntur Et valent per annum viginti marcas Et tenentur de domino Rege Et racione premissorum tria aratra ibidem deponuntur et viginti persone abinde recesserunt et in ocium ducebantur et dicta hameletta de Vpton totaliter destruitur.[1] Et dicunt quod Thomas Davers modo habet statum predicti Willelmi Davers in tenementis illis.

*Davers scr[ibat] Gilez r[espondere] quindena [a] Mich[ael]is

Et vlterius dicunt quod Edwardus Raughley Miles nuper fuit seisitus in dominico suo vt de feodo de vno Mesuagio et quadraginta acris terre arrabilis cum Mesuagio illo occupari locari et tradi consuete in Farnborowe in Comitatu predicto et sic inde seisitus duodecimo die Iulii anno regni domini Regis nunc septimo Mesuagium illud devastari et in decasum fore permisit et sic existit per quod quatuor persone que ibidem manere solebant abinde recesserunt et vagarunt Et quod Georgius Raulegh infra etatem e[xistens] [c] et in custodia d[omini] [d] Regis modo habet statum predicti Edwardi in tenementis predictis Et tenementa illa valent per annum vltra

†Raughley scr[ibat] Gilez r[espondere] quindena [a] Mich[ael]is

[a] MS. *xv*ᵗⁱ.   [b] Sic.   [c] Conjectural : MS. mutilated.   [d] MS. mutilated.

[1] This entry is of importance as giving us the exact size of a hamlet inclosed and destroyed as consisting of five houses and 220 acres. Dugdale adds, 'Which Will. [Danvers] depopulated 1 Mess. and inclosed xxviij Acres of Land and cc Acres of Pasture in this place (Inq. super Depop. 10 H. VIII.).'

reprisas quadraginta et quatuor solidos Et tenentur de domino Rege.

*Owen †
scr[ibat] Gilez
r[espondere]
quindena ᵇ
Michaelis*

Et dicunt quod Dauid Owen Miles ex[istit] ᵃ seisitus in dominico suo vt de feodo de vno Mesuagio et quadraginta acris terre arrabilis et annuatim arrari consuete et cum Mesuagio illo locate in Oxshelff¹ in Comitatu predicto et sic inde seisitus quarto die Octobris anno regni predicti nuper Regis decimo Mesuagium illud ad terram cadere et sic adhuc existere voluntarie permisit ob quod sex persone minuuntur et ab eorum occupacione in ocium uertuntur Et tenementa illa valent per annum vltra reprisas viginti et quatuor solidos Et tenentur de domino Rege.

Walssh †

Et Iuratores predicti dicunt quod agnes Walshe vidua nuper fuit seisita in dominico suo vt de feodo de vno Mesuagio vocato Booston house et viginti et quatuor acris terre arrabilis cum Mesuagio illo occupari locari et tradi consuete in Warwyke in Comitatu predicto et sic inde seisita tercio die Marcii anno regni predicti nuper Regis decimo septimo Mesuagium illud ad terram cadere voluntarie permisit per quod vnum aratrum deponitur et sex persone que ibidem manere solebant abinde recesserunt et vagarunt Et tenementa illa valent per annum viginti sex solidos et octo denarios Et tenentur de domino Rege.

*Matill[da] Rowse
scr[ibat] Gille[s]
litell darsyngton
quindena ᵇ pasche
in alio folio*

Et dicunt quod Matilda Rowse vidua² nuper fuit scisita pro termino vite sue de quinque Mesuagiis et ducentis acris terre. arrabilis et Cultui apte et annuatim arrate et cum Mesuagiis illis ante tunc vsualiter locat[is] ᶜ et dimissis scilicet

ᵃ MS. mutilated.   ᵇ MS. *xv*ᵃ.   ᶜ MS. *locat.*

¹ Oxhill, Dugdale. Octeselve in Domesday. The manor was granted to Sir David Owen July 2, 4 H. VII. (1489) after the attainder of W. Catesby by the Parliament of 1485 (Dugd. *Warw.* p. 430).

² 'But after the 4th of E. III. I have not found any farther Mention at all of it in Record till 9 H. VIII., that Maud Rous, widow, was certified to have converted cc Acres of Land, lying in this Place, from Tillage to Pasture in 17 H. VII. and decaying three Ploughs, being then possessed of the capitall Messuage (Inq. super Depop. 9 H. VIII.). From which Maud did descend Sir John Brome, of Ragley, kt. . . . who in 3 E. VI. possest it (Inq. super Depop. 3 E. VI.).' Dugdale, *Warw.* p. 497.

cum vnoquoque eorundem Mesuagiorum triginta acre terre arrabilis inde ad minus in hameletto **vocato** Darsyngton in parochia de Welford in Comitatu predicto reuersio [b] inde post ipsius Matilde mortem cuidam Thome Rowse et heredibus suis spectan[te] [c] et dicta Matilda sic inde seisita quarto die Marcii anno regni predicti [nuper Regis henrici] [d] septimi decimo septimo predicta Mesuagia voluntarie in ruinam et decasum extremum existere permisit et adhuc permittit et predictas terras ab vsu cultus et arrure pro granis ibidem seminandis in pasturam ouium [et aliorum animalium conuertit] [d] et illis sic extunc hucusque vsus [b] est ob quod iconomia et cultus eorundem tenementorum a dicto quarto die Marcii anno decimo septimo supradicto hucusque non habebatur sed penitus destruitur et totaliter . . . . . .[e] sex aratra deponuntur et viginti et quatuor persone que in Mesuagiis predictis adtunc moram traxerunt et circa Culturam et iconomiam illam ante predictum quartum diem Marcii sufficienter fuerunt . . . . .[e] predictis dicto quarto die Marcii anno predicto recesserunt et in ocium perducti sunt Et dicunt quod tenementa illa valent per annum vltra reprisas septem libras Et tenentur de domino Rege.

e. v.[a]
(Membrane 50)

vj

Et iidem Iur[atores dicunt quod] [d] . . .[e] **Kebyll** nuper aldermannus london [1] nuper fuit seisitus in dominico suo vt de feodo de septem Mesuagiis et vno Cotagio et ducentis acris terre arrabilis et vsualiter arrate et seminacioni granorum posite . . [Weston] [f] iuxta Cheryton in parochia de longcompton in Comitatu predicto et cum quolibet Mesuagio Mesuagiorum predictorum viginti et sex acre terre arrabilis

Kebyll

lxxxviij

[a] MS. *e v.* apparently corresponding to *f. vj.* of the next membrane.
[b] Sic.
[c] MS. *spectan.*
[d] Conjectural: MS. mutilated.
[e] MS. mutilated.
[f] MS. mutilated: name of place supplied from Dugdale's *Warwickshire,* p. 415.

[1] This Kebyll was probably Henry Keble, Lord Mayor of London in 1510. Dugdale makes no mention of this inclosure, but cites that of 350 acres of land, accompanied by the destruction of seven messuages and one cottage here, from the Inq. of 1518 : 'Being all that there were in this Village, except the Mannour House, wherewith lxxx Acres of Land were occupied' (*Warw.* p. 416). By the Return here 182 acres appear to have been attached to the seven messuages, and the rest—18 acres—to the cottage.

inde ad minus de terris predictis ad firmam . . . . .[a] in Cultura et iconomia a tempore quo cuius contrarii memoria hominum non existit solebant et fuerunt et sic inde seisitus sexto die decembris anno regni domini Regis nunc primo predict[a] . . . . devastari et destrui ac in ruinam cadere et sic adhuc existere fecit et permisit ita quod id quod de Mesuagio illo modo superest non sufficit ad iconomiam de terris illis manutenendam a[a] . . . . Culture in pasturam animalium conuertit et ille sic adhuc vtuntur per quod septem aratra deponuntur et triginta et octo persone laboribus mansionibus et occupacionibus carent et diu caruerunt [Et tenementa illa valent per][b] annum triginta libras Et tenentur de . . . .[c] Et quod [c] modo habet statum predicti henrici in tenementis predictis.

W Willington Barcheston scr[ibat] Gill[es] r[espondere] quindena [f] pasche

Et dicunt Iuratores predicti quod Willelmus Wyll[yngton nuper][d] fuit et adhuc existit s[eisitu]s[b] in dominico suo vt de feodo de Manerio de Barcheston in Comitatu predicto et de quatuor Mesuagiis et vno Cotagio quingentis et triginta acris terre arrabilis et arrari consuete [in Barcheston][e] predicta in Comitatu predicto parcella Manerii predicti et cum vno Mesuagio vocato Fraunceis Mese Mesuagiorum predictorum due virgate terre arrabilis et cum alio Mesuagio vocato William Torches Mese Mes[uagiorum predictorum due][e] virgate terre arrabilis et cum alio Mesuagio vocato lambertys Mese Mesuagiorum illorum due virgate terre arrabilis cum alio Mesuagio vocato persons Mese Mesuagiorum predictorum quatuor virgate [terre arrabilis a tempore de][b] quo non exstat memoria occupate in vsu iconomie locate fuerunt et quod quelibet earundem virgatarum terre continet in se viginti et duas acras terre arrabilis et annuatim arrate et Cotagium predictum [uocabatur Brayse][e] Et idem Willelmus Wyllyngton sic inde seisitus primo die Marcii anno regni predicti nuper Regis henrici septimi vicesimo quarto Mesuagia et Cotagium predicta voluntarie devastari et in ruinam [cadere et sic adhuc][e] exis-

[a] MS. illegible.
[b] Conjectural : MS. mutilated.
[c] Blank in MS.
[d] Conjectural : MS. illegible.
[e] MS. mutilated : text supplied from recital in Exch. Q. R. Mem. Roll 299, M. T. 11 H. VIII (1519), m. 22 dorso.
[f] MS. xv^a.

tere permisit et adhuc permittit terrasque arrabiles predictas cum Mesuagiis predictis occupatas et locatas ab vsu Culture et iconomie in pasturam aueriorum et animalium mutauit et conuertit et illas sic tenet hucusque Et [predictus Willelmus]^a Willyngton tantum vnum principale Manerium videlicet situm Manerii predicti et sexaginta et quatuor acras terre parcellam predictarum quingentorum ^b et triginta acrarum terre cum vno arratro ibidem in vsu Culture [et seminacionis]^a granorum et iconomie vtuntur et racione premissorum quasi totum hamelettum de Barcheston predictum desolatur et adnichilatur et quinque aratra que ibidem circa Culturam predicte terre arrabilis in . . . . .^c detrahuntur et viginti et quatuor persone de suis mansionibus expellentur et lacrimose de victu et opere evitantur et sic in miseria perducuntur Et tenementa predicta tenentur de domino Rege vt de . . .^c et tenementa predicta sic in decasu existentia et in pasturam conuersa valent per annum quadraginta marcas.[1]

Et dicunt quod Willelmus Compton Miles nuper fuit seisitus in dominico suo vt de feodo de duobus Me[suagiis]^c et Centum acris terre arrabilis et arrure et seminacioni granorum

Compton f[iat] s[ub] p[ena] bis

^a Conjectural: MS. mutilated.   ^b Sic.   ^c MS. mutilated.

[1] The tabulation of this entry, which is very confused, requires explanation. The 530 acres are divided among four messuages, with assigned areas amounting in all to 220 acres. This leaves 310 acres apparently attached to the manor house. Of these 64 were not converted to pasture, but maintained as arable, which leaves 246 acres inclosed to pasture. The evictions belong to the four messuages and the cottage, none of them being assigned to the demesne of 310 acres (cf. *Trans. R.H.S.* 1893, p. 246). In the case of the second messuage decayed, of which the acreage is illegible, I have ventured to supply, in brackets, [44], that being the acreage of the other two messuages, excepting the parsonage, and harmonising with the statistics of evictions &c. These I have conjecturally apportioned. In Dugdale, *Warw.* p. 425, the entry appears as follows: 'He (W. W.) depopulated the town in 24 H. VII., making Inclosure of 530 acres of land; so that there was no more than 64 acres left for Tillage, which were used by him as belonging to his Mannour-House there, and mannaged with one Plough (Inq. super Depop. 9 H. VIII.).' The incloser, he tells us, was 'a wealthy Merchant of the Staple.' For another example of a merchant incloser see *sub* Parua Bromwyche, p. 400, *supra*.

a tempore de quo non exstat memoria vsitate et posite in Compton[1] in Comitatu predicto et cum quolibet eorundem Mesuagiorum quadraginta [acre][a] terre inde ad minus per totum dictum tempus locari tradi et ocupari fuerunt[b] et solebant et predictus Willelmus sic inde seisitus vndecimo die Marcii anno regni domini Regis nunc quarto Mesuagia predicta in decasum et ruinam cadere permisit et adhuc permittit ac quinquaginta acras terre predicte parcelle palis et sepibus inclusit et parcum inde pro feris nutriendis fecit et illas imparcauit et parcum inde tenet et feras in eodem habet et quinquaginta acras terre residue ab vsu culture et seminacionis granorum in pasturam brutorum animalium posuit et conuertit et terre ille sic adhuc in pasturam vtuntur quibus de causis tria aratra que ibidem circa culturam terrarum illarum occupari solebant detrahuntur et viginti persone que circa illam culturam et iconomiam in terris predictis occupari solebant et in Mesuagiis illis domus habitarunt abinde recesserunt Et predictus Willelmus adhuc seisitus existit de tenementis illis et tenementa illa valent per annum octo libras tresdecim solidos et quatuor denarios et tenentur de [c]

Compton f[iat]

f vi
(Membrane 51)
vij

Et dicunt quod idem Willelmus Compton Miles **nuper** fuit seisitus in dominico suo vt de Feodo de vno Mesuagio et triginta acris terre arrabilis et annuatim arrate et c[um][a] Mesuagio illo per totum dictum tempus tradite locate et occupate in Compton in Comitatu predicto et [sic inde][d] seisitus sexto die Marcii anno regni predicti domini Regis henrici septimi decimo Mesuagium illud devastari et in ruinam poni Fecit per quod tres persone que in Mesuagio illo habitare solebant abinde recesserunt et idem Willelmus adhuc seisitus existit in forma predicta Et tenementa illa valent per annum octo solidos et tenentur de [c][2]

[a] Conjectural: MS. mutilated.   [b] Sic.   [c] Blank in MS.
[d] Conjectural: MS. illegible.

[1] 'Compton,' *i.e.* Compton-Winyate.
[2] It is noticeable that Dugdale (*Warw.* p. 394), though he mentions imparcations here by Sir W. Compton in 1519–20 from the licence in Pat. 11 H. VIII. p. 1, does not mention these two entries. But they are reproduced in his notes of this Inquisition (cf. p. 649, *infra*).

WARWICKSHIRE 419

ET DICUNT quod Willelmus Brown nuper fuit possessionatus[1] in dominico suo v[t de feodo de vno][b] Mesuagio et duodecim virgatis terre arrabilis in Braylys[2] in Comitatu predicto qualibet virgata inde sexdecim acras terre continente et que quidem terra a t[em]pore[d] cuius contrarii memoria hominum not exstat . . . .[e] culture et seminacionis granorum posite et vtebantur cum Mesuagio illo per totum idem tempus locate occupate et tradite fuerunt et idem Willelmus sic inde seisitus sexto die aprilis anno regni predicti [domini Regis][b] henrici septimi vndecimo Mesuagium predictum devastari et destrui ac in ruinam cadere et sic adhuc existere fecit et permisit et predictas terras arrabiles ab vsu prioris seminacionis granorum et arrure in pasturam br[utorum animalium][b] mutauit et illis terris sic adhuc vtitur per quod quatuor aratra que circa inde culturam occupari solebant deponuntur et sexdecim persone que circa eandem culturam similiter occupari et morare[f] in Mesuagio illo solebant abinde recessserunt et in ocium vagando se destinarunt ac tenementa illa valent per annum viginti libras et tenentur de domino Rege et Willelmus Wyllington vt Balliuus ad opus dicti Regis inde percipit exitus et proficua etc.

Brown *
Brayles [a]
scr[ibat] Gilez r[espondere] quindena [c] Mich[ael]is

ET DICUNT predicti Iuratores quod Ricardus Greneffeld gentilman nuper fuit seisitus in dominico suo vt de feodo de tribus Mesuagiis et vno Cotagio et Centum et viginti acris terre arrabilis cum pertinenciis in villa de Chelmyscote[3] in

Grenfeld
Chelmyscote
lxxxix
scr[ibat] Gill[es] r[espondere] quindena [c] pasche

[a] Thus struck through in MS.   [b] Conjectural : MS. illegible.
[c] MS. *xv*[a].   [d] MS. mutilated.   [e] MS. illegible.   [f] Sic.

[1] The phrase ' possessionatus in dominico suo vt de feodo' perhaps indicates a fee farm tenure. The word ' possessionatus ' is used of a leaseholder at Horborough and Ruyton (pp. 423, 430, *infra*), and generally appears to mean any kind of tenant : a use which unfortunately prevents any knowledge of the part played by copyholders as inclosers so far as the Warwickshire Returns are concerned. In the Returns for Bucks we find *sub* Wyllyn (p. 177, *supra*) ' quod Rogerus Couper qui de Johanne Mordaunt armigero tenet et a diu tenuit in feodo firma,' &c. Dugdale does not mention this inclosure (*Warw*. p. 396).

[2] ' Braylys.' Now Brailes. This manor had been in the Crown since 3 H. VII. (1488–89), *Warw. ibid.*

[3] Now Chelmscote. A hamlet within the parish of Brailes. It is mentioned by Rous as one of the places which were destroyed in his time, i.e. before 1491 (*Hist. Regum Angliæ*, 2nd ed. by T. Hearne, Oxon., 1745, fo. 110 b).

Comitatu predicto videlicet cum quolibet Mesuagio Mesuagiorum predictorum quadraginta acre terre arrabilis [1] in iconomia occupari tradi et locari a tempore de quo non exstat memoria fuerunt et solebant et idem Ricardus sic inde seisitus sexto die Nouembris anno regni domini Regis nunc secundo totam villam predictam sepibus et Fossis inclusit ac Mesuagia et Cotagium predicta devastari et destrui Fecit et permisit et in decasum adhuc fore permittit et terras predictas arrabiles in pasturam animalium posuit et sic illis adhuc vtitur per quod tria aratra que in Cultura terrarum illarum occupare [a] solebant detrahuntur et viginti sex persone que ibidem similiter occupari et infra Mesuagia et Cotagium predicta habitauerunt abinde lacrimose recesserunt [2] Et dicunt quod tenementa illa valent per annum sexdecim libras et tenentur de domino Rege vt de Comitatu suo Warrewici Et predictus Ricardus adhuc inde seisitus existit in Forma predicta etc.

Mag[ist]ro et fr[atr]ibus guilde s[an]cte Tri[nitatis] Warr[ewici] f[iat] s[ub] p[ena]

Et dicunt quod Magistri et Fratres Guilde siue Fraternitatis sancte Trinitatis et sancti Georgii in Warrewico in iure Guilde predicti [a] nuper fuerunt seisiti in dominico suo vt de Feodo de vno Mesuagio et vna Carucata terre arrabilis continente in se sexaginta acras terre in Chelmyscote predicta in Comitatu predicto que quidem terre cum Mesuagio predicto a tempore de quo non exstat memoria in iconomia et cultura occupari tradi et dimitti solebant et fuerunt vsque in sextum diem

[a] Sic.

[1] Note that no land is assigned to a cottage. Cf. 'tanquam cotagia' &c. on p. 383.

[2] 'I am of Opinion that the said Eustace de Grenevill began the Depopulation thereof; for our Countryman Rous (who lived in that Time) [*Hist. MS.* i. Rous, p. 144] complains of it. After which others followed his Example; for by the Inquisition taken in 9 H. VIII. it appears that Henry Grenefeild, Gent. depopulated 3 Messuages and 1 Cottage, inclosing cxx Acres of Land; the Master and Brethren of the Trinity and S. George his Gild in Warwick 1 Messuage with a Carucate of Land and a half, containing lx Acres, and the Chantry Priest here at Chelmescote 1 Messuage and 50 Acres of Land. . . . Will. Willington Esq. . . . in 1 E. VI. converted 4 Messuages here into Cottages, as also 200 Acres of Arable Land into Pasture, and being seized in fee simple of one Messuage and lx Acres of Land more, did the like by it [Inq. super Depop. 3 E. VI.]' (*Warw.* 398).

Ianuarii anno regni domini Regis nunc secundo quibus die et anno predicti Magistri et Fratres Mesuagium predictum devastari et in decasum fore permiserunt et permittunt in presenti terras que illas in pasturam animalium conuerterunt et sic adhuc illis vsi sunt et tenentur [a] et inde seisiti existunt in forma predicta et valent per annum tenementa illa quadraginta solidos et tenentur de [b]   et predicta occasione vnum aratrum deponitur et septem persone de suis occupacionibus et mansionibus impediuntur etc.

ET DICUNT quod Willelmus Brown Clericus ac perpetuus Capellanus Cantarie de Chelmescote fuit et adhuc seisitus existit de vno Mesuagio et quinquaginta acris terre arrabilis et annuatim arrari consuete ac cum Mesuagio illo vsualiter locate et tradite ad anuum valorem quinquaginta solidorum in Chelmescote predicta in Comitatu predicto et sic inde seisitus sexto die Nouembris anno regni domini Regis nunc secundo Mesuagium illud cum pertinenciis devastari et in ruinam fore voluntarie permisit et sic existit terras que illas in pasturam animalium produxit et fecit per quod vnum aratrum ibidem deponitur et sex persone a suis prioribus laboribus ibidem depriuantur et tenementa illa tenentur de domino Rege vt de Comitatu suo Warrewici etc.

Broun † s[c]r[ibat] [e] gilez r[espondere] quindena [d] Mich[ael]is

ET DICUNT quod Robertus Prior Prioratus siue domus sancti sepulcri Warrewici [1] nuper fuit et adhuc existit seisitus in dominico suo vt de feodo in iure eiusdem Prioratus de quateruiginti [2] acris terre arrabilis et annuatim arrate modo in

[a] Sic.   [b] Blank in MS.   [c] MS. *sr*.   [d] MS. *xv*[a].

[1] 'Robertus Prior' &c. is Robert Ichington, elected May 12, 1493 (Dugd. *Monast*. vi. 602).

[2] Apparently Dugdale here quotes the record incorrectly, reading 'quadringentis' for 'quateruiginti' (see his MS. notes of the Inq. of 1517), but apparently his mistake is corrected in his notes of that of 1518 : 'It also seems that much of the Lands they [the Prior and Canons of St. Sepulchre's, Warwick] had here in Warwick was antiently common, for by an Inquis. taken 9 H. VIII. I find that they had inclosed foure Hundred Acres here, and depopulated one Mess. whereunto eighty Acres belonged (Inq. super Depop.)' (*Warw.* p. 330). The last case appears to be identical with that of this entry. But in this record the 'domus' and the converted area are not distinctly associated

quatuor Clausis vocatis Lynelles Feeldes et in vno Clauso vocato Seynt Mighelles Feldes existentibus in Warwik predicta et sic inde seisitus in Festo sancti Michaelis archangeli anno regni domini Regis nunc Octauo terras illas ab vsu seminacionis granorum et arrure in pasturam animalium conuertit et mutauit et illis sic adhuc vsus est per quod duo aratra deponuntur et xj persone de laboribus suis impediuntur Et dicunt quod domus et edificia Prioratus siue domus predicte multipliciter ruine minantur et in decasum causa non reparacionis eorundem existunt et quod dominus Rex racione Comitatus sui Warwici est Fundator Prioratus predicti et omnia tenementa predicta tenentur de ipso Rege vt de Comitatu suo Warrewici et terre predicte valent per annum quinquaginta solidos.

<small>Robertus le strange Walton devill Scr[ibat] Gill[es] r[espondere] quindena^a pasche</small>

ET DICUNT quod Robertus le Straunge nuper fuit seisitus in dominico suo vt de feodo de septem Mesuagiis vno Cotagio et Centum et Sexaginta acris terre arrabilis et a tempore de quo non exstat memoria et [b] seminacioni granorum in iconomia vsitate et posite in villa de Walton Devyll [1] in Comitatu predicto et cum quolibet Mesuagio Mesuagiorum illorum viginti et quatuor acre terre [2] in Culturam et iconomiam occupari et tradi ad Firmam fuerunt et solebant et predictus Robertus sic inde seisitus septimo die Ianuarii anno regni predicti nuper Regis vicesimo quarto Mesuagia et Cotagium predicta in ruinam destruccionem et decasum cadere permisit et tenementa illa sic adhuc existunt terras que predictas arrabiles ab vsu seminacionis granorum in pasturam animalium conuertit que terre in huiusmodi vsu pasture **adhuc** vtuntur per quod tota villa predicta destruitur et septem aratra que circa inde culturam occupabantur depo-

<small>g. vii

(Membrane 52)

viij</small>

[a] MS. *xv^a*.   [b] Sic.

[1] Walton-D'Eivile, Dugdale.

[2] The first area returned here is that of 160 acres, but this does not agree with the later statement that each of the seven messuages had 24 acres attached to it. Dugdale mentions this inclosure as of 160 ac., as which it is tabulated, citing 'Inq. super Depop. 9 H. VIII.' (*Warw.* p. 411). It is, at any rate, clear that no land was assigned to the cottage. Cf. 'tanquam cotagia,' p. 383, *supra*.

nuntur et quadraginta persone que in Mesuagiis predictis diu habitauerunt et circa culturam predictam laborare et victum suum perquirere solebant lamentabiliter abinde recesserunt et occiosi [a] facti sunt et tenementa illa valent per annum decem libras et tenentur de domino Rege vt de Comitatu suo Warrewici et Edwardus Knyvett [1] et Iohannes le Straunge modo habent statum predicti Roberti in tenementis illis etc.

ET PREDICTI IURATORES DICUNT quod Iohannes Roose sexto die Marcii anno domini Regis nunc octauo tenet [a] et adhuc possessionatus existens pro termino annorum adhuc durancium reuercione inde cuidam [b] Corbett [2] gentilman post terminum illum completum spectante de et in viginti quatuor acris terre arrabilis et arrari consuete in Horborough [3] in Comitatu predicto terras illas dictis die et anno sepibus et Fossatis inclusit et adhuc sic tenet ac illas terras in pasturam animalium conuertit et mutauit per quod vnum aratrum ibidem deponitur terre que ille valent per annum duodecim solidos et tenentur de [b]

ET DICUNT QUOD Thomas Hall nuper fuit et adhuc existit possessionatus pro termino certorum annorum adhuc durancium de vno Mesuagio et viginti quatuor acris terre arrabilis cum Mesuagio illo locate in Horborough predicta in Comitatu predicto ad anuum valorem viginti quatuor sol[idorum] [c] et sic existens possessionatus sexto die Marcii anno regni domini Regis nunc septimo Mesuagium illud in ruinam et decasum fore et permanere permisit et adhuc permittit [4] et

[a] Sic.   [b] Blank in MS.   [c] Conjectural : MS. partly illegible.

[1] (Sir) Edward Knyvett was the second husband of Ann (*née* L'Estrange) widow of Sir Robert L'Estrange, who had died in 1511 (Blomefield's *Norfolk*, x. 114). According to Blomefield, John L'Estrange, her brother, became a judge of the Common Pleas, but his name does not appear in Foss's *Lives*.

[2] The lessor, Corbett, was lord of one moiety of the manor ; the family of Ferrers held the other (Dugd. *Warw.* p. 66).

[3] Harborow Magna, Dugd. Now Harborough Magna.

[4] (*a*) The number of inhabitants to a messuage in the case of leaseholds on ecclesiastical land = 6 (at Wollescote). (*b*) The average area to a messuage in such cases = 31·2 acres. These data give 5 persons (4·6) evicted here. (*c*) The average area per person evicted by leaseholders

dicunt quod P[rior]^a domus ordinis Cartusiensis in insula de
Exholme¹ modo seisitus existit de tenementis predictis vt in
iure domus sue predicte et tenentur de domino Rege vt de
ducatu suo lan[c]astrie.²

ET DICUNT quod Edwardus Belknap Miles nuper fuit
seisitus in dominico suo vt de feodo de duodecim Mesuagiis
et trescentis et sexaginta acris terre arrabilis et seminacioni
granorum apte et ad vsum illum a tempore de quo non exstat
memoria vsitate et posite in darsett et Byrton³ in Comitatu

Ex[equatu]r Exholme ^a scr[ibat] Gilez r[espondere] mense Mich[ael]is

lxxxx

^a Conjectural : MS. partly illegible.

from ecclesiastical land = 4·2 acres, which gives 6 persons (5·7) evicted.
(*d*) The average area per person evicted from the land of ecclesiastical
freeholders = 6·6 acres. This gives 4 evictions (3·6). I adopt [5] as a
mean number.

¹ The Priory was the Priory of Eppeworth, Lincolnshire, but no property of that house was returned as being in this place at the Dissolution (Dugd. *Monast.* vi. 28).

² Dugdale does not notice property of the duchy of Lancaster here, apparently freehold.

³ Derset and Burton-Dassett, Dugdale.

In Dugdale MSS. D. i. 443, this place is written ' Dorset alias Dasset, alias great Dorset alias great Dasset ' (Escæt. de aº xxv Rne Eliz.). In Exch. Q. R. Mem. Roll 312, M. T. 24 H. VIII. (1532), m. 25, it is spelt Dorsett.

Dugdale (*Warw.* p. 378) says of Sir Edward Belknap, lord of this manor, that Henry VII. ' by a speciall patent (Pat. 24 H. VII. p. 1, m. 17), dated 14 April 24 of his Raign, granted him Immunity from being troubled or questioned for that Inclosure and Depopulation, which he had made in this Lordship, contrary to the Statute in the Third of his Raign. . . . The Depopulation and Inclosure that he made within this Lordship, scil. in 14 H. VII., was of xij Mess. and ccclx acres of Land ; unto every of which Messuages 24 acres belonged : But by the Inquis. [Inq. super Depop. 9 & 10 H. VIII.] then taken I find it certified that this decay of Tillage was no Prejudice but Benefit to the Publique ; for whereas before that Time they were able to entertain but xx Strangers, upon Occasion they could afterwards entertain lx as well ; and that the Church and Ornaments were then in better condition than before, having since cost the Parish cc li. That there were also xxi Ploughs maintained in the Parish ; and whereas before the Inclosure they had but one Priest, then there were two. . . . That the Benefice was better, and more of Value to the Incumbent than when the Lands did lye in Tillage by iij li. or thereabouts : That the Children of the Parish were better taught, and better Houses kept ; and that there were then within the Precincts of the

predicto que quidem tenementa fuerunt et adhuc existunt parcella Manerii ipsius Edwardi de darsett quodque cum quolibet Mesuagio Mesuagiorum predictorum viginti et quatuor acre terre arrabilis de terris predictis per totum dictum tempus occupari locari et ad firmam tradi consueuerunt et predictus Edwardus sic de tenementis predictis seisitus existens vicesimo tercio die Octobris anno regni predicti nuper Regis Henrici septimi quartodecimo tenementa predicta vna cum aliis terris et tenementis ipsius Edwardi in dorsett[a] et Byrton predictis parcella Manerii sui predicti sepibus et fossatis inclusit et in separalitate fore et teneri et adhuc permanere fecit Mesuagia que predicta devastari et in ruinam et decasum fieri voluntarie permisit ac inde inhabitantes a suis mansionibus ibidem exire coegit predictas que terras arrabiles in pasturam animalium brutorum conuertit et a priore vsu culture mutauit et sic extunc hucusque vsi sunt[a] et existunt ob quod duodecim aratra que circa culturam terrarum illarum operari solebant deponuntur et adnichillantur et sexaginta persone que ibidem operabantur et in Mesuagiis predictis moram suam traxerunt abinde vagando recesserunt et ociosi deuenerunt et dicunt quod tenementa predicta tenentur de domino Rege in capite et quod valent per annum quadraginta libras Et dicunt quod idem Edwardus adhuc in forma predicta seisitus est de tenementis predictis.

Et iidem Iuratores dicunt quod predictus dominus Rex henricus nuper Rex anglie septimus diu post inclusionem vast[um][b] et decasum tenementorum predictorum per predictum Edwardum Belknap in forma predicta de predictis tenementis in Dorsett et Byrton parcella eiusdem Manerii de Dorsett in forma predicta fact[os][c] scilicet quartodecimo die aprilis anno regni ipsius nuper Regis vicesimo quarto literas suas patentes quarum irrotulamenti transcriptum manu

[a] Sic.   [b] MS. *vast*.   [c] MS. *fact*.

same Parish cxl Communicants.' The certificate which Dugdale quotes does not occur in this Inquisition.

As to Sir E. B. see the Act for the ' Restitucion of Sir Edward Belknapp knight' (6 H. VIII. c. 21, anno 1515).

Willelmi Nanson[1] vnius Clericorum Cancellarie domini Regis consignatum Iuratoribus predictis aperte super capcione huius Inquisicionis in euidenciis pro parte dicti Edwardi ostensum fuit per nomen dilecti et fidelis seruientis sui Edwardi Belknap tunc vnius armigerorum pro corpore suo ipso Edwardo tunc de tenementis predictis in Dorsett seisitus existens[a] in dominico suo vt de feodo fieri fecit in hec verba HENRICUS dei gracia Rex anglie et Francie et dominus hibernie Omnibus ad quos presentes litere peruenerint salutem Sciatis quod nos in consideracione boni et fidelis seruicii quod dilectus et fidelis seruiens noster Edwardus Belk[napp][b] vnus armigerorum pro corpore nostro nobis impendit et imposterum impendere intendit concessimus et per presentes concedimus sibi pro nobis et heredibus nostris quod nos nec heredes nostri vexemus nec [vllo][c] modo imposterum grauemus dictum Edwardum pro ruina aliquorum[d] domorum vel inclusarum aliquarum terrarum per ipsum facta siue fienda infra Manerium siue dominium de dorsett et omnium terrarum et tenementorum ipsius Edwardi cum suis pertinenciis in parochia de Whitechurch [2][e] in Comitatu Warrewici iacencium que de nobis tenentur nec pro aliqua alia causa per ipsum facta siue fienda de vel in predictis Manerio terris [et tenementis][f] vel in aliqua inde parcella contra formam et effectum cuiusdam statuti in parliamento nostro apud Westmonasterium anno regni nostri quarto[g] tenti et editi ruinam domorum et sustentacionem Culture et h[usbandrie][h] concernentis et quod nos nec heredes nostri non percipimus[i] redditus vel proficua alicuius parcelle dicti Manerii terrarum et tenementorum nec alicuius inde parcelle racione ruine aliquarum domorum vel inclausurarum ali[cuius parcelle][f] eorundem[a] siue alicuius alterius cause per ipsum Edwardum

[a] Sic.
[b] MS. partly illegible.
[c] MS. illegible: supplied from the Orig. Pat., 24 H. VII, p. 1, m. 19.
[d] Sic: but 'aliquarum' in Orig. Pat.
[e] 'Whitechirche' in Orig. Pat.
[f] MS. illegible: supplied from the Orig. Pat.
[g] 'tercio' in Orig. Pat.
[h] MS. partly illegible: supplied from the Orig. Pat.
[i] 'perciperemus' in Orig. Pat.

[1] See General Introduction, p. 77, *supra*.
[2] See Dugdale, *Warw.* p. 443.

contra formam et effectum statuti predicti facte siue fiende Et quod idem Edwardus et heredes sui habeant omnia eadem forisfacturas proficua vel avantagia [a] [que][b] heredibus nostris infra Manerium terras et tenementa predicta pertinebunt aut pertinere debent [c] aut spectarent racione quacumque per ipsum facta siue imposterum fienda contra formam statuti predicti Ea [d] quod expressa mencio de [certitudine vel valore][b] dicti Manerii terrarum et tenementorum aut de ea [e] que ad nos ea parte spectarent aut de aliis donis siue concessionibus per nos prefato Edwardo factis siue alicuius forisfacture vel proficui in hac parte que nondum nobis aspect[ant siue accidunt][f] aut aliquo statuto ordinacione siue prouisione incontrarium facto non obstante   In cuius rei etc. Teste Rege apud Knoll decimo quarto die aprilis [g] anno regni regis henrici septimi xxiiij^{to}.[1]   h. viij

ET DICUNT QUOD Willelmus C[lerke][h] . . .[i] in dominico   (Membrane 53) suo vt de feodo de vno Mesuagio et triginta acris terre   ix arrabilis et annuatim arrari consuete et cum Mesuagio illo   Will[elmu]s C[lerke][h] locari et occupari a tempore de quo non exstat memoria   f[iat] s[ub] p[ena] solebant et fuerunt in Bysshopshampton [2] in Comitatu predicto et sic seisitus tercio die Iulii anno regni domini Regis nunc tercio Mesuagium illud in decasum et ruinam fieri et cadere voluntarie permisit ita quod inhabitantes in eodem ab eodem Mesuagio causa illa recesserunt [3] et tenementa illa valent per annum septem solidos et tenentur de [j]

ET DICUNT QUOD Robertus [Halles]w[orth][k] . . [ad][k]huc possessionatus existit de vno Mesuagio et de decem acris

[a] 'advantagia' in Orig. Pat.
[b] MS. illegible: supplied from Orig. Pat.
[c] 'deberent' in Orig. Pat.
[d] Sic: but 'eo' in Orig. Pat.
[e] Sic: and also in Orig. Pat.
[f] MS. partly illeg ble: supplied from Orig. Pat.
[g] The Orig. Pat. ends here.
[h] MS. illegible: supplied from MS. Dugdale, D. 1, fo. 545.
[i] MS. illegible.
[j] Blank in MS.
[k] Conjectured from next entry: MS. illegible.

[1] *I.e.* 1509. Notwithstanding that this pardon extends to future acts, Sir E. B. in 1519 procured a fresh one. See p. 478, *infra*.

[2] Hampton-upon-Avon, Dugdale. Now Hampton Lucy. A manor of the Bishops of Worcester (Dugd. *Warw.* p. 471, and cp. John Brogden's case, p. 428, *infra*).

[3] Following the reasoning in Grafton (2), p. 406, *n*. 1, *supra*, upon the data of (*a*) and (*b*), we get 5 persons (4·9) evicted here. By (*c*) we get 7·3 evictions. By (*d*) we get 5 (4·7) evictions. I adopt [6] as a mean number

terre et annuatim arrari consuete et cum Mesuagio illo locate et tradite Et sic seisitus . . . .ᵃ existens decimo die Nouembris anno regni predicti nuper Regis Henrici septimi tercio Mesuagium predictum in ruinam et decasum fore voluntarie permisit et . . .ᵃ terras que illas a seminacione granorum et arrura in pasturam ovium et aliorum animalium conuertit et sic extunc hucusque vsus est et tenet ita quod ea de causa vnum aratrum deponitur et sex persone que ibidem occupari et manere solebant abinde recesserunt etc.

<small>Turnour f[iat] s[ub] p[ena]
lxxxxj</small>

Et dicunt quod Simon Turnour Clericus fuit seisitus de vno Mesuagio vocato the deyrye et de triginta acris terre arrabilis et annuatim arrari consuete et cum Mesuagio illo locate ad anuum valorem sex solidorum et octo denariorum in Bysshopshamton predicta in Comitatu predicto et sic inde seisitus quarto [die] ᵇ Octobris anno regni predicti nuper Regis sextodecimo Mesuagium illud in decasum cadere et fore voluntarie permisit ob quod iiij^or persone minuuntur et ab eorum occupacione in ocium vertuntur et dicunt [quod] ᵇ predictus Robertus hallesworth modo seisitus existit in tenementis predictis et tenentur de ᶜ

ET DICUNT predicti Iuratores quod Frater Iohannes Brogden[1] minister domus Fratrum ordinis sancte Trinitatis de Thellesford et vicarius perpetuus de Newbold [2] in Comitatu Warrici tenet et per tres annos elapsos tenuit ad firmam Rectoriam de Snytterfeld in Comitatu predicto ad anuum valorem viginti librarum ex dimissione Rectoris ibidem aceciam per duodecim annos vltimo elapsos tenuit et adhuc tenet Manerium de

<small>Ep[iscop]us Wigor[niensis] Ex[equatu]r Brogden scr[ibat] Gilez r[espondere] quindena ᵈ Mich[ael]is</small>

ᵃ MS. illegible.   ᵇ Conjectural: MS. illegible.   ᶜ Blank in MS.   ᵈ MS. *xvᵃ*.

[1] One of those cases of clerical farming against which the statute of 1529 (21 H. VIII. c. 13) was directed. The 'domus' &c. was the House of the Trinitarian or Maturin friars of Thelesford, Warwickshire, the head of which was termed Prior or 'Minister.' John Brokeden had been elected in 7 H. VII. (1491–92). At the surrender, which was postponed till 1530, although 'it was a small house, the head subscribed himself Edw. Davie, minister' (Dugd. *Warw.* p. 363, *Monast.* vi. 1564).

[2] *I.e.* Newbold Pacy, the neighbouring parish to Bysshopshamton. John Brocden was presented to the living by Queen's College, Oxford, May 20, 1512 (Dugd. *Warw.* p. 360).

Bysshopshampton[1] in eodem Comitatu ad anuum valorem viginti marcarum simul cum aliis terris et tenementis Et predictus Frater Iohannes secundo die Octobris anno regni domini Regis nunc quarto voluntarie permisit[a] vnum Mesuagium in Bysshopshampton predicta cum quo quadraginta acre terre arrabilis et arrari consuete per ipsum Iohannem et alios ante ipsum inde Firmarios in iconomia fuerunt occupate devastari fecit[a] et in decasum fieri et sic adhuc permittit et existit per quod sex persone a mansione sua ibidem recedere coacte fuerunt et tenementa illa valent per annum quadraginta solidos et tenentur per Episcopum Wigorniensem inde seisitum in dominico suo vt de feodo vt parcella Manerii sui de Bysshopshampton de domino Rege.

ET DICUNT quod predictus Frater Iohannes Brogden fuit et adhuc seisitus existit de duobus aliis Mesuagiis et de vno Cotagio et quadraginta et quinque acris terre arrabilis et annuatim arrate et cum vtroque Mesuagio Mesuagiorum predictorum viginti acre terre occupari et locari solebant ad anuum valorem viginti duo solidorum in Bysshopshamton predicta in Comitatu predicto et sic inde seisitus sexto die Nouembris anno primo domini Regis nunc Mesuagia et Cotagium illa voluntarie permisit in ruinam cadere et sic extunc hucusque permanere fecit et racione premissorum duodecim persone que circa agriculturam in Mesuagiis predictis occupabantur a suis Mansionibus ibidem expelluntur et tenentur de domino Rege vt supra. *ex[equatu]r t Brogden scr[ibat] giles r[espondere] quindena [b] Mich[ael]is*

Et Iuratores predicti dicunt quod Thomas Prior hospitalis sancti Iohannis Iherusalem in anglia [2] in iure eiusdem hospitalis nuper fuit et adhuc existit seisitus in dominico suo vt de *Prior s[an]cti Ioh[ann]is Ier[usa]lem in angl[ia]*

---
[a] Sic.   [b] MS. *xv*[a].

[1] At the average rentals of farm tenancies of ecclesiastical land in Warwickshire of 10¼*d*. per acre, the area of the Snytterfeld farm would be [468] acres, and that of the manor of Bysshopshampton [312] acres.

[2] 'Thomas,' *i.e.* Sir Thomas Docwra, Grand Prior 1501–27 (*Hist. of the Knights of Malta*, W. Porter, 1858, vol. ii. p. 284). The manor belonged to the Order. 'Against whom [the Hospitalers] in 9 H. VIII. it was certified that they had inclosed here three hundred Acres of Land, and that by this Decay of Husbandry, if Remedy were not provided, the Church there would fall to Ruin' (*Warw.* p. 33; cf. next page).

Wilmer
Ruyton

feodo de trescentis acris terre arrabilis cum pertinenciis in Ruyton[1] in Comitatu predicto que terre a tempore de quo non exstat memoria arrate fuerunt et in vsu seminacionis granorum posite scilicet ducente et viginti acre terre inde vsque duodecimum diem Decembris anno regni domini Regis nunc quarto Et residuum earundem terrarum vsque quartum diem Marcii anno regni ipsius domini Regis nunc octauo ante quem quidem duodecimum diem Decembris predictus Prior apud Ryton predictam in Comitatu predicto terras illas cum aliis terris Ricardo Wylmer dimisit pro certo termino annorum adhuc durancium virtute cuius idem Ricardus fuit et adhuc existit inde possessionatus et sic possessionatus idem Ricardus predictas ducentas et viginti acras terre predicto decimo[a] die Decembris dicto anno quarto et predicto quarto die Marcii dicto anno octauo predictas octoginta acras terre residuum sepibus et Fossatis circumclausit et claudere[a] fecit et in separalitate sibimet a terris apertis et arrabilibus[2] tenuit et adhuc tenet et terras illas a seminacione granorum arratura et cultura quibus antea vsi[a] fuerunt in pasturam animalium brutorum conuertit et mutauit et adhuc illas sic tenet per quod ceteri parochiani et inhabitantes parochie de Ruyton predicta qui in terris illis certis temporibus communiam pasture pro aucriis suis ibidem habere consueuerunt ab eadem Communia habenda impediuntur et ea de causa maxime depauperantur et ex verisimili a suis tenuris ibidem recedere infra breue tempus coartentur necnon ecclesia ibidem parochialis in desolacionem fiet nisi cito remedium inde prouideatur Et dicunt quod ea occasione quinque aratra que circa inde culturam occupari solebant deponuntur[3] Et

[a] Sic.

[1] Rietone, Domesday. Rieton super Dunsmore, Dugdale. Now Ryton on Dunsmore.

[2] Note the references to the open fields and the common lands.

[3] Although no mention is made of persons displaced from their labour by the putting down of the ploughs, it is clear that this must have been as necessary an incident as the eviction of inhabitants from a destroyed house. The average number of persons to an aratrum for Warwickshire is 6 (no figures for leaseholds being available), and I have therefore entered [24] and [6] persons displaced by the putting down of the (4) and (1) ploughs respectively.

dicunt quod predicte ducente et viginti acre terre valent per annum septem libras sex solidos et octo denarios et predicte quateruiginti acre terre valent per annum quinquaginta tres solidos et quatuor denarios Et predicte trescente acre terre tenentur de domino Rege etc.

Et Iuratores predicti dicunt quod henricus Smyth nuper fuit seisitus in dominico suo vt de feodo de duodecim Mesuagiis et quatuor Cotagiis Sexcentis et quadraginta acris terre arrabilis ad anuum valorem quinquaginta quinque librarum cum pertinenciis in Stretton super Strete[1] in Comitatu predicto et cum quolibet Mesuagio Mesuagiorum predictorum quadraginta acre terre arrabilis et culture apte et vsualis locari et tradi ad firmam et occupari a tempore de quo non exstat memoria solebant[2] idemque henricus Smyth sic inde seisitus sexto die decembris anno regni predicti nuper Regis henrici septimi nono Mesuagia Cotagia et terras sepibus et fossis circumclusit eadem que Mesuagia et Cotagia prosterni et devastari voluntarie fecit et ab occupacione culture et iconomie in pasturam brutorum animalium conuertit et illa sic hucusque tenentur ob quod duodecim aratra **que** ibidem circa culturam terrarum illarum occupata fuerunt detrahuntur et octoginta persone que circa eandem culturam similiter ocupari et eciam in Mesuagiis et Cotagiis predictis moram trahere solebant lamentando abinde inuiti recedere coacti fuerunt et ociosi exinde permanerunt et sic miseram vitam extunc duxerunt et ex veri-

henr[ico] Smyth non scr[ibat]
Stretton super Strete
scr[ibat] Gil[es] †
r[espondere]
tres a
sept[imanas]

I. ix

(Membrane 54)

x

^a Sic.

---

[1] Stretton Baskervile, Dugdale.

[2] It is probable that the clause assigning forty acres to each messuage is merely common form, to show the case to be within the Act 4 H. VII. c. 19, 'For kepyng up of houses for husbandrie.' It apparently leaves forty acres for each cottage, which is very unusual, though there seems to be a parallel case in Flechamsted (p. 440, *infra*).

Dugdale's words are : ' In whose [John de Twyford's] family it continued till H. VII. Time that Thomas Twyford, having begun the Depopulation thereof, in 4 H. VII. decaying 4 messuages, and three cottages, whereunto clx Acres of Errable Land belonged, sold it to Henry Smith Gentleman. Which Henry following that Example, in 9 H. VII. enclosed, &c. [according to this entry]. [Inq. super Depop. 9. H. VIII. and 3 E. VI.]' (*Warw.* p. 36).

simili sic misere obierunt et quod magis dolendum est ecclesia parochialis ea occasione de Stretton predicta in ruinam et decasum existit ita quod congregacio Christianorum que ibidem pro diuinis officiis audiendis venire solebant vlterius ibidem non habetur et Cultus dei ibidem penitus cassatur animalia in ecclesia illa ab tempestatibus aeris protegantur ac animalia bruta super sepulturas corporum Christianorum in Cemiterio ecclesia [a] illius sepultorum pascuntur et ecclesia et Cimiterium illa in omnibus prophanantur in malum exemplum aliorum in tali casu se habere disponentium.[1] Et quod Walterus Smyth filius et heres predicti henrici et in custodia domini Regis existens racione minoris etatis modo seisitus existit in tenementis predictis in dominico suo vt de feodo Et tenementa illa tenentur de [b]

Comes Salop[ie]   Et dicunt quod Georgius Comes Salopie nuper fuit et adhuc seisitus existit in dominico suo vt de feodo de duobus Mesuagiis et sexaginta acris terre arrabilis cum pertinenciis in Wylly [2] in Comitatu predicto et cum quolibet Mesuagio triginta acre terre arrabilis locari et ocupari solebant et sic inde seisitus ante quartum diem Nouembris anno decimonono predicti nuper Regis henrici septimi predictus Comes cuidam henrico Salisbery predicta duo Mesuagia cum dictis sexaginta acris terre ad firmam dimisit habenda sibi pro termino certorum annorum adhuc non finitorum virtute cuius dimissionis dictus henricus inde possessionatus existens quarto die Marcii anno regni predicti nuper Regis anglie septimi decimo[nono] [c] predicta Mesuagia voluntarie proici et devastari fecit et sic adhuc permanere permisit ac terras predictas cum alio Mesuagio ibidem tradi [3] et ocupari fecit ob quod octo persone

[a] Sic.   [b] Blank in MS.   [c] MS. partly illegible: inferred from preceding.

[1] This entry fully justifies the language of the preamble of the Act 7 H. VIII. c. 1 ('Thacte advoidyng pullyng downe of Townes'), 'wherby the husbandry which is the greatyst commodite of this realme for sustenance of man ys greatly decayed, Churches destrued, the servyce of God wythdrawen,' &c.

[2] The earl was lord of a manor here (*Warw.* pp. 51-53).

[3] The average area to a messuage upon leaseholds of lay land in Warwickshire being 28 acres, this gives a total ingrossing of [88] acres.

que in Mesuagiis illis manere solebant abinde vagando recesserunt et tenementa illa valent per annum viginti et sex solidos et quatuor denarios   Et tenentur de [a]

ET DICUNT QUOD Nicholaus Mallory nuper fuit seisitus in dominico suo vt de feodo de vno Mesuagio et triginta acris terre arrabilis et vsualiter arrate in Eysenell [1] in comitatu predicto que cum Mesuagio illo locari tradi et ocupari solebant et fuerunt et sic inde seisitus vicesimo die Nouembris anno regni Regis henrici septimi tercio Mesuagium illud in decasum fore et existere voluntarie permisit   Ita quod Mesuagium illud ad sustentacionem iconomie non manutenetur sed in ruina positum fuit et existit terras que predictas ab vsu culture in pasturam animalium conuertit et posuit et ea occasione vnum aratrum deponitur et sex persone que ibidem inhabitare solebant abinde recesserunt et tenementa illa tenentur de   [a]   Et valent per annum quadraginta solidos   Et dicunt quod Edwardus Cave in iure dorothee vxoris sue filie et heredis predicti Nicholai Malory modo seisitus existit in dominico suo vt de feodo de tenementis predictis.

Mallory lxxxxij

Cave f[iat] s[ub] p[lena]

ET DICUNT QUOD   [a]   harvy nuper fuit seisitus in dominico suo vt de feodo de vno Mesuagio et viginti quatuor acris terre arrabilis et vsualiter arrate in Bulkyngton [2] in Comitatu predicto que cum Mesuagio illo locari et ocupari solebant et fuerunt et sic inde seisitus secundo die . . . .[b] anno regni domini Regis nunc secundo Mesuagium illud in decasum fore et existere voluntarie permisit ita quod Mesuagium illud ad sustentacionem iconomie non manutenetur sed in ruinam positum fuit et existit [terras que][c] predictas cum alio Mesuagio [3] ibidem tradi et ocupari fecit et ea occasione quatuor persone que ibidem inhabitare solebant

harvy

[a] Blank in MS.   [b] MS. illegible.   [c] Conjectural : MS. illegible.

[1] Esenhull, Dugd. Now Easenhall. The family of Mallory were lords of the manor (Dugd. *Warw.* 57). For the Cave-Mallory pedigree see *ib.* p. 58.

[2] Bochintone, Domesday. Bulkinton, Dugdale. Now Bulkington. The manor belonged to Lord Zouche of Haringworth (*Warw.* p. 4).

[3] Following the reasoning in the parallel case of Grafton (p. 405, *n.* 3, *supra*), this gives a total area of [56] acres ingrossed.

abinde recesserunt   Et tenementa illa tenentur de   [a]
Et valent per annum sexdecim sol[idos][b] cuiusquidem harvy statum de et in tenementis predictis fratres hospitalis sancti Iohannis in Couentre modo habent.

Quyncy[c] f[iat] s[ub] p[ena]

ET DICUNT quod Ricardus Quyney[c] nuper fuit et adhuc seisitus existit in dominico suo vt de feodo de vno Mesuagio et quadraginta acris terre arrabilis et vsualiter arrate in Wolvehamcote[1] in Comitatu predicto que cum Mesuagio illo locari tradi et ocupari solebant et sic inde seisitus septimo die Marcii anno regni domini Regis nunc primo Mesuagium illud in decasum fore et sic adhuc existere voluntarie permisit ita quod ad sustentacionem iconomie non manutenentur[c] sed in ruinam positum et sic existit   Et dicunt quod ea occasione sex persone [que][d] ibidem [inhabitare solebant abinde recesserunt et tenementa illa tenentur de   [a]   Et valent per annum sexdecim solidos.

Ferrers f[iat] s[ub] p[ena]

ET DICUNT quod Iohannes Ferrers Miles nuper fuit seisitus in dominico suo [vt de][d] feodo de vno Mesuagio et triginta acris terre arrabilis et vsualiter arrate in parochia de Wolvehamcote[2] predicta in Comitatu predicto que cum Mesuagio illo locari ocupari et tradi solebant et sic inde seisitus quinto die Marcii [anno][d] regni nuper Regis henrici septimi sextodecimo Mesuagium illud in decasum fore et existere permisit ita quod ad sustentacionem iconomie non manutenetur sed in ruinam cecidit et sic existit et ea occasione sex persone que ibidem inhabitare solebant abinde recesserunt Et tenementa illa valent per annum duodecim solidos et tenentur de   [a]   Et quod   [a]   Ferrers filius et heres predicti Iohannis Ferrers Militis nunc existit seisitus in tenementis predictis in dominico suo vt de feodo et est in custodia domini Regis racione minoris etatis sue.

[a] Blank in MS.   [b] Conjectural: MS. partly illegible.   [c] Sic.
[d] Conjectural: MS. illegible.

[1] Wolphamcote or Ovencote, Dugd.   Now Wolthamcote.   This manor belonged to the family of Peto (*Warw.* p. 214).

[2] 'Wolvehamcote.' Here, as elsewhere, I interpret the formula mentioning the disuse of 'iconomia' as indicating conversion to pasture, as stated more distinctly in the next entry. See General Introduction, p. 37, *supra*. Rous mentions Wulhampcote as a place destroyed before 1491 (*Hist. Reg. Angl.* fo. 110 b).

WARWICKSHIRE

Et dicunt quod Willelmus Pereson de Banbery nuper fuit et adhuc seisitus existit in dominico suo vt de feodo de vno Mesuagio et viginti octo acris [terre]^a arrabilis et vsualiter arrate in alseley¹ in Comitatu predicto que cum Mesuagio illo locari tradi et ocupari solebant et sic inde seisitus decimo die Marcii anno regni domini Regis nunc quarto Mesuagium illud in decasum fore et existere voluntarie permisit ita quod ad sustentacionem iconomie non manutenetur sed in ruinam cecidere^b et sic existere permissum est ac terras illas a vsu culture in pasturam animalium conuertit et sic illas adhuc tenet et ea occasione vnum aratrum depon[itur et]^a . . . .^c persone² que ibidem inhabitare solebant abinde recesserunt Et tenementa illa valent per annum quadraginta solidos Et tenentur de ^d

[margin: Pereson f[iat] s[ub] p[ena]]

Et dicunt quod Willelmus Smyth nuper fuit seisitus in dominico suo vt de feodo de v[no]^e Mesuagio et viginti acris terre arrabilis et vsualiter arrate in allesley predicta in Comitatu predicto que cum Mesuagio predicto locari tradi et ocupari solebant et fuerunt et sic inde seisitus sexto die Marcii anno regni domini Regis nunc sexto Mesuagium illud in decasum fore et existere voluntarie permisit Et terras illas ab vsu culture in pasturam animalium conuertit et sic adhuc tenet et ea occasione sex persone que ibidem inhabitare solebant abinde recesserunt et tenementa et terre [ille]^a valent per annum quadraginta solidos Et tenentur de Georgio Nevell domino de Burgauenny et idem dominus de Burgauenny

[margin: Smyth]

^a Conjectural: MS. illegible.   ^b Sic.   ^c MS. illegible.
^d Blank in MS.   ^e Conjectural: MS. partly illegible.

¹ 'Alseley.' Allesley, Dugdale. The manor was in the hands of the family of Nevill. See next entry and *Warw.* p. 90.

² Following the reasoning in Grafton (2), p. 406, *n.* 1, *supra*, by (*a*) and (*b*) we get 4 (4·3) persons evicted. (*c*) The average area per person evicted by lay freeholders from inclosed pasture in Warwickshire = 8·3 acres, which gives 3 (3·3) evictions. (*d*) The average area per person evicted from the land of lay freeholders = 6·37 acres, which gives 4 (4·3) evictions. (*e*) The average number of persons to an aratrum on lay freeholders' land = 5, but the average number of acres to an aratrum = 41·16; which data give 3 (3·4) evictions here. I adopt [4] as a mean number.

illas tenet vlterius de domino Rege Et dicunt quod predictus dominus de Burgavenny racione illa aliqu[a] . . . . . **redditus** exitus seu proficua de tenementis illis hucusque non percepit aut habuit nec in presenti habet etc.

ET DICUNT quod Iohannes hugford nuper fuit et adhuc seisitus existit in dominico suo vt de feodo de duobus Mesuagiis et quinquaginta acris terre arrabilis et vsualiter arrate in pryncethorp[1] in Comitatu predicto que cum Mesuagiis illis locari tradi et ocupari solebant et fuerunt scilicet cum quolibet ipsorum Mesuagiorum viginti acre terre inde ad minus et sic inde seisitus quarto die Februarii anno regni domini Regis nunc tercio Mesuagia illa in decasum fore et existere voluntarie permisit ita quod ad sustentacionem iconomie non manutenetur[b] et ea occasione vnum aratrum deponitur et octo persone que in mansionibus predictis inhabitare solebant ab eisdem Mansionibus exire coartebantur et compellebantur Et tenementa illa valent per annum viginti quinque solidos Et vnum Mesuagium cum viginti acris terre parcella dictarum quinquagintarum[b] acrarum terre tenetur de domino Rege et aliud Mesuagium cum triginta acris terre residuum tenetur de[c]

ET DICUNT quod Thomas Shukborugh armiger nuper fuit et adhuc seisitus existit in dominico suo vt de feodo de vno Capitali Mesuagio et septuaginta acris terre arrabilis et vsualiter arrate et cum Mesuagio illo locate in Napton[2] in Comitatu predicto et sic inde seisitus Mesuagium illud quarto die Marcii anno regni henrici septimi nuper Regis anglie quinto in ruinam et decasum cadere et sic adhuc existere voluntarie permisit ita quod ea occasione duodecim persone que ibidem morare[b] solebant abinde exire cohortebantur[d] Et tenementa illa valent per annum quinque libras et tenentur de[c]

[a] MS. illegible. [b] Sic. [c] Blank in MS. [d] Sic : and in following entries.

[1] Prinsthorpe, Dugd. Now Prince Thorpe. John Hugford was lord of the manor (*Warw.* p. 31).

[2] Neptone, Domesday. Now Napton-on-the-Hill. T. S. was lord of the manor. For other inclosures by him see Nethershukborough, p. 411, *supra* (*Warw.* p. 235).

WARWICKSHIRE

ET DICUNT quod Thomas Catesby armiger nuper fuit et adhuc seisitus existit de vno Mesuagio et triginta acris terre arrabilis et vsualiter arrate et cum Mesuagio illo locate et ad firmam tradite in Wollescote[1] in Comitatu predicto in dominico suo vt de feodo et sic inde seisitus Mesuagium illud octauo die Ianuarii anno decimo octauo predicti nuper Regis henrici septimi in ruinam cadere et in decasum fore et sic adhuc existere voluntarie permisit ita quod ea occasione septem persone que ibidem inhabitare solebant abinde exire cohortebantur et compellebantur Et tenementa illa valent per annum viginti solidos Et tenetur[a] de[b]   *Catesby lxxxxiij*

ET DICUNT quod predictus Thomas Catesby armiger nuper fuit et adhuc seisitus existit de vno Mesuagio et triginta acris terre arrabilis vsualiter arrate ac cum Mesuagio illo tradite et locate in Grenborugh[2] in Comitatu predicto et sic seisitus existens vicesimo die Marcii anno sexto domini Regis nunc Mesuagium illud in ruin[am et][c] decasum fore et existere voluntarie permisit ita quod ea occasione sex persone que ibidem inhabitare solebant abinde exire cohortebantur Et tenementa illa valent per annum viginti solidos Et tenentur de[b]   *Catesby bis f[iat] s[ub] p[ena]*

ET DICUNT [quod][d] Iohannes Rodbourne nuper fuit possessionatus de vno Mesuagio et triginta acris terre arrabilis et vsualiter arrari consuete et cum illo Mesuagio locari et tradi consuete in Wollescote predicta et sic possessionatus existens sexto die Ianuarii [anno][d] septimo predicti nuper Regis henrici septimi Mesuagium illud in ruinam et decasum fore et existere voluntarie permisit ita quod modo ad sustentacionem iconomie non manutenetur per quod vnum aratrum deponitur et sex persone que ibidem inhabitare solebant abinde exire cohortebantur et compellebantur Et tenementa illa valent per annum viginti solidos et tenetur[a]   *Couentre Rodbourne f[iat] s[ub] p[ena]*

[a] Sic.   [b] Blank in MS.   [c] MS. partly illegible
[d] Conjectural : MS. illegible.

[1] Woscote, Dugdale. Now Wolscot. The manor was in the family of Catesby (*Warw.* p. 221).

[2] Granborough, Dugdale. The manor was in the family of Catesby (*Warw.* p. 220).

438 THE DOMESDAY OF INCLOSURES, 1517

Couentre

de   a   Et quod Iohannes prior Monasterii Beate Marie de Couentre de tenementis illis nunc seisitus existit in iure eiusdem Monasterii in dominico suo vt de feodo.

ET DICUNT quod Willelmus Banwell de Couentre nuper fuit seisitus in dominico suo vt de feodo de vno Mesua[gio et] [b] viginti acris terre arrabilis vsualiter arrate ac cum Mesuagio illo tradite et locate in Bobenhill [1] in Comitatu predicto et sic seisitus existens quinto die Nouembris anno regni predicti nuper Regis henrici septimi duodecimo Mesuag[ium illud in] [c] ruinam et decasum fore et existere voluntarie permisit per quod sex persone que ibidem inhabitare solebant abinde exire cohortebantur Et tenementa illa valent per annum quatuordecim solidos et tenentur de   a   [Et di]cunt [b] q[uod] [b] Willelmi Banwell statum de et in tenementis predictis Thomas Mountford modo habet.

f[iat] s[ub] p[ena] Mountford

f[iat] s[ub] p[ena] Draper

ET DICUNT quod Thomas Draper nuper fuit possessionatus de duobus Mesuagiis et quadraginta acris terre arrabilis vsualiter arrate ac cum Mes[uagiis] [b] illis locate et tradite in Bobenhull [d] predicta reuercione inde Edwardo Belknap Militi spectante et sic possessionatus existens tercio die Februarii anno regni domini Regis nunc quarto Mesuagia illa ab vsu et sustentacione ic[onomie] [b] in Cotagiis conuertit et adhuc existunt [2] sic quod modo ad sustentacionem iconomie non

---

[a] Blank in MS.   [b] MS. partly illegible.   [c] Conjectural: MS. illegible.   [d] Sic.

[1] 'Bobenhull,' Dugdale. Now Bubenhall. The manor was in the family of Crofte (*Warw.* p. 35).

[2] The number of inhabitants to a messuage in the case of farm tenants on lay land in Warwickshire = 16. But this is the unique case of Braylys (p. 419). It is better, therefore, to take (*a*) the average number of inhabitants of a messuage on lay property, which = 6. (*b*) The average area to a messuage on lay land = 31·4 acres. From these data we may infer 8 (7·6) persons to have been evicted here, supposing the two messuages actually destroyed. (*c*) The average area per person evicted from land inclosed to pasture by lay freeholders = 8·3 acres, which, on the same supposition, gives 5 (4·8) evictions. (*d*) The average area per person evicted from the land of lay freeholders = 6·37 acres, which, again on the same supposition, gives 6 (6·2) evictions here. I take 6, therefore, as the number which would have been evicted from these two messuages had they been totally destroyed. But they were converted into cottages. I deduct, therefore, 4 from the total number of evictions, which leaves two inhabitants to each cottage and [2] persons evicted.

Manutenentur Et tenementa illa valent per annum triginta sex solidos et quatuor denarios et tenentur de [a]

E[T DICU]NT [b] quod Edwardus Belknap Miles de tenementis predictis modo seisitus existit in dominico suo vt de feodo.

Et iidem Iuratores DICUNT quod Iohannes Turnour de Couentre Bocher nuper fuit et adhuc existit seisitus de septuaginta acris terre arrabilis et arrari consuete in Eythorp [1] in Comitatu predicto que quidem terre locari et ocupari solebant cum quodam Mesuagio ipsius Iohannis vocato Marteyns house et de triginta acris terre arrabilis in Eythorp predicta que locari et ocupari solebant in iconomia cum vno Mesuagio ipsius Iohannis vocato hyllys house in Eythorp predicta in Comitatu predicto et sic seisitus sexto die Septembris anno regni domini Regis nunc octauo terras illas a Mesuagiis illis separauit [2] et dimisit eas cuidam Edwardo lapworth pro termino certorum annorum adhuc durancium Et quod tenementa predicta valent per annum quatuor libras sexdecim solidos et octo denarios et ea racione quod terras predictas a Mesuagiis predictis sep[arauit] [c] duo aratra deponuntur et sex persone diminuuntur et tenementa illa tenentur de domino Rege.

Turnour

ET DICUNT QUOD Nicholaus Malory armiger nuper fuit seisitus in dominico suo vt de feodo de vno Mesuagio et viginti acris terre arrabilis et arrari consuete in payleton [3] in Comitatu predicto et cum Mesuagio illo ocupate et locate Et sic seisitus sexto die aprilis anno regni predicti nuper Regis henrici septimi septimo terras illas in pasturam animalium ab

f [iat] s[ub] p[ena] Malory

[a] Blank in MS. [b] MS. partly illegible. [c] Conjectural : MS. partly illegible.

[1] 'Eythorp.' Eathorp, Dugdale. The manor was not in the Crown, but in the family of Hugford (*Warw.* p. 208).

[2] The separation of the land from the houses was probably interpreted by the commissioners as involving a statutory decay of the houses under 4 H. VII. c. 19, or, at least, an offence against the proclamation of 1514 (see p. 7, *supra*). I have therefore tabulated the two messuages as decayed.

[3] Paylington, Dugdale. Now Pailton. The manor was in the family of Andrews (*Warw.* p. 58).

(Membrane 56) xii

Smyth

lxxxiiij [c]

vsu iconomie conuertit ita quod tres persone **ibidem** labore carent et tenementa illa valent per annum tresdecim solidos et quatuor denarios et tenentur de [a]

ET DICUNT quod Iohannes Smyth nuper de Flechamsted [1] gentylman nuper fuit [seisitus in dominico] [b] suo vt de feodo de Centum acris pasture cum pertinenciis in Flechamsted in parochia de Stonley et sic inde seisitus sexto die Marcii anno regni predicti nuper Regis henrici septimi octauo terras illas sepibus et fossis [inclusit] [b] et imparcauit et parcum nouum inde fecit et feras in eodem posuit et fere ibidem adhuc nutriuntur et pascuntur et pastura illa tenetur de domino Rege tempore imparcacionis illius fuit de anuo valore Centum . . . . [d]

[ET] [b] DICUNT quod henricus Smyth filius et heres predicti Iohannis Smyth nuper fuit seisitus de duobus Mesuagiis vno Cotagio et quadraginta [e] acris terre arrabilis et arrari annuatim consuete in Flechamsted in [parochia de] [b] Stoneley predicta in Comitatu predicto in dominico suo vt de feodo et cum vtroque eorundem Mesuagiorum quadraginta [e] acre terre inde ad firmam locari tradi et ocupari in Cultura solebant Et idem henricus [de tenementis] [b] illis seisitus existens cum tenementis illis elargauit parcum predictum et illas imparcauit et inclusit palis et Fossis et sic illas tenet Mesuagia et Cotagium illa in decasum et ruinam voluntarie permisit et adhuc permittit et terras [illas] [b] in pasturam ferarum et aliorum animalium Conuertit et illis sic adhuc vsus est ob quod duo aratra detrahuntur et viginti persone suis laboribus et mansionibus Carent et Mesuagia et terre ille valent per annum quadraginta . . . [d] et predicta Cotagia sex solidos [2] Et tenentur de [a]

[a] Blank in MS.   [b] Conjectural: MS. illegible.   [c] Sic: struck through in text.
[d] MS. illegible.   [e] Sic.

[1] Nether-Flechamsted, Dugdale.   Now Fletchamstead.
[2] Dugdale's account of these two inclosures is as follows (*Warw.* p. 184): 'John Smith, a wealthy Citizen of Coventre, (living in the Spon-Street) purchased this [Esc. 3 H. VII.] and other lands of good Value. . . To whom succeeded Henry his Son and Heir, who in 12 H. VII. made [Inq. super Depop. 3 E. VI.] a Park of the one half of this Lord-

Et quod idem henricus Smyth sexto die Maii anno regni predicti nuper Regis duodecimo tunc et adhuc seisitus existens in dominico suo vt de feodo de duobus Mesuagiis et sexaginta acris terre arrabilis et arrari annuatim consuete in Flechamsted in parochia de Stoneley predicta in Comitatu predicto cum vtroque Mesuagiorum illorum triginta acre terre occupari et locari solebant . . . .[a] in Cotagia absque terris cum eisdem . . at[is][b] Conuertit[1] et illa in vsu manutenencie iconomie vlterius non tenet et terras illas ab vsu iconomie in pasturam animalium conuertit et mutauit per quod duo aratra detrahuntur sex persone . . .[a] depriuantur tenementa que illa valent per annum quadraginta sex solidos et octo denarios et tenentur de domino Rege Et quod Walterus Smyth filius et heres predicti henrici in custodia domini Regis existens

[a] MS. illegible.   [b] MS. mutilated.

ship, converting [*ibid.*] the Rest into Pasture, whereby 4 of the 5 Messuages there being, went to Decay. In that Park he then also made a Pool [*ibid.*] of certain Ground that had formerly been a Medow; and in 20 H. VII. obtain'd in Exchange [Pat. 20 H. VII. p. 2] from the Abbot of Stonley, for other Lands, all that belong'd to the Monks of that House in this Flechamsted.'

It will be seen that the quotation of Dugdale differs from this Return in important particulars. Nothing is said in the Chancery MS. to lead to the inference that there were only five messuages in the place. It appears by Dugdale's original note from the Inquisition of 3 E. VI. that in 1548 fresh evidence was taken of inclosures made as far back as 1497, a proceeding which was within Hales's commission; and in the case of Astley we find that it actually took place. See Strype, *Eccl. Mem.* II. ii. 360 (Oxford, 1822). Dugdale's note of this entry appears to be due to a hasty reading of the MS., which is itself obscure; but his statement that one half of the lordship was imparked certainly favours my reading of 120 acres as against his own of 40 acres.

This Return supplies particulars for the pedigree of the family not given in Dugdale.

For the murder of (Sir) Walter Smith, here mentioned, by his wife in 1554 see Dugd. *Warw.* pp. 40-41.

[1] I have taken the presentment of the conversion of two messuagia into cotagia, which could only have been through the decay or pulling down of part of them, as equivalent for statistical purposes to a presentment of their decay. For a parallel see the case of Retherfeld Pypaid Oxon., p. 383, *supra*.

racione minoris etatis de predictis parco et cotagiis ᵃ predicta modo seisitus existit in dominico suo vt de feodo.

hastynges

ET DICUNT quod Ricardus hastynges nuper fuit seisitus in dominico suo vt de feodo de vno Capitali Mesuagio et ducentis acris terre arrabilis et vsualiter arrate in Draknage¹ in parochia de W[hita]ker ᵇ in Comitatu predicto que cum Mesuagio illo locari tradi et ocupari solebant et fuerunt et sic inde seisitus sexto die Marcii anno regni predicti nuper Regis henrici septimi duodecimo Mesuagium illud in decasum fore et existere voluntarie permisit Et dictas ducentas acras terre arrabilis ab vsu culture et iconomie in pasturam animalium conuertit et sic adhuc tenet per quod duo aratra detrahuntur et duodecim persone circa eandem culturam terrarum illarum ocupati fuerunt et in Mesuagio predicto moram trahere solebant lamentando abinde inuiti recedere coacti sunt et ociosi exinde permanserunt Et quod tenementa illa valent per annum quinque libras sex solidos et octo denarios et tenentur de ᶜ

assheby f[iat] s[ub] p[ena]

ET DICUNT [quod] ᵈ Thomas assheby nuper fuit seisitus in dominico suo vt de feodo de vno Mesuagio vocato Barnys place et triginta acris terre arrabilis et arrari consuete in lapworth in Comitatu predicto et cum Mesuagio illo in iconomia locate et tradite et sic seisitus quarto die Februarii anno regni predicti nuper Regis henrici septimi duodecimo Mesuagium illud cum pertinenciis devastari et in ruinam fore voluntarie permisit et sic existit per quod sex persone a suis prioribus laboribus depriuantur² et valent per annum tenementa illa viginti solidos et tenentur de ᶜ ³

ᵃ MS. illegible. ᵇ MS. partly illegible. ᶜ Blank in MS. ᵈ Conjectural : MS. illegible.

¹ Drakenedge, Dugd. Dugdale quotes this Return as here set out (*Warw.* p. 752).

² The phrase 'a suis prioribus laboribus depriuantur' is obviously a litotes for eviction, and seems to imply conversion. It is almost unprecedented in this Inquisition in this connexion, though it occurs again in Kingeswod, Wollescote, and Ichyngton, pp. 444, 517, *infra*, and probably in Flechamsted where an hiatus occurs on the preceding page. It illustrates the want of uniformity with which these Returns were made that no mention occurs in this case of the putting down of a plough, though it does in the next, as in that of Kingeswod, p. 444.

³ The manor was in the family of Catesby (*Warw.* p. 555).

ET DICUNT quod Iasper leke nuper fuit et adhuc seisitus [a] in dominico suo vt de feodo de vno Mesuagio et triginta acris terre arrabilis et arrari consuete in Phyllyngley[1] in Comitatu predicto et cum Mesuagio illo in iconomia diu locate tradite et ocupate et sic inde seisitus quinto die Nouembris anno regni domini Regis nunc tercio Mesuagium illud cum pertinenciis devastari et in ruinam voluntarie permisit et sic adhuc fore existit per quod vnum aratrum deponitur et sex persone abinde recedere coacti sunt et ociosi facti sunt Et tenementa illa valent per annum triginta sex solidos et octo denarios Et tenentur de [b]

leke f[iat] s[ub] p[ena]

ET DICUNT quod Decanus et Capitulum Collegii beate Marie in Warwico[2] nuper fuerunt et adhuc seisiti existunt de vno Mesuagio et triginta acris terre arrabilis et arrari consuete in Woluerton in Comitatu predicto et cum Mesuagio illo in iconomia diu ocupate locate et tradite et sic seisiti existentes nono die Marcii anno regni predicti nuper Regis henrici septimi octauo Mesuagium illud devastari et in ruinam cadere voluntarie permiserunt et sic adhuc fore permittunt ita [quod] [c] ea occasione quinque persone a suis mansionibus ibidem abinde recesserunt et in ocium perducuntur Et tenementa illa valent per annum duodecim solidos Et tenentur de domino Rege vt de Comitatu suo Warrewici.

decanus Warwici [a] scr[ibat] Gilez r[espondere] Crastino a[n]imarum

ET IURATORES PREDICTI DI[CUNT][d] quod Willelmus Medley[3] nuper fuit seisitus in dominico suo vt de feodo de duobus Mesuagiis et quadraginta acris terre arrabilis et arrari consuete in Whitnasshe in Comitatu predicto et cum quolibet Mesuagio Mesuagiorum illorum viginti acre terre locate et diu in iconomia tradite et ocupate fuerunt et sic inde seisitus sexto die Nouembris anno regni predicti nuper Regis henrici septimi

Medley [a] Gilez r[espondeat] crastino a[n]imarum

[a] Sic: verb omitted.   [b] Blank in MS.   [c] Conjectural: MS. illegible.
[d] Conjectural: MS. partly illegible.

[1] Now Fillongley (*Warw.* pp. 725-33).
[2] The Dean and Canons of the Collegiate Church of St. Mary, Warwick, were lords of the manor (*Warw.* p. 468).
[3] For the incloser, William Medley, who was lord of the manor, see *sub* Tachebroke Malory, p. 407, *supra*.

vicesimo secundo Mesuagia predicta . . .^a Cotagia[1] ab vsu mansionis pro iconomia voluntarie fieri fecit et illa sic adhuc tenet ita quod ad sustentacionem iconomie [b] manutenentur nec sustentantur et ea occasione duo aratra deponuntur et duodecim persone que ibidem inhabitare solebant a suis mansionibus recedere coacti fuerunt et in ocium perducuntur (Membrane 57) Et tenementa illa [valent per annum] [c] **viginti** solidos Et tenentur de domino Rege. ET DICUNT quod Thomas Marchio Dorsett modo seisitus existit in tenementis predictis vt in iure domine Margarete [2] vxoris sue.

m\rchio
Dors[ett]

Bewfo   ET DICUNT quod Iohannes Bewffo armiger fuit seisitus in
Ferrers
f[iat] s[ub]   dominico suo vt de feodo de vno Capitali Mesuagio et
p[ena]   sexaginta acris terre arrabilis et arrari consuete in Kingeswod [3]

lxxxv   in Comitatu predicto que cum Mesuagio illo locate et in iconomia ocupate fuerunt et [sic inde] [c] seisitus existens decimo die aprilis anno regni predicti nuper Regis henrici septimi vicesimo tercio Mesuagium predictum cum pertinenciis in decasum et ruinam cadere voluntarie permisit et sic adhuc existit terras que illas ab vsu iconomie et culture in pasturam animalium conuertit et sic adhuc tenet et ea occasione vnum aratrum deponitur et sex persone a suis prioribus laboribus abinde recesserunt et a suis mansionibus ibidem recedere coacti fuerunt et in ocium perducuntur Et tenementa illa valent per annum quinquaginta tres solidos et quatuor denarios Et tenentur de   [d]   Et Iohannes Bewffo filius et heres predicti Iohannis [4] modo habet statum in tenementis predictis et est infra etatem et in custodia Edwardi Ferrers Militis per literas patentes domini Regis nunc sibi concessas.

^a MS. illegible.   ^b A long erasure here.   ^c Conjectural : MS. illegible.   ^d Blank in MS.

[1] For the conversion to cottages as equivalent to a decaying of the houses see note to Flechamsted, p. 441, *n.* 1, *supra*.

[2] See p. 408, *n.* 1, *supra*.

[3] Kingwode-juxta-Badsley and Clinton, Dugdale. The manor had been in the family of Brome, and in this year (9 H. VIII.) passed by marriage of an heiress into that of Ferrers (Dugd. *Warw.* pp. 557, 675). The term 'capitale messuagium,' therefore, does not necessarily mean a manor house.

[4] The family of Beaufo, as it appears in Dugdale, was of some consequence in the county. This incloser died Sept. 29, 1516 (*Warw.* p. 197).

ET DICUNT quod Willelmus huett nuper fuit et adhuc possessionatus existit de vno Mesuagio et sexaginta acris terre arrabilis et annuatim arrari consuete ac cum Mesuagio illo vsualiter locate et tradite in Wollescote[1] in Comitatu predicto pro termino certorum annorum adhuc durancium reuercione inde Thome Priori domus siue prioratus de Rounton[2] et successoribus suis spactante[a] post terminum illum completum Et sic possessionatus existens quarto die Marcii anno Regni domini Regis nunc sexto Mesuagium predictum in quoddam Cotagium ab vsu iconomie conuertit aceciam in ruinam cadere permisit ita quod ad sustentacionem iconomie non manutenetur nec sustentatur per quod vnum aratrum deponitur et sex persone a suis mansionibus et suis prioribus laboribus ibidem depriuantur Et tenementa illa valent per annum triginta solidos Et tenentur de [b]

ET VLTERIUS DICUNT quod Thomas Catesby nuper fuit et adhuc existit seisitus in dominico suo vt de feodo de vno Mesuagio et quadraginta acris terre arrabilis et vsualiter arrate ac cum Mesuagio illo tradite et locate in Grendborugh in Comitatu predicto et sic seisitus existens sexto die Februarii anno regni predicti nuper Regis henrici septimi octauo Mesuagium illud in ruinam et decasum fore et existere voluntarie permisit ita quod ea occasione vnum aratrum deponitur et sex persone que ibidem inhabitare solebant abinde exire cohortebantur Et tenementa illa valent per annum sexdecim solidos Et tenentur de [b] *Catesby f[iat] s[ub] p[ena]*

ET DICUNT quod Edwardus Odyngselles nuper fuit seisitus in dominico suo vt de feodo de vno Mesuagio et triginta acris terre arrabilis et singulis annis arrate ac arrari et seminari consuete et cum Mesuagio illo locate ocupate et tradite *Odyngsellis*

---

[a] Sic. [b] Blank in MS.

[1] Woscote, Dugdale. See p. 441, *n.* 1, *supra*.
[2] Thome' &c. was perhaps Thomas Alton, who was prior in 1534 (Dugd. *Monast.* vi. 257). The Priory was that of Ronton or Ronthon, co. Staff. No property appears to have been held by it here at the time of the Dissolution (*ibid.* and cf. *Warw.* p. 221).

in Ichyngton¹ in Comitatu predicto et sic inde seisitus septimo die Nouembris anno regni predicti nuper Regis henrici septimi vicesimo secundo Mesuagium illud devastari et destrui fecit et terras illas in pasturam animalium conuertit per quod vnum aratrum ibidem subtrahitur et sex persone a suis prioribus laboribus ibidem depriuantur tenementa que illa tenentur de domino Rege et valent per annum viginti solidos etc.

Nobull

Et quod Iohannes Nobull sexto die Februarii anno Regni predicti nuper Regis henrici septimi vicesimo tercio tunc seisitus existens in dominico suo vt de feodo de vno Mesuagio et viginti acris terre arrabilis et arrate ab antiquo et cum Mesuagio illo locate in Ichyngton predicta in Comitatu predicto et dictis die et anno Mesuagium illud in quoddam Cotagium et ab vsu mansionis pro iconomie ᵃ voluntarie fieri fecit per quod vnum aratrum deponitur et sex persone occupacione sua carent² et tenementa illa tenentur de ᵇ Et valent per annum sexdecim solidos Et Edwardus Odyngselles modo habet statum in tenementis predictis.

ET DICUNT quod Iohannes Bukmere nuper fuit seisitus in dominico suo vt de feodo de vno Mesuagio et viginti et quatuor acris terre arrabilis et vsualiter arrari consuete et cum Mesuagio illo locate et tradite in Ichyngton in Comitatu predicto et sic inde seisitus sexto die Marcii anno regni domini Regis nunc octauo Mesuagium illud in Cotagium fieri fecit ita quod ad sustentacionem iconomie non manutenetur et terras illas aliis habitantibus eiusdem ville dimisit per quod vnum aratrum deponitur et due persone ocupacione carent³ et valent tenementa illa per annum decem et octo solidos Et tenentur de Edwardo Odynselles et ipse vlterius de domino

ᵃ Sic. ᵇ Blank in MS.

¹ Long-Ichington, Dugdale. Now Long Itchington. The incloser (Odyngsells) was lord of the manor (*Warw.* p. 239).

²,³ As I have explained under Flechamsted, p. 441, *n.* 1, *supra*, I have for statistical purposes tabulated the conversion of this messuagium into a cotagium as equivalent to the decay of a messuagium. It appears, however, from the form of the entry that no evictions took place, the inhabitants remaining in the reduced house, and being thrown out of employment by the conversion to pasture.

Rege qui quidem Edwardus nichil de exitibus reuencionibus redditibus et proficuis tenementorum illorum racione predicta adhuc percepit etc.

ET DICUNT quod Iohannes Whore nuper fuit seisitus de vno Mesuagio et octuaginta acris terre arrabilis et arrari consuete in dominico suo vt de feodo in Ichyngton predicta in Comitatu predicto et cum Mesuagio illo in iconomia locate diu ocupate et tradite et sic seisitus sexto die Marcii anno regni regis henrici septimi vicesimo Mesuagium illud cum pertinenciis devastari et in ruinam fore voluntarie permisit et sic . . .[a] terras que illas in pasturam animalium perduxit et fecit per quod vnum aratrum deponitur et quatuor persone a suis prioribus laboribus ibidem depriuantur Et valent tenementa illa per annum tres libras Et tenentur de [b]

ET DICUNT quod Iohannes dominus Clynton nuper fuit seisitus in dominico suo vt de feodo de vno Capitali Messuagio vocato bowlhall et de ducentis acris terre ad anuum valorem xx marcarum in Amyngton[1] in Comitatu predicto et sic seisitus existens iiij° die Marcii anno regni Regis predicti nuper henrici septimi secundo Messuagium illud in ruinam cadere voluntarie permisit per quod ij[a] aratra deponuntur et decem persone abinde recesserunt et ociose facte sunt et tenementa illa tenentur de [b]

(Membrane 58) Clynton

Et dicunt quod Thomas Vnderhill nuper fuit et adhuc Seisitus[2] existit de duobus Mesuagiis et quadraginta acre[c] terre arabilis et arari consuete ad annuum valorem xxiiij s. in honyngham[3] in Comitatu predicto et sic seisitus existens

[a] MS. illegible.   [b] Blank in MS.   [c] Sic.

[1] Amington, Dugdale. The name of 'hall' being given to this house points to its being the manor house. If so, this entry sets at rest the question raised by Dugdale as to the time at which the manor house passed from the family of Clinton to that of Repington (*Warw.* p. 812).

[2] 'Seisitus' is evidently here intended, as in the following entry, for the full form usual, ' in dominico suo vt de feodo.'

[3] Huningeham, Domesday. Now Honingham. T. U. was lord of the manor (*Warw.* p. 251).

448 THE DOMESDAY OF INCLOSURES, 1517

xxxxvj

vj⁽ᵗᵒ⁾ die Februarii anno regni domini Regis nunc Secundo Messuagia predicta in duobus cotagiis ab vsu iconomie fieri fecit ita quod ad sustentacionem iconomie non manutenentur per quod vnum aratrum deponitur et octo persone a suis Mansionibus recedere coacte fuerunt et tenementa illa tenentur de ᵃ

holier

Et dicunt quod Ricardus holyer nuper fuit seisitus de vno Mesuagio et triginta acre ᵇ terre arabilis eidem Messuagio adiacentis ad annuum valorem xxvj s. viij d. in Bentley ¹ in Comitatu predicto et sic seisitus ix° die Marcii anno regni predicti nuper Regis henrici septimi decimo Messuagium predictum in ruinam cadere voluntarie permisit per quod dimidium aratrum deponitur et iiij⁽ᵒʳ⁾ persone abinde ociosi recesserunt et tenementa illa tenentur de ᵃ

Nullus processus fiet versus infra-scr[iptum] laurencium Robynson pro eo quod mesuag[ium] infrascr[iptum] Pendit ᵇ in canc[ellaria] d[o]m[i]ni Regis indecis[um] quousque discuss[um] fuerit per mandatum commissionar[iorum] ³

Et dicunt quod laurencius Robinson nuper fuit seisitus de vno Messuagio et xx ᵇ acre terre arabilis eidem Mesuagio adiacentis ad annuum valorem xxij s. in Solyhu(ll)ᶜ in Comitatu predicto ² et sic Scisitus iiij⁽ᵗᵒ⁾ die aprilis anno vj⁽ᵗᵒ⁾ predicti nuper Regis henrici septimi Messuagium illud in decasum fore voluntarie permisit per quod vnum aratrum deponitur et octo persone a suis laboribus . .ᵈ mansionibus ibidem depriuantur Et predictus laurencius modo seisitus existit in tenementis predictis et valent per annum xx s.⁴ et tenentur de ᵃ

herthill

ET DICUNT quod Thomas herthill nuper fuit possessionatus de duobus Mesuagiis et quadraginta acre ᵇ terre arabilis iisdem messuagiis adiacentis ad annuum valorem quadraginta soli-

ᵃ Blank in MS.   ᵇ Sic.   ᶜ MS. partly illegible.   ᵈ MS. mutilated.

¹ The manor was in the family of De L'Isle (*Warw.* p. 740).
² The manor was at this time in the Crown (*Warw.* p. 665).
³ The marginal 'stet processus' shows that proceedings were in some cases begun, possibly on the initiative of the commissioners, perhaps only when set in motion by an inhabitant. See *sub* Clyff, next page.
⁴ This entry gives two statements as to the value of the 'tenementa,' a phrase which includes the messuagium. It is scarcely possible that the result of the inclosure, coupled with the decay of the house, should have been a fall in rental value from 22s. to 20s., nor is there any similar instance in these Inquisitions. I have taken 22s. as the correct figure.

WARWICKSHIRE

dorum in Clyff¹ in parochia de Kemysley² in Comitatu predicto et sic possessionatus iiij^{to} die Marcii anno regni Regis predicti nuper henrici septimi decimo Messuagia illa in cotagia ab vsu iconomie peruertit³ et terras illas in pasturam animalium conuertit et Iohannes coton modo habet statum in tenementis predictis et tenentur de ^a   *Coton*

Et dicunt quod Iohannes bracebrige⁴ armiger nuper fuit seisitus in dominico suo vt de feodo de tribus Messuagiis et sexaginta acre^b terre arrabilis et arrari consuete et cum Mesuagiis illis locate et tradite in Kynnysbury in Comitatu predicto et sic seisitus existens iiij° die Marcii anno regni predicti nuper regis henrici vij xij° Messuagia predicta in ruinam cadere voluntarie permisit per quod duo aratra deponuntur et octodecem persone a suis Mansionibus depriuantur Et Thomas bracebrigge modo seisitus existit in tenementis predictis et valent [per]^d annum v libras Et tenentur de domino Rege.   *Bracebrige† s[c]r[ibat] r[espondere] quindena· Mich[ael]is*

Et dicunt quod abbas de stanley⁵ fuit et adhuc existit seisitus in Iure sui Monasterii de vno capitali Messuagio et   *Stanley* s[c]r[ibat] gilez r[espondere] crastino a[n]i[m]arum*

^a Blank in MS.   ^b Sic.   ^c MS. *xv*ⁱ.   ^d Conjectural : MS. illegible.

¹ Cliffe, Dugdale. 'Of it I have not seen other mention than that Thomas Herthill was [Esc. 10 H. VIII.] presented in 10 H. VIII. for depopulating two messuages and inclosing xl Acres of Land here' (*Warw.* p. 752). The appearance in the Escheator's accounts points to the freehold as being in the Crown, 'possessionatus' indicating that the incloser was a tenant. See *sub* Braylys, p. 419, *n.* 1, *supra*.

² 'Kemysley' is, as Dugdale's notes show, for Kingsbury, in Domesday Chinesburie. Cf. the spelling of the same parish in the next entry (*Warw.* p. 746).

³ The number of [2] persons evicted here is arrived at by the process in Bobenhull (p. 438, *n.* 2, *supra*).

⁴ J. B. was lord of the manor (*ibid.*). For an imparcation by him see p. 451, *infra*, and for another inclosure by him in 1504 see Inq. 3 E. VI., p. 664, *infra*.

⁵ Stonely or Stoneley, Dugdale. Now Stoneleigh. 'Stonlei' the ancient name (*Warw.* p. 176). On p. 180 Dugdale gives a list of the Abbots, and to the names of the last three, Rob. Sutton (10 H. VII.), Thom. Hodskinson (probably this incloser), and Thom. Tutbury (27 H. VIII.), he appends a reference 'Inq. super Depop. 3 E. VI.'; but he does not mention this inclosure nor refer to this Inquisition. It appears however, in his transcript of this Inquisition, fo. 547.

II.   F

ccc acris arabiles[a] et arari consuetas[a] in stanley in Comitatu predicto et sic seisitus vj[to] die Marcii anno regni domini Regis nunc primo Messuagium illud in ruinam voluntarie permisit per quod ij⁰ aratra deponuntur et sexdecim persone a suis Mansionibus depriuantur Et acre[a] acrarum predictarum in pasturam animalium conuertit et messuagium illud valet per annum vij Marcas et tenetur de domino Rege.

Kyllyngworth Radulphus nuper abbas de Kyllyngworth[1] imparcauit de novo[2] vnum parcum vocatum wrygfyn[3] in anno iiij[to] predicti nuper Regis henrici septimi et in parco illo quadraginta acre[a] terre arabiles[a] paliis[a] circumclusit cum aliis terris pratis et pasturis de terris suis dominicalibus pro feris ibidem nutriendis et feras nunc in eodem habet.

Throgmorton Et dicunt quod Robertus throgmorton miles imparcauit et palis circumclvsit in anno secundo nuper Regis henrici septimi viginti dimidio[b] acras terre arabiles[a] cum aliis terris pratis pascuis et pasturis de terris dominicalibus eiusdem Roberti Throgmorton et novum parcum inde fecit pro feris nutriendis in cougheton.[4]

Et dicunt quod Thomas nuper marchio dorset de novo

[a] Sic. [b] Sic : MS. apparently dio[e] without a contraction. In Dugdale's transcript xx[d].

[1] For 'Radulphus' see note to Tachebroke Malory, p. 406, *supra*. Dugdale cites this inclosure as from Inq. super Depop. 9 H. VIII. (*Warw.* p. 176).

[2] The phrase 'de novo' seems to imply that a former imparcation had been put down. It occurs again at Astley, on next page.

[3] Rudfen, Dugdale. The name appears at the Dissolution as Wrydefine, the annual rental of the farm of the manor being 10*l*. (Dugd. *Monast.* vi. 225).

[4] 'Coctune, Domesday. Coughton, Dugdale 'In 2 H. VII. Robert [Throkmorton] made [Inq. super Depop. 9 H. VIII.] the Park here at Coughton, inclosing [Inq. super Depop. 3 E. VI.] therewith a certain Common Ground called Wike-Wood, wherunto he afterwards added [*ibid.*] Samburn Heath and Spiney's-Leys, lying within the said lordship of Samburne' (*Warw.* p. 525). The entry in this MS. is another instance of evidence being taken for a time antecedent to the date of the inquiry fixed by the Commission (see p. 441, *n.* 2, *supra*). Dugdale has made an error in attributing the entire inclosures here to Sir Robert Throkmorton. His notes of the Inquisition of 1549 show

imparcauit et palis circumclusit triginta acras bosc(is)[a] pascuis et pasturis[b] de terris dominicalibus et elargauit alium parcum cum octo decem acris terre in Astley.[1]

Et dicunt quod henricus smyth imparcauit et palis circumclusit triginta acras arabiles et centum acras terre bosc[is][a] pasturis[c] in anno primo Regis nunc in shyrford.[2] *Smyth*

Et dicunt quod Iohannes Bracebryge elargauit parcum in Kynnysbery cum decem acris terre. Bawdewynus hethe[3] imparcauit de novo vnum parcum in parochia de wotton et in parco illo inclusit viginti iiij^{or} acre[c] terre arabiles[c] cum aliis terris pascuis et pasturis in anno xiiij° predicti nuper Regis henrici septimi. *Bracebrige*

ET DICUNT quod Willelmus Wodeward nuper fuit et adhuc existit possessionatus pro termino certorum annorum adhuc durancium de vno Mesuagio et viginti quatuor acris terre arrabilis cum Mesuagio illo locate in harborugh[4] predicta in *(Membrane 59) xv xiiij Wodeward*

[a] MS. *bosc.*   [b] Sic : ablative cases.   [c] Sic.

that Samburn Heath and Spiney's-Leys, at any rate, were inclosed by his successor, Sir George Throkmorton, in 1527, R. T. having died on pilgrimage to Jerusalem in 1520 (*Warw.* p. 523).

[1] Here again we have an extract in Dugdale varying from this entry, while reference is made to this Inquisition : 'Which Thomas impaled [Inq. 9 H. VIII. super Depop.] 30 Acres of Wood and Pasture, for to make that Parke, here at Astley, now called the Little Parke ; and enlarg'd [Inq. super Depop. 3 E. VI.] the Great Parke there, with 90 Acres of Land, in 12 H. VII. taken out of the Precincts of Arley' (*Warw.* p. 79).

The former of these references may perhaps be explained by supposing that Dugdale's eye overlooked the mention of the 18 acres (cf. *sub* Shyttyngton, Castell Bromyche, and Tachebroke Malory, pp. 396, *n.* 1, 401, *n.* 2, 406, *n.* 3, *supra*), and he may himself, as an inhabitant of the neighbourhood, have added the statement about the Little Park. For the second reference see p. 663, *infra*. See *sub* Flechamsted, p. 440, *n.* 1, *supra*.

[2] Shirforde, Dugdale. In 37 H. VIII. (1545–46) this incloser bought the manor from the family of Purefey (*Warw.* p. 40). At the time of making the inclosure, therefore, he was probably a freeholder.

[3] 'Bawdewynus Hethe.' This person is mentioned in Dugd. *Warw.* p. 575, as being about this time lord of the manor of Forde-hall in Aspley. As an imparker he was presumably lord of this manor.

[4] Harborow Magna, Dugd. The manor was in the family of Ferrers (*Warw.* p. 66).

Comitatu predicto ad anuum valorem viginti solidorum et sic existens possessionatus sexto die Marcii anno regni domini Regis nunc secundo Mesuagium illud in quoddam Cotagium ab vsu mansionis iconomie voluntarie fieri fecit et sic adhuc permittit per quod vnum aratrum deponitur et quinque persone a suis mansionibus et laboribus ibidem recedere coacti fuerunt et in ocium ducuntur et tenementa [illa][a] tenentur de [b] Et quod Domina Dorothia Ferrers vidua modo habet statum in terris et tenementis predictis.

Ferrers

Et dicunt quod omnia et singula predicta Mesuagia domus et edificia que superius in hac Inquisicione per eosdem Iuratores de et pro ruina et vasto in eisdem Mesuagiis domibus et edificiis permissis factis perpetratis siue habitis presentantur ita ruinose [c] et vastata [c] existunt et quodlibet eorundem existit quod id illorum Mesuagiorum domorum et edificiorum quod superest siue ibidem remanet non sufficit pro mansura iconomie nec ad manutenciam iconomie et culture que de terris arrabilibus cum Mesuagiis domibus et edificiis illis requiruntur et fieri deberent.

lxxxxvij

Et Iuratores predicti dicunt quod omnia predicta decasus ruine Mesuagiorum inclusiones terrarum arrabilium et conuercio inde in pasturam animalium ac diminuciones populorum et quamplurima alia supradicta per eos superius presentata facta perpetrata et permissa sunt et a diu fuerunt contra formam diuersorum statutorum inde editorum ac in regni domini Regis depauperacionem et populi sui diminucionem Ecclesiarum que desolacionem ad magnum dampnum dicti [d] domini Regis in Comitatu predicto et partibus vicinis huic Comitatui comorantis ac in malum et pernisiosum exemplum aliorum in consimilibus casubus delinqu[entiu]m [e] se disponentium nisi cicius in hac parte 'de premissis prouideatur remedium congruum.

IN CUIUS rei testimonium tam Sigilla predictorum Comissionariorum vni parti presentis Inquisicionis cum predicto

[a] Conjectural: MS. mutilated.
[b] Blank in MS.
[c] Sic.
[d] In Oxon this recital has 'populi,'
which is consistent with what follows.
'Dicti' makes nonsense in connexion with 'comorantis.'
[e] MS. delinqm.

henrico Squier primo Iuratorum predictorum remanenti quam Sigilla predictorum Iuratorum alteri inde parti prefatis Comissionariis per ipsos Iuratores deliberate presentibus sunt appensa Data apud allesley predictam vicesimo secundo die Septembris anno regni Regis Henrici octaui nono supradicto.

NOTE.—For the Inquisition of 1517 for Cheshire, see p. 640, *infra*. pars xv

INQUISITION OF 1518

BEDFORDSHIRE

INTRODUCTION

IN 1518 two commissioners sat for Bedfordshire in substitution for Sir Andrew Wyndesore. They were Richard Dicons and John Hales.[1] Of these, Richard Dicons was perhaps the same as Queen Katharine's secretary of that name. He had, as Richard Decons, in 1509, been appointed joint keeper of the writs and rolls of the Common Pleas, probably for him a sinecure office. (S. P. Dom. H. VIII. i. 125.) In the same year he was appointed porter of Berkehamstede Castle, Herts, and of the lands called Ambrelayns in the same manor (*ibid.* 126) and also keeper of the great park of Fasterne, and of Bradon Forest, Wilts (*ibid.* 128). All these three appointments were made on May 22, 1509, the name being uniformly spelt. In 1511 he received a grant in survivorship of a corrody in the monastery of Warden (*ibid.* 1595), and in 1516 (when his name is spelt Dycons but the identity established by his description of 'keeper of writs in the Common Pleas') he received a life pension of 6*l.* 13*s.* 4*d.* (*ibid.* ii. 2736). He attended the Queen at the Field of the Cloth of Gold in 1520 (*ibid.* ii. 704). He appears to have continued as Queen Katharine's secretary, at any rate down to 1529 (*ibid.* iv. 6121). There were two families of the name in Bedfordshire, at Marston and Samford respectively, to one of which he probably belonged. He was certainly a landowner, for among Cromwell's papers in 1533 and in 1534 are several notes of an office or inquisition to be taken of the lands of Richard Dicons (*ibid.* vi. 299, ix., vii. 923, x. &c.). It

[1] P. 459.

seems improbable that Cromwell would have concerned himself with the devolution of these lands had they fallen to the Crown by escheat in default of heirs, and the existence of these notes, which disclose nothing, suggests the inference that Dicons had fallen into disgrace through his association with the Queen, from whom Henry had separated in 1531, and that his lands had been seized by the Crown. His name does not subsequently occur in the Domestic State Papers. No nominations to the commission of 1518 have been found. The commissioners' names and the dates and places of their sittings are taken from the recitals of these Returns and from the subsequent proceedings in the Court of Exchequer.

The other new commissioner was John Hales. He belonged to the parent stock of the family of Hales, settled in Kent (Hasted's 'Kent,' iv. 440, ed. 1799), and was himself a purchaser of land near Canterbury in the year 1529 (MS. R. O. Exch. Q. R. Mem. Roll 308, H. T. 20 H. VIII. inter commissiones, literas patentes, &c.) On Nov. 4, 1522, he was admitted to the office of third Baron of the Exchequer, being simply described as 'dilecto nobis Johanni Hales' (*ibid.* Roll 302, M. T. 14 H. VIII. m. 1), but he had for a year previously enjoyed an annuity of 80 marks during pleasure, payable out of the petty customs and subsidies of the port of London (*ibid.* Roll 303, E. T. 15 H. VIII. inter brevia), a sum which apparently he found some difficulty in extracting (*ibid.* Roll 306, E. T. 18 H. VIII. m. 1 dorso). In 1529, on the death of William Wutton, he was appointed second Baron (*ibid.* Roll 308, E. T. 20 H. VIII. m. 29) and was admitted on May 17 of that year in the presence of the Chancellor, Cardinal Wolsey, 'et aliorum magnatum de consilio domini Regis.' His name occurs in the proceedings of the Exchequer in 1536 (*ibid.* Roll 316, T. T. 28 H. VIII.) and 1538 (*ibid.* Roll 319, E. T. 30 H. VIII.). In Roll 319, M. T. 30 H. VIII. m. 60 dorso, is a recital of Letters Patent of the king, 'factis Johanni Smyth de officio secundi baronis huius Scaccarii,' in which it is stated that on May 14, 20 H. VIII. (1529), the king by Letters Patent bestowed the office of second Baron on John Hales. The operative part then grants to John Smyth the reversion of the office on its vacancy by death, resignation, or deposition of John Halys (*sic*). This, at any rate, suggests that John Hales, though alive, was not expected to live long, and, as a matter of fact, his name does not appear upon later Rolls of the Court of Exchequer. John Smyth sits in his place in the succeeding Term (cp. Foss, 'Lives of the Judges,' v. 185). These details are given because the chairman of Somerset's commission of 1549 was also John Hales, of the county of Warwick, who again has been confused by Strype, and Dugdale following him, with another John Hales, clerk of the Hanaper under Queen Mary. See p. 4, *n.* 1, *supra.*

The objects and character of the Inquisition of 1518 will be discussed in the Appendix, where Dugdale's notes of the Inquisitions of 1517 and 1518 for Warwickshire will be found printed. This Inquisition is plainly largely supplementary, filling up those particulars as to tenure of which pressure of time had probably prevented the investigation in 1517. Scanty though they are, the Returns are probably complete as they stand. It is an indication of the supplementary character of this Return that seven out of the nine Hundreds are represented, which makes it the more to be regretted that the original Inquisition for 1517 has not been preserved, seeing that it left so few *lacunae* to be made good. In conformity with the model followed in the case of other counties a Table has been prepared showing the proportions borne by the areas inclosed to the areas of the Hundreds, but this presents nothing instructive in view of the fragmentary nature of the Returns.

The proportion of inclosures to arable and pasture, the total being 822 acres, are 31·3 and 68·6 per cent. respectively. The Table 'Yearly Progress of Inclosures' shows the same decline in inclosures, both arable and pasture alike, on ecclesiastical estates as has appeared elsewhere, and the same significantly larger decline of ecclesiastical pasture inclosed immediately prior to the Inquisition. These figures are an answer to those who maintain that legislation was entirely inoperative to check the movement. The proportion to the whole of the total area of ecclesiastical land, however, was lower than in other counties, being only 7·29 per cent. It is impossible upon such scanty data to hazard a conjecture whether this truly represented the participation of lay and ecclesiastics respectively in the inclosing movement in Bedfordshire. The evictions of six persons from ecclesiastical land correspond very closely to this proportion.

The Table showing the 'Number of Inclosures and Distribution of Areas' suggests that the agricultural economy of Bedfordshire was rather one of small ownerships than of great estates, only 25 per cent. of the land in owners' hands belonging to lay lords of manors. In this respect Beds, Oxon, and Berks stand together, the other counties exhibiting a larger area of inclosures by lords of manors. Lay copyholds figure upon a small scale in Bedfordshire, but while there are no farm tenancies, leaseholds of lay land are 81·81 per cent· of all lay land let.

Upon ecclesiastical estates there was no inclosure of arable. The Table 'Status of actual Inclosers' shows that there was not much difference in the rigour with which laymen and ecclesiastics respectively carried out their improvements. The data showing the average number of persons connected with messuages and ploughlands are too scanty to justify any conclusions.

The Table of Rental Values shows that inclosed arable in Bedfordshire commanded 1s. an acre as against $9\frac{1}{4}d$. for pasture. In this respect Bedfordshire resembles Berks, for there also arable was valued higher, viz. at $9d$. as against $7\frac{3}{4}d$. for pasture. It is to be observed, on the other hand, that though Berkshire wool was rated in 1454 at 93s. 4d. a sack and Bedfordshire wool at only 80s., the pasture rents of Berkshire, like the arable, were lower than those of Bedfordshire. While, in conformity with the better rents for inclosed arable, the proportion of inclosures of arable was greater in Berks, in Beds, though with that exception greater than in other counties, it was only 31·3 to 68·6, a sign that the quantity of land superior in remunerativeness as inclosed arable was comparatively limited. The lowest rental value is that of 8*d*. for inclosed pasture in the hand of an ecclesiastical freeholder, the highest 1*s*. 2*d*. for arable in the hand of lay lords of manors.

INQUISITION OF 1518

BEDFORDSHIRE

INQUISICIO INDENTATA capta apud Bedford in predicto Comitatu Bedfordie sextodecimo die augusti anno regni Regis henrici octaui decimo coram Iohanne Veysy Clerico Decano Capelle domini Regis Ricardo Dycons Rogero Uygeston et Iohanne hales Commissionariis predicti domini Regis virtute literarum patentium eiusdem domini Regis eisdem Decano Ricardo Rogero et Iohanni hales et aliis in eisdem literis patentibus nominatis directarum et vni parti presentis Inquisicionis consutarum ad inquirendum per sacramentum proborum et legalium hominum de predicto Comitatu Bedfordie inter alios plenius veritatem de et super certis articulis in predictis literis patentibus specificatis per Sacramentum Willelmi Gostwyk gentilman Iohannis Golston gentilman Iohannis Bendowe gentilman Willelmi Iordon henrici Wythed Iohannis Warner Willelmi lawrens Ricardi lorimer Willelmi Cole Iohannis Strachen Ricardi Falde Iohannis Bromham Roberti Scyle Willelmi Pancost· Thome Scott Willelmi Paton et Iohannis Belcott de lyttyllyngton proborum et legalium hominum de predicto Comitatu Bedfordie Qui dicunt super sacramentum suum quod Prior Monasterii de Bisshmede[1] in Comitatu predicto nuper fuit seisitus in domi-

(Membrane 40)[a] Bed[fordia]

Prior de Byshmede

---

[a] At the bottom of this membrane is
By me Willm Gostweke pro aliis Iur.

[1] Bisshmede, Bissemede, or Bushmead, a priory of Austin Canons. The Prior appears to have let the land to himself and Burgoyn as co-tenants. This was a freehold, one manor here being in the family of Enderby (Lysons, i. 139), another in the duchy of Lancaster. See next entry.

460 THE DOMESDAY OF INCLOSURES, 1518

Sutton
Welles
scr[ibat][a]

nico suo vt de feodo in iure Monasterii predicti de vno Mesuagio in quo iconomia a tempore de quo non extat memoria haberi vti et sustentari solebat et de sexaginta acris terre arrabilis et arrari consuete cum pertinenciis in Sutton in Comitatu predicto que terre cum Mesuagio predicto ad firmam tradite dimisse et locate ac in iconomia occupate fuerunt et predictus prior sic inde seisitus vicesimo die Octobris anno regni domini henrici nuper Regis anglie septimi decimo octauo Mesuagium predictum in ruinam et decasum voluntarie fieri et sic deinceps hucusque existere fore permisit et adhuc permittit ita quod iconomia ibidem vti nec manutenere [b] non potest vt decet et solet contra formam statuti in huiusmodi casu nuper editi et prouisi ob quod vnum aratrum [1] deletur [c] sex persone laboribus et occupacionibus carent tenementa illa valent per annum quadraginta solidos sed de quo aut de quibus tenementa illa tenentur Iuratores predicti penitus ignorant Et dicunt quod predictus Prior et quidam Iohannes Burgoyn gentilman tenementa predicta ex dimissione predicti prioris modo tenentes exitus et proficua tenementorum predictorum a predicto vicesimo die Octobris hucusque perceperunt et habuerunt et adhuc percipiunt et habent Idemque Prior de tenementis illis in forma predicta seisitus existit et ad quorum dampnum vel ad quod Iuratores predicti ignorant.

Thomas Morgan
Sutton
Welles
scr[ibat][a]

Et Iuratores predicti dicunt quod Thomas Morgan gentilman qui de domino Rege nunc tenet per Copiam Curie ad voluntatem domini Regis vt de Manerio suo de Sutton [2] in Comitatu predicto vnde predictus nuper Rex et Dominus Rex nunc seisitus existit in dominico suo vt de feodo vt

---

[a] In MS. *scī*. Apparently an instruction to Welles, as clerk, to write to the persons presented.   [b] Sic.   [c] 'et' omitted.

[1] The putting down of a plough indicates conversion to pasture. Cf. the more explicit form 'ut antea' *sub* Eversoll, *infra*. See Introduction, p. 33, *supra*.

[2] 'Sutton.' This entry confirms the 'current tradition,' which, according to Lysons (i. 138), 'appears to be totally destitute of foundation,' that a manor here at one time belonged to the duchy of Lancaster. The name of Burgoyn coupled with the recital of the proprietorship of the duchy of Lancaster sufficiently identifies this place (see Lysons, *l.c.*), but it is diffi-

parcella Ducatus sui lancastrie vnum ^a Mesuagium vocatum Gibbis in quo iconomia a toto tempore de quo non exstat memoria vti et manuteneri solebant^a ac de quadraginta acris terre arrabilis et arrari consuete et cultui apte in Sutton predicta in Comitatu predicto que quidem terre cum Mesuagio illo a toto dicto tempore in vsu iconomie vti et occupari fuerunt et solebant et predictus Thomas Mesuagium predictum et terras sic inde tenens quarto die Octobris anno regni predicti nuper Regis vicesimo secundo et deinceps Mesuagium illud in ruinam et decasum existere permisit et sic adhuc permittitur ita quod iconomia que ibidem manuteneri et haberi solebat sustentari et vti extunc non potuit nec potest vt decet et solet contra formam statuti in huiusmodi casu editi et prouisi tenementa que illa valet ^a per annum viginti et sex solidos et octo denarios predictus que Thomas Morgan exitus et proficua tenementorum illorum a predicto quarto die Octobris hucusque percepit et habuit et adhuc percepit ^a et habet et occasione predicta vnum aratrum deletum existit et sex persone mansionibus et laboribus suis priuantur qui eciam ea de causa dampnificantur et nichil de incremento redditus predicto priori occasione predicta peruenit etc.

Et dicunt super sacramentum suum quod Iohannes lee nuper fuit seisitus in dominico suo vt de feodo de vno Mesuagio et triginta acris terre arrabilis et cultui apte et vsitate cum pertinenciis in Eversoll¹ in Comitatu predicto in quo quidem Mesuagio a tempore de quo non extat memoria iconomia vti et occupari solebat que terre et pasture cum Mesuagio illo a toto tempore cuius contrarii memoria hominum non existit ad firmam tradi et locari ac cum Mesuagio illo in iconomia et Cultura occupari solebant et idem Iohannes lee sic inde seisitus quarto die Ianuarii anno regni domini

Iohannes lee Eversoll Scr[ibe] r[esponsum] scr[ibat]^b scr[ibat]^b

^a Sic.
^b In MS. *scr̄ r̄ scr̄*, and in line following *scr̄* under the last *scr̄* of the line preceding, the blank being apparently intended for the clerk's name. Cf. ^a on p. 53.

cult to see why the entry concludes with a reference to the Prior of Bushmead, unless the clerk were a stranger to the county and confused with the preceding entry. The complementary presentments show that Thomas Morgan was also an incloser elsewhere (p. 473, *infra*).

¹ Now Eversholt.

henrici[a] nuper Regis anglie septimi decimo sexto Mesuagium illud voluntarie ad terram prosterni et devastari fecit per quod iconomia ibidem que in Mesuagio illo haberi et occupari solebat ibidem extunc manuteneri nec vti potuit nec adhuc potest vt antea solet et debuit habitacio que hominum que ibidem fieri solebat ea de causa deserta et vacua deuenit contra formam statuti in ea parte editi et prouisi tenementa que illa valent per annum triginta tres solidos et quatuor denarios Cuius quidem Iohannis lee statum de et in predictis tenementis cum pertinenciis quidam Georgius henton modo habet Et dicunt quod predictus Iohannes lee exitus et proficua tenementorum predictorum a tempore predicti decasus vastacionis et ruine vsque sextum diem Octobris anno regni domini Regis nunc quinto percepit et habuit Et quod predictus Georgius henton exitus et proficua tenementorum illorum ab eodem sexto die Octobris hucusque percepit et habuit et adhuc percepit[b] et habet et ea occasione vnum aratrum deponitur[c] sex persone mansionibus et occupacionibus carent et eorum victu et vestitu depauperantur et sic dampnificantur Et tenementa illa tenentur de domino Rege.

Iohannes Rufford Westnyng f[iat] s[ub][d] p[ena]

 Et dicunt quod Iohannes Rufford[1] gentilman nuper fuit seisitus in dominico suo vt de feodo de vno Mesuagio et octuaginta acris terre arrabilis et arrari consuete cum pertinenciis in Westnyng[2] in Comitatu predicto in quo Mesuagio iconomia a toto tempore de quo non extat memoria vti consueuit terre que ille cum Mesuagio illo a toto dicto tempore ad firmam tradi occupari et in Cultura et iconomia vti et occupari solebant predictus que Iohannes sic de Mesuagio et terris predictis seisitus existens quarto die Septembris anno regni .predicti nuper Regis vicesimo mesuagium predictum ad terram prosterni et voluntarie destrui fecit et permisit et

[a] MS. 'h' only.   [b] Sic.   [c] 'et' omitted.   [d] MS. *f.s.p.*

[1] J. Rufford had been presented in the Inquisition of 1517. See p. 472, *infra*, and p. 160, *supra*.
[2] Now Weston-Ing or Westoning.

sic existere adhuc permittit [et]^a terras predictas sepibus et fossatis circumquaque inclusit et in pasturam animalium conuertit et illis sic adhuc vtitur contra formam statuti in ea parte editi et prouisi et idem Iohannes Rufford inde adhuc seisitus existit qua occasione vnum aratrum deletur et septem persone mansionibus et occupacionibus carent et tenementa illa valent per annum sexaginta solidos idemque Iohannes Rufford exitus et proficua **tenementorum** illorum a predicto quarto die Septembris hucusque percepit et habuit et adhuc percepit^b et habet Et tenementa illa tenentur de¹ Iohanne Zouche Milite et idem Iohannes Zouche illa vlterius tenet de domino Rege. (Membrane 41)

ij

Et dicunt quod Ricardus lantowe de Dunstabill houghton nuper fuit seisitus in dominico suo vt de feodo de vno Mesuagio cum pertinenciis in Maldoun² in Comitatu predicto in quo Mesuagio a tempore die^b quo non exstat memoria iconomia vtebatur et fruebatur ac de viginti et quatuor acris terre arrabilis et arrari consuete et cultui apte cum pertinenciis in Maldoun predicta in Comitatu predicto que terra cum mesuagio illo a toto dicto tempore ad firmam tradita dimissa et in vsu iconomie vsitata fuit et predictus Ricardus sic inde seisitus quarto die Maii anno regni henrici nuper Regis anglie septimi vicesimo mesuagium predictum devastari et destrui permisit et sic adhuc existit contra formam statuti in ea^b casu editi et prouisi³ et ea occasione premissa tres persone mansionibus et laboribus carent et abinde recesserunt tenementa que illa valent per annum vltra reprisas viginti sex solidos et octo

Ricardus lantowe Maldoun Welles no[t]a

^a Conjectural: MS. illegible. ^b Sic.

[1] This formula, which in the case of Berkshire was reserved for manorial lords, is perhaps here applied to freeholders, since the family of Zouche are known to have held the manor (Lysons, i. 149).

[2] Now Maulden.

[3] There is no mention here of an abandonment of 'iconomia.' I interpret this, therefore, as a case of consolidation of holdings. Cf. the formula used in the case of Batlesden, p. 465, *infra*. Another inclosure apparently by the same tenant is mentioned of land held of the Abbess of Ellenstowe, p. 473, *infra*. That this latter inclosure is other than that here presented is apparent both from the preamble to the complementary presentments and from a comparison of the presentment of Thomas Morgan on p. 460 with that on p. 473.

denarios Et dicunt quod predictus Ricardus exitus et proficua tenementorum predictorum a predicto quarto die Maii hucusque percepit et habuit et adhuc percepit ᵃ et habet et inde adhuc seisitus existit in forma predicta tenementaque illa tenentur de abbatissa Monasterii de Elmestowe sed de quo vel de quibus eadem abbatissa tenementa illa vlterius tenet aut quot sunt inde medii inter ipsam abbatissam et dominum Regem et ad cuius vel quod dampnum existunt penitus ignorant.

> Dominus Rex
> Wrestlyngworth
> Welles
> no[t]a
> Cristoferus
> Johnson
> scr[ibat]

Et dicunt quod Dominus henricus nuper Rex anglie septimus nuper fuit et dominus Rex nunc est seisitus in dominico suo vt de feodo vt parcella de Richemond Fee[1] de duobus principalibus Mesuagiis et Centum et quateruiginti acris terre arrabilis et arrari consuete cum pertinenciis in Wrestlyngworth in Comitatu predicto vt parcella propartis sue Manerii de Wrestlyngworth in eodem Comitatu in quibus Mesuagiis iconomia a toto tempore de quo non exstat memoria vsitata fuit ac Centum acre ᵃ de terris predictis parcella cum vno eorundem Mesuagiorum Et quateruiginti acre terre residuum cum alio inde messuagio a toto dicto tempore ad firmam tradite et in vsu iconomie et culture occupate fuerunt et predictus nuper Rex de tenementis illis sic seisitus existens Mesuagia et terras predictas a festo sancti Michaelis anno regni sui vicesimo tercio Mesuagia et terras predictas dimisit cuidam Cristoforo Johnson habendum sibi pro termino certorum annorum adhuc durancium virtute cuius dimissionis idem Cristoferus fuit et adhuc existit inde possessionatus et sic possessionatus sexto die Ianuarii anno regni domini Regis nunc quinto mesuagia predicta voluntarie in decasu et extrema ruina existere permisit et ea sic deinceps et hucusque permittit ita quod habitaciones siue iconomia ibidem vti nec haberi non potest sicut solet et debet contra formam statuti in ea parte editi et prouisi per quod vnum aratrum deletum est et decem persone mansionibus et habitacionibus carent tene-

ᵃ Sic.

[1] For the relations of the earldom of Richmond to the duchy of Lancaster, see *The Charters of the Duchy of Lancaster*, W. Hardy, London, 1845.

BEDFORDSHIRE

menta que illa valent per annum septem libras et predictus Cristoferus exitus et proficua tenementorum illorum a predicto sexto die Ianuarii anno quinto predicto percepit et habuit et adhuc percepit^a et habet.

Et dicunt quod Edmundus Bray[1] Miles nuper fuit seisitus in dominico suo vt de feodo de vno Mesuagio et triginta acris terre arrabilis cum pertinenciis in Batlesden in Comitatu predicto in quo quidem Mesuagio iconomia a toto tempore de quo non exstat memoria vsitata fuit terreque predicte cum Mesuagio predicto a toto dicto tempore ad firmam tradite et locate ac cum Mesuagio illo in vsu iconomie in Culture^a per totum dictum tempus vsitate fuerunt et predictus Edmundus sic inde seisitus duodecimo die augusti anno regni domini Regis nunc quinto mesuagium predictum prosterni et devastari fecit et sic adhuc fore permisit terrasque predictas cum aliis Mesuagiis[2] extra villam predictam occupari fecit contra formam statuti in huiusmodi casu editi et prouisi ob quod septem persone que ibidem manere potuissent habitacionibus et occupacionibus carent tenementaque illa tenentur de domino Rege et valent per annum viginti et quatuor solidos et predictus Edmundus exitus et proficua tenementorum illorum a predicto duodecimo die augusti hucusque percepit et habuit et adhuc percepit^a et habet. Ed[mund]us Bray Miles Batlesden scr[ibe] bill[am

Et Iuratores predicti dicunt quod Iohannes harper nuper fuit seisitus in dominico suo vt de feodo de vno mesuagio et Iohannes harper ^b Vaux Bromeham Welles scr[ibat]

^a Sic.   ^b Sic: name struck through in MS.

[1] 'Edmundus Bray' was doubtless Edmund Bray, nephew and heir to the Bedfordshire manors of his uncle, Sir Reginald Bray, to which he succeeded in 1510. He was afterwards (1529) Lord Bray. See Manning and Bray's *Hist. of Surrey*, i. 517, 518, from which it appears that this was not among the manors so inherited. The property was probably, therefore, freehold.

[2] A messuage being 'a dwelling house, with some adjacent land assigned to the use thereof' (Cowel), this implies that E. B. held at least three farms ingrossed. The average area attached to a messuage in Bedfordshire on land in the hand of lay freeholders = 37 (36·9) acres. This nearly approaches the average obtained from the Returns of seven counties, viz. 38 acres (pp. 49, 50, *supra*), and I therefore adopt it here and tabulate in the column of areas ingrossed [104] acres, being 30 + [37] + [37] acres.

quadraginta et octo acris terre arrabilis cum pertinenciis in Bromeham in Comitatu predicto in quo quidem Mesuagio iconomia a tempore de quo non exstat memoria vsitata fuit et terre predicte cum Mesuagio illo a tempore de quo non exstat memoria cum mesuagio illo [a] ad firmam tradite et locate et ad vsum arrure seminacionis et iconomie posite fuerunt et sic inde seisitus terciodecimo die Iulii anno regni predicti nuper Regis terciodecimo Mesuagium predictum ad terram prosterni et devastari voluntarie fecit et sic adhuc fore permittitur contra formam statuti in ea [b] casu editi et prouisi per quod octo persone que ibidem occupari et inhabitare solebant abinde exire et occupacione carere compellebantur tenementa illa tenentur de domino Rege et valent per annum vltra reprisas viginti et sex solidos et octo denarios Cuius quidem Johannis harper statum de et in tenementis illis Nicholaus Vaus Miles modo habet predictusque Johannes harper exitus et proficua tenementorum predictorum a predicto terciodecimo die Iulii vsque sextum diem aprilis anno regni domini Regis nunc octauo percepit et habuit et ab eodem sexto die aprilis predictus Nicholaus Vaus exitus et proficua inde hucusque percepit et habuit et adhuc percepit [b] et habet.

Et dicunt quod [c] nuper fuit seisitus in dominico suo vt de feodo de vno Mesuagio et viginti acris terre arrabilis et cultui apte et sic vsitate cum pertinenciis [1][c] in Comitatu predicto quod quidem Mesuagium cum terris predictis in vsu iconomie et culture a tempore de quo non exstat memoria insimul traditum et locatum ac occupatum fuerunt [b] et idem Willelmus sic inde **seisitus** nono die augusti anno regni domini Regis nunc quarto Mesuagium predictum devastari et in ruinam existere voluntarie permisit

(Membrane 42)
iij

[a] Sic : repeated. [b] Sic. [c] Blank in MS.

[1] Probably Goldyngton, of which this prior held the manor (Dugd. *Monast.* vi. 377), and which is about midway between Bromeham and Northell. Goldyngton had belonged to the Mowbrays (Lysons, i. 88). Thomas Howard, created Duke of Norfolk in 1514, was the representative of that family through his mother Margaret Mowbray (Nicolas, *Hist. Peerage* [ed. Courthope], p. 352). Goldyngton, therefore, unites all the characters attributed to the place of which this inclosure is recorded.

et sic adhuc Mesuagium illud in decasum exist[it terrasque] [a] predictas [b] . . . . .[b] contra formam statuti inde editi et prouisi conuertit idemque exitus et proficua inde vsque sextum diem Septembris anno regni domini Regis nunc nono percepit et habuit quo die idem . . . .[b] obiit post cuius mortem [b] tenementa illa intrauit et inde seisitus existit in dominico suo vt de feodo et exitus et proficua a predicto die obitus predicti Willelmi Mylys[1] percepit et habuit et adhuc percepit [c] et habet tenementaque illa valent per annum [b] et octo denarios et tenementa illa tenentur de priore de Newnam idemque Prior vlterius tenet tenementa illa de Thoma Duce Norffolcie Et idem Dux vlterius tenet tenementa illa de domino Rege et occasione predicta [b] carent etc.

Et dicunt quod Johannes Barneston nuper fuit seisitus in dominico suo vt de feodo de vno mesuagio vocato Tomsyns et viginti acris terre arrabilis cum pertinenciis in Nort[he]ll [d] in Comitatu predicto quod quidem Mesuagium pro vsu iconomie a toto tempore de quo non exstat memoria vsum fuit quodque terre predicte cum Mesuagio illo a toto dicto tempore tr[adi]te [d] et locate ac in vsu iconomie et Culture occupate fuerunt et predictus Johannes Barmeston [c] sic inde seisitus septimo die Februarii anno regni domini Regis nunc quinto Mesuagium predictum voluntarie destrui et devastari fecit et sic adhuc existit contra formam statuti in ea parte editi et prouisi terrasque predictas cum aliis Mesuagiis occupari fecit[2] et idem Iohannes adhuc de tenementis illis seisitus existit in forma predicta eaque de causa tres persone mansionibus et occupacionibus carent tenementaque illa valent per annum vltra reprisas viginti solidos et tenentur de domino Rege et predictus Iohannes exitus et proficua

Iohannes Barneston Northell Welles scr[ibat]

[a] Conjectural: MS. mutilated.
[b] An erasure in MS.　　[c] Sic.　　[d] MS. mutilated.

[1] W. Mylys had been presented in the Inquisition of 1517. See p. 470 *infra*.

[2] This phrase apparently means that he has consolidated this with other holdings. See note to Batlesden, p. 465, *n.* 2, *supra*. Following that reasoning I have tabulated [94] acres in the column of areas ingrossed.

tenementorum predictorum a predicto septimo die Februarii anno quinto predicto hucusque percepit et habuit et adhuc percepit ª et habet.

Townesend
Sharpenho
Welles^c
scribat ^c

Et dicunt quod ^b Townesend armiger nuper fuit et adhuc existit seisitus in dominico suo vt de feodo de vno principali Mesuagio Manerii sui de Sharpenho in Sharpenho et centum acris terre arrabilis viginti acris prati et sexdecim acris pasture cum pertinenciis in Stretley parcella Manerii predicti in quo quidem Mesuagio iconomia vsitata et occupata a tempore de quo non exstat memoria fuit ac predicte terre pratum et pastura cum Mesuagio illo a toto eodem tempore ad firmam tradite et dimissa ª fuerunt in vsum iconomie et Culture occupate fuerunt et predictus ^b Townesend sic inde seisitus decimo die Marcii anno regni predicti nuper Regis sextodecimo Mesuagium predictum prosterni et devastari fecit et sic adhuc devastatum et desolatum tenet contra formam statuti in ea parte editi et prouisi tenementaque illa valent per annum octo libras et tenentur de Comite Kancie et idem Comes vlterius illud tenet ^d de domino Rege et occasione predicta octo persone mansionibus suis carent et predictus ^b Townesend exitus et proficua tenementorum predictorum a predicto decimo die Marcii hucusque percepit et habuit et adhuc percepit ^e et habet.

Johannes lokke
gentilman
Stretley
Welles
scr[ibat]

Et dicunt quod Iohannes lokke gentilman nuper fuit et adhuc existit seisitus in dominico suo vt de feodo de vno Mesuagio et quadraginta acris terre cum pertinenciis in Stretley in Comitatu predicto in quo Mesuagio iconomia a tempore cuius contrarii memoria hominum non existit vtebatur ac terre predicte cum Mesuagio illo a toto eodem tempore tradite et locate fuerunt et in iconomia vsitate et occupate fuerunt et predictus Iohannes lokke sic de tenementis illis seisitus existens decimo die Iulii anno regni predicti nuper Regis duodecimo Mesuagium predictum ita in ruina et decasu fore permisit et adhuc permittit quod iconomia que

---

ª Sic. Blank in MS. ^e Sic: struck through in MS.
^d Sic: from 'de' after 'tenentur' to 'tenet' inclusive underlined in MS.

BEDFORDSHIRE

ibidem vti et haberi solebat sustentari non potest[1] contra formam statuti in ea parte editi et prouisi et tenementa illa valent per annum viginti solidos.

    Et dicunt quod idem Iohannes lokke nuper fuit et adhuc existit seisitus in dominico suo vt de feodo de vno Mesuagio et viginti acris terre arrabilis cum pertinenciis in Sharpenho in Comitatu predicto que terre cum Mesuagio illo in vsu iconomie et Culture a tempore de quo non extat memoria tradite locate vsitate et occupate fuerunt et sic inde seisitus predicto decimo die Iulii anno duodecimo predicto Mesuagium predictum ita in ruinam et decasum existere permisit et adhuc permittit quod iconomia que ibidem haberi et frui consueuit extunc manuteneri non potest nec potuit contra formam statuti in ea parte editi et prouisi et tenementa illa valent per annum viginti solidos. Et omnia tenementa predicti Iohannis lokke predicta tenentur de predicto [b] Townesend et idem [b] Townesend vlterius tenet tenementa illa de predicto Comite Kancie Et idem Comes Kancie vlterius tenet eadem tenementa de domino Rege Et predictus Iohannes lokke exitus et proficua tenementorum predictorum a predicto decimo die Iulii hucusque percepit et habuit et adhuc percepit[c] et habet et occasione illa sex persone mansionibus et occupacionibus carent etc.

idem Iohannes lokke Sharpenho ~~*Welles*~~[a] *scribat*

    ET Iuratores predicti dicunt quod ipsi super capcionem huius Inquisicionis vnam partem cuiusdam Inquisicionis indentate in Custodia Iohannis Warner remanentem primo apud Bedford in Comitatu Bedfordie decimo die augusti anno regni domini Regis nunc nono coram predicto Decano et sociis suis tunc Commissionariis predicti domini Regis nunc pretextu literarum patencium eiusdem domini Regis

(Membrane 43)

iiij

---

[a] Thus struck through in MS.   [b] Blank in MS.   [c] Sic.

[1] This recital differs from the previous by its express mention of the fact that 'iconomia sustentari non potest.' This has been tabulated, as at Chilworth and Combe, Oxon, and elsewhere, as all conversion to pasture. For the justification see General Introduction, p. 24, *supra*. The following complementary presentments, since they afford no clue either to the areas of the inclosures or the places where they were made, are only of occasional interest to genealogists.

eis confectarum et directarum ad inquirendum de certis
articulis in Inquisicione predicta specificatis assignatis per
Sacramentum predicti Iohannis Warner et aliorum proborum
et legalium hominum de Comitatu predicto in inquisicione
illa nominatorum et deinde assensu et requestu eorundem
Iuratorum vsque sextum diem octobris anno nono predicto
apud Turvey in Comitatu predicto adiornat[e] et tunc ibidem
per Sacramentum eorundem Iuratorum accepte inspexerunt
Inquisicio que illa et inde contenta predictis nunc Iuratoribus
super capcionem huius inquisicionis publice et aperte lecta
fuerunt Et quia in quibusdam et diuersis presentamentis in
predicta prima Inquisicione specificatis in quibus Ricardus
Vyce Iohannes Broun Macfitz William Iohannes Colt Michael
Fyssher Willelmus Mylys Johannes Enderby Iohannes Rufford Willelmus Kyng Willelmus Dey henricus punter Iohannes Shepard Ricardus lawnt Thomas Morgan Ricardus
Cosyn henricus Ioye Thomas atkynson Iohannes Ellys
Thomas Wy Johanna Woghton Robertus a pryce Robertus
Gyfford et Nicholaus Wadell nominantur et specificantur
omittitur et minime reperitur vel continetur de quo vel
de quibus terre et tenementa in presentamentis illis contentis ^a tenentur nec quod in eisdem presentamentis et aliis in
predicta prima inquisicione contentis nulla fit mencio quis
vel qui exitus et proficua tenementorum in eisdem inquisicionibus specificatorum post tempus prostracionis devastacionis
decasus et ruine Mesuagiorum et domorum vnde in eisdem
presentamentis fit mencio factorum siue permissorum percepit et habuit perceperunt vel habuerunt sic quod quamplura
presentamenta in dicta prima inquisicione specificata tam in
articulis illis quam in aliis incerta et inperfecta existunt predicti nunc Iuratores dicunt super Sacramentum suum quod
tenementa in predicta prima Inquisicione specificata que
nuper fuerunt predicti Ricardi Vyce tenentur immediate de
heredibus Ricardi Godfrey et iidem heredes vlterius tenent
eadem tenementa de domino Rege Et dicunt quod predictus
Ricardus Vyce exitus et proficua eorundem terrarum et tene-

<small>Vice f[iat] s[ub] p[ena]</small>

^a Sic.

mentorum a vicesimo octauo die Nouembris anno regni predicti nuper Regis sexto vsque primum diem Maii anno regni predicti nuper Regis vicesimo percepit et habuit et quod Cecilia Bedon in eadem prima inquisicione nominata exitus et proficua eorundem tenementorum que fuerunt predicti Ricardi Vyce a predicto primo die Maii vsque diem capcionis huius inquisicionis percipit ᵃ et habuit et adhuc percipit et habet.

Et dicunt quod tenementa in dicta prima Inquisicione specificata nuper predicti Iohannis Browne immediate tenentur de Episcopo lincoln idem que Episcopus vlterius tenet tenementa illa de domino Rege et dicunt quod· predictus Iohannes Brown exitus et proficua tenementorum illorum a secundo die Ianuarii anno regni predicti nuper Regis quinto hucusque percepit et adhuc percipit etc.

Et dicunt quod predictus Nicholaus hardyng exitus et proficua dictorum tenementorum suorum in predicta prima Inquisicione specificatorum a duodecimo die Nouembris anno regni domini Regis nunc quinto hucusque percepit et habuit et adhuc percipit et habet etc. — hardyng

Et dicunt quod predictus Macfitz William exitus et proficua tenementorum suorum predictorum in predicta prima Inquisicione specificatorum sexto die Maii anno regni predicti nuper Regis quintodecimo hucusque percepit et habuit et adhuc percipit tenementaque illa tenentur de priore hospitalis sancti Iohannis Iherusalem in anglia et idem prior vlterius illa tenet de domino Rege. — Prior sancti Iohannis

Et dicunt quod tenementa predicti Iohannis Colt in dicta prima inquisicione comperta tenentur de dicto priore predicti hospitalis abbate de Wardon et Thoma Duce Norffolcie. Et quod predictus Johannes Colt exitus et proficua tenementorum illorum a decimo die Iunii anno regni domini Regis nunc secundo hucusque percepit et adhuc percipit etc. — idem prior

Et dicunt quod predicta tenementa predicti Michaelis Fyssher in predicta prima inquisicione specificata tenentur de predicto priore predicti hospitalis sancti Johannis et idem prior vlterius tenet tenementa illa de domino Rege quodque idem Michael exitus et proficua eorundem tenementorum a duodecimo die Nouembris anno regni domini Regis nunc primo percepit et habuit et adhuc percipit et habet.

Et dicunt quod tenementa predicta in predicta prima inquisicione specificata nuper predicti Iohannis Enderby tenentur de Georgio Comite Salop et idem Comes ea vlterius tenet de domino Rege Et quod predictus Johannes Enderby exitus et proficua eorundem tenementorum a temporibus decasus vastacionis et ruine Mesuagiorum et domorum in predicta prima inquisicione specificatorum vsque sextum diem Iulii anno regni domini Regis nunc quarto percepit et habuit et quidam Thomas pigott seruiens domini Regis ad legem ab eodem sexto die Iulii vsque diem capcionis huius inquisicionis racione custodie alianore filie et heredis predicti Iohannis Enderby infra etatem sexdecim annorum et in Custodia predicti Thome pygott existentis exitus et proficua eorundem tenementorum percepit et habuit et adhuc percipit et habet etc.

Et dicunt quod tenementa in predicta prima inquisicione specificata predicti Iohannis Rufford tenentur de Iohanne Souche Milite et idem Iohannes illa vlterius tenet de domino Rege Et quod predictus Iohannes Rufford exitus et proficua tenementorum illorum a tercio die Maii anno regni predicti nuper Regis decimo octauo hucusque percepit et habuit et adhuc percipit et habet.

Et dicunt omnia et singula predicta tenementa in predicta prima inquisicione specificata predictorum Willelmi Kyng Willelmi Dey henrici punter et Iohannis Shepard tenentur de domina alianora Melton Et dicunt quod quilibet predictorum Willelmi Kyng Willelmi Dey henrici punter et Johannis Shepard exitus et proficua tenementorum suorum in predicta prima Inquisicione specificatorum scilicet quilibet eorum per se de tenementis suis a temporibus prostracionis vastacionis et ruine Mesuagiorum domorum et edificiorum in inquisicione illa specificatorum hucusque percepit et habuit et adhuc percipit et habet.

Et Iuratores predicti dicunt quod quilibet predictorum

BEDFORDSHIRE 473

Ricardi launt Ricardi Cosyn henrici Ioye Thome atkynson Iohannis Ellys Thome Wy Iohanne Woghton Roberti a pryce Roberti Gyfford et Nicholai Wadell scilicet quilibet eorum per se exitus et proficua de terris et tenementis suis que in predicta prima inquisicione presentantur exitus et proficua inde a separalibus temporibus quibus prostracio decasus vastum et ruina Mesuagiorum domorum et edificiorum in eadem prima inquisicione compertorum fieri dicitur hucusque percepit et habuit et adhuc percipit et habet. <small>Ricardus Cosyn</small>

Et predicti nunc Iuratores dicunt quod tenementa predicti Ricardi launt tenentur de abbatissa de Ellenstowe.

et tenementa predicti Thome Morgan tenentur de domino Rege vt de Ducatu suo lancastrie.

Et predicta tenementa predicti Cosyn tenentur de Georgio harvy Milite.

Et predicta tenementa separatim predictorum henrici Ioy et Thome atkynson tenentur de Michaele Fyssher.

Et predicta tenementa predicti Iohannis Ellys tenentur de Thoma Duce Norffolcie et idem Dux illa **vlterius** tenet de domino Rege. <small>(Membrane 44) v.</small>

Et predicta tenementa predicti Thome Wy tenentur de heredibus Iohannis Broughton.

Et predicta tenementa separatim predictorum Johanne Woghton et Roberti a pryce tenentur de henrico Duce Bukinghamie et idem Dux vlterius tenet tenementa illa de domino Rege.

Et predicta tenementa separatim predictorum Roberti Gyfford et Nicholai Wadell tenentur de Nicholao Odell.

Et dicunt quod predictus Thomas Morgen exitus et proficua tenementorum suorum in predicta prima Inquisicione specificatorum a septimo die Octobris anno regni predicti nuper Regis duodecimo percepit et habuit et adhuc percipit et habet.

Et dicunt quod abbas de Woborn exitus et proficua tenementorum predictorum in predicta prima inquisicione specificatorum a quarto die Nouembris anno regni predicti nuper Regis quarto hucusque percepit et habuit et adhuc percipit et habet.

Sancti Iohannis Ierusalem

Et Iuratores predicti dicunt quod de quo vel de quibus predicti prior hospitalis sancti Iohannis Iherusalem in anglia abbas de Wardon domina alianora Melton abbatissa de Ellenstowe Georgius harvye Miles Michael Fyssher heredes Johannis Broughton et Nicholaus Odell tenementa predicta de ipsis vel de eorum aliquo vt superius presentatur separatim tenta vlterius tenent ac eorum aliquis tenet ac quot sunt medii inde inter dominum Regem et ipsos vel eorum aliquem Iuratores predicti ignorant.

[a] Et dicunt quod [b] nuper fuit seisitus in dominico suo vt de feodo de vno Mesuagio et quinquaginta et quatuor acris terre arrabilis cum pertinenciis in Southwell [1] in Comitatu predicto in quo Mesuagio iconomia a tempore de quo non exstat memoria vsa fuit et terre predicte cum Mesuagio illo per totum dictum tempus tradite et occupate pro vsu iconomie et Culture fuerunt et sic inde seisitus sexto die Maii anno regni predicti nuper Regis vicesimo Mesuagium predictum in decasum et ruinam fore permisit ita quod iconomia ibidem vti non potest et sic adhuc existit contra formam statuti in huiusmodi casu editi et prouisi per quod octo persone mansionibus Carent tenementaque illa valent per annum sexaginta solidos et tenentur de abbate de Wardon sed de quo vel de quibus tenementa illa vlterius tenetur [c] ac quot sunt inde medii inter dominum Regem et ipsum abbatem Iuratores predicti ignorant Cuius quidem Ricardi Vys . y [d] statum in tenementis illis hugo heres h . g . . . [d] broughton [d] modo habet predictus Ricardus Vys . y [d] exitus et proficua eorundem tenementorum a predicto sexto die Maii vsque septimum diem augusti anno regni domini Regis nunc septimo percepit et habuit a quo quidem septimo die Maii predictus hugo heres h . g . . . [d] broughton exitus et proficua inde percepit et habuit etc.

[a] The whole of this entry is underlined the MS.
[b] Name erased in MS.   [c] Sic.
[d] These names are erased in the MS., but are nevertheless not quite illegible.

[1] Southwell. Now Southill.

Et dicunt quod Willelmus lord nuper fuit seisitus in dominico suo vt de feodo de vno Mesuagio et quadraginta acris terre arrabilis cum pertinenciis vocate Davys in Bydenham in Comitatu predicto in quo quidem Mesuagio iconomia a tempore de quo non exstat memoria vtebatur terreque predicte a toto eodem tempore cum Mesuagio illo occupate tradite et locate fuerunt pro vsu Culture et iconomie et sic inde seisitus sexto die Marcii anno regni predicti nuper Regis sexto Mesuagium predictum voluntarie devastari et destrui fecit et Mesuagium illud sic adhuc vastatum et prostratum existit per quod iconomia ibi vti non potest contra formam statuti in huiusmodi casu editi et prouisi et ea occasione quatuor persone abinde recedere coacti fuerunt et mansionibus Carent tenementaque illa valent per annum vltra reprisas viginti et sex solidos et octo denarios et tenentur de domino Rege et dicunt quod predictus Willelmus in iure predicte alicie vxoris sue exitus et proficua tenementorum predictorum vsque decimum diem aprilis anno regni domini Regis nunc septimo percepit et habuit quo die idem Willelmus lord obiit et predicta alicia vxor eius ipsum superuixit et exitus et proficua tenementorum predictorum a predicto decimo die aprilis hucusque percepit et habuit et adhuc percipit et habet et eadem alicia de tenementis illis adhuc seisita existit in dominico suo vt de feodo. Willelmus lord Bydenham f[iat] s[ub] p[ena]

Et Iuratores predicti dicunt quod omnia et singula predicta Mesuagia domus et edificia que superius in hac inquisicione per eosdem Iuratores prosterni dicuntur necnon per eosdem Iuratores de et pro ruina et vastacione in eisdem Mesuagiis domibus et edificiis permissis factis perpetratis siue habitis presentantur ita in decasu ruina et devastatione existunt et quo[d]libet eorundem existit quod id illorum Mesuagiorum domorum et edificiorum quod superest siue remanet non sufficit ad manutenenciam iconomie et Culture que de terris arrabilibus cum Mesuagiis domibus et edificiis illis occupatis siue dimissis aut que occupari et dimitti solebant requiruntur et fieri deberent nec quod iconomi in domibus et edificiis illis ... [ad]huc *

* MS. mutilated : qu. *adhuc*.

pro Cultura et iconomia ibidem vtendis vt dicent [a] Moram ibidem habere nequiunt.[a]

Et Iuratores predicti dicunt quod omnia decasus ruine Mesuagiorum inclusiones terrarum arrabilium et conuercio inde in pasturam animalium ac diminucio populorum quam plurima alia supradicta per eos superius presentata facta perpetrata et permissa sunt et a diu fuerunt contra formam diuersorum statutorum inde editorum et regni domini Regis depauperacionem et populi domini Regis in Comitatu predicto et partibus vicinis huic Comitatui Commorantis ac in malum et pernisiosum exemplum in consimilibus Casubus delinq[uentiu]m [b] se disponent[ium] nisi cicius in hac parte de premissis prouideatur remedium congruum.

In Cuius rei testimonium vni parti presentis Inquisicionis tam predicti Decanus Ricardus Dycons Rogerus Wygeston et Iohannes hales quam Iuratores predicti sigilla sua apposuerunt alteri vero inde parti cum prefato Willelmo Gostwyk primo Iuratorum predictorum remanenti predicti Decanus Ricardus Dycons Rogerus Wygeston et Iohannes hales sigilla sua apposuerunt.

Data apud Bedford in predicto Comitatu Bedfordie predicto sextodecimo die augusti anno regni Regis henrici octaui decimo predicto.

[a] Sic.   [1] MS. *delinqm*.

APPENDICES

I.

S. Papers, Foreign and Dom. Henry VIII.
Vol. II. Appendix 53
(1518)[1]

xij^{mo} die Iulii anno x^{mo} Regis Henrici viij Redditum fuit Iudicium subscriptum per Reuerendum in Christo patrem Thomam Cardinalem Eboracensem Archiepiscopum Cancellarium Anglie et de eius mandato in plena Curia Cancellarie publice et solempniter proclamatum fuit &c.

It is decreed and adjuged by the moost reverent fader in god, my Lord Cardinall Chauncellor of Englande and the Courte of the Kingys Chauncerie. That all maner of persons that hathe pleted the Kingys generall pardon or submitted them selffs to the Kingys mercy and grace for enclosures. That thei within xl^{ti} daies nexte affter this present proclamation made, pull doun and lay abrode all suche enclosures and diches whiche were made and don sithin the firste yere of the Reigne of our late souveraigne Lord King Henry the Seventh. And the lande so layde abrode to converte to tyllage as it was used before the said first yere upon payne to every such personne doing contrairie hereunto to forfaicte unto the King our souveraigne lord c li. Except he or thei whiche shall not pull doun the said closure for ther part w^{t}in the tyme above prefixed shall bring sufficient prove before the King in his Chaunceryе at the quindena of seint Mighel nexte convenyent that suche enclosur and the standing of the same shalbe more beneficiall for the commonwelth of this realme then the pulling downe theroff or that it may stande wth the lawes and statutys again the decaye of houses and turnyng of tyllage to pastoure heretofore provided.

T. Car^{lis} Ebor.

[1] See p. 10, *supra*.

II.

Patent Roll 11 Henry VIII. (1519) Part II, m. 20[1]

(S. P. Dom. Hen. VIII. iii. 278)

Rex Omnibus ad quos &c. salutem. Sciatis quod nos de gratia nostra speciali ac ex certa sciencia & mero motu nostris ac eciam pro laudabili & acceptabili seruicio tam precharissimo patri nostro quam nobis per dilectum seruientem nostrum Edwardum Belknapp militem pro corpore nostro diuersimode impenso pardonauimus remisimus & relaxauimus ac per presentes pardonamus remittimus & relaxamus prefato Edwardo omnes & omnimodas Ruinas decasus prosternaciones & voluntarias deuastaciones omnium & singulorum domorum mesuagiorum & cotagiorum aceciam inclausuram omnium & singulorum terrarum & tenementorum que in cultura erant per prefatum Edwardum vel per aliquem alium siue aliquos alios ad eius Vsum infra manerium de Dorset alias dictum Chepyng Dorset & Byrton parcellam manerij predicti seu eorum aliquo[a] qualitercumque factas siue perpetratas Necnon conuercionem ad pasturam siue in pasturam posicionem eorundem terrarum & tenementorum ac custodiam & occupacionem eorundem terrarum & tenementorum in pastura[2] Aceciam omnes & omnimodos contemptus transgressiones & offensiones contra formam & effectum cuiusdam statuti in parliamento predicti patris nostri apud Westmonasterium Anno regni sui quarto tento editi ruinam domorum & sustentacionem Culture & husbondrie concernentis aceciam omnes & omnimodos sectas forisfacturas debitas adiudicatas vel non adiudicatas compotus exitus & proficua penas pecuniarum & denariorum summas quascumque imprisomenta[b] fines amerciamenta & redempciones & omne id quod ad nos pertinet pro premissis vel aliquo premissorum Nolentes quod

[a] Sic. [a] Sic.

[1] See p. 426, *supra*.

[2] Seeing that the pardon of 1509 extended to future acts, I can only surmise that these clauses, which do not appear there, were thought necessary for the incloser's legal security, and account for his procuring a fresh pardon.

idem Edwardus nec heredes sui pro premissis vel aliquo premissorum molestetur seu grauetur molestentur seu grauentur Et vlterius de vberiori gratia nostra concessimus ac per presentes concedimus pro nobis & heredibus nostris prefato Edwardo & heredibus suis quod nos nec heredes nostri non vexemus nec ullomodo imposterum grauemus dictum Edwardum nec heredes suos pro Ruina prosternacione decasu siue voluntaria deuastacione aliquarum domorum vel inclausura aliquarum terrarum vel conuercione eorundem terrarum & tenementorum siue alicuius inde parcelle ab vsu culture & iconomie aut in pasturam posicione eorundem terrarum & tenementorum vel alicuius inde parcelle nec pro occupacione eorundem in vsu pasture nec pro aliqua alia re causa vel materia quacumque per ipsum Edwardum facta siue fienda de vel in predicto manerio vel aliqua inde parcella aut de vel in predictis terris & tenementis vel aliqua inde parcella contra formam & effectum statuti predicti Et vlterius concedimus per presentes pro nobis et heredibus nostris quod nos nec heredes nostri percipiemus redditus exitus vel proficua dicti manerij nec alicuius inde parcelle neque dictorum terrarum & tenementorum nec alicuius inde parcelle pro Ruina prosternacione decasu siue voluntaria deuastacione aliquarum domorum vel inclausura aliquarum terrarum vel conuercione eorundem terrarum & tenementorum siue alicuius inde parcelle ab vsu culture & iconomie aut in pasturam posicione eorundem terrarum & tenementorum vel alicuius inde parcelle siue pro occupacione eorundem in pastura aut aliqua alia causa per ipsum Edwardum vel aliquem alium contra formam & effectum statuti predicti facta siue fienda Et vlterius de vberiori gratia nostra dedimus & concessimus ac per presentes damus & concedimus pro nobis & heredibus nostris prefato Edwardo heredibus & assignatis suis omnia eadem forisfacturas exitus proficua fines amerciamenta interesse & auauntagia quecumque que nobis aut heredibus nostris infra manerium terras & tenementa predicta vel aliquam parcellam inde pertinent pertinebunt aut pertinere debent vel deberent aut spectarent seu spectare poterint ratione quacumque per ipsum Edwardum

facta siue imposterum fienda contra formam statuti predicti
seu alicuius alterius statuti siue imposterum fienda habenda
percipienda & tenenda prefato Edwardo heredibus & assignatis suis tam per manus suas proprias quam per manus
tenencium siue aliquorum occupatorum quorumcumque
predictorum maneri[j][a] terrarum & tenementorum vel alicuius
inde parcelle Et hoc absque compoto vel aliquo alio nobis vel
heredibus nostris inde reddendo soluendo vel faciendo Eo
quod expressa mencio de vero valore annuo dictorum manerij
terrarum & tenementorum aut predictorum forisfacturarum
exituum proficuorum finium amerciamentorum & auaunta-
giorum aut de certitudine premissorum aut de eo quod ad nos
in ea parte pertinet aut pertineret vel spectaret seu de aliis
donis siue concessionibus per nos prefato Edwardo prius factis
in presentibus minime facta existit aut aliquo statuto actu
ordinacione restrictione seu prouiso incontrarium ordinato siue
facto aut aliqua alia re causa vel materia quacumque in aliquo
non obstante. In cuius &c. Teste Rege apud Westmonasterium xxij die maij

per ipsum Regem & de dato &c.

III.

NORTHAMPTON.

BREVE DE MAGNO SIGILLO THESAURARIO ET BARONIBUS
DIRECTUM DE SUPERSEDENDO PRO ABBATE DE
CROYLAND [1]

[Exch. Q. R. Memoranda, Roll 299, M. T. 11 Hen. VIII. (1519) membrane 9]

DOMINUS REX mandavit hic [2] breve suum sub magno sigillo suo Thesaurario et Baronibus huius scaccarij directum
cuiusquidem brevis tenor sequitur in hec verba : Henricus
dei gratia Rex anglie & Francie & Dominus hibernie
Thesaurario & Baronibus omnibus suis de scaccario salutem

---

[a] Erasure, probably of 'maneriorum,' and substitution of contraction for 'manerii.'
[1] See p. 282, *n.* 1, *supra.*   [2] *I.e.* to the Exchequer.

APPENDIX III. 481

Cum nuper pendente placito coram nobis in Cancellaria nostra inter nos & Johannem Abbatem monasterij de Croylond de medietate exituum & proficuorum duorum mesuagiorum vocatorum marahams landes & Georgys landes & octuaginta acrarum terre Arrabilis & cum mesuagiis illis locate tradite & occupate in Elmyngton in Comitatu Northamptonie a tercio die Aprilis Anno regni domini henrici nuper Regis anglie septimi patris nostri decimo nono crescencium & de medietate viginti Acrarum terre vocate Goswong in Elmyngton predicta a quarto die Nouembris Anno regni dicti patris nostri sexto ac de medietate exituum & proficuorum duorum mesuagiorum quorum vnum vocatum Browneshous a quinto die Octobris Anno regni dicti patris nostri decimo & alterum vocatum Conyngtons hous a sexto die Decembris Anno regni nostri quinto & octuaginta Acrarum terre Arabilis cum messuagiis illis tradi & dimitti solite in Elmyngton predicta similiter crescencium que pretextu cuiusdam Inquisitionis capte apud Northamton in Comitatu predicto terciodecimo die Augusti Anno regni nostri nono coram Johanne Veysey tunc decano Capelle nostre Andrea Wyndesore milite & Rogero Wygston nuper de leicester Commissionariis nostris virtute literarum nostrarum patentium eis directarum & in Cancellariam nostram predictam retornate per quam inter alia erat compertum quod Abbas monasterij de Croyland nuper fuit seisitus in dominico suo vt de feodo in iure monasterij sui predicti de duobus mesuagiis vocatis marahams landes & Georgys land & octuaginta Acrarum terre Arrabilis & cum mesuagiis illis locate tradite & occupate in Elmyngton in Comitatu predicto scilicet cum vtroque eorundem mesuagiorum triginta Acrarum terre Arrabilis ad minus & sic inde seisitus tercio die Aprilis anno regni dicti nuper Regis decimo nono predicta duo mesuagia ad terram prosterni fecit ac illa in ruinam fore & remanere voluntarie permisit Et quod predictus Abbas nuper fuit seisitus in dominico suo vt de feodo in iure monasterij sui predicti de viginti Acris terre Arrabilis vocate Goswong cultui vsitate & pro seminacione

II. II

omnium apte in Elmyngton in Comitatu predicto & sic inde seisitus quarto die Nouembris Anno regni predicti patris nostri sexto viginti Acras terre predicte in pasturam animalium conuertit & inclusit Et quod predictus Abbas nuper fuit seisitus in dominico suo vt de feodo in iure monasterij sui predicti de duobus mesuagiis quorum vnum vocatur Browneshous & alterum vocatur Conyngtons hous & octuaginta Acrarum terre Arabilis & cultui vsitate & apte & que cum mesuagiis illis a tempore de quo non extat memoria hominum tradi & dimitti & occupari solebant in Elmyngton predicta Scilicet cum vtroque mesuagio illorum triginta acre terre Arabilis ad minus per totum idem tempus tradi locari & occupari solebant Et sic inde seisitus quinto die Octobris Anno regni predicti nuper Regis decimo predictum mesuagium vocatum Browneshous ad terram prosterni fecit illum in decasum fore voluntarie permisit Et predictum mesuagium vocatum Conyngtons hous sexto die Decembris anno regni nostri quinto in decasum & ruinam existere & ad terram prosterni voluntarie fieri fecit contra formam statuti in parliamento dicti nuper Regis Apud Westmonasterium anno regni sui quarto tento inde editi & prouisi & nobis respondere deberent ac per aliam Inquisicionem captam apud Northampton in Comitatu predicto decimo die Augusti anno regni nostri decimo coram Iohanne Veysey clerico tunc decano capelle nostre Abbate sancti Iacobi Rogero Wigston & Iohanne hales Commissionariis nostris pretextu literarum nostrarum patentium eis directarum & in Cancellariam nostram similiter retornatam inter alia erat compertum quod Abbas monasterij de Croyland nuper fuit seisitus in dominico suo vt de feodo de & in manerio siue hameletto de Elmyngton in parochia de Oundell in Comitatu predicto in iure monasterij sui predicti infra quod quidem manerium idem Abbas nuper habuit septem mesuagia in separales habitaciones pro Agricolis & iconomis & ducentas & sexaginta acras terre arabilis & prati cum mesuagiis illis ab octauo die Aprilis Anno regni predicti nuper Regis decimo & pro octo annos [a]

[a] Sic.

APPENDIX III. 483

tunc proxime elapsos pro vsu iconomie & seminacionis granorum traditas & ad firmam occupatas & quidam Ricardus Clerke totum hamelettum predictum tempore capcionis Inquisicionis predicte tenuit ad firmam de prefato Abbate quodque idem Ricardus clerke in vno mesuagio mesuagiorum predictorum modo manet & in residuis mesuagiis illorum nullo modo fit nec pro quatuor annos [a] tunc proxime preteritos fuit habitacio iconomorum in eisdem Et predictus Abbas sic de manerio siue tenemento illo seisitus existens duo mesuagia scilicet cum quorum vtroque de predictis mesuagiis triginta acre terre predicto tercio die aprilis Anno regni predicti nuper Regis decimo nono tradite & ad firmam fuerunt sexto die maij anno decimo nono predicto in cotagia conuertit & illa pro habitacione operiarorum [a] tenet & vnam aulam & vnum selarium [b] alterius mesuagii de mesuagiis predictis cum quo quadraginta & due Acre terre Arabilis per tempus predictum ad firmam tradite & occupate fuerunt predicto sexto die maij deuastari fecit & aliud inde mesuagium cum quo triginta Acre terre predicto octauo die aprilis ad firmam tradite fuerunt sexto die maij anno decimo predicto per ignem casualiter fuit combustum Ita quod in eisdem quatuor mesuagiis habitacio iconomorum non habetur contra formam statuti predictam & super hoc prefatus Abbas coram nobis in Cancellaria nostra personaliter constitutus vicesimo tercio die Nouembris Anno vltimo preterito recognouerit se debere nobis Centum libras soluendas ad certum diem in dicta recognicione specificatum sub tali condicione scilicet quod idem Abbas reedificaret aut reedificari & reparari faceret omnia & singula mesuagia in Elmyngton versus ipsum in Inquisicionibus predictis comperta esse fore vastata & terras ibidem ab vsu seminacionis granorum per ipsum Abbatem aut tenentes suos in pasturam Animalium conuersa in culturam & vsum iconomie citra festum purificationis beate marie virginis tunc proxime futurum exceptis illis terris que propter inundacionem aquarum ibidem multociens insurgencium arari & seminari non potuissent redigeret Idem

[a] Sic.   [b] Sic. : for *solarium*.

Abbas iuxta condicionem recognicionis predicte in Cancellaria nostra predicta sufficienter probauit ipsum omnia & singula in condicione recognicionis predicte contenta perimplesse & performasse & hoc ante festum predictum ac pro eo quod similiter nobis constat quod dicta quatuor mesuagia & terre predicte eisdem mesuagiis nuper tradite & locate Et predicte viginti acre terre vocate Goswong in Elmyngton predicta in dicta prima Inquisicione specificate Et predictum manerium siue hamellettum in Elmyngton necnon dicta septem mesuagia in Elmyngton predicta quorum vnum sufficienter reparatur & cum tenente in iconomia occupatur & duo ab dictis septem mesuagiis in cotagia conuersa & tria alia mesuagia comperta esse fore vastata necnon aliud mesuagium residuum de predictis septem mesuagiis compertum esse casualiter fore combustum & terre predicte ibidem in dicta secunda Inquisicione specificate sunt eadem & non alia neque diuersa Nos volentes [a] ipsum abbatem super huius[modi] Inquisicionibus indebite pregrauari vobis mandamus quod cuicunque processui siue demande tam prefato abbati quam nunc vicecomiti aut nuper vicecomiti Comitatus predictis seu eorum alicui ad respondendum nobis tam de medietate exituum & proficuorum dictorum quatuor mesuagiorum & terrarum in Elmyngton predicta in dicta prima Inquisicione quam de medietate exituum & proficuorum predictorum septem mesuagiorum & terre in Elmyngton predicta in dicta secunda Inquisicione specificatorum seu ad computandum de exitubus & proficuis eorundem nobis a predicto Festo purificacionis beate marie hucusque crescentibus siue emergentibus per summonicionem processum siue oneracionem scaccarij nostri predicti factum vel fiendum extunc vsque nunc donec aliud a nobis habueritis in mandatis supersedeatis omnino Salua nobis medietate exituum & proficuorum dictorum mesuagiorum & terrarum in dicta secunda Inquisicione specificatorum a tempore decasus & ruine mesuagiorum illorum usque dictum festum purificacionis beate marie nobis spectantium siue

[a] Sic.

emergentium Teste meipso apud Westmonasterium quinto die Nouembris anno regni nostri vndecimo.[1]

TUNSTALL.

IV.

(1519 ?)[2]
EARL SPENCER'S MSS.

In most humble wyse shewith vnto your grace your dayly Oratour John Spencer of Wormeleighton in the Countie of Warr[ewick] that where oon sir Symond Mountford knight was seasid of the maner of Wormeleighton forseid, and so seasid was atteynted for treason doon ayenst the noble prince king Henry the viith by reason wherof the seid maner with all other londes and tenementes whiche were the seid Symondes were forfayt to his grace, and he so beyng therof seasid, by his lettres patentes graunted the seid maner of Wormeleighton to oon William Coope then being Cofforer to his grace, to haue to hym his heyres and assignes for evir, paying therfore to the king and to his heyres yerely xx markes, Whiche was then but of the valew of viij li., and so the Rent was encreased to the king by the seid William when he inclosed the seid maner to xx markes a yere, and so duly payd yerely, and the same William Coope afore the tyme of Inclosur purchasid of the meane lordes within the same lordship all the rest of the londes and tenementes within the seid lordship And so the said William Coope inclosid the same lordship of Wormleighton long tyme byfore the seid John Spencer bought the seid lordship of the seid William Coope to his great cost and charge whiche hathe cost hym to the seid William and his Executours xx hundreth poundes wherupon he made hym a dwelling place, where he had noon to inhabit hym self in his countrey where he was borne, for at

[1] 1519. At this time Cuthbert Tunstall was Master of the Rolls (1516–22), afterwards Bishop of London (1522) and of Durham (1530), d. 1559.

[2] See pp. 285, 404, *supra*. The date is conjectured from the proceedings in the Exchequer in that year. Exch. Q. R. Mem. Roll 299, M. T. 11 H. VIII. m. 17 dorso.

Hodnell where he dwelt byfore he had yt no longer but duryng the nanage of his vnkyls son whiche now there dwellith and hathe doon this iij yeris, and so this iij yeris the seid John Spencer hathe be in bylding in Wormeleighton to his great cost and charge.

And first in bilding and mayntenyng of the Churche and bought all Inhornamentes, as Crosse, Bookes, Coope, Vestementes, Chalisis, and Sensers, for all the Churche gere that was within the Churche at the tyme when hubandsmen were there inhabyted was not worthe vj li. for they had neuir seruis by note for they were so poore and lyvd so poorely that they had no bookes to syng seruis on in the Churche. And where they neuir had but one preste, I haue had and intende to haue ij or iij. And also he hathe byldid and inhabitid iiij howsis. And men women and childryn dwelling in them. And so what with his owne hows, and the other iiij howsis ther ys within xx persons asmoche people as was in the towne byfore. And where ther ys noo wood nor tymber growing within xij or xiiij myle of the same lordship the seid John Spencer hathe there set trees and sowyn Acornys for tymber and wood, and doble dykyd and set with almaner of wood bothe in the heggerowes, and also betwixt the hegges adioynyng to the old hegges that William Coope made before in the seid lordship wherupon now growith moche wood whiche ys all redy growen to the profute of all them that shuld dwell in the said lordship, as also to the Cuntrey adioynyng thervnto, for in those partes ther ys no wood, so that the pore men of the cuntrey are fayne to bren the strawe that theire cattell shuld lyve by, therfore yt were a great losse to dystroy those hegges for yt ys a gretter commodyte then eyther corne or grasse in thoo partes, for they were set to the most Increce of wood that myght be devysid at the great cost and charge of the seid John Spenser as furst in purchasing bylding hegging and dyching of the same whiche hathe byn to hym a mervelous charge aboue all men and most losse shal haue yf ye be not good and gracios lord to hym in the same for he hathe noon othcr pastur lefte hym now in his cuntrey but the same. Whiche yf now shuld be put in tyllage and noon cf that reseruyd that when tyllage for pastur seuerall reseruyd for his cattell yt shuld be to his vttour vndoyng for his lyuyng ys and hathe byn by the brede of cattell in his pastures, for he ys neythir byer nor seller in comon markettes as other grasyers byn, but lyuyth by his owne brede of the same pastures, and sold yt when it was fatt to the Citie of London and other places yerely as good chepe in all this v or vi yeris past as he dyd in other yeres when they were best chepe within ij s in a beste, and ij d in a shepe, and he hathe bred and fed within the said lordship whiche was neuir good for corne as the cuntrey will testefye more cattell this vi yeres then was bred in the lordship when the towne was inhabit in xx yeres afore or shalbe in xx yeres after yt shalbe inhabytid.

[Indorsed] (*In contemporary hand*) WORMLEYGHTON. A supplycation to King Henry viii by JOHN SPENCER of Wormeleton, Esq. In this his vncle's son.[1]

V.

(1522 ?) [2]

EARL SPENCER'S MSS.

In most humble wyse shewith vnto your grace John Spencer of Wormeleighton in the Countie of Warr[ewick] besechith your grace in the wey of charyte, that he put not his lond all in tyllage in so short space as your grace hath geuyn Iniunccion which ys by Candylmas next and also to putt downe his heggis and dychis by the same day whiche

---

[1] *I.e.* his uncle's son's legal representative. But the text seems to show that this is a mistake, so far as Wormeleighton is concerned.

[2] See p. 404, *supra.* The date is conjectured from the proceedings in the Exchequer in that year. Exch. Q. R. Mem. Roll 301, H. T. 13 H. VIII. m. 8.

he cannot do in so short space to folow the Iniunccion but to
his vndoing, for he shall dystroy all his cattell that ys going
on the same grounde for lak of mete, for yf he shuld sell his
cattell now in the ded tyme of wyntyr, he shuld lose and sell
yt for half the money that yt ys worthe, for he hathe no maner
of fatt cattell now lefte hym at this tyme but his brede. And
to put downe his hegges that be now redy growen whiche be
now xx yeris olde whiche be now growyn full of almaner of
wood, to great proffute and oone of the grettest commodyte
in that cuntrey, above corne or grasse, And also to the greate
proffute of the tenauntes that shall Inhabyte within the seyd
lordship for ther ys very lytill wood growing within xiiij myle
of the same. And for that wood ys oone of the grettest com-
modytees in those parties, the seyd John Spencer dyd sett
and doble dyched and doble hegged and set yt with wood as
well betwixt the dychis as also in the hegges to his great cost
and charge, Whiche yf now shuld be throwen downe, shuld
not be only a greate losse to the seyd John Spencer, but also
to the Cuntrey and also to the tenauntes that shall Inhabyte
the same, for ther ys noon other entyrcomoners within the
seyd lordship, but only the Lord and tenauntes of the same
And yf the hegges were throwen downe, yt shuld cause
moche varyaunce betwixt the tenauntes of the same Lordship
and townys adjoynyng therunto whiche haue no right of
comon there. Therfore the seyd John Spencer besechith
your grace that the hegges may stond unto suche tyme as
your grace may have dve profe whedyr yt be to a more commodyte and comon weale for the Cuntrey there that the
said hegges to stond or to be throwen downe, and also to
haue a Resonable tyme to put the lond in tyllage that ys the
oone half betwixt this and Estur, and to make the oone half
of the howsyng betwixt this and Michelmas, and the other
half of the lond to be put in tyllage by Estyr come twelve-
monythis, and the other half of the howsys to be made by
Michelmas come twelvemonyth. And to all as afforseyd the
seyd John Spencer ys content to folow and perfourme as your
grace shall appoynt hym, trusting that your grace will con-

sydre hym aboue all other in somyche as he neuyr Inclosyd yt, and bought yt of a high price as William Coope Inprowed yt, And also hathe byn at great coste with the Churche whiche he found greatly in decay, And also byldyd him a manour place where was noon before but a sory thached hows to his great cost and charge wherin he now dwellith with lytyll lak of lx persons, And that the lond be not all put in tyllage, but some to be reserued for serten cattell for the mayntenaunce of his hows. And he shall dayly pray for the preseruacion of your noble grace.

VI.

HARL. MS. 442, F. 76

Anno xviii Henrici Octavi (1526)[1]

A proclamacon demaunding such as were summoned to appeare in the Chauncery concerning Enclosures to make their appearaunce there accordinglie.

The King our Souveraigne Lord straightly chargeth and demaundeth all and singular persons sommoned by his writt of subpena or by his comissioners or otherwise warned to appeare in the Kings Chauncery for Enclosures that they and euerie of them appeare in his said Chauncery on ffriday next coming Or else writts of Attachment shalbe awarded against them and euerie of them w'hout further delay.

Proclaimed in the Court of Chauncery
21 Novembris xviii H. viii.

[1] See p. 11, *supra*.

VII.

Harl. MS. 442, f. 76 b

(1526)[1]

A Proclamation for the appearaunce in the Chauncery of such persons as are to become bound in recognizaunce concerninge Enclosures.

The King o^r Souveraigne Lord straightlie chargeth and demaundeth all and singular persons called into his court of Chauncerie by writts or other processe or by Comaundem^t for enclosures And as yet have not entered into the Recognizaunce made and devised for reformacon of the same that they and ev^{r}y of them so not bound by recognizaunce appeare before the commissioners appointed in that behalf from daie to daie And by the same comissioners to be ordered and not to departe upon paine of ffyve hundred markes.

Nov. 28, 1526

Proclaimed in the Court of Chauncery the xxviii of November Anno xviii H. viii.

VIII.

Exch. Q. R. Mem. Roll 310, H. T. 22 Henry VIII.[2]
(1531), m. 3.

Pro Rogero Wigston

Rex Thesaurario et Baronibus suis salutem Cum nos decimo octauo die Maii Anno regni nostri decimo nono per literas nostras patentes de gracia nostra speciali dederimus et concesserimus Dilecto seruienti nostro Rogero Wigston armigero medietatem siue dimidiam partem omnium et singulorum exituum reuercionum reddituum et proficuorum vnius mesuagii et triginta acrarum terre arrabilis cum pertinenciis in hogshawe in Comitatu nostro Bukinghamie necnon vnius mesuagii vocati Sompnerhouse et triginta acrarum

[1] See p. 12, *supra*.   [2] See p. 75, *supra*.

APPENDIX VIII. 491

arabilium cum eodem mesuagio nuper traditarum locatarum et ocupatarum et alterius mesuagii vocati Richard hughes house et viginti acrarum terre arabilis cum eodem mesuagio nuper tradite locate et ocupate Acociam Alterius mesuagii vocati hichemanyshouse et viginti Acrarum terre arabilis cum pertinenciis cum eodem mesuagio nuper tradite locate et occupate in ffulbroke in dicto Comitatu nostro Bukinghamie Ac totum ius interesse et titulum in predicta medietate siue dimidia parte Que quidem separalia mesuagia predicta simulcum terris predictis separaliter in vsu iconomie et seminacionis granorum nuper tradita locata et ocupata fuerunt et de quibus quidem mesuagiis et terris cum pertinenciis Johannes Kendale nuper prior hospitalis sancti Iohannis Ierusalem in Anglia nuper fuit seisitus in dominico suo vt de feodo in iure hospitalis sui predicti et eadem mesuagia et terras cum pertinenciis de domino henrico nuper Rege Anglie septimo patre nostro immediate tenuerit Ipsoque nuper Priore sic inde seisito existente quidam Radulphus lane omnia mesuagia et terras predicta cum pertinenciis de dicto nuper Priore tunc tenuerit pro termino certorum annorum mesuagia predicta prosterni et deuastari fecit terrasque predictas in pasturam animalium conuertit contra formam statuti inde editi et prouisi et que quidem medietas siue dimidia pars exituum reuercionum reddituum et proficuorum mesuagiorum et terre predicte cum pertinenciis ad summam sexaginta nouem solidorum et quatuor denariorum attingerit[a] Ac ad nos racione decasus et ruine mesuagiorum predictorum pertinuerit et pertinere debuerit videlicet a duodecimo die Nouembris Anno regni nostri septimo vsque dictum decimum octauum diem maii proueniens crescens siue emergens Ac nobis aliquo modo racione seu occasione debita pertinens siue spectans habenda leuanda recipienda et percipienda eandem medietatem siue dimidiam partem dictorum exituum reuercionum reddituum mesuagiorum et terre predicte cum pertinenciis prefato Rogero Wigston et assignatis suis videlicet a dicto duodecimo die Nouembris predicto anno regni nostri septimo

[a] Sic.

vsque dictum decimum octauum diem maii prouenientem siue crescentem ac prouenturam siue crescituram quousque dicta mesuagia bene et sufficienter reparata et reedificata essent et terre in iconomiam pro iconomis et culturam posite et redacta [a] forent prout eidem [a] terre ante conuersionem earundem in pasturam animalium vse et occupate essent secundum vsum patrie ibidem tam per manus suas proprias quam per manus nuper tunc vicecomitis et Escaetoris in Comitatu predicto Ac quorumcumque balliuorum ffirmariorum siue aliorum tenencium siue occupatorum eorundem mesuagiorum et terre cum pertinenciis pro tempore existentium Absque compoto seu aliquo alio nobis pro premissis seu aliquo premissorum reddendo soluendo seu faciendo prout in eisdem literis plenius continetur Et per breve nostrum precipimus Thome Weyston nunc priori hospitalis predicti quod eidem Rogero id quod ei a retro fuit de predicta medietate siue dimidia parte predictorum exituum reuercionum reddituum mesuagiorum et terrarum predictorum cum pertinenciis a dicto duodecimo die Nouembris predicto anno regni nostri septimo proueniens siue crescens solueret iuxta tenorem literarum nostrarum predictarum Vobis mandamus quod viso mandato nostro predicto id quod vobis constare poterit prefatum nunc priorem hospitalis predicti eidem Rogero pretextu mandati nostri predicti racionabiliter soluisse eidem nunc priori inde in compoto suo ad Scaccarium nostrum debite allocetis Recipientes a prefato nunc Priore literas acquietancie ipsius Rogeri que pro nobis sufficientes fuerint in hac parte Teste me ipso apud Westmonasterium xxvj die Januarii Anno regni nostri vicesimo secundo [b]

TAILER.[1]

[a] Sic. [b] *I.e.* 1531.

[1] John Tailer, Master of the Rolls 1527-34.

IX.

CHANCERY FILES, BUNDLE 879

(1537)

HENRICUS OCTAUUS dei gratia Anglie et Francie Rex fidei defensor Dominus Hiberniae et in terra Supremum caput Anglicane ecclesie Vicecomiti Norhamtonie salutem Cum per quandam Inquisicionem captam apud Norhampton in Comitatu tuo tercio decimo die Augusti anno regni nostri nono coram Johanne Veysy clerico tunc decano Capelle nostre et aliis Commissionariis nostris pretextu litterarum nostrarum patentium eis directarum et in Cancellariam nostram retornatam inter alia sit compertum quod Johannes Goylyn [1] nuper fuit seisitus in dominico suo vt de feodo de quinque mesuagiis et ducentis acris terre arabilis que [quidem a tempore] de quo non exstat memoria in cultura occupate fuerunt et que cum mesuagiis illis tradi locari et dimitti solebant et consueuerunt in Waltone in Comitatu predicto scilicet cum quolibet . . . quadraginta acre terre ad minus occupate et locate fuerunt et sic inde seisitus vicesimo quarto die Marcii Anno regni domini H[enrici] nuper Regis Anglie septimi patris nostri praecarissimi secundo mesua[gia predicta] ad terram prosterni et deuastari fecit ac terras predictas sepibus et fossis circumquaque inclusit et ab vsu culture et iconomie in pasturam animalium conuertit et sic adhuc tenet per quod quinque aratra deponuntur et quaterviginti persone minuuntur Et tenementa predicta valent per annum quadraginta vnam libras Et quod Elianora Goylyn vidua nuper vxor predicti Johannis modo habet statum predicti Johannis Goylyn in tenementis predictis et quod tenentur de nobis Et quod omnia et singula predicta mesuagia domos [a] et edificia que superius in hac inquisicione per eosdem Juratos prosterni dicuntur . . . eosdem Juratos de et pro ruina et vasto in eisdem mesuagiis domibus et edificiis premissis facta

Transcript

Aug. 13, 1517

Mar. 24, 1486 7

[a] Sic.

[1] Cf. p. 316, *supra*.

perpetrata siue habita presentantur ita in decasu ruina
deuastacione existunt et quodlibet eorundem existit quod id
illorum mesuagiorum domorum et edificiorum quod superest
siue remanet non sufficit ad manutenenciam iconomie et
culture que ad terras arabiles cum mesuagiis domibus et
edificiis illis occupatas siue dimissas aut que occupari et
dimitti solebant requiruntur et fieri deberent nec quod
iconomie in domibus et edificiis illis pro cultura et iconomia
ibidem vtendis conuenienter moram ibidem habere nequiunt
Et Jurati predicti dicunt quod omnia predicta decasus ruine
mesuagiorum inclusiones terrarum arabilium et conuersio
inde in pasturam animalium et diminucio populorum et
quamplurima alia supradicta per eos superius presentata
facta perpetrata et commissa sunt et a diu fuerunt, contra
formam statutorum diuersorum inde editorum ac [a] regni nostri
depauperacionem et populi diminucionem ecclesiarum que
desolucionem [b] ad magnum dampnum populi nostri in Comitatu predicto et partibus vicinis huic Comitatui commorantis ac in malum et perniciosum exemplum in consimilibus casubus delinquent[ium] se disponentium nisi citius
in hac parte de premissis prouideatur remedium congruum
prout in inquisicione predicta plenius continetur Et nuper
tibi precepimus quod scire faceres prefate Elianore quod esset
coram nobis in dicta Cancellaria nostra ad certum diem iam
preteritum ad ostendendum si quid pro se haberet vel dicere
sciret quare medietas annui valoris exituum et proficuorum
mesuagiorum et terrarum predictorum a dicto quarto [a] die
Marcii anno secundo predicti nuper Regis vsque nunc et
exnunc donec et quousque mesuagia predicta sufficienter
reedificarentur et terra predicta in pristinum statum culture
redigatur nobis responderi non deberet [iuxta] vim formam
et effectum cuiusdam actus in parliamento dicti nuper Regis
patris nostri apud Westmonasterium Anno regni sui quarto
tento in huiusmodi casu editi et prouisi et ad faciendum
vlterius et recipiendum quod Cura nostra consideraret in ea
parte Et quod haberes ibi nomina illorum per quos ei scire

[a] 'ad' omitted. [b] Sic.

APPENDIX IX. 495

faceres et breve nostrum predictum   Ac tu coram nobis in dicta Cancellaria nostra retornaueris quod predicti Johannes Golyn[a] et Elianora mortui sunt et quod Ricardus Fermer de Londonia Grocer est tenens mesuagiorum terrarum et tenementorum predictorum tibi precipimus quod scire facias prefato Ricardo Fermer quod sit coram nobis in dicta Cancellaria nostra in Crastino purificacionis beate Marie proximo futuro vbicumque tunc fuerit ad ostendendum si quid pro se habeat vel dicere sciat quare medietas annui valoris exituum et proficuorum mesuagiorum et terrarum predictorum a dicto quarto[a] die Marcii dicto Anno secundo predicti nuper Regis vsque nunc et exnunc donec et quousque mesuagia predicta sufficienter reedificantur et terra predicta in pristinum statum culture redigatur nobis responderi non debeat iuxta vim formam et effectum cuiusdam actus in parliamento dicti nuper Regis patris nostri apud Westmonasterium Anno regni sui quarto tento in huiusmodi casu editi et prouisi et ad faciendum vlterius et recipiendum quod Curia nostra consideraucrit in hac parte   Et habeas ibi nomina illorum per quos ei scire feceris et hoc breve   Teste me ipso apud Westmonasterium xiiij die Januarii anno regni nostri vicesimo octauo.   Jan. 14, 1537

HALES.[1]

[Indorsed]   Scire feci infranominatum RICARDUM FERMER per JOHANNEM DOO RICARDUM ROO JOHANNEM DENNE THOMAM FENNE probos et legales homines.   WILLELMUS NEWENHAM MILES Vicecomes

Et super hoc modo ad hunc diem venit predictus Ricardus Fermour qui per Vicecomitem Comitatus predicti retornatus est terram tenens predicti Johannis Goylyn in inquisicione predicta nominati per Willelmum Jesson attornatum suum

[a] Sic.

[1] *I.e.* Christopher Hales, late A.-G., appointed July 10, 1536, 'custodem siue Magistrum Rotulorum librorum & Recordorum Cancellarie nostre.'   Recital in Exch. Mem. Roll 316, H. T. 28 H. VIII. (1537), m. 20, where he is also styled 'Cancellarie Registrario.'

et habito Auditu inquisicionis predicte Dicit quod ipse non intendit quod dominus Rex ipsum Ricardum Fermour hiis occacionibus seu eorum aliqua inquietare aut grauare velit aut debet quia pro placito Dicit quod predictus Johannes Goylyn in dicta inquisicione nominatus predicto vicesimo quarto die Marcii in dicta inquisicione specificato nec antea siue postea predicta quinque Messuagia in dicta inquisicione specificata nec aliquam inde parcellam ad terram prosterni et deuastari fecit nec terras arrabiles predictas in dicta inquisicione specificatas nec aliquem inde parcellam sepibus et fossis circumquaque vnquam inclusit nec ab vsu culture et iconomie in pasturam animalium conuertit nec sic tempore capcionis dicte inquisicionis tenuit per quod quinque aratra ibidem deponabantur [a] aut die inquisicionis predicte capte deponabantur [a] modo et forma prout in dicta inquisicione specificatur absque hoc quod quater viginte [a] persone racione premissorum ibidem vnquam miniabantur [a] aut minuuntur Et absque hoc quod predicta tenementa valent per annum quadraginta vnum libris [a] Et absque hoc quod tenementa predicta tenentur aut die capcionis dicte inquisicionis tenebantur siue aliqua inde parcella tenetur de domino Rege prout in inquisicione predicta specificatur Et absque quod omnia et singula predicta mesuagia domus et edificia in dicta inquisicione specificata ita ruinosa deuastata et in decasu tempore dicte inquisicionis capte existebant et quodlibet eorundem existebat quod id illorum mesuagiorum domorum et edificiorum quod superest siue tunc remanebat aut remanet non sufficit ad manutenenciam iconomie et culture que ad terras arabiles cum mesuagiis domibus et edificiis illis occupatas siue dimissas aut quod occupari et dimitti solebant requiruntur et fieri deberent nec quod iconomie in domibus et edificiis illis pro cultura et iconomia ibidem vtendis conuenebant [a] aut convenient ita quod moram ibidem habere nequiebant aut nequiunt [a] contra formam aliquorum statutorum inde editorum aut [b] huius regni Anglie depauperacionem et populi diminucionem communem ecclesiarum que desolacionem in magnum

[a] Sic.   [b] 'ad' omitted.

APPENDIX IX

dampnum populi domini Regis in dicto Comitatu Northamtonie et partibus vicinis huic Comitatui comorantis in malum et in pernisicionum[a] exemplum in consimilibus casubus delinquentium modo et forma prout in inquisicione predicta specificatur et continetur que omnia et singula premissa predictus Ricardus Fermour paratus est verificare prout in Curia &c. vnde petit iudicium quod ipse de premissis per Curiam hic dimittitur &c.

Et Johannes Baker[1] qui pro domino Rege sequitur in hac parte pro eodem Domino Rege Dicit quod predicto vicesimo quarto die Marcii Anno Regni Domini Henrici nuper Regis Anglie septimi secundo Predictus Johannes Goylyn predicta quinque mesuagia in dicta inquisicione specificata ad terram prosterni et deuastari fecit et dictas ducentas acras terre arabilis in dicta inquisicione specificatas sepibus et fossis circumquaque inclusit et ab vsu culture et iconomie in pasturam animalium conuertit et ea sic tenuit per quod quinque aratra ibidem deponuntur et quod quatuor viginti persone ratione premissorum ibidem miniuntur[a] et quod predicta tenementa valent per annum quadraginta vnam libras prout per eamdem inquisicionem compertum existit Et quod predicta tenementa tenentur et tempore inquisicionis predicte capte tenebantur de eodem Domino Rege prout per eandem inquisicionem similiter compertum existit et quod omnia et singula predicta mesuagia domos[a] et edificia in dicta inquisicione specificata ita ruinosa deuastata et in decasu tempore dicte inquisicionis capte existebant et quilibet[a] eorum existebat quod id illorum mesuagiorum domorum et edificiorum quod superest non remanent[a] nec sufficiunt[a] ad manutenciam[a] iconomie et culture que ad terras arabiles cum mesuagiis domibus et edificiis illis occupatas siue dimissas aut quod[a] occupari et dimitti solebant requiruntur et fieri deberent nec quod iconomie in domibus et edificiis illis pro cultura et iconomia ibidem vtendis conueniebant aut convenient ita

[a] Sic.

[1] Attorney-General 1535-40; Chancellor of the Exchequer, 1545. See *Dict. Nat. Biog.*

quod moram ibidem habere nequiebant aut nequiunt contra formam aliquorum statutorum inde editorum aut huius Regni Anglie depauperacionem et populi diminucionem communem ecclesiarum que desolacionem in magnum dampnum populi Domini Regis in dicto Comitatu Norhamtonie et partibus vicinis huic Comitatui Comorantis in malum et perniciosum exemplum in consimilibus casibus delinquentium modo et forma prout in inquisicione predicta similiter compertum existit Et hoc pro eodem Domino Rege petit quod inquiratur per primam [a] Et predictus Ricardus dimittitur.

JOHANNES BAKER.

Ideo dies datus est prefato Ricardo Fermour coram prefato domino Rege in Octaua Sancte Trinitatis vbicumque tunc fuerit in Anglia [b] . . . . faciendum et recipiendum quod iustum fuerit in premissis Et preceptum est Vicecomiti Norhamtonie quod venire faciat coram eodem Domino Rege ad diem illum xxiiij tam Milites quam alios probos et legales homines de visneto de Waltona qui prefatum Ricardum nulla affinitate attingant ad recognoscendum super eorum sacramentum premissorum plenam veritatem.

[a] Sic : for *patriam*.   [b] MS. much damaged.

TABLES

LIST OF TABLES[1]

I. Tabular view of the Inquisition of 1517: Berks, Bucks.

II. Table showing the Hundreds from which inclosures are returned. Inferred figures included. Berks, Bucks.

III. Analysis of the preceding Tables, showing (1) the areas of the Hundreds of the County included in the Returns and the areas inclosed in each Hundred; (2) the proportions of the total areas returned as inclosed to the total areas of the Hundreds from which returns are made; (3) the proportions of the total areas returned as inclosed in each Hundred to the total areas of the several Hundreds; and (4) the proportions of the total areas remaining arable and inclosed to pasture in each Hundred. Inferred figures included. Berks, Bucks.

IV. Yearly progress of inclosures, classified according to the status of landlords responsible for them, and showing whether land held in hand of owner at time of inclosure or upon what tenancy demised. Inferred figures included. Berks, Bucks.

V. Number of inclosures and distribution of areas inclosed according to tenures and tenancies. Inferred figures included. Berks, Bucks.

VI. Status of landlords responsible for inclosures, objects of inclosure and number of persons evicted and displaced from labour. Inferred figures included. Berks, Bucks.

VII. Status of actual inclosers, together with evictions and displacements from labour on inclosed arable and pasture land respectively. Inferred and doubtful figures excluded. Berks, Bucks.

VIII. Evictions and displacements from labour, area of evicted lands &c., and status of landlords responsible. Inferred figures excluded. Berks, Bucks.

[1] See General Introduction, p. 4, *n.* 1, *supra.*

LIST OF TABLES 501

IX. Number of acres to a messuagium, cotagium, &c., classified according to tenures and tenancies. Inferred and doubtful figures excluded. Berks, Bucks.

X. Number of inhabitants of a messuagium, cotagium, manerium, and mansio respectively, classified according to tenures and tenancies. Inferred figures excluded. Berks, Bucks.

XI. Number of persons and acres to an aratrum, classified according to tenures and tenancies. Inferred and doubtful figures excluded. Berks, Bucks.

XII. Rental values of inclosed arable and pasture. Land classified according to tenures and tenancies. Inferred figures excluded. Berks, Bucks.

XIII. Selected inclosures exceeding an area of 300 acres in one place or parish, showing the proportion per cent. of the inclosures to the total area of the place or parish in which such inclosures were made. Berks, Bucks.

XIV. The area of the virgate and carucate. Berks, Bucks.

XV. Comparative Table of the numeration of the MS. Berks, Bucks.

THE DOMESDAY OF INCLOSURES, 1517

I. GENERAL ANALYSIS OF THE CHANCER[Y]

Reference[1]	Ingrossing of Farms				Parishes	Total areas presented as inclosed	Inclosures			Condition of inclosers				
								Objects of inclosure						
	No. of farms ingrossed	No. of cases of ingrossing	Area ingrossed	Areas consolidated with farms			Park	Inclosure of arable	Pasture	Lay lords of manors	Lay freeholders	Ecclesiastical lords of manors	Other ecclesiastics	Lay
P. 101	—	—	acr..s —	acres —	Fulscot . . .	acres 160	acr. —	acres 160	acr. —	—	—	—	—	1
	3	1	240	—	Fulscot	40	—	40	—	—	—	—	—	1
	—	—	—	—	Fulscot	40	—	40	—	—	—	—	—	1
	—	—	—	—	Catmar	400	—	200	200	—	—	—	—	?
	—	—	—	—	Westyllesley .	40	—	40	—	—	—	—	—	?
	—	—	—	—	Westyllysley . .	[107]	—	[107]	—	—	—	—	—	?
	—	—	—	—	Ferneburghe . .	20	—	20	—	—	—	—	—	?
104	—	—	—	—	Compton . . .	200	—	140	60	—	—	—	—	?
	—	—	—	—	Aldeworth . . .	200	—	150	50	—	—	—	—	?
	—	—	—	—	Chilton . . .	30	—	30	—	—	—	—	—	?
	—	—	—	—	Bastelden . . .	20	—	20	—	—	—	—	—	?
	—	—	—	—	Stretley . . .	60	—	60	—	—	—	—	—	?
	—	—	—	—	Stretl y . . .	60	—	60	—	—	—	—	—	?
	—	—	—	—	Stretley . . .	40	—	40	—	—	—	—	—	?
	—	—	—	—	Vpton . . .	20	—	20	—	—	—	—	—	?
	—	—	—	—	Brightwell . .	40	—	40	—	—	—	—	—	?
	—	—	—	—	Chilrey . . .	20	—	20	—	1	—	—	—	?
107	—	—	—	—	Wantage . . .	55	—	—	55	—	1	—	—	?
	—	—	—	—	Esthenrede . . .	20	—	—	20	—	1	—	—	?
	—	—	—	—	Spersholt . .	40	—	—	40	—	—	—	—	?
	—	—	—	—	Spersholt . .	40	—	—	40	—	—	—	—	?
	—	—	—	—	Lekehamstede . .	30	—	30	—	—	1	—	—	?
	—	—	—	—	Yatyndon . .	40	—	—	40	1	—	—	—	?
	2	1	[80]	[40]	[Yatyndon] . .	—	—	—	—	—	—	—	—	?
	—	—	—	—	Yatendone . .	10	10	—	—	1	—	—	—	?
	—	—	—	—	[Yatendone] . .	10	10	—	—	1	—	—	—	?
	—	—	—	—	Hampstede Norreys	30	30	—	—	1	—	—	—	?
	—	—	—	—	Hampstede Norreys	40	—	40	—	—	1	—	—	?
111	—	—	—	—	Cbyveley . . .	20	—	20	—	—	—	—	—	?
	—	—	—	—	Bedone . . .	40	—	40	—	—	—	—	—	?
	—	—	—	—	Chadlyngworth .	40	—	40	—	—	—	1	—	?
	3	1	300	—	Chadlyngworth .	40	—	40	—	—	—	1	—	?
	—	—	—	—	Wolley (Chaddelworth)	120	—	—	120	—	—	1	—	?
	—	—	—	—	Chaddelworth .	40	—	40	—	—	1	—	—	?
	—	—	—	—	Easthenrede . .	24	—	24	—	—	—	—	—	?
	—	—	—	—	Westhenrede . .	180	—	180	—	2	—	—	—	?
	—	—	—	—	Grove (Wantage) .	30	—	30	—	—	—	—	—	?
	—	—	—	—	Grove (Wantage) .	24	—	24	—	—	1	—	—	?
	—	—	—	—	Easthanney . .	42	—	—	42	1	—	—	—	?
115	—	—	—	—	Easthanney . .	20	—	20	—	—	—	1	—	?

[1] Each page to which reference is made in this colum[n]
[2] The numbers of evicted persons are printed in round brackets where they represent an appor[tionment] from employment, not being evict[ed]

BERKSHIRE

RETURNS OF THE INQUISITION OF 1517 FOR BERKSHIRE

ploughs put down	Displacement of population[2]	No. of houses decayed	No. of churches decayed	Annual rental value £ s. d.	Date of inclosure	Memorabilia
—	persons (15)	1 messuagium	—	8 0 0	1515 (10 May)	The three 'messuagia' are also called 'tres separales firmas et mansiones.' The three inclosures involved eviction of twenty-nine persons taken together
—	(7)	1 ,,	—	2 0 0	1501 (16 July)	
—	(7)	1 ,,	—	2 0 0	1507 (11 Jan.)	
1	14	—	—	10 0 0	1510 (6 March)	Incloser a leaseholder of the 'manerium'
—	6	1 messuagium	—	1 0 0	1497 (16 July)	Ecclesiastical glebe
—	10	1 ,,	—	3 0 0	1515 (10 May)	,, ,,
—	3	1 ,,	—	0 12 0	1511 (6 March)	Incloser a leaseholder. Constructive decay
1	12	1 ,,	—	10 0 0	1507 (8 Jan.)	Incloser a leaseholder. Rental of 200 acres
1	5	1 ,,	—	6 0 0	1509 (6 Jan.)	Incloser a leaseholder. Rental of 200 acres
—	8	1 ,,	—	2 0 0	1510 (18 July)	Female incloser.
—	2	1 ,,	—	0 10 0	1501 (10 March)	—
—	4	1 ,,	—	0 12 0	1504 (16 Feb.)	Incloser a copyholder
—	6	1 ,,	—	2 13 4	1512 (11 Oct.)	—
—	6	1 ,,	—	1 0 0	1508 (7 June)	—
—	4	1 ,,	—	0 17 0	1512 (6 March)	—
—	5	1 ,,	—	1 0 0	1514 (6 Sept.)	Incloser a leaseholder
—	4	1 ,,	—	0 16 0	1497 (10 March)	—
1	*4*	—	—	1 10 0	1501 (1 Feb.)	—
½	*2*	—	—	0 13 0	1492 (6 March)	—
—	—	—	—	1 0 0	1488 (6 Dec.)	—
½	3	—	—	1 0 0	1506 (11 Oct.)	—
—	4	1 messuagium	—	0 10 0	1490 (26 Feb.)	A female incloser
1	5	1 ,,	—	0 18 0	1495 (18 July)	—
—	4	1 ,,	—	not given	1517	Incloser 'tenet ad firmam ... duo mesuagia et tantum in vno fit habitacio'
—	—	—	—	not given	1515 (2 March)	'de communi terra'
—	—	—	—	not given	1515 (2 March)	'alibi in communi'
—	—	—	—	0 10 0	1515 (16 Feb.)	—
—	[4]	1 messuagium	—	0 5 0	1499 (7 March)	—
—	2	1 ,,	—	0 10 0	1505 (10 July)	Incloser a copyholder of Abbey of Abingdon
—	3	1 ,,	—	0 10 0	1505 (6 June)	Incloser a female copyholder
—	(*6*)	1 ,,	—	(1 0 0)	1493 (6 April)	The two holdings grouped as of the rental value of 2l. and the destruction of the messuages as involving the eviction of twelve persons
—	(6)	1 ,,	—	(1 0 0)	1497 (7 Jan.)	
—	—	—	—	4 0 0	1509 (16 Nov.)	—
—	6	1 messuagium	—	2 0 0	1516 (6 April)	Incloser a Justice of the K. B.
—	3	1 ,,	—	0 12 0	1511 (2 Oct.)	—
—	12	1 manerium	—	10 0 0	1512 (7 June)	Inclosers probably feoffees to uses
—	2	1 messuagium	—	1 10 0	1510 (7 Nov.)	Incloser a copyholder
—	2	1 ,,	—	0 13 4	1498 (16 July)	—
½	*4*	—	—	1 0 0	1513 (8 March)	Incloser lady of the manor
—	4	1 messuagium	—	0 14 0	1502 (8 August)	—

ncident with the beginning of a membrane.
nt of totals given in the text; in square brackets where they are conjectural. Displacements indicated by italic numerals.

THE DOMESDAY OF INCLOSURES, 1517

I. General Analysis of the Chancery Returns

| Reference | Ingrossing of Farms | | | | Parishes | Total areas presented as inclosed | Inclosures | | | Condition of inclosers | | | | |
| | No. of farms ingrossed | No. of cases of ingrossing | Area ingrossed | Areas consolidated with farms | | | Park | Objects of inclosure | | Lay lords of manors | Lay freeholders | Ecclesiastical lords of manors | Other ecclesiastics | Lay |
								Inclosure of arable	Pasture					
P.			acres	acres		acres	acr.	acres	acr.					
115	—	—	—	—	Ardyngton	50	—	—	50	—	—	—	—	1
	—	—	—	—	Westlokhenges	20	—	20	—	—	—	—	—	1
	—	—	—	—	Estlokhenges	30	—	30	—	—	—	—	—	1
	—	—	—	—	Beaterton	35	—	—	35	—	—	—	—	1
	—	—	96	—	Estgynge	36	—	—	36	—	1	—	—	—
	3	1	96	—	Estgynge	30	—	—	30	—	1	—	—	—
	—	—		—	Estgynge	30	—	30	—	—	1	—	—	—
	—	—	—	—	Greneham	26	—	26	—	—	—	—	—	1
118	—	—	—	—	Greneham	20	—	—	20	—	1	—	—	—
	—	—	—	—	Greneham	80	—	—	80	—	1	—	—	—
	—	—	—	—	Wynterbourn	40	—	20	20	—	1	—	—	—
	—	—	—	—	Boxforth	40	—	40	—	—	1	—	—	—
	—	—	—	—	Bynfeld	80	—	80	—	—	1	—	—	—
	—	—	—	—	Bynfeld	26	—	26	—	—	1	—	—	—
	—	—	—	—	Langford in Cleware	60	—	—	60	—	—	—	—	2
	—	—	—	—	Ray	40	—	—	40	—	—	—	—	2
	—	—	—	—	Clewer	60	—	—	60	—	—	—	—	2
	—	—	—	—	Bustellesham	10	10	—	—	—	—	1	—	—
	—	—	—	—	Hurst	60	60	—	—	—	1	—	—	—
	—	—	—	—	Erley	40	—	—	40	—	1	—	—	—
121	—	—	—	—	Bray	20	—	—	20	—	1	—	—	—
	—	—	—	—	Harwell	20	—	20	—	—	—	—	—	—
	—	—	—	—	Westyllysley	60	—	60	—	—	—	—	1	—
	—	—	—	—	Farnham	100	—	100	—	—	—	—	—	—
	—	—	—	—	Fernham	30	—	30	—	—	—	—	—	—
	2	1	30	—	Compton	30	—	30	—	—	—	—	—	—
	—	—	—	—	Burton	20	—	20	—	—	—	—	—	2
	—	—	—	—	Knyghton	40	—	40	—	—	—	—	—	2
	—	—	—	—	Crokeham	20	—	20	—	—	—	—	1	—
125	2	1	140	—	Westsandford	60	—	60	—	—	—	—	—	2
				—	Westsandford	80	—	80	—	—	—	—	—	2
	—	—	—	—	Kenyngton	44	—	44	—	—	1	—	—	—
	5	1	112	80	Shalyngford	112	—	32	80	—	—	—	—	2
	—	—	—	—	Shalyngford	50	—	50	—	—	—	—	—	2
	—	—	—	—	Shalyngford	30	—	30	—	—	—	—	—	2
	—	—	—	—	Shalyngford	30	—	30	—	—	—	—	1	—

BERKSHIRE

OF THE INQUISITION OF 1517 FOR BERKSHIRE—(continued)

	Consequences of inclosure				Inclosures	
ploughs put down	Displace- ment of population	No. of houses decayed	No. of churches decayed	Annual rental value	Date of inclosure	Memorabilia
	persons			£ s. d.		
—	4	1 messuagium	—	1 9 0	1506 (6 Sept.)	'messuagium . . . in bercariam pro ouibus conuertit.' Incloser a copyholder
—	3	1 ,,	—	0 13 4	1510 (10 June)	Incloser a copyholder
—	4	1 ,,	—	1 6 8	1510 (11 Nov.)	Incloser a female copyholder
—	3	1 ,,	—	0 15 0	1498 (17 June)	'de mesuagio illo quandam bercariam erexit.' Incloser a copyholder
—	(3)	1 ,,	—	(1 1 6)	1512 (6 May)	The rental value of the two together returned as 40s., and the evicted persons as 6. 'In quoddam horreum conuerti . . . fecit'
—	(3)	1 ,,	—	(0 18 6)	1512 (6 May)	
—	4	1 ,,	—	1 10 0	1515 (4 June)	
—	6	1 ,,	—	1 0 0	1512 (6 March)	Incloser a leaseholder
—	2	1 ,,	—	1 0 0	1516 (6 May)	—
1	4	—	—	1 10 0	1511 (7 Dec.)	—
—	4	1 messuagium	—	1 0 0	1495 (7 April)	A holding of 40 acres
—	6	1 ,,	—	1 0 0	1511 (10 April)	—
—	8	1 ,,	—	4 13 4	1507 (10 May)	Two legal owners, of whom one acted
—	4	1 ,,	—	1 4 0	1503 (6 March)	—
2	12	—	—	5 0 0	1507 (7 March)	Incloser a copyholder
1	6	1 messuagium manerii	—	2 13 8	1508 (6 Dec.)	'non custodit mansum in mesuagio'
—	5	1 messuagium manerii	—	2 0 0	1514 (6 March)	—
—	—	—	—	0 5 0	1517	—
—	—	—	—	1 10 0	1506 (10 Feb.)	—
—	8	—	—	1 0 0	1505 (6 July)	—
—	3	1 messuagium	—	1 0 0	1501 (6 March)	—
—	2	1 ,,	—	0 10 0	1510 (16 Aug.)	Incloser a leaseholder
—	6	1 ,,	—	3 0 0	1505 (10 May)	Ecclesiastical glebe
—	4	1 ,,	—	6 13 4	1487 (16 July)	Incloser a leaseholder
—	3	1 ,,	—	0 18 0	1503 (6 Sept.)	Incloser a copyholder
—	[4]	2 messuagia	—	1 0 0	1498 (16 March)	Incloser a leaseholder. Two virgates, 'qualibet virgata quindecim acras terre in se continente'
—	4	1 messuagium	—	1 0 0	1498 (12 April)	—
—	6	1 messuagium	—	2 0 0	1507 (12 July)	Incloser a leaseholder
—	7	1 ,,	—	0 9 0	1515 (6 Mar.)	Incloser an ecclesiastical freeholder. Leasehold at time of Inquisition
—	[7]	1 ,,	—	0 11 0	1509 (10 July)	Incloser a copyholder
—	6	1 ,,	—	0 12 0	1508 (7 Nov.)	,, ,,
—	6	1 ,,	—	5 0 0	1513 (18 June)	—
—	8	4 messuagia	—	3 13 4	1506 (10 Oct.)	Incloser a leaseholder. The 112 acres belong to 5 messuagia. Rental value of 80 acres only
—	3	1 messuagium	—	1 6 8	1510 (3 Oct.)	Incloser a copyholder
—	[4]	1 ,,	—	1 0 0	1515 (6 May)	,, ,,
—	3	1 'mansio Rectorie'	—	1 10 0	1511 (8 April)	Incloser a clerical farming tenant of a rectory

THE DOMESDAY OF INCLOSURES, 1517

I. GENERAL ANALYSIS OF THE CHANCERY RETURNS

Reference	Ingrossing of Farms				Parishes	Total areas presented as inclosed	Inclosures			Condition of inclosures				
								Objects of inclosure						
	No. of farms ingrossed	No. of cases of ingrossing	Area ingrossed	Areas consolidated with farms			Park	Inclosure of arable	Pasture	Lay lords of manors	Lay freeholders	Ecclesiastical lords of manors	Other ecclesiastics	Lay
P.			acres	acres		acres	acr.	acres	acr.					
128	—	—	—	—	Henton	45	—	45	—	—	—	—	—	1
	—	—	—	—	Bukland . . .	40	—	—	40	—	1	—	—	—
	—	—	—	—	Bukland . . .	40	—	40	—	—	1	—	—	—
	—	—	—	—	Cokeham . . .	20	—	20	—	—	1	—	—	—
	—	—	—	—	Wynkefeld . . .	50	—	50	—	—	1	—	—	—
	—	—	—	—	Wynkefeld . . .	20	—	—	20	—	1	—	—	—
	—	—	—	—	Berkeham . . .	100	—	—	100	1	—	—	—	—
	—	—	—	—	Bray	60	—	—	60	—	1	—	—	—
131	—	—	—	—	Stephyngton . .	40	—	40	—	—	1	—	—	—
	—	—	—	—	Stephyngton . .	40	—	—	40	—	1	—	—	—
	—	—	[1,200]	—	Milton . . .	—	—	—	—	—	—	—	—	2
	—	—	—	—	Milton	120	—	—	120	—	—	—	—	2
		⎧	[600]	—	Drayton	—	—	—	—	—	—	—	—	1
	2	1 ⎨	[300]	—	Garford . . .	—	—	—	—	—	—	—	—	1
		⎩	—	—	Garford . . .	60	—	—	60	—	—	—	—	1
	—	—	—	—	Drayton	20	—	20	—	—	—	—	—	1
	—	—	—	—	Wittnam . . .	20	—	—	20	—	—	—	—	1
	—	—	—	—	Newbrigg (Kyngeston Bagpues)	60	—	60	—	—	—	—	—	1
	—	—	—	—	Lyford	40	—	—	40	—	1	—	—	—
	—	—	—	—	Southcote . .	100	—	—	100	—	1	—	—	—
135	—	—	—	—	Hampstede Marshall .	100	100	—	—	1	—	—	—	—
	2	1	[89]	—	(Hampstede Marshall) .	—	—	—	—	—	—	—	—	1
			[178]	—	(Hampstede Marshall) .	—	—	—	—	—	—	—	—	1
	—	—	—	—	Kentbury . . .	30	—	—	30	—	—	—	—	1
	—	—	—	—	Huddon	100	—	20	80	—	—	—	—	1
	—	—	—	—	Wilde . . .	40	—	40	—	—	—	—	—	1
	—	—	—	—	Wilde	50	50	—	—	1	—	—	—	—
	—	—	—	—	Warfild . . .	40	—	—	40	—	1	—	—	—
	—	—	—	—	Wargrave . . .	40	—	—	40	—	—	—	—	1
	—	—	—	—	Oxynham . . .	30	—	30	—	—	1	—	—	—
	2	1	60	—	Sandhurst . .	60	—	—	60	—	1	—	—	—
139	1	1	[80]	[80]	Fyfeld	40	—	40	—	—	1	—	—	—
	1	1	[80]	[80]	Frylford . . .	[80]	—	[80]	—	—	—	—	—	—
	a	a	[a]	—	(Garford a	—	—	—	—	—	—	—	—	1
	b	b	[b]	—	Drayton b	—	—	—	—	—	—	—	—	1
	—	—	—	—	Marcham . . .	40	—	—	40	—	—	—	—	1
	—	—	—	—	Sutton Curttenay .	40	—	40	—	—	1	—	—	—
	—	—	—	—	Appelford . . .	40	—	40	—	—	—	—	—	1
	—	—	—	—	(Bukland . . .	40	—	40	—	—	—	—	—	1
	—	—	—	—	Bukland . . .	60	—	60	—	—	—	—	—	1
	2	1	40	—	Newynton (Bukeland)	20	—	20	—	—	—	—	—	1
				—	Bukland . . .	20	—	20	—	—	—	—	—	1

a, b. These two farms have been already returned (m. 75, *supra*), and their areas are therefore n ingrossed with them. MS. here by mistake Brayton.

BERKSHIRE 507

OF THE INQUISITION OF 1517 FOR BERKSHIRE—(continued)

ploughs put down	Displacement of population	No. of houses decayed	No. of churches decayed	Annual rental value	Date of inclosure	Memorabilia
				INCLOSURES		
		Consequences of inclosure				
	persons			£ s. d.		
—	6	1 manerium	—	2 6 8	1515 (6 May)	Incloser a copyholder on a Crown manor
—	4	1 messuagium	—	1 0 0	1515 (16 Feb.)	—
—	3	1 ,,	—	1 0 0	1510 (6 July)	—
—	2	1 ,,	—	1 0 0	1510 (10 July)	—
—	6	1 ,,	—	2 0 0	1493 (14 Feb.)	—
—	6	1 ,,	—	1 0 0	1510 (11 Jan.)	—
—	8	1 ,,	—	1 13 4	1516 (4 Mar.)	—
1	5	1 ,,	—	3 0 0	1492 (10 Jan.)	—
—	4	1 ,,	—	2 0 0	1498 (4 Jan.)	—
—	6	1 ,,	—	2 0 0	1499 (6 July)	—
—	—	—	—	20 0 0	1499 (6 Oct.) }	Inclosers lessees of the manor, of which the 120 acres inclosed formed part
2	13	1 manerium	—	2 0 0	1499 (6 Oct.) }	
—	12	1 messuagium manerii	—	20 0	1506 (1 Oct.)	Constructive decay of both manor houses
—	6	1 manerium	—	8 } £ 10	1506 (1 Oct.)	Incloser a lessee of the manors. The rental value refers to the 240 acres
—	—	—	—	2 }	1506 (1 Oct.)	The total rental value is £10 for 300 acres
—	4	1 messuag'um	—	0 12 6	1501 (6 June)	Incloser a copyholder
—	3	1 ,,	—	0 13 4	1516 (10 July)	,, ,,
—	4	1 ,,	—	1 4 0	1506 (11 Oc..)	,, ,,
2	8	—	—	2 0 0	1517 (6 July)	—
2	10	—	—	5 0 0	1507 (6 Mar.)	—
—	—	—	—	2 0 0	1505 (1 Dec.)	—
—	—	—	—	3 6 8	1517 }	'tenet duas firmas'
—	—	—	—	6 13 4	1517 }	
1	4	1 messuagium	—	1 0 0	1506 (10 June)	—
1	4	1 ,,	—	4 0 0	1509 (6 Oct.)	Incloser a leaseholder. Rental value of 100 acres
—	[5]	1 ,,	—	0 13 4	1513 (10 July)	—
—	4	—	—	0 12 0	1514 (6 Jan.)	—
1	4	—	—	2 0 0	1516 (9 Jan.)	—
—	4	1 messuagium	—	1 0 0	1514 (6 Mar.).	Incloser a female copyholder
—	4	1 ,,	—	1 10 0	1499 (13 June)	—
—	6	2 messuagia	—	1 6 8	1515 (6 July)	Each holding of 30 acres
—	4	1 messuagium	—	0 13 0	1514 (14 Jan.)	—
—	4	1 ,,	—	3 0 }	1517	Constructive decay of messuage Date records subsisting lease
—	—	—	—	10 a }	1517	,, ,, ,,
—	—	—	—	20 b }	1517	
—	12	1 messuagium	—	2 0 0	1501 (7 Aug.)	Incloser a copyholder
—	8	1 ,,	—	0 13 4	1510 (7 July)	—
—	8	1 ,,	—	1 0 0	1508 (7 May)	Incloser a copyholder
—	8	1 ,,	—	0 18 0	1510 (7 May)	—
—	6	1 ,,	—	1 10 0	1510 (12 Oct.)	'le personage lande'
—	4	1 ,,	—	0 18 0	1512 (3 Feb.)	—
—	4	1 ,,	—	0 11 0	1511 (7 May)	—

ain entered in the total of this column, though Frylford, as intended by the MS., is reckoned as

I. General Analysis of the Chancery Returns

Reference	Ingrossing of Farms				Parishes	Total areas presented as inclosed	Objects of inclosure			Condition of inclosers					
	No. of farms ingrossed	No. of cases of ingrossing	Area ingrossed	Areas consolidated with farms			Park	Inclosure of arable	Pasture	Lay lords of manors	Lay freeholders	Ecclesiastical lords of manors	Other ecclesiastics	Lay	
P.			acres	acres		acres	acr.	acres	a:r.						
143	—	—	—	—	Sotwell	60	—	60	—	—	—	—	—	—	1
	—	—	—	—	Sotwell	40	—	40	—	—	—	—	—	—	1
	—	—	—	—	⎰ Southmorton	20	—	20	—	—	—	—	—	—	1
	—	—	—	—	⎱ Southmorton	20	—	20	—	—	—	—	—	—	1
	—	—	—	—	Dudcote	30	—	—	30	—	—	—	—	—	1
	—	—	—	—	Dudcote	20	—	20	—	—	—	—	—	—	1
	—	—	—	—	Mylford	60	—	60	—	—	—	—	—	—	1
	—	—	—	—	Aston Turrold	30	—	30	—	—	—	—	—	1	—
	—	—	—	—	⎰ Aston Turrold	30	—	30	—	—	—	—	—	—	1
	—	—	—	—	⎱ Aston Turrold	30	—	30	—	—	—	—	—	—	1
	—	—	—	—	Harwell	100	—	100	—	—	—	—	—	1	—
146	—	—	—	—	Crokam	60	—	—	60	1	—	—	—	—	—
	—	—	—	—	Pangbourn	20	—	20	—	—	—	1	—	—	—
	—	—	—	—	Tyleherst	30	—	30	—	—	—	—	—	—	1
			—	20	⎧ Westhagbourn	20	—	20	—	—	—	—	—	—	1
	7	1			⎨										
			[281]	[130]	⎩ (Westhagbourn, &c.)	—	—	—	—	—	—	—	—	—	1
	[3]	1	[287]	200	Burghfeld Regis	200	—	200	—	—	—	—	—	—	1
	—	—	—	—	Hartley	40	—	—	40	—	—	—	—	—	1
	—	—	—	—	Hartley	15	—	—	15	—	1	—	—	—	—
	—	—	—	—	Bradfeld	4	4	—	—	1	—	—	—	—	—
				—	⎰ Wolhamton	20	—	20	—	1	—	—	—	—	—
	2	1	50												
				—	⎱ Wolhampton	30	—	30	—	—	—	—	—	—	1
	41	15	4163	550	Totals	6615	274	4068	2273	12	33	4	5	7	

¹ Ev. = Evictions, D = Displacement from employment, the latter represen⸺

BERKSHIRE

OF THE INQUISITION OF 1517 FOR BERKSHIRE—(continued)

ploughs put down	Displace-ment of population	No. of houses decayed	No. of churches decayed	Annual rental value	Date of inclosure	Memorabilia
				Inclosures		
	Consequences of inclosure					
	persons			£ s. d.		
—	10	1 messuagium	—	1 0 0	1515 (16 Oct.)	Incloser a leaseholder
—	4	1 ,,	—	1 0 0	1508 (6 June)	—
—	3	1 ,,	—	1 0 0	1507 (19 April)	Incloser a female leaseholder
—	3	1 ,,	—	1 0 0	1507 (7 July)	Incloser a leaseholder
—	3	1 ,,	—	2 0 0	1516 (7 April)	,, ,,
—	2	1 ,,	—	0 15 0	1505 (10 June)	Incloser a copyholder
—	6	1 ,,	—	1 0 0	1497 (6 May)	Incloser a leaseholder
—	4	1 ,,	—	1 0 0	1515 (7 June)	Incloser the Rector
—	3	1 ,,	—	1 4 0	1512 (16 July)	—
—	3	1 ,,	—	0 18 10	1516 (7 April)	—
—	8	1 ,,	—	2 13 4	1514 (6 May)	Incloser a clerical farmer
▪	[6]	—	—	1 0 0	1514 (10 Mar.)	Incloser Margaret, Countess of Salisbury
—	6	1 messuag'nm	—	0 10 0	1505 (20 May)	—
—	5	1 ,,	—	0 10 0	1505 (10 July)	—
—	[2]	1 ,,	—	1 13 4	1517	'domum molendini.' Rental value apparently includes both mill and house. 'Et sex alias firmas in diuersis locis'
—	[15]	3 messuagia	—	Not given	1517	'permittit tres de aliis firmis suis . . . in decasum & ruinam fore'
—	12	1 messuagium	—	10 0 0	1500 (10 Oct.)	Incloser a leaseholder, and 'similiter alias firmas tenet'
▪	4	1 ,,	—	1 0 0	1497 (10 Jan.)	House legally decayed
—	[0]	1 ,,	—	0 5 0	1515 (4 May)	House legally decayed. Two inmates left
—	—	—	—	0 1 4	[1508]	Incloser, who 'nuper inclusit,' died 1509. 'More' land
—	[2]	1 messuagium	—	0 10 0	1501 (10 July)	Incloser of next also farmer of this holding
—	2	1 ,,	—	0 10 0	1517	'Ponit in mesuagio illo pauperem . . . in quo tres persone habitare possunt
4½	Ev.¹| D.¹ 590+80 ——— 670	111 mess. 7 maneria 1 mansio	—	—	—	—

italic figures. The two together constitute Displacement of Population.

II.

TABLE SHOWING THE HUNDREDS[1] FROM WHICH INCLOSURES ARE RETURNED.
INFERRED FIGURES INCLUDED

	LAY OWNERSHIP					ECCLESIASTICAL OWNERSHIP				
				Inclosures					Inclosures	
Hundred	Parish	Total area	Inclosures of arable	Conversions to pasture		Hundred	Parish	Total area	Inclosures of arable	Conversions to pasture
		acres	acres	acres				acres	acres	acres
Moreton	Fulscot	240	240	—						
,,	Bastelden	20	20	—						
,,	Stretley	60	60	—						
,,	Stretley	60	60	—						
,,	Stretley	40	40	—						
,,	Vpton	20	20	—						
						Moreton	Brightwell	40	40	—
						,,	Harwell	20	20	—
,,	Sotwell	60	60	—		,,	Sotwell	40	40	—
,,	{ Southmorton	20	20	—						
,,	{ Southmorton	20	20	—						
,,	Dudcote	30	—	30						
,,	Dudcote	20	20	—						
,,	Mvlford	60	60	—						
						,,	Aston Turrold	30	30	—
,,	{ Aston Turrold	30	30	—						
,,	{ Aston Turrold	30	30	—						
,,	Harwell	100	100	—						
,,	Westhagbourn	20	20	—						
—	—	830	800	30		—	—	130	130	—
Compton	Catmar	400	200	200		Compton	Westyllesley	40	40	—
,,						,,	Westyllysley	[107]	[107]	—
						,,	Ferneburghe	20	20	—
,,	Compton	200	140	60						
,,	Aldeworth	200	150	50						
,,	Chilton	30	30	—						
						,,	Westyllysley	60	60	—
—	—	830	520	310		—	—	227	227	—
Wanting or Wantage	Chilrey	20	20	—						
,,	Wantage	55	—	55						
,,	Esthenrede	20	—	20		Wanting or Wantage	Easthenrede	24	24	—
Carried	forward	95	20	75		Carried	forward	24	24	—

[1] As is shown by the Returns for Cheshire, as also by the Lansd. MS. for Norfolk, the presentments were made by the Hundreds.

BERKSHIRE

TABLE SHOWING THE HUNDREDS FROM WHICH INCLOSURES ARE RETURNED. INFERRED FIGURES INCLUDED—(*continued*)

	LAY OWNERSHIP				ECCLESIASTICAL OWNERSHIP				
			Inclosures					Inclosures	
Hundred	Parish	Total area	Inclosures of arable	Conversions to pasture	Hundred	Parish	Total area	Inclosures of arable	Conversions to pasture
		acres	acres	acres			acres	acres	acres
Brought	forward	95	20	75	Brought	forward . .	24	24	—
Wanting or	Westhenrede .	180	180	—					
Wantage	Grove (Wantage	30	30	—					
,,	Grove (Wantage	24	24	—					
,,	Easthanney .	42	—	42	Wanting or	Easthanney .	20	20	—
,,	Ardyngton .	50	—	50	Wantage				
					,,	Westlokhenges	20	20	—
					,,	Estlokhenges .	30	30	—
					,,	Beaterton .	35	—	35
,,	Estgynge .	66	—	66 ⎫					
,,	Estgynge .	30	30	— ⎭					
—	—	517	284	233	—	—	129	94	35
Shrivenham	⎧ Spersholt .	40	—	40					
,, .	⎨ Spersholt .	40	—	40					
,, .	Farnham .	130	130	—					
,, .	Compton [1] .	30	30	—					
,, .	Burton . .	20	20	—					
,, .	Knyghton .	40	40	—					
—	—	300	220	80					
Faircross .	Lekehamstede	30	30	—					
,, .	Yatyndon .	40	—	40					
,, .	Yatendone .	20	—	20					
,, .	Hampstede Norreys	30	—	30					
,, .	Hampstede Norreys	40	40	—					
					Faircross .	Chyveley .	20	20	—
,, .	Bedone . .	40	40	—					
,, .	Greneham .	26	26	—					
,, .	Greneham .	20	—	20					
,, .	Greneham .	80	—	80					
,, .	Wynterbourn .	40	20	20					
,, .	Boxforth . .	40	40	—					
					,, .	Crokeham .	20	20	—
					,, .	Wilde .	40	40	—
,, .	Wilde . .	50	—	50					
,, .	Crokam . .	60	—	60					
—	—	516	196	320	—	—	80	80	—

[1] *I.e.* Compton Beauchamp.

II. Table showing the Hundreds from which Inclosures are returned. Inferred Figures included—(*continued*)

Lay Ownership					Ecclesiastical Ownership				
			Inclosures					Inclosures	
Hundred	Parish	Total area	Inclosures of arable	Conversions to pasture	Hundred	Parish	Total area	Inclosures of arable	Conversions to pasture
		acres	acres	acres			acres	acres	acres
					Kintbury Eagle	Chadlyngworth	80	80	—
					Kintbury Eagle	Wolley (Chaddelworth)	120	—	120
Kintbury Eagle	Chaddelworth	40	40	—					
Kintbury Eagle	Hampstede Marshall	100	—	100					
					Kintbury Eagle	Kentbury	30	—	30
					Kintbury Eagle	Huddon	100	20	80
—	—	140	40	100	—	—	330	100	230
Cookham	Bynfeld	80	80	—					
,,	Bynfeld	26	26	—					
,,	Ray	40	—	40					
,,	Cokeham	20	20	—					
—	—	166	126	40					
Ripplesmere	Langford in Cleware	60	—	60					
,,	Clewer	60	—	60					
,,	Wynkefeld	50	50	—					
,,	Wynkefeld	20	—	20					
—	—	190	50	140					
					Beynhurst	Bustellesham	10	—	10
					—	—	10	—	10
Charlton	Hurst	60	—	60					
,,	Erley	40	—	40					
,,	Berkeham	100	—	100					
—	—	200	—	200					

II. Table showing the Hundreds from which Inclosures are returned. Inferred Figures included—(*continued*)

	Lay Ownership				Ecclesiastical Ownership				
			Inclosures					Inclosures	
Hundred	Parish	Total area	Inclosures of arable	Conversions to pasture	Hundred	Parish	Total area	Inclosures of arable	Conversions to pasture
		acres	acres	acres			acres	acres	acres
Bray	Bray	20	—	20					
,,	Bray	60	—	60					
—	—	80	—	80					
					Hormer	Westsandford	60	60	—
					,,	Westsandford	80	80	—
Hormer	Kenyngton	44	44	—					
—	—	44	44	—	—	—	140	140	—
					Ganfield	Shalyngford	112	32	80
					,,	Shalyngford	50	50	—
					,,	Shalyngford	30	30	—
					,,	Shalyngford	30	30	—
Ganfield	Henton	45	45	—					
,,	Bukland	40	40	40					
,,	Bukland	40	40	—					
,,	Bukland	40	40	—					
					,,	Bukland	60	60	—
,,	Newynton (Bukeland)	20	20	—					
,,	Bukland	20	20	—					
—	—	205	165	40	—	—	282	202	80
Ock	Stephyngton	40	40	—					
,,	Stephyngton	40	—	40					
					Ock	Milton	120	—	120
					,,	Garford	60	—	60
					,,	Drayton	20	20	—
,,	Wittnam	20	—	20					
,,	Newbrigg (Kyngeston Bagpues)	60	60	—					
,,	Lyford	40	—	40					
,,	Fyfeld	40	40	—					
,,	Frylford	[80]	[80]	—					
					,,	Marcham	40	—	40
,,	Sutton Curttenay	40	40	—					
					,,	Appelford	40	40	—
—	—	360	260	100	—	—	280	60	220

TABLE SHOWING THE HUNDREDS FROM WHICH INCLOSURES ARE RETURNED.
INFERRED FIGURES INCLUDED—(*continued*)

Lay Ownership			Inclosures		Ecclesiastical Ownership			Inclosures	
Hundred	Parish	Total area	Inclosures of arable	Conversions to pasture	Hundred	Parish	Total area	Inclosures of arable	Conversions to pasture
Reading	Southcoote	acres 100	acres —	acres 100	Reading ,,	Pangbourn Tyleherst	acres 20 30	acres 20 } 30 }	acres — —
—	—	100	—	100	—	—	50	50	—
Wargrave	Warfild	40	—	40	Wargrave	Wargrave	40	—	40
—	—	40	—	40	—	—	40	—	40
Sonning	Okynham Sandhurst	30 60	30 —	— 60					
—	—	90	30	60					
Theale ,, ,, ,, , ,,	Burghfeld Regis Hartley Hartley Bradfeld Wolhamton Wolhampton	200 40 15 4 20 30	200 — — — 20 } 30 }	— 40 15 4 — —					
—	—	309	250	59					

BERKSHIRE

III

ANALYSIS OF THE PRECEDING TABLES, SHOWING (1) THE AREAS OF THE HUNDREDS OF THE COUNTY INCLUDED IN THE RETURNS AND THE AREAS INCLOSED IN EACH HUNDRED; (2) THE PROPORTIONS OF THE TOTAL AREAS RETURNED AS INCLOSED TO THE TOTAL AREAS OF THE HUNDREDS FROM WHICH RETURNS ARE MADE; (3) THE PROPORTIONS OF THE TOTAL AREAS RETURNED AS INCLOSED IN EACH HUNDRED TO THE TOTAL AREAS OF THE SEVERAL HUNDREDS, AND (4) THE PROPORTIONS OF THE TOTAL AREAS REMAINING ARABLE AND INCLOSED TO PASTURE IN EACH HUNDRED. INFERRED FIGURES INCLUDED.

Hundred	Area of Hundred	Total area inclosed	Inclosures remaining arable	Conversions and inclosures to pasture	Proportion per cent. of total area inclosed to area of Hundred	Proportion per cent. of inclosures remaining arable to area of Hundred	Proportion per cent. of conversions and inclosures to pasture to area of Hundred
	acres	acres	acres	acres			
Moreton	28,700	960	930	30	3·34	3·24	·10
Compton	18,190	1,057	747	310	5·81	4·10+	1·70+
Wanting, or Wantage	28,160	646	378	268	2·29	1·34	·95
Shrivenham	34,490	300	220	80	·86	·63	·23
Faircross	46,130	596	276	320	1·29	·59+	·69+
Kintbury Eagle	43,940	470	140	330	1·06	·31	·75
Cookham	14,330	166	126	40	1·15	·87+	·27+
Ripplesmere	17,430	190	50	140	1·09	·28	·81
Beynhurst	13,020	10	—	10	·07	—	·07
Charlton	12,940	200	—	200	1·55	—	1·55
Bray	8,900	80	—	80	·89	—	·89
Hormer	21,460	184	184	—	·08	·08	—
Ganfield	17,020	487	367	120	2·86	2·15+	·70+
Ock	28,250	640	320	320	2·26	1·13	1·13
Reading	37,510	150	50	100	·39	·13	·26
Wargrave	11,220	80	—	80	·71	—	·71
Sonning	21,830	90	30	60	·41	·13+	·27+
Theale	26,690	309	250	59	1·15	·93	·22
Totals	430,210[1]	6,615	4,068	2,547	1·53	·94	·59

[1] The Hundreds from which no returns are made are Faringdon (9,880 acres), which includes six parishes, and Lambourn (19,400 acres), including two parishes. Remenham, the place of meeting of the commissioners, is in Beynhurst Hundred (13,020 acres), from which one return (Bustellesham) is made. The areas are from the Census of 1831, since which period some changes have taken place in the areas of some of the Hundreds.

IV

YEARLY PROGRESS OF INCLOSURES CLASSIFIED ACCORDING TO STATUS OF LAND-
LORDS RESPONSIBLE FOR THEM, AND SHOWING WHETHER LAND HELD IN
HAND OF OWNER AT THE TIME OF INCLOSURE OR UPON WHAT TENANCY
DEMISED.[1] INFERRED FIGURES INCLUDED

| Year | Tenure or tenancy | Lay Ownership | | Lords of manors | | Freeholders | | Tenure or tenancy | Ecclesiastical Ownership | | Lords of manors | | Freeholders | |
		Parish	Hundred	Arable	Pasture	Arable	Pasture		Parish	Hundred	Arable	Pasture	Arable	Pasture
				acr.	acr.	acr.	acr.				acr.	acr.	acr.	acr.
1485		Nil												
1486		Nil												
1487	L.	Farnham	Shrivenham	100	—	—	—							
1488	F.T.	Spersholt	,,	—	40	—	—							
1489		Nil												
1490	H.F.	Lekehamstede	Faircross	—	—	30	—							
1491		Nil												
1492	H.F.	Esthenrede	Wantage	—	—	—	20							
,,	H.F.	Bray	Bray	—	—	—	60							
1493								H.M.[2]	Chadlyngworth	Kintbury Eagle	40	—	—	—
,,	H.F.	Wynkefeld	Ripplesmere	—	—	50	—							
1494		Nil												
1495	H.M.	Yatyndon	Faircross	—	40	—	—							
,,	H.F.	Wynterbourn	,,	—	—	20	20							
1496		Nil												
1497								F.T.	Westyllesley	Compton	—	—	40	—
,,	H.M.	Chilrey	Wantage	20	—	—	—							
,,								H.M.[2]	Chadlyngworth	Kintbury Eagle	40	—	—	—
,,	L.	Mvlford	Moreton	—	—	60	—							
,,	F.T.	Hartley	Theale	—	—	—	40							
1498	H.F.	Grove (Wantage)	Wantage	—	—	24	—							
,,								C.	Beaterton	Wantage	—	35	—	—
,,	L.	Compton	Shrivenham	30	—	—	—							
,,	F.T.	Burton	,,	20	—	—	—							
,,	H.F.	Stephyngton	Ock	—	—	40	—							
1499	H.F.	Hampstede Norreys	Faircross	—	—	40	—							
,,	H.F.	Stephyngton	Ock	—	—	—	40							
,,								L.	Milton	Ock	—	120	—	—
,,	H.F.	Okynham	Sonning	—	—	30	—							
1500	L.	Burghfeld Regis	Theale	200	—	—	—							
1501	F.T.	Fulscot	Moreton	40	—	—	—							
,,	F.T.	Bastelden	,,	20	—	—	—							
,,	H.F.	Wantage	Wantage	—	—	—	55							

[1] H.M. = In hand of lord of manor.; H.F. = In hand of freeholder; C = Copyhold; L = Leasehold; F.T. = Farm tenancy.   [2] H.M. at time of inclosure.

BERKSHIRE

IV. YEARLY PROGRESS OF INCLOSURES CLASSIFIED—(continued)

Year	Tenure or tenancy	Lay Ownership						Tenure or tenancy	Ecclesiastical Ownership					
		Parish	Hundred	Lords of manors		Freeholders			Parish	Hundred	Lords of manors		Freeholders	
				Arable	Pasture	Arable	Pasture				Arable	Pasture	Arable	Pasture
				acr.	acr.	acr.	acr.				acr.	acr.	acr.	acr.
1501	H.F.	Bray . .	Bray .	—	—	—	20							
,,								C.	Drayton .	Ock . .	20	—	—	—
,,	F.T.	Wolhamton	Theale .	20	—	—	—	C.	Marcham .	,, . .	—	40	—	—
1502								H.M.	East Hanney	Wantage	20	—	—	—
1503	H.F.	Bynfeld .	Cookham	—	—	26	—							
,,	C.	Fernham .	Shrivenham	30	—	—	—							
1504	F.T.	Stretley .	Moreton	60	—	—	—							
1505								C.	Chyveley .	Faircross	20	—	—	—
,,	C.	Bedone. .	Faircross	40	—	—	—							
,,	H.F.	Erley . .	Charlton	—	—	—	40							
,,								H.F.	Westyllysley	Compton	—	—	60	—
,,	H.M.	Hampstede Marshall	Kintbury Eagle	—	100	—	—							
,,	C.	Dudcote .	Moreton	20	—	—	—							
,,								H.M.	Pangbourn	Reading	20	—	—	—
,,								F.T.	Tyleherst	,,	30	—	—	—
1506	F.T.	Spersholt .	Shrivenham	—	40	—	—							
,,	C.	Ardyngton	Wantage	—	50	—	—							
,,	H.F.	Hurst . .	Charlton	—	—	—	60							
,,								L.	Shalyngford	Ganfield	32	80	—	—
,,								L.	Garford .	Ock . .	—	60	—	—
,,	C.	Newbrigg (Kyngeston Bagpues)	Ock . .	60	—	—	—							
,,								F.T.	Kentbury.	Kintbury Eagle	—	30	—	—
1507	F.T.	Fulscot .	Moreton	40	—	—	—							
,,	L.	Compton .	Compton	140	60	—	—							
,,	H.F.	Bynfeld .	Cookham	—	—	80	—							
,,	C.	Langford in Cleware	Ripplesmere	—	60	—	—							
,,	L.	Knyghton	Shrivenham	—	—	40	—							
,,	H.F.	Lyford .	Ock . .	—	—	—	40							
,,	H.F.	Southcote.	Reading	—	—	—	100							
,,	F.T.	Southmorton	Moreton	20	—	—	—							
,,	F.T.	Southmorton	,,	20	—	—	—							
1508	F.T.	Stretley .	,,	40	—	—	—							
,,	F.T.	Ray . .	Cookham	—	40	—	—							
,,								C.	Westsandford	Hormer	80	—	—	—
,,								C.	Appelford	Ock . .	40	—	—	—
,,								F.T.	Sotwell .	Moreton	—	—	40	—
,,	H.M.	Bradfeld[1] .	Theale .	—	4	—	—							

[1] The MS. in this case says of the incloser that he 'nuper inclusit.' He is known to have died in 1509. I have therefore taken 1508 as the nearest possible date to 1517. The omission of the precise date is, as will be seen, quite exceptional in the Returns for Berkshire, while the area inclosed is so small that the conjecture does not materially affect the result.

IV. Yearly Progress of Inclosures Classified—(continued)

| Year | Tenure or tenancy | Lay Ownership | | Lords of manors | | Free-holders | | Tenure or tenancy | Ecclesiastical Ownership | | Lords of manors | | Free-holders | |
		Parish	Hundred	Arable	Pasture	Arable	Pasture		Parish	Hundred	Arable	Pasture	Arable	Pasture
				acr.	acr.	acr.	acr.				acr.	acr.	acr.	acr.
1509	L.	Aldeworth	Compton	—	—	150	50							
,,								F.T.	Wolley (Chaddelworth)	Kintbury Eagle	—	120	—	—
,,								C.	Westsandford	Hormer	60	—	—	—
,,								L.	Huddon	Kintbury Eagle	20	80	—	—
1510	L.	Catmar	Compton	200	200	—	—							
,,	F.T.	Chilton	,,	30	—	—	—							
,,	C.	Grove (Wantage)	Wantage	30	—	—	—							
,,								C.	Weslokhenges	Wantage	20	—	—	—
,,								C.	Estlokhenges	,,	30	—	—	—
,,								L.	Harwell	Moreton	—	—	20	—
,,								C.	Shalyngford	Ganfield	50	—	—	—
,,	H.F.	Bukland	Ganfield	—	—	40	—							
,,	H.F.	Cokeham	Cookham	—	—	20	—							
,,	H.F.	Wynkefeld	Ripplesmere	—	—	—	20							
,,	H.F.	Sutton Curttenay	Ock	—	—	40	—							
,,	F.T.	Bukland	Ganfield	40	—	—	—							
,,								F.T.	Bukland	Ganfield	—	—	60	—
1511								L.	Ferneburghe	Compton	20	—	—	—
,,								F.T.	Easthenrede	Wantage	—	—	24	—
,,	H.F.	Greneham	Faircross	—	—	—	80							
,,	H.F.	Boxforth	,,	—	—	40	—							
,,								C.	Shalyngford	Ganfield	—	—	30	—
,,	F.T.	Bukland	Ganfield	20	—	—	—							
1512	F.T.	Stretley	Moreton	60	—	—	—							
,,	F.T.	Vpton	,,	20	—	—	—							
,,	H.M.	Westhenrede	Wantage	180	—	—	—							
,,	H.F.	Estgynge	,,	—	—	—	36							
,,	H.F.	Estgynge	,,	—	—	—	30							
,,	L.	Greneham	Faircross	26	—	—	—							
,,	F.T.	Newyngton (Bukeland)	Ganfield	20	—	—	—							
,,	F.T.	Aston Turrold	Moreton	30	—	—	—							
1513	H.M.	Easthanney	Wantage	—	42	—	—							
,,	H.F.	Kenyngton	Hormer	—	—	44	—							
,,								F.T.	Wilde	Faircross	—	—	40	—
1514								L.	Brightwell	Moreton	40	—	—	—
,,	F.T.	Clewer	Ripplesmere	—	60	—	—							
,,								C.	Wargrave	Wargrave	—	40	—	—
,,	H.F.	Fyfeld	Ock	—	—	40	—							

BERKSHIRE

IV. YEARLY PROGRESS OF INCLOSURES CLASSIFIED—(continued)

| Year | Tenure or tenancy | Lay Ownership | | Lords of manors | | Free-holders | | Tenure or tenancy | Ecclesiastical Ownership | | Lords of manors | | Free-holders | |
		Parish	Hundred	Arable	Pasture	Arable	Pasture		Parish	Hundred	Arable	Pasture	Arable	Pasture
				acr.	acr.	acr.	acr.				acr.	acr.	acr.	acr.
1514	F.T.	Harwell	Moreton	100	—	—	—							
,,	F.T.	Crokam	Faircross	—	60	—	—							
,,	H.M.	Wilde	,,	—	50	—	—							
1515	F.T.	Fulscot	Moreton	160	—	—	—							
,,								F.T.	Westyllysley	Compton	—	—	[107]	—
,,	H.M.	Yatendone	Faircross	—	20 }	—	—							
,,	H.M.	Hampstede Norreys	,,	—	30 }	—	—							
,,	H.F.	Estgynge	Wantage	—	—	30	—							
,,								L.	Crokeham	Faircross	—	—	20	—
,,								C.	Shalyngford	Ganfield	30	—	—	—
,,	C.	Henton	Ganfield	45	—	—	—							
,,	H.F.	Bukland	,,	—	—	—	40							
,,	H.F.	Sandhurst	Sonning	—	—	—	60							
,,	L.	Sotwell	Moreton	60	—	—	—							
,,								H.F.	Aston Turrold	Moreton	—	—	30	—
,,	H.F.	Hartley	Theale	—	—	—	15							
1516	H.F.	Chaddelworth	Kintbury Eagle	—	—	40	—							
,,	H.F.	Greneham	Faircross	—	—	—	20							
,,	H.M.	Berkeham	Charlton	—	100	—	—							
,,	C.	Wittnam	Ock	—	20	—	—							
,,	H.F.	Warfild	Wargrave	—	—	—	40							
,,	L.	Dudcote	Moreton	—	—	—	30							
,,	F.T.	Aston Turrold	,,	30	—	—	—							
1517								H.M.	Bustellesham	Beynhurst	—	10	—	—
,,	F.T.	Frylford	Ock	[80]	—	—	—							
,,	F.T.	Westhagbourn	Moreton	20	—	—	—							
,,	F.T.	Wolhamton	Theale	—	—	30	—							
—	—	—	—	2,071	1,016	914	916	—	—	—	612	615	471	0

	acres		acres
Total lay arable	2,985	Total ecclesiastical arable	1,083
Total lay pasture	1,932	Total ecclesiastical pasture	615
	4,917		1,698

	acres
Total arable	4,068
Total pasture	2,547
Total area	6,615

IV. YEARLY PROGRESS OF INCLOSURES CLASSIFIED ACCORDING TO THE STATUS OF THE LANDLORDS RESPONSIBLE FOR THEM. ALL INFERRED AND DOUBTFUL CASES INCLUDED

Year	Lay ownership		Ecclesiastical ownership		Totals	
	Arable	Pasture	Arable	Pasture	Arable	Pasture
	acres	acres	acres	acres	acres	acres
1485	—	—	—	—	—	—
1486	—	—	—	—	—	—
1487	100	—	—	—	100	—
1488	—	40	—	—	—	40
1489	— —	— —	—	—	—	—
1490	30	—	—	—	30	—
1491	—	—	—	—	—	—
1492	—	80	—	—	—	80
1493	50	—	40	—	90	—
1494	—	—	—	—	—	—
1495	20	60	40	—	60	60
1496	—	—	—	—	—	—
1497	80	40	40	—	120	40
1498	114	— —	—	35	114	35
1499	70	40	—	120	70	160
1500	200	—	—	— —	200	—
1501	80	75	20	40	100	115
1502	—	—	20	—	20	—
1503	56	—	—	—	56	—
1504	60	—	—	—	60	—
1505	60	140	130	—	190	140
1506	60	150	32	170	92	320
1507	340	260	—	—	340	260
1508	40	44	160	—	200	44
1509	150	50	80	200	230	250
1510	400	220	180	—	580	220
1511	60	80	74	—	134	80
1512	336	66	—	—	336	66
1513	44	42	40	—	84	42
1514	140	170	40	40	180	210
1515	295	165	187	—	482	165
1516	70	210	—	—	70	210
1517	130	—	—	10	300	10
	2,985	1,932.	1,083	615	4,068	2,547

BERKSHIRE

IV. Yearly Progress of Inclosures classified according to the Status of the Landlords responsible for them. All Inferred and Doubtful Cases included

Years	Lay ownership		Ecclesiastical ownership		Totals	
	Arable	Pasture	Arable	Pasture	Arable	Pasture
	acres	acres	acres	acres	acres	acres
1485–1490	130	40	—	—	130	40
1491–1500	534	220	120	155	654	375
1501–1510	1,246	939	622	410	1,868	1,349
1511–1517	1,075	733	341	50	1,416	783
	2,985	1,932	1,083	615	4,068	2,547

Percentage of Increase and Decrease of Inclosure

Years	Lay ownership		Ecclesiastical ownership		Totals	
	Arable	Pasture	Arable	Pasture	Arable	Pasture
1485–1490	—	—	—	—	—	—
1491–1500	+310·76	+450	—	—	+403·07	+837·5
1501–1510	+133·3	+326·81	+418·3	+164·51	+185·62	+259·73
1511–1517	−18·72	−21·93	−45·17	−87·80	−24·19	−41·95

Percentage of Total Increase and Decrease of Inclosure

Years	Per cent.
1485–1490	—
1491–1500	+505·29
1501–1510	+212·62
1511–1517	−31·62

V

NUMBER OF INCLOSURES AND DISTRIBUTION OF AREAS INCLOSED ACCORDING TO TENURES AND TENANCIES. INFERRED FIGURES INCLUDED

I. Land in hands of lords of manors [1]

	LAY OWNERSHIP					ECCLESIASTICAL OWNERSHIP			
No. of inclosures[2]	Parish	Total	Arable	Pasture	No. of inclosures	Parish	Total	Arable	Pasture
1	Chilrey	20	20	—					
1	Yatyndon	40	—	40					
1	Yatendone	10	—	10					
1	[Yatendone]	10	—	10					
1	Hampstede Norreys	30	—	30					
1	Westhenrede	180	180	—					
1	Easthanney	42	—	42					
					1	East Hanney	20	20	—
					1	Bustellesham	10	—	10
1	Berkeham	100	—	100					
1	Hampstede Marshall	100	—	100					
1	Wilde	50	—	50					
					1	Pangbourn	20	20	—
1	Bradfeld	4	—	4					
11		586	200	386	3		50	40	10

[1] In the cases of Crokam (60 acres of pasture) and Wolhamton (20 acres of arable), though the land had been inclosed by the manorial lords, it was at the time of the Inquisition held in farm tenancies, and is classified accordingly.

[2] The principle adopted has been to reckon inclosures by the number of ploughs put down, a half plough being taken as one inclosure; but where no ploughs are mentioned, the number is supplied from that of the houses destroyed; where neither is returned, the inclosure returned is reckoned as one unless otherwise specified in the text.

V. Number of Inclosures, &c.—(continued)

II. Land in hands of freeholders

	Lay Ownership				Ecclesiastical Ownership			
No. of inclosures[2]	Parish	Total	Arable	Pasture	No. of inclosures	Parish	Total	Arable	Pasture
1	Wantage.	55	—	55					
1	Esthenrede	20	—	20					
1	Lekehamstede.	30	30	—					
1	Hampstede Norreys	40	40	—					
1	Chaddelworth.	40	40	—					
1	(Grove) Wantage	24	24	—					
1	Estgynge	36	—	36					
1	Estgynge	30	—	30					
1	Estgynge	30	30						
1	Greneham	20	—	20					
1	Greneham	80	—	80					
1	Wynterbourn	40	20	20					
1	Boxforth.	40	40	—					
1	Bynfeld.	80	80	—					
1	Bynfeld.	26	26	—					
1	Hurst	60	—	60					
1	Erley	40	—	40					
1	Bray	20	—	20	1	Westyllysley	60	60	—
1	Kenyngton	44	44	—					
1	Bukland.	40	—	40					
1	Bukland.	40	40	—					
1	Cokeham	20	20	—					
1	Wynkefeld	50	50	—					
1	Wynkefeld	20	—	20					
1	Bray	60	—	60					
1	Stephyngton	40	40	—					
1	Stephyngton	40	—	40					
2	Lyford	40	—	40					
2	Southcoote	100	—	100					
1	Warfild	40	—	40					
1	Okynham	30	30	—					
1	Sandhurst	60	—	60					
34	Carried forward	1335	554	781	1	Carried forward	60	60	0

[1] In the case of Crokeham (20 acres of arable) the incloser is an ecclesiastical freeholder, but it was a leasehold at the time of the Inquisition, and is so classified.
[2] See note 2 on preceding page.

V. NUMBER OF INCLOSURES, &C.—(*continued*)

II. Land in hands of freeholders—(*continued*)

LAY OWNERSHIP					ECCLESIASTICAL OWNERSHIP				
No. of inclosures	Parish	Total	Arable	Pasture	No. of inclosures	Parish	Total	Arable	Pasture
34	Brt. forward	1335	554	781	1	Brt. forward	60	60	0
1	Fyfeld . .	40	40	—					
1	Sutton Curttenay	40	40	—					
					1	Aston Turrold.	30	30	—
1	Hartley . .	15	—	15					
37		1,430	634	796	2		90	90	0

III. Copyholds

LAY OWNERSHIP					ECCLESIASTICAL OWNERSHIP				
No. of inclosures[1]	Parish	Total	Arable	Pasture	No. of inclosures	Parish	Total	Arable	Pasture
1	Stretley . .	60	60	—					
					1	Chyveley .	20	20	—
1	Bedone . .	40	40	—					
1	Grove (Wantage	30	30	—					
1	Ardyngton .	50	—	50					
					1	Westlokhenges	20	20	—
					1	Estlokhenges .	30	30	—
					1	Beaterton .	35	—	35
2	Langford in Cleware	60	—	60					
1	Fernham . .	30	30	—					
					1	Westsandford .	60	60	—
					1	Westsandford .	80	80	—
					1	Shalyngford .	50	50	—
					1	Shalyngford .	30	30	—
1	Henton . .	45	45	—					
					1	Drayton . .	20	20	—
1	Wittnam .	20	—	20					
1	Newbrigg (Kyngeston Bagpues)	60	60	—					
					1	Wargrave .	40	—	40
					1	Marcham .	40	—	40
					1	Appelford .	40	40	—
1	Dudcote . .	20	20	—					
11		415	285	130	12		465	350	115

[1] See as to the principles of enumeration note 2 on p. 522, *supra*.

BERKSHIRE

V. NUMBER OF INCLOSURES, &C.—(*continued*)

IV. Leaseholds

No. of inclosures[1]	Lay Ownership Parish	Total	Arable	Pasture	No. of inclosures	Ecclesiastical Ownership Parish	Total	Arable	Pasture
1	Catmar .	400	200	200					
					1	Ferneburghe .	20	20	—
1	Compton	. 200	140	60					
1	Aldeworth	. 200	150	50					
					1	Brightwell	. 40	40	—
1	Greneham	. 26	26	—					
					1	Harwell .	. 20	20	—
1	Farnham	. 100	100	—					
1	Compton	. 30	30	—					
1	Knyghton	. 40	40	—					
					1	Crokeham	. 20	20	—
					2	Shalyngford	. 112	32	80
					2	Milton .	. 120	—	120
					1	Garford .	. 60	—	60
					1	Huddon .	. 100	20	80
1	Sotwell .	. 60	60	—					
1	Southmorton .	20	20	—					
1	Southmorton .	20	20	—					
1	Dudcot .	. 30	—	30					
1	Mvlford .	. 60	60	—					
1	Burfeld Regis .	200	200	—					
13		1,386	1,046	340	10		492	152	340

[1] See as to the principles of enumeration note 2 on p. 122, *supra*.

V. Farm tenancies [1]

No. of inclosures[2]	Lay Ownership Parish	Total	Arable	Pasture	No. of inclosures	Ecclesiastical Ownership Parish	Total	Arable	Pasture
1	Fulscot .	. 160	160	— ⎫[3]					
1	Fulscot .	. 40	40	— ⎬					
1	Fulscot .	. 40	40	— ⎭					
					1	Westyllesley .	40	40	—
					1	Westyllysley	. [107]	[107]	—
3	Carried forward	240	240	0	2	Carried forward	147	147	0

[1] In the cases of Chadlyngworth and Wolley (80 acres of arable and 120 acres of pasture) and Crokam (60 acres of pasture) the incloser held the manor, but at the time of the Inquisition these were farm tenancies, *i.e.* holdings from year to year or at will at common law.

[2] See as to the principles of enumeration note 2 on p. 522, *supra*.   [3] Same landlord.

V. Number of Inclosures, &c.—(*continued*)

V. Farm tenancies—(*continued*)

Lay Ownership					Ecclesiastical Ownership				
No. of inclosures	Parish	Total	Arable	Pasture	No. of inclosures	Parish	Total	Arable	Pasture
3	Brt. forward	240	240	0	2	Brt. forward	147	147	0
1	Chilton . .	30	30	—					
1	Bastelden	20	20	—					
1	Stretley . .	60	60	—					
1	Stretley . .	40	40	—					
1	Vpton . .	20	20	—					
1	Spersholt .	40	—	40					
1	Spersholt .	40	—	40					
					1	Chadlyngworth	40	40	—
					1	Chadlyngworth	40	40	—
					1	Wolley (Chaddelworth)	120	—	120
					1	Easthenrede .	24	24	—
1	Ray . .	40	—	40					
1	Clewer . .	60	—	60					
1	Burton . .	20	20	—					
					1	Shalyngford [1] .	30	30	—
					1	Kentbury .	30	—	30
					1	Wilde . .	40	40	—
1	Frylford . .	[80]	[80]	—					
1	Bukland . .	40	40	—	1	Bukland . .	60	60	—
1	Newyngton (Bukeland)	20	20	—					
1	Bukland . .	20	20	—					
					1	Sotwell . .	40	40	—
1	Aston Turrold	30	30	—					
1	Aston Turrold	30	30	—					
1	Harwell . .	100	100	—					
1	Crokam [1]. .	60	—	60					
					1	Tyleherst .	30	30	—
1	Westhagbourn.	20	20	—					
1	Hartley . .	40	—	40					
1	Wolhamton [2] .	20	20	—					
1	Wolhampton .	30	30	—					
25		1,100	820	280	12		601	451	150

[1] Incloser a clerical farming tenant of a rectory.
[2] Inclosed by lord of manor, but held at the time of the Inquisition on a farm tenancy.

BERKSHIRE

V. Number of Inclosures, &c.—(*continued*)

General Total

Lay Ownership				Ecclesiastical Ownership			
No. of inclosures	Total	Arable	Pasture	No. of inclosures	Total	Arable	Pasture
97	4,917	2,985	1,932	39	1,698	1,083	615

Total arable 4,068
Total pasture 2,547
                              ─────
                              6,615

Summary of the Distribution of Areas according to Tenures and Tenancies. Inferred Areas included

A. TENURES

I. Land in owners' hands

	Lay		Ecclesiastical		
	Total area acres	Percentage of total area in lay owners' hands		Total area acres	Percentage of total area in ecclesiastical owners' hands
1. In hands of lay lords of manors .	586	29·06	1. In hands of ecclesiastical lords of manors . .	50	35·7
2. In hands of lay freeholders . .	1,430	70·93	2. In hands of ecclesiastical freeholders .	90	62·4
	2,016	99·99		140	99·9

II. Total areas held in hand by both lay and ecclesiastical owners, and proportions per cent. of total areas so held in hand by lay and ecclesiastical owners respectively

	Total area acres	In hands of lay lords of manors acres	In hands of ecclesiastical lords of manors acres	Proportion per cent. in hands of lay lords of manors	Proportion per cent. in hands of ecclesiastical lords of manors
1. In hands of lords of manors . .	636	586	50	92·13	7·86

	Total area acres	In hands of lay freeholders acres	In hands of ecclesiastical freeholders acres	Proportion per cent. in hands of lay freeholders	Proportion per cent. in hands of ecclesiastical freeholders
2. In hands of freeholders . .	1,520	1,430	90	94·07	5·92

V. NUMBER OF INCLOSURES, &C.—(continued)

	Total area	In hands of lay owners	In hands of ecclesiastical owners	Proportion per cent. in hands of lay owners	Proportion per cent. in hands of ecclesiastical owners
	acres	acres	acres		
3. Totals in hands of lords of manors and freeholders	2,156	2,016	140	93·5	6·49

B. TENANCIES

III. Land let and in hands of tenants

	LAY			ECCLESIASTICAL	
	Total area	Proportion of total area of lay land let		Total area	Proportion of total area of ecclesiastical land let
	acres			acres	
1. Copyholds	415	14·3		465	29·84
2. Leaseholds	1,386	47·77		492	31·57
3. Farm tenancies	1,100	37·92		601	38·57
Total area of lay land let	2,901	99·99	Total area of ecclesiastical land let	1,558	99·98

IV. Proportion per cent. of total areas of land in hands of owners and land let to tenants respectively

	LAY		ECCLESIASTICAL	
	Total area	Proportion per cent.	Total area	Proportion per cent.
	acres		acres	
1. Land in owners' hands	2,016	41·00	140	8·24
2. Land let to tenants	2,901	58·99	1,558	91·75
	4,917	99·99	1,698	99·99

V. Total areas and relative proportion per cent. of lay and ecclesiastical lands

	LAY		ECCLESIASTICAL	
Total areas	Total area	Proportion per cent.	Total area	Proportion per cent.
acres	acres		acres	
6,615	4,917	74·33	1,698	25·66

BERKSHIRE

V. Number of Inclosures, and Areas of Inclosures of Arable and Pasture according to Tenures and Tenancies

Summary of Numbers and Areas of Inclosures of Arable and Pasture according to Tenures and Tenancies—(continued)

	Lay									Ecclesiastical							
	Arable			Pasture			Total arable and pasture			Arable			Pasture			Total arable and pasture		
	No. of inclosures	Area	Average area of inclosures	No. of inclosures	Area	Average area of inclosures	No. of inclosures	Area	Average area of inclosures	No. of inclosures	Area	Average area of inclosures	No. of inclosures	Area	Average area of inclosures	No. of inclosures	Area	Average area of inclosures
		acres	acres		acres	acres		acres	acres		acres	acres		acres	acres		acres	acres
I. Land in owners' hands																		
1. Lords of manors	2	200	100	9	386	42·8	11	586	53·27	2	40	20	1	10	10	3	50	16·6
2. Freeholders	17	634	39·29	21	796	37·90	38[1]	1,430	37·63	2	90	45	—	—	—	2	90	45
II. Land let																		
1. Copyholds	7	285	40·71	4	130	32·5	11	415	37·72	9	350	38·8	3	115	38·3	12	465	38·75
2. Leaseholds	12	1,046	87·16	4	340	85	16[2]	1,386	86·62	6	152	25·3	4	340	85	10	492	49·2
3. Farm tenancies	19	820	42·10	6	280	46·5	25	1,100	44	10	451	45·1	2	150	75	12	601	50·08
III. Totals and Total Averages							101	4,917	48·64							39	1,698	43·53

IV. Totals of lay and ecclesiastical land together .
No. of inclosures . . . 140
Area . . . acres 6,615
Average area of inclosures . acres 47·25

[1] Inclosures of arable and pasture together at Wynterbourn reckoned as *two* inclosures for the purposes of this Table.
[2] Inclosures of arable and pasture together at Catmar, Compton, and Aldeworth reckoned as *two* inclosures in each instance. This accounts for the slight variations between the totals here and on pp. 525, 527.

VI.

STATUS OF LANDLORDS RESPONSIBLE FOR INCLOSURE, OBJECTS OF
FROM LABOUR.[1] ALL

		LAY OWNERSHIP					
Parish	Hundred	Total	Inclosures of arable	Parks and inclosures to pasture	No. of persons evicted	No. of persons displaced from labour	Landl respons Lord of manor
Fulscot	Moreton	acres 240	acres 240	acres —	29	—	1
Catmar	Compton	400	200	200	—	14	1
Compton	,,	200	140	60	12	—	1
Aldeworth	,,	200	150	50	5	—	—
Chilton	,,	30	30	—	8	—	[1]
Bastelden	Moreton	20	20	—	2	—	1
Stretley	,,	60	60	—	4	—	1
Stretley	,,	60	60	—	6	—	1
Stretley	,,	40	40	—	6	—	1
Vpton	,,	20	20	—	4	—	1
Chilrey	Wantage	20	20	—	4	—	1
Wantage	,,	55	—	55	—	4	—
Esthenrede	,,	20	—	20	—	2	—
Spersholt	Shrivenham	40	—	40	—	—	1
Spersholt	,,	40	—	40	3	—	1
Lekehamstede	Faircross	30	30	—	4	—	—
Yatyndon [2]	,,	40	—	40	5	—	1
Yatendone	,,	20	—	20	—	—	1
Hampstede Norreys	,,	30	—	30	—	—	1
Hampstede Norreys	,,	40	40	—	[4]	—	
Bedone	,,	40	40	—	3	—	1
Chaddelworth	Kintbury Eagle	40	40	—	6	—	—
Westhenrede	Wantage	180	180	—	12	—	1
Grove (Wantage)	,,	30	30	—	2	—	1
Grove (Wantage)	,,	24	24	—	2	—	—
Easthanney	,,	42	—	42	—	4	1
Ardyngton	,,	50	—	50	4	—	1

[1] In cases where joint owners, probably co-feoffees to uses, were responsibl really for the presum
[2] The eviction of four persons from [Yatyndon] appears to have been due to the consolidation of f. order to arrive at accurate averages of evictions specifically associated with inclosure, such as belor do not comprise many cases.

BERKSHIRE

VI.

NCLOSURE, AND NUMBER OF PERSONS EVICTED AND DISPLACED
NFERRED FIGURES INCLUDED

Parish	Hundred	Total	Inclosures of arable	Parks and inclosures to pasture	No. of persons evicted	No. of persons displaced from labour	Landlord responsible Lord of manor	Freeholder
		acres	acres	acres				
styllesley	Compton .	40	40	—	6	—	—	1
styllysley	,,	[107]	[107]	—	10	—	—	1
neburghe	,,	20	20	—	3	—	1	—
htwell	Moreton .	40	40	—	5	—	1	—
eley .	Faircross .	20	20	—	2	—	1	—
lyngworth	Kintbury Eagle	80	80	—	12	—	1 }	—
ey (Chaddel-rth)	,, ,,	120	—	120	—	—	1 }	—
heurede	Wantage .	24	24	—	3	—	—	1
Hanney .	,,	20	20	—	4	—	1	—

sures, it has not been thought necessary to state the number, such acts being
itage of one beneficiary.
ngrossing rather than to inclosure. The total evictions on all accounts appear in Table I. but in
returned for consolidation and ingrossing are excluded from this Table. These two latter classes

L 2

THE DOMESDAY OF INCLOSURES, 1517

VI. STATUS OF LANDLORDS RESPONSIBLE

Parish	Hundred	Total	Inclosures of arable	Parks and inclosures to pasture	No. of persons evicted	No. of persons displaced from labour	Lord of manor	Land responsible
		acres	acres	acres				
Estgynge	Wantage	{66	—	66}	6	—	—	
Estgynge	,,	{30	30	—}	4	—	—	
Greneham	Faircross	26	26	—	6	—	1	
Greneham	,,	20	—	20	2	—	—	
Greneham	,,	80	—	80	—	4	—	
Wynterbourn	,,	40	20	20	4	—	—	
Boxforth	,,	40	40	—	6	—	—	
Bynfeld	Cookham	80	80	—	8	—	—	
Bynfeld	,,	26	26	—	4	—	—	
Langford in Cleware	Ripplesmere	60	—	60	—	12	1	
Ray	Cookham	40	—	40	6	—	[1]	
Clewer	Ripplesmere	60	—	60	5	—	1	
Hurst	Charlton	60	—	60	—	—	—	
Erley	,,	40	—	40	—	8	—	
Bray	Bray	20	—	20	3	—	—	
Farnham	Shrivenham	130	130	—¹	7	—	1	
Compton	,,	30	30	—	[4]	—	1	
Burton	,,	20	20	—	4	—	1	
Knyghton	,,	40	40	—	6	—	—	
Kenyngton	Hormer	44	44	—	6	—	—	
Henton	Ganfield	45	45	—	6	—	1	
Bukland	,,	40	—	40	4	—	—	
Bukland	,,	40	40	—	3	—	—	
Cokeham	Cookham	20	20	—	2	—	—	
Wynkefeld	Ripplesmere	50	50	—	6	—	—	
Wynkefeld	,,	20	—	20	6	—	—	
Berkeham	Charlton	100	—	100	8	—	1	
Bray	Bray	60	—	60	5	—	—	
Stephyngton	Ock	40	40	—	4	—	—	
Stephyngton	,,	40	—	40	6	—	—	

¹ The other evictions at Drayton appear to have been due, not to inclosures, but to

BERKSHIRE

FOR INCLOSURE, &C.—(continued)

Parish	Hundred	Total	Inclosures of arable	Parks and inclosures to pasture	No. of persons evicted	No. of persons displaced from labour	Landlord responsible	
							Lord of manor	Freeholder
		ECCLESIASTICAL OWNERSHIP						
		acres	acres	acres				
stlokhenges	Wantage	20	20	—	3	—	1	—
okhenges	,,	30	30	—	4	—	1	—
terton	,,	35	—	35	3	—	1	—
ellesham	Beynhurst	10	—	10	—	—	1	—
vell	Moreton	20	20	—	2	—	—	1
yllysley	Compton	60	60	—	6	—	—	1
eham	Faircross	20	20	—	7	—	—	1
tsandford	Hormer	60	60	—	[7]	—	1	—
tsandford	,,	80	80	—	6	—	1	—
yngford	Ganfield	112	32	80	8	—	1	—
yngford	,,	50	50	—	3	—	1	—
yngford	,,	30	30	—	[4]	—	1	—
ngford	,,	30	30	—	3	—	—	1
n	Ock	120	—	120	18	—	1	—
rd	,,	60	—	60	6	—	1	—
ton [1]	,,	20	20	—	4	—	1	—

tion or ingrossing of farms. The total evictions on all accounts appear in Table I.

THE DOMESDAY OF INCLOSURES, 1517

VI. STATUS OF LANDLORDS RESPONSIBLE

Parish	Hundred	Total	Inclosures of arable	Parks and inclosures to pasture	No. of persons evicted	No. of persons displaced from labour	Landl< respons< Lord of manor
		acres	acres	acres			
Wittnam . . .	Ock . . .	20	—	20	3	—	1
Newbrigg (Kyngeston Bagpues)	,,	60	60	—	4	—	1
Lyford . . .	,,	40	—	40	—	8	—
Southcoote . .	Reading . .	100	—	100	—	10	—
Hampstede Marshall	Kintbury Eagle .	100	—	100	—	—	1
Wilde . . .	Faircross . .	50	—	50	—	4	1
Warfild . . .	Wargrave . .	40	—	40	—	4	—
Okynham . .	Sonning . .	30	30	—	4	—	—
Sandhurst . .	,,	60	—	60	6	—	—
Fyfeld . . .	Ock . . .	40	40	—	4	—	—
Frylford . . .	,,	[80]	[80]	—	4	—	[1]
Sutton Curttenay .	,,	40	40	—	8	—	—
Bukland . . .	Ganfield . .	{40	40	—	8	—	1}
Newynton (Bukeland)	,,	{20	20	—	4	—	1}
Bukland . . .	,,	{20	20	—	4	—	1}
Sotwell . . .	Moreton . .	60	60	—	10	—	1
Southmorton . .	,,	{20	20	—	3	—	1
Southmorton . .	,,	{20	20	—	3	—	1
Dudcote . . .	,,	30	—	30	3	—	—
Dudcote . . .	,,	20	20	—	2	—	1
Mvlford . . .	,,	60	60	—	6	—	—
Aston Turrold .	,,	30	30	—	3	—	1}
Aston Turrold .	,,	30	30	—	3	—	1}
Harwell . . .	,,	100	100	—	8	—	1
Crokam . . .	Faircross . .	60	—	60	—	[6]	1
Westhagbourn .	Moreton . .	20	20	—	[2]	—	[1]
Burghfeld Regis .	Theale . .	200	200	—	12	—	[1]
Hartley . . .	,,	40	—	40	4	—	—
Hartley . . .	,,	15	—	15	[0]	—	—
Bradfeld . . .	,,	4	—	4	—	—	1
Wolhamton . .	,,	20	20	—	[2]	—	1
Wolhampton . .	,,	30	30	—	2	—	—
Totals . . .		4,917	2,985	1,932	368	80	44

BERKSHIRE

OR INCLOSURE, &C.—(continued)

Parish	Hundred	Ecclesiastical Ownership					Landlord responsible	
		Total	Inclosures of arable	Parks and inclosures to pasture	No. of persons evicted	No. of persons displaced from labour	Lord of manor	Freeholder
		acres	acres	acres				
tbury	Kintbury Eagle.	30	—	30	4	—	1	—
don .	,, ,,	100	20	80	4	—	1	—
de .	Faircross .	40	40	—	[5]	—	—	1
grave	Wargrave.	40	—	40	4	—	1	—
cham	Ock .	40	—	40	12	—	1	—
elford	,,	40	40	—	8	—	1	—
land .	Ganfield .	60	60	—	6	—	—	1
ell .	Moreton .	40	40	—	4	—	—	1
n Turrold .	,,	30	30	—	4	—	—	1
bourn	Reading .	20	20	—		—	1 ⎫	—
herst	,,	30	30	—	5		1 ⎭	—
		1,698	1,083	615	191	—	23	10

VI. Status of Landlords responsible

Lay Ownership				Ecclesiastical Ownership			
Arable inclosed		Pasture inclosed		Arable inclosed		Pasture inclosed	
Total arable inclosed on land of lords of manors	Total arable inclosed on land of freeholders	Total pasture inclosed on land of lords of manors	Total pasture inclosed on land of freeholders	Total arable inclosed on land of lords of manors	Total arable inclosed on land of freeholders	Total pasture inclosed on land of lords of manors	Total pasture inclosed on land of freeholders
acres 2,071	acres 914	acres 1,016	acres 916	acres 612	acres 471	acres 615	acres 0
2,985		1,932		1,083		615	

Proportionate Analysis of the above

Proportion per cent. of total arable inclosed on lay land		Proportion per cent. of total pasture inclosed on lay land		Proportion per cent. of total arable inclosed on ecclesiastical land		Proportion per cent. of total pasture inclosed on ecclesiastical land	
69·38	30·61	52·5	47·4	56·50	43·49	100	0

Total arable inclosed	Proportion per cent. of arable inclosed to total area inclosed	Total pasture inclosed	Proportion per cent. of pasture inclosed to total area inclosed
acres 4,068	61·04	acres 2,547	38·5

Proportion per cent. of lay arable inclosed to total arable inclosed	Proportion per cent. of lay pasture inclosed to total pasture inclosed	Proportion per cent. of ecclesiastical arable inclosed to total arable inclosed	Proportion per cent. of ecclesiastical pasture inclosed to total pasture inclosed
73·37	75·8	26·62	24·1

Total inclosures	Total lay land inclosed	Total ecclesiastical land inclosed
acres 6,615	acres 4,917	acres 1,698

BERKSHIRE

FOR INCLOSURES, &C.—(continued)

Proportion per cent. of lay land inclosed to total inclosures	Proportion per cent. of ecclesiastical land inclosed to total inclosures
74·33	25·66

EVICTIONS AND DISPLACEMENTS FROM LABOUR

LAY OWNERSHIP				ECCLESIASTICAL OWNERSHIP			
Land of lords of manors		Land of freeholders		Land of lords of manors		Land of freeholders	
Total evictions	Total displacements from labour	Total evictions	Total displacements from labour	Total evictions	Total displacements from labour	Total evictions	Total displacements from labour
persons 225	persons 40	persons 143	persons 40	persons 135	persons 0	persons 56	persons 0

Total evictions on lay land	Total displacements from labour on lay land	Total evictions on ecclesiastical land	Total displacements from labour on ecclesiastical land
persons 368	persons 80	persons 191	persons 0
448		191	

PROPORTIONATE ANALYSIS OF THE ABOVE

LAY OWNERSHIP				ECCLESIASTICAL OWNERSHIP			
Land of lords of manors		Land of freeholders		Land of lords of manors		Land of freeholders	
Proportion per cent. of evictions to total evictions on lay land	Proportion per cent. of displacements from labour to total displacements from labour on lay land	Proportion per cent. of evictions to total evictions on lay land	Proportion per cent. of displacements from labour to total displacements from labour on lay land	Proportion per cent. of evictions to total evictions on ecclesiastical land	Proportion per cent. of displacements from labour to total displacements from labour on ecclesiastical land	Proportion per cent. of evictions to total evictions on ecclesiastical land	Proportion per cent. of displacements from labour to total displacements from labour on ecclesiastical land
61·14	50	38·85	50	70·68	0	29·31	0

VI. STATUS OF LANDLORDS RESPONSIBLE FOR INCLOSURES, &C.—(*continued*)

Summary

Total evictions	Total displacements from labour
persons 559	persons 80
639	

PROPORTIONATE ANALYSIS OF THE ABOVE

Proportion per cent. of evictions on lay land to total evictions	Proportion per cent. of displacements from labour on lay land to total displacements from labour	Proportion per cent. of evictions on ecclesiastical land to total evictions	Proportion per cent. of displacements from labour on ecclesiastical land to total displacements from labour
65·83	100	34·16	0

Proportion per cent. of evictions and displacements from labour on lay land to total ditto	Proportion per cent. of evictions and displacements from labour on ecclesiastical land to total ditto
70·10	29·89

VII.

STATUS OF ACTUAL INCLOSERS, TOGETHER WITH THE EVICTIONS AND DISPLACEMENTS FROM LABOUR ON INCLOSED ARABLE AND ON PASTURE RESPECTIVELY. INFERRED FIGURES EXCLUDED [1] [2]

1. Lords of manors holding land in hand

Parish	Lay Ownership					Parish	Ecclesiastical Ownership				
	Total	Inclosure of arable	Evictions and displacements from labour	Parks and inclosures to pasture	Evictions and displacements from labour		Total	Inclosure of arable	Evictions and displacements from labour	Parks and inclosures to pasture	Evictions and displacements from labour
	acr.	acr.	persons	acres	persons		acr.	acr.	persons	acres	persons
1. Chilrey	20	20	4	—	—						
2. Yatyndon	'40	—	—	40	5						
3. Yatendone	70	—	—	20)	—						
4. Hampstede Norreys	30	—	—	30)	—						
						1. Chadlyngworth [3]	80	80	12	—	—
						2. Wolley (Chaddelworth)	120	—	—	120	—
5. Easthanney	42	—	—	42	*4*	3. East Hanney	20	20	4	—	—
						4. Bustellesham	10	—	—	10	—
6. Berkeham	100	—	—	100	8						
7. Hampstede Marshall	100	—	—	100	—						
8. Wilde	50	—	—	50	*4*						
9. Crokam	60	—	—	60	—						
						5. Pangbourn	20	20	6	—	—
10. Bradfeld	4	—	—	4	—						
	466	20	E. 4 / D. —	446	E. 13 / D. 8 21		250	120	E. 22 / D. —	130	—

[1] Where an area is returned as inclosed, but unaccompanied by evictions, it is entered in this Table. Inferred cases, *i.e.* cases where, as at Yatyndon, the number of evictions, but not the area, is given, excluded.

[2] Figures of displacement from labour in italics.

[3] The evictions, &c., at Chadlyngworth, were by the lady of the manor.

VII. STATUS OF ACTUAL INCLOSERS, TOGETHER WITH THE EVICTIONS AND DISPLACEMENTS FROM LABOUR ON INCLOSED ARABLE AND ON PASTURE RESPECTIVELY. INFERRED FIGURES EXCLUDED [1] [2] [3]—(*continued*)

2. Freeholders holding land in hand

	LAY OWNERSHIP						ECCLESIASTICAL OWNERSHIP				
Parish	Total	Inclosure of arable	Evictions and displacements from labour	Parks and inclosures to pasture	Evictions and displacements from labour	Parish	Total	Inclosure of arable	Evictions and displacements from labour	Parks and inclosures to pasture	Evictions and displacements from labour
	acr.	acr.	persons	acres	persons		acr.	acr.	persons	acres	persons
1. Wantage	55	—	—	55	4						
2. Esthenrede	20	—	—	20	2						
3. Lekehamstede	30	30	4	—	—						
4. Chaddelworth	40	40	6	—	—						
5. Grove (Wantage)	24	24	2	—	—						
6. Estgynge	66	—	—	66	6						
7. Estgynge	30	30	4	—	—						
8. Greneham	20	—	—	20	2						
9. Greneham	80	—	—	80	4						
10. Boxforth	40	40	6	—	—						
11. Bynfeld	80	80	8	—	—						
12. Bynfeld	26	26	4	—	—						
13. Hurst	60	—	—	60	—						
14. Erley	40	—	—	40	8						
15. Bray	20	—	—	20	3						
						1. Westyllysley	60	60	6	—	—
16. Kenyngton	44	44	6	—	—						
17. Bukland	40	—	—	40	4						
18. Bukland	40	40	3	—	—						
19. Cokeham	20	20	2	—	—						
20. Wynkefeld	50	50	6	—	—						
21. Wynkefeld	20	—	—	20	6						
22. Bray	60	—	—	60	5						
23. Stephyngton	40	40	4	—	—						
24. Stephyngton	40	—	—	40	6						
25. Lyford	40	—	—	40	8						
26. Southcote	100	—	—	100	10						
27. Warfild	40	—	—	40	4						
28. Okynham	30	30	4	—	—						
29. Sandhurst	60	—	—	60	6						
30. Fyfeld	40	40	4	—	—						
31. Sutton Curttenay	40	40	8	—	—						
32. Hartley	15	—	—	15	—						
						2. Aston Turrold	30	30	4	—	—
Totals	1350	574	E. 71 / D. --	776	E. 38 / D. 40 = 78	Totals	90	90	E. 10 / D. —	—	—

[1] [2] See notes 1 and 2 on p. 539, *supra*.
[3] Where, as at Wynkebourn, part of the holding has been inclosed to pasture and part consolidated and a messuage destroyed and persons evicted, it has been thought better to omit the case from these Tables on account of the uncertainty as to the operation to which the evictions should be assigned.

BERKSHIRE

VII. STATUS OF ACTUAL INCLOSERS, TOGETHER WITH THE EVICTIONS AND DISPLACEMENTS FROM LABOUR ON INCLOSED ARABLE AND ON PASTURE RESPECTIVELY. INFERRED FIGURES EXCLUDED [1] [2] [3]—(*continued*)

3. Copyholders

Parish	Lay Ownership					Parish	Ecclesiastical Ownership				
	Total	Inclosure of arable	Evictions and displacements from labour	Parks and inclosures to pasture	Evictions and displacements from labour		Total	Inclosure of arable	Evictions and displacements from labour	Parks and inclosures to pasture	Evictions and displacements from labour
	acr.	acr.	persons	acres	persons		acr.	acr.	persons	acres	persons
1. Stretley	60	60	4	—	—	1. Chyveley	20	20	2	—	—
2. Bedone	40	40	3	—	—						
3. Grove (Wantage)	30	30	2	—	—						
4. Ardyngton	50	—	—	50	4						
						2. Westlokhenges	20	20	3	—	—
						3. Estlokhenges	30	30	4	—	—
						4. Beaterton	35	—	—	35	3
5. Langford in Cleware	60	—	—	60	12						
6. Fernham	30	30	3	—	—	5. Westsandford	80	80	6	—	—
						6. Shalyngford	50	50	3	—	—
						7. Shalyngford	30	30	3	—	—
7. Henton	45	45	6	—	—						
8. Wittnam	20	—	—	20	3	8. Drayton	20	20	4	—	—
9. Newbrigg (Kyngeston Bagpues)	60	60	4	—	—						
						9. Wargrave	40	—	—	40	4
						10. Marcham	40	—	—	40	12
						11. Appelford	40	40	8	—	—
10. Dudcote	20	20	2	—	—						
	415	285	E. 24 / D. 0	130	E. 7 / D. 12 — 19		405	290	E. 33 / D. —	115	E. 19 / D. 0

4. Leaseholders

						1. Ferneburghe	20	20	3	—	—
						2. Brightwell	40	40	5	—	—
1. Greneham	26	26	6	—	—	3. Harwell	20	20	2	—	—
2. Farnham	100	100	4	—	—						
3. Knyghton	40	40	6	—	—	4. Crokeham	20	20	7	—	—
						5. Milton	120	—	—	120	1
4. Sotwell	60	60	10	—	—						
5. Southmorton	20	20	3	—	—						
6. Southmorton	20	20	3	—	—						
7. Dudcote	30	—	—	30	3						
8. Mylford	60	60	6	—	—						
9. Burghfeld Regis	200	200	12	—	—						
	556	526	E. 50 / D. —	30	E. 3 / D. 0		220	100	E. 17 / D. —	12	E. 18 / D. 0

[1] [2] See notes 1 and 2 on p. 539, *supra*.   [3] See note 3 on p. 54 *supra*

VII. Status of actual Inclosers, together with the Evictions and Displacements from Labour on Inclosed Arable and on Pasture respectively. Inferred Figures excluded [1] [2] [3]—(*continued*)

5. Farm tenants

Parish	Lay Ownership					Parish	Ecclesiastical Ownership				
	Total	Inclosure of arable	Evictions and displacements from labour	Parks and inclosures to pasture	Evictions and displacements from labour		Total	Inclosure of arable	Evictions and displacements from labour	Parks and inclosures to pasture	Evictions and displacements from labour
	acr.	acr.	persons	acres	persons		acr.	acr.	persons	acres	persons
1. Fulscot	240	240	29	—	—						
						1. Westyllesley	40	40	6	—	—
2. Chilton	30	30	8	—	—						
3. Bastelden	20	20	2	—	—						
4. Stretley	60	60	6	—	—						
5. Stretley	40	40	6	—	—						
6. Vpton	20	20	4	—	—						
7. Spersholt	40	—	—	40	—						
8. Spersholt	40	—	—	40	3						
						2. Esthenrede	24	24	3	—	—
9. Ray	40	—	—	40	6						
10. Clewer	60	—	—	60	5						
11. Burton	20	20	4	—	—						
						3. Shalyngford	30	30	3	—	—
						4. Garford	60	—	—	60	—
						5. Kentbury	30	—	—	30	4
12. Bukland	40	40	8	—	—						
						6. Bukland	60	60	6	—	—
13. Newynton (Bukeland)	20	20	4	—	—						
14. Bukland	20	20	4	—	—						
						7. Sotwell	40	40	4	—	—
15. Aston Turrold	30	30	3	—	—						
16. Harwell	100	100	8	—	—						
						8. Tyleherst	30	30	5	—	—
17. Hartley	40	—	—	40	4						
18. Wolhampton	30	30	2	—	—						
	890	670	E. 88 / D. —	220	E. 18 / D. —		314	224	E. 27 / D. —	90	E. 4 / D. —

[2] See notes 1 and 2 on p. 539, *supra*.   See note 3 on p. 540, *supra*.

BERKSHIRE

VII. Status of actual Inclosers, together with the Evictions and Displacements from Labour on Inclosed Arable and on Pasture respectively—(continued)

Summary

	Lay Ownership									Ecclesiastical Ownership								
	1. Total area per person evicted and displaced	2. Total area per person evicted	3. Total area per person displaced	4. Total area of inclosed arable per person evicted and displaced	5. Total area of inclosed arable per person evicted[1]	6. Total area of inclosed arable per person displaced[2]	7. Total area of inclosed pasture per person evicted and displaced	8. Total area of inclosed pasture per person evicted[1]	9. Total area of inclosed pasture per person displaced[2]	1. Total area per person evicted and displaced	2. Total area per person evicted	3. Total area per person displaced	4. Total area of inclosed arable per person evicted and displaced	5. Total area of inclosed arable per person evicted[1]	6. Total area of inclosed arable per person displaced	7. Total area of inclosed pasture per person evicted and displaced	8. Total area of inclosed pasture per person evicted[1]	9. Total area of inclosed pasture per person displaced
	acres	acres	acres	acres	acres	acres	acres	acres	acres	acres	acres	acres	acres	acres	acres	acres	acres	acres
1. Lords of manors holding land in hand	18·6	27·4	58·2	5	5	—	21·2	10·7	11·5	11·3	11·3	—	5·4	5·4	—	—	—	—
2. Freeholders holding land in hand	9·06	12·3	33·7	8·08	8·08	—	9·9	8·5	9·3	9	9	—	9	9	—	—	—	—
3. Copyholders	9·6	13·3	34·6	11·8	11·8	—	6·8	10	5	7·7	7·7	—	8·7	8·7	—	6·06	6·06	—
4. Leaseholders	10·4	10·4	—	10·5	10·5	—	10	10	—	6·2	6·2	—	5·8	5·8	—	6·6	6·6	—
5. Farm tenants	8·39	8·39	—	7·6	7·6	—	12·2	10	—	10·1	10·1	—	7·2	7·2	—	22·5	22·5	—

[1] Taking the areas only from which evictions took place. [2] Taking the areas only from which displacements from labour took place.

VIII

EVICTIONS AND DISPLACEMENTS FROM LABOUR, AREA OF EVICTED LANDS, AND STATUS OF LANDLORDS RESPONSIBLE. INFERRED AND DOUBTFUL FIGURES EXCLUDED [1] [2] [3]

LAY OWNERSHIP						ECCLESIASTICAL OWNERSHIP					
Lords of manors			Freeholders			Lords of manors			Freeholders		
Place	Area acres	Population displaced persons	Place	Area acres	Population displaced persons	Place	Area acres	Population displaced persons	Place	Area acres	Population displaced persons
Fulscot	240	29									
Catmar	400	14									
Compton	200	12	Aldeworth	200	5	Ferneburghe	20	3	Westyllesley		
Chilton	30	8									
Bastelden	20	2									
Stretley	160	16									
Upton	20	4				Brightwell	40	5			
Chilrey	20		Wantage	55	4						
			Esthenrede	20	2						
Spersholt	40	3	Lekehamstede	30	4						
Yatyndon	40	9[4]				Chyveley	20	2			
Bedone	40	3	Chaddelworth	40	6	Chadlyngworth	80	12			
Westhenrede	180	12							Easthenrede	24	3

BERKSHIRE

II.								
Grove (Wantage)	30	2	Grove (Wantage)	24				
East Hanney	42	*4*						
Ardyngton	50	4			2	Easthanney	20	
			Estgynge	96	10			
Greneham	26	6	Greneham	20	2	Westlokhenges	20	3
			Greneham	80	4	Estlokhenges	30	4
			Wynterbourn	40	4	Beaterton	35	3
			Boxforth	40	6			
			Bynfeld	106	12			
Langford in Cleware	60	*12*						
Ray	40	6	Erley	40	8			
Clewer	60	5	Bray	20	3			
Farnham	130	7				Harwell	20	2
Burton	20	4				Westyllysley	60	6
			Knyghton	40	6	Crokeham	20	7

[1] All conjectural areas and numbers are excluded. [2] This Table differs from 'Status of Landlords' ultimately responsible for Inclosures' in omitting those areas from which no evictions or displacement from occupation took place, and the cases where the numbers are not specified. [3] Figures in brackets, inferred; figures in italics cases of deprival of occupation, not actual eviction. [4] One inclosure of 40 acres accompanied by eviction of five persons and destruction of their house, one destruction of house and eviction of four persons without inclosure.

M

546 THE DOMESDAY OF INCLOSURES, 1517

VIII. EVICTIONS AND DISPLACEMENTS FROM LABOUR, &c.—(*continued*)

LAY OWNERSHIP						ECCLESIASTICAL OWNERSHIP					
Lords of manors			Freeholders			Lords of manors			Freeholders		
Place	Area acres	Population displaced persons	Place	Area acres	Population displaced persons	Place	Area acres	Population displaced persons	Place	Area acres	Population displaced persons
Henton	45	6									
Bukland	80	7	Kenyngton	44	6	Westsandford	80	6			
Berkeham	100	8	Cokeham	20	2	Shalyngford	162	11	Shalyngford	30	3
			Wynkefeld	70	12						
			Bray	60	5	Milton	120	18			
			Stephyngton	80	10	Drayton	20	4			
Wittnam	20	3	Lyford	40	*8*	Kentbury	30	4			
Newbrigg (Kyngeston Bagpues)	60	4	Southcoote	100	*10*	Huddon	100	4			
Wilde	50	*4*	Warfild	40	*4*	Wargrave	40	4			

BERKSHIRE

Place			Place			Place		
Bukland	40	8	Okynham	30	4			
Newynton (Bukland)	20	4	Sandhurst	60	6			
Bukland	20	4	Fyfeld	40	4			
Sotwell	60	10	Sutton Curtenay	40	8	Marcham	40	12
						Appelford	40	8
Southmorton	40	6				Bukland	60	6
Dudcote	20	2	Dudcote	30	3			
			Mvlford	60	6	Sotwell	40	4
Aston Turrold	60	6				Aston Turrold	30	4
Harwell	100	8						
Burghfeld Regis	200	12	Hartley	40	4	Pangbourn	20	6
			Wolhamton	30	2	Tyleherst	30	5
	2763	258[1]		1635	172[1]		947	118[1]
							324	41[1]

[1] It is to be understood that the total number of evictions and displacements from labour is given in Table I., which includes all cases of an inferential character, and amounts to 590 evictions and 74 displacements from labour, in all, £64 cases, or, roughly, 11½ acres per person evicted and put out of employment. This Table, which excludes doubtful cases, is constructed for the purpose of obtaining an average

VIII. Evictions and Displacements, &c.—(continued)

Summary

	Lay Ownership								Ecclesiastical Ownership							
	Lords of manors				Freeholders				Lords of manors				Freeholders			
	Areas from which evictions took place	Persons evicted	Areas of dis-placement from employment	Persons dis-placed from employment	Areas from which evictions took place	Persons evicted	Areas of dis-placement from employment	Persons dis-placed from employment	Areas from which evictions took place	Persons evicted	Areas of dis-placement from employment	Persons dis-placed from employment	Areas from which evictions took place	Persons evicted	Areas of dis-placement from employment	Persons dis-placed from employment
1	acres 2,211	224	acres 552	34	acres 1,260	132	acres 375	40	acres 947	118	acres 0	0	acres 324	41	acres 0	0
2	No. of acres per person evicted		No. of acres per person displaced from employment		No. of acres per person evicted		No. of acres per person displaced from employment		No. of acres per person evicted				No. of acres per person evicted			
	9.8		16.2		9.8		9.3		8				7.9			
3	Total acres	Persons evicted	Persons evicted and displaced from employment	Persons evicted and displaced from employment	acres		Persons evicted and displaced from employment		acres	Persons evicted			acres	Persons evicted and displaced from employment		
	2,763	258	1,635	172					947	118			324	41		

Total number of acres per person evicted and displaced from employment	Total number of acres evicted and displaced from employment	Total number of acres per person evicted	Total number of acres per person evicted
acres 10.7	acres 9.5	acres 8	acres 7.9

Total number of acres from which evictions took place (lay and ecclesiastical lands together)	Total number of persons evicted (lay and ecclesiastical together)	Total number of acres from which displacements of labour took place	Total number of persons displaced from employment
acres 4,730	515	acres 927	74

5

6

Total number of acres per person evicted (lay and ecclesiastical lands together)			Total number of acres per person displaced from employment
9.2			12.5

7

Total number of acres from which evictions and displacement from employment took place (lay and ecclesiastical lands together)			Total number of persons evicted and displaced from employment (lay and ecclesiastical lands together)
5,669			589

8

Total number of acres per person evicted and displaced from employment (lay and ecclesiastical lands together)
9.6

IX

NUMBER OF ACRES TO A MESSUAGIUM (MANOR HOUSES AND INFERRED CASES EXCLUDED) CLASSIFIED ACCORDING TO TENURES AND TENANCIES

I. Land in hands of lords of manors

LAY OWNERSHIP

Parish	Number of messuages	Acres
1. Chilrey	1	20
2. Yatyndon	1	40
3. Hampstede Norreys	1	40
4. Berkeham	1	100
5. Wolhamton	1	20
	5	220

Average number of acres to a messuagium . . . 44

ECCLESIASTICAL OWNERSHIP

Parish	Number of messuages	Acres
1. Chadlyngworth	2	80
2. East Hanney	1	20
	3	100

Average number of acres to a messuagium . . . 33·3

II. Land in hands of freeholders

LAY OWNERSHIP

Parish	Number of messuages	Acres
1. Lekehamstede	1	30
2. Hampstede Norreys	1	40
3. Chaddelworth	1	40
4. Grove (Wantage)	1	24
5. Estgynge	1	36
6. Estgynge	1	30
7. Estgynge	1	30
8. Greneham	1	20
9. Wynterbourn	1	40
10. Boxforth	1	40
11. Bynfeld	1	80
12. Bynfeld	1	26
13. Bray	1	20
14. Kenyngton	1	44
15. Bukland	1	40
16. Bukland	1	40
17. Cokeham	1	20
18. Wynkefeld	1	50
19. Wynkefeld	1	20
20. Bray	1	60

ECCLESIASTICAL OWNERSHIP

Parish	Number of messuages	Acres
1. Westyllysley	1	60

BERKSHIRE

IX. Number of Acres to a Messuagium (Manor Houses and Inferred Cases excluded) classified according to Tenures and Tenancies—(continued)

II. Land in hands of freeholders—(continued)

Lay Ownership			Ecclesiastical Ownership		
Parish	Number of messuages	Acres	Parish	Number of messuages	Acres
21. Stephyngton	1	40			
22. Stephyngton	1	40			
23. Okynham	1	30			
24. Sandhurst	2	60			
25. Fyfeld	1	40			
26. Sutton Curttenay	1	40			
			2. Aston Turrold	1	30
27. Hartley	1	15			
	28	995		2	90

Average number of acres to a messuagium . . . 35·5

Average number of acres to a messuagium . . . 45

III. Copyholds

Lay Ownership			Ecclesiastical Ownership		
Parish	Number of messuages	Acres	Parish	Number of messuages	Acres
1. Stretley	1	60			
			1. Chyveley	1	20
2. Bedone	1	40			
3. Grove (Wantage)	1	30			
4. Ardyngton	1	50			
			2. Westlokhenges	1	20
			3. Estlokhenges	1	30
			4. Beaterton	1	35
5. Fernham	1	30			
			5. Westsandford	1	60
			6. Westsandford	1	80
			7. Shalyngford	1	50
			8. Shalyngford	1	30
			9. Drayton	1	20
6. Wittnam	1	20			
7. Newbrigg (Kyngeston Bagpues)	1	60			
			10. Wargrave	1	40
			11. Marcham	1	40
			12. Appelford	1	40
8. Dudcote	1	20			
	8	310		12	465

Average number of acres to a messuagium . . . 38·7

Average number of acres to a messuagium . . . 38·7

IX. NUMBER OF ACRES TO A MESSUAGIUM (MANOR HOUSES AND INFERRED CASES EXCLUDED) CLASSIFIED ACCORDING TO TENURES AND TENANCIES—(continued)

IV. Leaseholds

LAY OWNERSHIP

Parish	Number of messuages	Acres
1. Compton	1	200
2. Aldeworth	1	200
3. Greneham	1	26
4. Farnham	1	100
5. Compton	2	30
6. Knyghton	1	40
7. Sotwell	1	60
8. Southmorton	1	20
9. Southmorton	1	20
10. Dudcote	1	30
11. Mvlford	1	60
12. Burghfeld Regis	1	200
	13	986

Average number of acres to a messuagium . . . 75·8

ECCLESIASTICAL OWNERSHIP

Parish	Number of messuages	Acres
1. Ferneburghe	1	20
2. Brightwell	1	40
3. Harwell	1	20
4. Crokeham	1	20
5. Huddon	1	100
	5	200

Average number of acres to a messuagium . . . 40

V. Farm tenancies

LAY OWNERSHIP

Parish	Number of messuages	Acres
1. Fulscot	3	240
2. Chilton	1	30
3. Bastelden	1	20
4. Stretley	1	60
5. Stretley	1	40
6. Vpton	1	20
7. Burton	1	20
8. Bukland	1	40

ECCLESIASTICAL OWNERSHIP

Parish	Number of messuages	Acres
1. Westyllesley	1	40
2. Chadlyngworth [1]	2	80
3. Easthenrede	1	24
4. Shalyngford	1	30
5. Kentbury	1	30
6. Wilde	1	40

[1] The inclosures had been carried out by the lady of the manor. At the time of the Inquisition the two farm tenancies had been consolidated.

BERKSHIRE

IX. NUMBER OF ACRES TO A MESSUAGIUM (MANOR HOUSES AND INFERRED CASES EXCLUDED) CLASSIFIED ACCORDING TO TENURES AND TENANCIES—*(continued)*

V. Farm tenancies—*(continued)*

LAY OWNERSHIP

Parish	Number of messuages	Acres
9. Newynton (Bukeland)	1	20
10. Bukland	1	20
11. Aston Turrold	1	30
12. Aston Turrold	1	30
13. Harwell.	1	100
14. Hartley.	1	40
15. Wolhampton.	1	30
	17	740

Average number of acres to a messuagium . . . 43·5

ECCLESIASTICAL OWNERSHIP

Parish	Number of messuages	Acres
7. Bukland	1	60
8. Sotwell	1	40
9. Tyleherst	1	30
	10	374

Average number of acres to a messuagium . . . 37·4

Total

LAY OWNERSHIP
messuagia   acres
71   3,251

ECCLESIASTICAL OWNERSHIP
messuagia   acres
32   1,229

Average number of acres to a messuagium

acres   acres
45·7   38·4

Total average number of acres to a messuagium

acres
44·4

The manor houses are associated with the following areas:

Place	Acres
Catmar	400
Westhenrede	180
Henton	45
Total	625

This gives an average of 208 acres to a manor house; but the variations between the data are so great, and the data themselves so few, that the result cannot be taken as satisfactory. The areas of the manors of Milton, Drayton and Garford, each associated with a manor house, are inferred from the rents.

X

NUMBER OF INHABITANTS OF A MESSUAGIUM (MANOR HOUSES AND DOUBTFUL CASES OMITTED) CLASSIFIED ACCORDING TO TENURES AND TENANCIES. INFERRED AND DOUBTFUL FIGURES EXCLUDED

I. Land in hands of lords of manor

LAY OWNERSHIP

Parish	No. of messuages	Inhabitants
1. Chilrey	1	4
2. Yatyndon	1	5
3. (Yatyndon)	1	4
4. Berkeham	1	8
	4	21
Average number of inhabitants of a messuagium		5

ECCLESIASTICAL OWNERSHIP

Parish	No. of messuages	Inhabitants
1. East Hanney	1	4
2. Pangbourn	1	6
	2	10
Average number of inhabitants of a messuagium		5

II. Land in hands of freeholders

LAY OWNERSHIP

Parish	No. of messuages	Inhabitants
1. Lekehamstede	1	4
2. Chaddelworth	1	6
3. Grove (Wantage)	1	2
4. Estgynge	2	6
5. Estgynge	1	4
6. Greneham	1	2
7. Wynterbourn	1	4
8. Boxforth	1	6
9. Bynfeld	1	8
10. Bynfeld	1	4
11. Bray	1	3
12. Kenyngton	1	6
13. Bukland	1	4
14. Bukland	1	3
15. Cokeham	1	2
16. Wynkefeld	1	6
17. Wynkefeld	1	6
18. Bray	1	5

ECCLESIASTICAL OWNERSHIP

Parish	No. of messuages	Inhabitants
1. Westyllysley	1	6

BERKSHIRE

X. Number of Inhabitants of a Messuagium (Manor Houses and Doubtful Cases omitted) classified according to Tenures and Tenancies. Inferred and Doubtful Figures excluded—(*continued*)

II. Land in hands of freeholders—(*continued*)

Lay Ownership

Parish	No. of messuages	Inhabitants
19. Stephyngton	1	4
20. Stephyngton	1	6
21. Okynham	1	4
22. Sandhurst	2	6
23. Fyfeld	1	4
24. Sutton Curttenay	1	8
	26	113

Average number of inhabitants of a messuagium   4

Ecclesiastical Ownership

Parish	No. of messuages	Inhabitants
2. Aston Turrold	1	4
	2	10

Average number of inhabitants of a messuagium   5

III. Copyholds

Lay Ownership

Parish	No. of messuages	Inhabitants
1. Stretley	1	4
2. Bedon	1	3
3. Grove (Wantage)	1	2
4. Ardyngton	1	4
5. Fernham	1	3
6. Wittnam	1	3
7. Newbrigg (Kyngeston Bagpues)	1	4
8. Dudcote	1	2
	8	25

Average number of inhabitants of a messuagium   3

Ecclesiastical Ownership

Parish	No. of messuages	Inhabitants
1. Chyveley	1	2
2. Westlokhenges	1	3
3. Estlokhenges	1	4
4. Beaterton	1	3
5. Westsandford	1	6
6. Shalyngford	1	3
7. Drayton	1	4
8. Wargrave	1	4
9. Marcham	1	12
10. Appelford	1	8
	10	49

Average number of inhabitants of a messuagium   5[1]

---

[1] The omission of Marcham, an item which is entirely exceptional and disturbing to the average, leaves the number of inhabitants of 9 messuages as 37, an average of slightly more than 4 persons to a messuagium.

X. NUMBER OF INHABITANTS OF A MESSUAGIUM (MANOR HOUSES AND DOUBTFUL CASES OMITTED) CLASSIFIED ACCORDING TO TENURES AND TENANCIES, &C.—(*continued*)

IV. Leaseholds

LAY OWNERSHIP			ECCLESIASTICAL OWNERSHIP		
Parish	No. of messuages	Inhabitants	Parish	No. of messuages	Inhabitants
1. Compton	1	12	1. Ferneburghe	1	3
2. Aldeworth	1	5			
3. Greneham	1	6	2. Brightwell	1	5
4. Farnham	1	4	3. Harwell	1	2
5. Knyghton	1	6			
			4. Crokeham	1	7
			5. Shalyngford	4	8
			6. Haddon	1	4
6. Sotwell	1	10			
7. Southmorton	1	3			
8. Southmorton	1	3			
9. Dudcote	1	3			
10. Mvlford	1	6			
11. Burghfeld Regis	1	12			
	11	70		9	29
Average number of inhabitants of a messuagium		6	Average number of inhabitants of a messuagium		3

V. Farm tenancies

LAY OWNERSHIP			ECCLESIASTICAL OWNERSHIP		
Parish	No. of messuages	Inhabitants	Parish	No. of messuages	Inhabitants
1. Fulscot	3	29			
			1. Westyllesley	1	6
2. Chilton	1	8			
3. Bastelden	1	2			
4. Stretley	1	6			
5. Stretley	1	6			
6. Vpton	1	4			
			2. Chadlyngworth	2	12
			3. Eastheurede	1	3
7. Burton	1	4			
			4. Shalyngford	1	3
			5. Kentbury	1	4
8. Bukland	1	8			
			6. Bukland	1	6

BERKSHIRE

X. NUMBER OF INHABITANTS OF A MESSUAGIUM (MANOR HOUSES AND DOUBTFUL CASES OMITTED) CLASSIFIED ACCORDING TO TENURES AND TENANCIES, &C.—(*continued*)

V. Farm tenancies—(*continued*)

LAY OWNERSHIP			ECCLESIASTICAL OWNERSHIP		
Parish	No. of messuages	Inhabitants	Parish	No. of messuages	Inhabitants
9. Newynton (Bukeland)	1	4			
10. Bukland . . .	1	4			
			7. Sotwell . . .	1	4
11. Aston Turrold .	1	3			
12. Aston Turrold .	1	3			
13. Harwell . . .	1	8			
			8. Tyleherst . .	1	5
14. Hartley . . .	1	4			
15. Wolhampton . .	1	2			
	17	95		9	43
Average number of inhabitants of a messuagium		5	Average number of inhabitants of a messuagium		5

SUMMARY

I

	LAY OWNERSHIP	ECCLESIASTICAL OWNERSHIP
	Average number of inhabitants to a messuagium	Average number of inhabitants to a messuagium
1. Land in hands of lords of manors .	5	5
2. Land in hands of freeholders . .	4	5
3. Copyholds	3	5
4. Leaseholds	6	3
5. Farm tenancies	5	5

II. Total messuages and inhabitants [1]

LAY OWNERSHIP		ECCLESIASTICAL OWNERSHIP	
Messuages	Inhabitants	Messuages	Inhabitants
66	324	32	141
Average number of inhabitants of a messuagium	5	Average number of inhabitants of a messuagium	4

[1] *I.e.* excluding manor houses, houses from which only a partial displacement took place, and houses the number of inhabitants of which is not specified.

X. NUMBER OF INHABITANTS OF A MESSUAGIUM, &C.—(*continued*)

III. Total messuages and inhabitants[1] on lay and ecclesiastical land taken together

Messuages	Inhabitants
98	465

Average number of inhabitants of a messuagium, 5

Number of inhabitants of manor houses ('manerium,' 'messuagium manerii')

Parish	Inhabitants
1. Westhenrede	12
2. Ray	6
3. Clewer	5
4. Henton	6
5. Milton	20
6. Drayton	14
7. Garford	6
Total	69

Average number of inhabitants of a manor house, 10

[1] See note on preceding page.

XI

NUMBER OF PERSONS AND ACRES TO AN ARATRUM CLASSIFIED ACCORDING TO TENURES AND TENANCIES. INFERRED FIGURES EXCLUDED

		Lay Ownership						Ecclesiastical Ownership			
Parish	Aratra	Land in hands of lords of manors	Land in hands of free-holders	Copy-holds	Lease-holds	Farm tenancies	Parish	Aratra	Land in hands of lords of manors	Land in hands of free-holders	Copy-holds	Lease-holds	Farm tenancies
		acr. per.	acr. per.	acr. per.	acr. per.	acr. per.			acr. per.	acr. per.	acr. per.	acr. per.	acr. per.
1. Catmar	1	—	—	—	200 14	—							
2. Compton	1	—	—	—	60 12	—							
3. Aldeworth	1	—	—	—	50 5	—							
4. Wantage	½–½	—	55 4	—	—	—							
5. Esthenrede	½–½	—	20 2	—	—	—							
6. Spersholt													
7. Yatyndon	1	40 5	—	—	—	40 3							
8. East Hanney	½	42 4	—	—	—	—							
9. Greneham	1	—	80 4	—	—	—							
10. Langford in Cleware	2	—	—	60 12	—	—							
11. Ray	1	—	—	—	—	—							
12. Shalyngford	2	—	—	—	80 8	40 6							
13. Bray	1	—	60 5	—	—	—	1. Milton	2	—	—	—	120 18	—
14. Lyford	2	—	40 8	—	—	—	2. Kentbury	1	—	—	—	—	30 4
15. Southcoote	2	—	100 10	—	—	—	3. Huddon	1	—	—	—	80 4	—
16. Warfld	1	—	40 4	—	—	—							
17. Hartley[1]	1	—	—	—	—	40 4							
	19½	82 9	395 37	60 12	390 39	120 13		4	—	—	—	200 22	30 4

Note the maintenance of the proportion of labour to the aratrum, varying with the extent of the latter. The only exception is the lay copyhold, and that is a solitary instance.

[1] Crokam is omitted, because quite exceptionally, while the plough is said to have been put down, no eviction nor displacement of labour is returned.

XI. NUMBER OF PERSONS AND ACRES TO AN ARATRUM CLASSIFIED ACCORDING
TO TENURES AND TENANCIES—(*continued*)

Total number of aratra put down, acres assigned thereto, and persons evicted displaced thereby

LAY OWNERSHIP			ECCLESIASTICAL OWNERSHIP		
Aratra	Acres	Persons	Aratra	Acres	Persons
19½	1,047	110	4	230	26

	Land in hands of lords of manors	Land in hands of freeholders	Copyholds	Leaseholds	Farm tenancies		Land in hands of lords of manors	Land in hands of freeholders	Copyholds	Leaseholds	Farm tenancies
Number of aratra	1½	8½	2	5	2½	Number of aratra	0	0	0	3	1
Average number of persons to an aratrum	6	4·3	6	7·8	5·2	Average number of persons to an aratrum	0	0	0	7·3	4
Average number of acres to an aratrum	54·6	46·4	30	78	48	Average number of acres to an aratrum	0	0	0	66·6	30

General average

Average number of persons to an aratrum . . . . . 5·6
Average number of acres to an aratrum . . . . . 53·6

Average number of persons to an aratrum . . . . . 6·5
Average number of acres to an aratrum . . . . . 57·5

Total general average (lay and ecclesiastical property together)

Average number of persons to an aratrum . . . 5·6
Average number of acres to an aratrum . . . 54·2

BERKSHIRE

XII

RENTAL VALUES [1] [2] OF INCLOSED ARABLE AND PASTURE. LAND CLASSIFIED ACCORDING TO TENURES AND TENANCIES. INFERRED FIGURES EXCLUDED

I. Land in hand of lords of manors

LAY OWNERSHIP

Parish	Total area inclosed	Arable	Parks and inclosures to pasture	Total rental value	Rental value per acre
	acr.	acr.	acr.	£ s. d.	d.
Chilrey . . .	20	20	—	0 16 0	9½
Yatyndon . .	40	—	40	0 18 0	5½ [3]
Hampstede Nor-reys	30	—	30	0 10 0	4
Westhenrede . .	180	180	—	10 0 0	13½
Easthanney . .	42	—	42	1 0 0	5¾
Berkeham . .	100	—	100	1 13 4	4
Hampstede Marshall	100	—	100	2 0 0	4¾ [4]
Wilde . . .	50	—	50	0 12 0	2¾
Bradfeld . .	4	—	4	0 1 4	4
Totals . .	566	200	366	17 10 8	—

Average rental value per acre = 7¼d.

ECCLESIASTICAL OWNERSHIP

Parish	Total area inclosed	Arable	Parks and inclosures to pasture	Total rental value	Rental value per acre
	acr.	acr.	acr.	£ s. d.	d.
East Hanney .	20	20	—	0 14 0	8½
Bustellesham .	10	—	10	0 5 0	6
Pangbourn . .	20	20	—	0 10 0	6
	50	40	10	1 9 0	—

Average rental value per acre = 7d.

---

[1] In this and in the other Tables of rental values, those cases are necessarily excluded where no rental values are returned. Hence, though these calculations involving the areas are indispensable to arrive at the rental values of land and their averages in the several tenures and tenancies, the distribution of areas including all entries must be sought in Table V. p. 522, *supra*.

[2] Reduced to nearest whole farthing. Inferred areas excluded. The term 'rental value' is throughout adopted in preference to 'rent' on account of the areas thus held in hand by owners.

[3] Same owner.   [4] Pasture inclosed as a park.

XII. Rental Values[1] of Inclosed Arable and Pasture. Land classified according to Tenures and Tenancies. Inferred Figures excluded—(*continued*)

II. Land in hand of freeholders

Lay Ownership

Parish	Total area inclosed	Arable	Parks and inclosures to pasture	Total rental value	Rental value per acre
	acr.	acr.	acr.	£ s. d.	s. d.
Wantage	55	—	55	1 10 0	0 6½
Esthenrede	20	—	20	0 13 0	0 7¾
Lekehamstede	30	30	—	0 10 0	0 4
Hampstede Norreys	40	40	—	0 5 0	0 1½
Chaddelworth	40	40	—	2 0 0	1 0
Grove (Wantage)	24	24	—	0 13 4	0 6½
Estgynge	66	—	66	2 0 0	0 7¼[2]
Estgynge	30	30	—	1 10 0	1 0
Greneham	20	—	20	1 0 0	1 0
Greneham	80	—	80	1 10 0	0 4½
Boxforth[3]	40	40	—	1 0 0	0 6
Bynfeld	80	80	—	4 13 4	1 2
Bynfeld	26	26	—	1 4 0	0 11
Hurst	60	—	60	1 10 0	0 6
Erley	40	—	40	1 0 0	0 6
Bray	20	—	20	1 0 0	1 0
Kenyngton	44	44	—	5 0 0	2 3¼
Bukland	40	40	—	1 0 0	0 6
Bukland	40	—	40	1 0 0	0 6
Cokeham	20	20	—	1 0 0	1 0
Wynkefeld	50	50	—	2 0 0	0 9½
Wynkefeld	20	—	20	1 0 0	1 0
Bray	60	—	60	3 0 0	1 0
Stephyngton	40	—	40	2 0 0	1 0
Stephyngton	40	40	—	2 0 0	1 0
Lyford	40	—	40	2 0 0	1 0
Southcote	100	—	100	5 0 0	1 0
Warfild	40	—	40	2 0 0	1 0
Okynham	30	30	—	1 10 0	1 0
Sandhurst	60	—	60	1 6 3	0 5¼
Fyfeld	40	40	—	0 13 0	0 3¼
Sutton Curttenay	40	40	—	0 13 4	0 4
Hartley	15	—	15	0 5 0	0 4
	1,390	614	776	53 6 8	—

Average rental value per acre = 9*d*.

Ecclesiastical Ownership

Parish	Total area inclosed	Arable	Parks and inclosures to pasture	Total rental value	Rental value per acre
	acr.	acr.	acr.	£ s. d.	s. d.
Westyllysley	60	60	—	3 0 0	1 0[4]
Aston Turrold	30	30	—	1 0 0	0 8
	90	90	—	4 0 0	—

Average rental value per acre = 10¾*d*.

[1] Reduced to nearest whole farthing. Inferred areas excluded. The term 'rental value' is throughout adopted in preference to 'rent' on account of the area thus held in hand by owners.
[2] Same owner.
[3] As the relative rental values of arable and pasture are inferred at Wynterbourn (No. 11), the figures for that place have been excluded.
[4] Rector's glebe.

BERKSHIRE

XII. RENTAL VALUES[1] OF INCLOSED ARABLE AND PASTURE. LAND CLASSIFIED ACCORDING TO TENURES AND TENANCIES. INFERRED FIGURES EXCLUDED—(*continued*)

III. Copyholds

LAY OWNERSHIP

Number of holdings	Parish	Total area inclosed	Arable	Parks and inclosures to pasture	Total rental value			Rental value per acre	
		acr.	acr.	acr.	£	s.	d.	s.	d.
1	Stretley	60	60	—	0	12	0	0	2¼
1	Bedone	40	40	—	0	10	0	0	3
1	Grove (Wantage)	30	30	—	1	10	0	1	0
1	Ardyngton	50	—	50	1	9	0	0	6¼
1	Langford in Cleware	60	—	60	5	0	0	1	8
1	Fernham	30	30	—	0	18	0	0	7
1	Henton	45	45	—	2	6	8	1	0¼
1	Wittnam	20	—	20	0	13	4	0	8
1	Newbrigg (Kyngeston Bagpues)	60	60	—	1	4	0	0	4¾
1	Dudcote	20	20	—	0	15	0	0	9
10	Total	415	285	130	14	18	0	—	

Average rental value per acre = 8¼d.
Average area of holding = 41·5

ECCLESIASTICAL OWNERSHIP

Number of holdings	Parish	Total area inclosed	Arable	Parks and inclosures to pasture	Total rental value			Rental value per acre	
		acr.	acr.	acr.	£	s.	d.	s.	d.
1	Chyveley	20	20	—	0	10	0	0	6
1	Westlokhenges	20	20	—	0	13	4	0	8
1	Estlokhenges	30	30	—	1	6	8	0	10¼
1	Beaterton	35	—	35	0	15	0	0	8
1	Westsandford	60	60	—	0	11	0	0	2
1	Westsandford	80	80	—	0	12	0	0	1¾
1	Shalyngford	50	50	—	1	6	8	0	6¼
1	Shalyngford	30	30	—	1	0	0	0	8
1	Drayton	20	20	—	0	12	6	0	7½
1	Wargrave	40	—	40	1	0	0	0	6
1	Marcham	40	—	40	2	0	0	1	0
1	Appelford	40	40	—	1	0	0	0	0
12	Total	465	350	115	11	7	2	—	

Average rental value per acre = 5¾d.
Average area of holding = 38·7

---

[1] Reduced to nearest whole farthing. Inferred areas excluded. The term 'rental value' is throughout adopted in preference to 'rent,' because many of the acreages in the Returns are of lands held by owners.

XII. RENTAL VALUES OF INCLOSED ARABLE AND PASTURE. LAND CLASSIFIED ACCORDING TO TENURES AND TENANCIES. INFERRED AREAS EXCLUDED — (*continued*)

IV. Leaseholds

LAY OWNERSHIP

Number of holdings	Parish	Total area inclosed	Arable	Parks and inclosures to pasture	Total rental value			Rental value per acre	
		acr.	acr.	acr.	£	s.	d.	s.	d.
1	Catmar [1].	[400	200	200	10	0	0	6][1]	
	Compton [1]	[200	140	60	10	0	0	1	0][1]
	Aldeworth [1]	[200	150	50	6	0	0	7][1]	
1	Greneham	26	26	—	1	0	0	0	9
1	Farnham	100	100	—	6	13	4	1	4
2	Compton	30	30	—	1	0	0	0	8
1	Knyghton	40	40	—	2	0	0	1	0
1	Sotwell	60	60	—	1	0	0	0	4
1	Southmorton	20	20	—	1	0	0	1	0
1	Southmorton	20	20	—	1	0	0	1	0
1	Dudcote	30	—	30	2	0	0	1	4
1	Mvlford	60	60	—	1	0	0	0	4
1	Burghfeld Regis	200	200	—	10	0	0	1	0
14	Total	586	556	30	26	13	4	—	

Average rental value per acre = $10\frac{3}{4}d$.
Average area of holding = 99 acres

ECCLESIASTICAL OWNERSHIP

Number of holdings	Parish	Total area inclosed	Arable	Parks and inclosures to pasture	Total rental value			Rental value per acre	
		acr.	acr.	acr.	£	s.	d.	s.	d.
1	Ferneburghe	20	20	—	0	12	0	7	
1	Brightwell	40	40	—	1	0	0	6	
1	Harwell	20	20	—	0	10	0	6	
1	Crokeham	20	20	—	0	9	0	$5\frac{1}{4}$ [1]
(5) 4	Shalyngford [2]	80	—	80	13	4		11	
1	Milton [3]	120	—	120	2	0	0	4	
1	Garford [3]	60	—	60	2	0	0	8	
1	Huddon [1]	[100	20	80	4	0	0	$9\frac{1}{2}$]	
10	Total	360	100	260	10	4	4	—	

Average rental value per acre = $6\frac{3}{4}d$.
Average area of holding [2] [3] = 31·2 acres

---

[1] Catmar, Compton, Aldeworth and Huddon are excluded, except in calculation of average area holding, as rental values of arable and pasture are inferred figures.

[2] The number of holdings at Shalyngford was 5 with 112 acres. The rental value given is for four holdings only, and 80 acres of pasture. The average area is calculated on 5 holdings and 112 acres.

[3] Milton and Garford are excluded from the calculation of the average area of holdings, because each the areas there inclosed represents a portion of a larger leasehold holding, the extent of which is an inferred figure.

XII. Rental Values[1] of Inclosed Arable and Pasture. Land classified according to Tenures and Tenancies. Inferred Figures excluded—(continued)

V. Farm tenancies[2]

Lay Ownership

Number of holdings	Parish	Total area inclosed	Arable	Parks and inclosures to pasture	Total rental value	Rental value per acre
		acr.	acr.	acr.	£ s. d.	s. d.
1	Fulscot .	160	160	—	8 0 0	1 0 ⎫[3]
1	Fulscot .	40	40	—	2 0 0	1 0 ⎬
1	Fulscot .	40	40	—	2 0 0	1 0 ⎭
1	Chilton .	30	30	—	2 0 0	1 4
1	Bastelden	20	20	—	0 10 0	0 6
1	Stretley .	60	60	—	2 13 4	0 10½
1	Stretley .	40	40	—	1 0 0	0 6
1	Vpton .	20	20	—	0 17 0	0 10
1	Spersholt	40	—	40	1 0 0	0 6
1	Spersholt	40	—	40	1 0 0	0 6
1	Ray .	40	—	40	2 13 8	1 4
1	Clewer .	60	—	60	2 0 0	0 8
1	Burton .	20	20	—	1 0 0	1 0
1	Bukland .	40	40	—	0 18 0	0 5¼
1	Newynton (Bukeland)	20	20	—	0 18 0	0 10¾
1	Bukland .	20	20	—	0 11 0	0 6½
1	Aston Turrold	30	30	—	1 4 0	0 9½
1	Aston Turrold	30	30	—	0 18 10	0 7½
1	Harwell .	100	100	—	2 13 4	0 6¼
1	Crokam[7]	60	—	60	1 0 0	0 4
1	Westhagbourn[8]	20	20	—	1 13 4	1 8
1	Hartley .	40	—	40	1 0 0	0 6
1	Wolhamton	20	20	—	0 10 0	0 6[7]
1	Wolhampton	30	30	—	0 10 0	0 4
24	Total .	1020	740	280	38 10 6	—

Average rental value per acre = 9d.
Average area of holding = 42·5

Ecclesiastical Ownership

Number of holdings	Parish	Total area inclosed	Arable	Parks and inclosures to pasture	Total rental value	Rental value per acre
		acr.	acr.	acr.	£ s. d.	s. d.
1	Westyllesley .	40	40	—	1 0 0	0 6
2	Chadlyngworth	80	80	—	2 0 0	0 6 ⎫[4]
1	Wolley (Chaddelworth)	120	—	120	4 0 0	0 8 ⎭
1	Easthenrede	24	24	—	0 12 0	0 6
1	Shalyngford	30	30	—	1 10 0	1 0[5]
1	Kentbury .	30	—	30	1 0 0	0 8
1	Wilde .	40	40	—	0 13 4	0 4
1	Bukland .	60	60	—	1 10 0	0 6[6]
1	Sotwell .	40	40	—	1 0 0	0 6
1	Tyleherst	30	30	—	0 10 0	0 4
11	Total .	494	344	150	13 15 4	—

Average rental value per acre = 6¾d.
Average area of holding = 44·9

---

[1] Reduced to nearest whole farthing. Inferred areas excluded. The term 'rental value' is throughout adopted in preference to 'rent,' because many of the acreages in the Returns are of land held in hand by owners.

[2] Farm tenancy, from year to year or at will at common law. See *Trans. R.H.S.* 1892, pp. 196, 197, 255.

[3] Same landlord.

[4] Inclosed by the ecclesiastical lady of the manor, but held at the time of the Inquisition as a farm tenancy, and valued on that basis.

[5] Rector's glebe. [6] Rector's glebe.

[7] Inclosed by lord of manor, but held at the time of the Inquisition as a farm tenancy and valued on that basis.

[8] The rental value here perhaps includes both mill and house.

XII. Rental Values of Inclosed Arable and Pasture. Land classified according to Tenures and Tenancies. Inferred Figures excluded—(*continued*)

Summary

I. Land in owners' hand

	Lay Ownership							Ecclesiastical Ownership						
	Arable	Parks and inclosure to pasture	Total rental value of arable	Total rental value of pasture	Average rental value of arable per acre	Average rental value of pasture per acre	Arable	Parks and inclosure to pasture	Total rental value of arable	Total rental value of pasture	Average rental value of arable per acre	Average rental value of pasture per acre
	acres	acres	£ s. d.	£ s. d.	s. d.	s. d.	acres	acres	£ s. d.	£ s. d.	s. d.	s. d.
1. In hand of lords of manors	200	366	10 16 0	6 14 8	1 1	0 4½	40	10	1 4 0	0 5 0	0 7¼	0 6
2. In hand of freeholders	614	776	25 12 0	27 14 8	0 10	0 8½	90	—	4 0 0	—	0 10¾	—
Totals . .	814	1,142	36 8 0	34 9 4	—	—	130	10	5 4 0	0 5 0	—	—

	Total arable d.	Total pasture d.		Total arable d.	Total pasture d.
Average rental value . .	10¾	7¼		9½	6

II. Lands let, and in hands of tenants

	Lay Ownership							Ecclesiastical Ownership						
	Arable	Parks and inclosure to pasture	Total rental value of arable	Total rental value of pasture	Average rental value of arable per acre	Average rental value of pasture per acre	Arable	Parks and inclosure to pasture	Total rental value of arable	Total rental value of pasture	Average rental value of arable per acre	Average rental value of pasture per acre
	acres	acres	£ s. d.	£ s. d.	s. d.	s. d.	acres	acres	£ s. d.	£ s. d.	s. d.	s. d.
1. Copyholds .	285	130	7 15 8	7 2 4	0 6½	1 1	350	115	7 12 2	3 15 0	0 5¼	0 7¾
2. Leaseholds .	556	30	24 13 4	2 0 0	0 10¾	1 4	100	260	2 11 0	7 13 4	0 6	0 7
3. Farm tenancy .	740	280	29 16 10	8 13 8	0 9¾	0 7½	344	150	8 15 4	5 0 0	0 6	0 8
Totals . .	1,581	440	62 5 10	17 16 0	—	—	794	525	18 18 6	16 8 4	—	—

	Total arable d.	Total pasture d.		Total arable d.	Total pasture d.
Average rental value . .	9½	9¾		5¾	7½

Per acre
Total average value of pasture let (lay and ecclesiastical together) . . 8½d.

BERKSHIRE

XII. RENTAL VALUES OF INCLOSED ARABLE AND PASTURE, &C.—(continued)

Summary—(continued)

III. Total areas and rental values

	LAY OWNERSHIP						ECCLESIASTICAL OWNERSHIP					
—	Arable	Parks and inclosure to pasture	Total rental value of arable	Total rental value of pasture	Average rental value of arable per acre	Average rental value of pasture per acre	Arable	Parks and inclosure to pasture	Total rental value of arable	Total rental value of pasture	Average rental value of arable per acre	Average rental value of pasture per acre
(I. and II.)	acres 2,395	acres 1,582	£ s. d. 98 13 10	£ s. d. 52 5 4	d. 9	d. —	acres 924	acres 535	£ s. d. 24 2 6	£ s. d. 16 13 4	d. 6	d. —

IV. Total areas and rental values of arable and pasture in owners' hands (lay and ecclesiastical together)

	LAY OWNERSHIP						ECCLESIASTICAL OWNERSHIP		
—	Total arable	Total rental value of arable	Average rental value of arable per acre	Total pasture	Total rental value of pasture	Average rental value of pasture per acre	Total arable and pasture	Total rental value of arable and pasture	Average rental value of arable and pasture together per acre
(I.)	acres 944	£ s. d. 41 12 0	d. 10½	acres 1,152	£ s. d. 34 14 4	d. 7¼	acres 2,096	£ s. d. 76 6 4	d. 8¼

V. Total areas and rental values of land let, both arable and pasture (lay and ecclesiastical together)

	LAY OWNERSHIP						ECCLESIASTICAL OWNERSHIP		
—	Total arable	Total rental value of arable	Average rental value of arable let per acre	Total pasture	Total rental value of pasture	Average rental value of pasture let per acre	Total arable and pasture	Total rental value of arable and pasture	Average rental value of arable and pasture let together per acre
(II.)	acres 2,375	£ s. d. 81 4 4	d. 8¼	acres 965	£ s. d. 34 4 4	d. 8½	acres 3,340	£ s. d. 115 8 8	d. 8¼

XII. Rental Values of Inclosed Arable and Pasture, &c.—(continued)

Summary—(continued)

VI. Total areas and rental values of land, both arable and pasture (lay and ecclesiastical together)

	Lay Ownership						Ecclesiastical Ownership		
	Total arable	Total rental value of arable	Average rental value of arable per acre	Total pasture	Total rental value of pasture	Average rental value of pasture per acre	Total arable and pasture	Total rental value of arable and pasture	Average rental value of arable and pasture together per acre
(IV. and V.)	acres 3,319	£ s. d. 122 16 4	d. 9	acres 2,117	£ s. d. 68 18 8	d. 7¾	acres 5,436	£ s. d. 191 15 0	d. 8½

XIII

Selected Inclosures exceeding an Area of 300 Acres in one Place or Parish, showing the Proportion per cent. of the Inclosures to the Total Area of the Place or Parish in which such Inclosures were made

No. of inclosures	Place or Parish	Area of parish	Total area inclosed	Proportion of total area inclosed to area of parish &c.	Area inclosed. Arable	Proportion of arable inclosed to total area of parish &c.	Area inclosed. Pasture	Proportion of pasture inclosed to total area of parish &c.
1	Catmar	acres 680	acres 400	58·8	acres 200	29·4	acres 200	29·4

XIV

The Area of the Virgate in Berkshire

Place	Returns		Acres to a virgate
	Virgates	Acr	
Compton	2	—	15

No other virgates and no carucates are mentioned in this county.

XV

Comparative Table of Numerations of MS.

Page	Modern numeration. Membrane	Marginal numeration (1)	Marginal numeration (2)	Marginal numeration (3)
100	83	—	—	—
101	—	xlvj	—	—
104	84	—	—	—
105	—	xlvij	—	—
107	82	—	iij	—
108	—	xlviij	—	—
111	81	xlix	iij	—
115	80	lj [1]	—	C
116	—	—	—	D
118	79	—	—	S
121	78	—	iiij	—
122	—	lij [2]	—	—
125	77	—	—	—
126	—	liij	—	F
127	—	—	—	G
127	—	—	—	H
128	76	—	—	I
129	—	liiij	—	—
131	75	—	—	—
132	—	lv	—	—
135	74	—	—	—
136	—	lvj	—	—
139	73	—	—	—
140	—	lvij	—	l
141	—	—	—	o
143	72	lviij	—	—
146	71	—	xiiij	—
147	—	lix	—	—

[1] This suggests the loss of a membrane between xlix and lj. But this is not the case, for membrane 80 continues a presentment of membrane 81, the two being beyond doubt consecutive; moreover, lower in the same membrane and page occurs the figure l, showing a consciousness of some confusion.

[2] This suggests that membrane 78 should follow membrane 80. But membranes 80 and 79 run on consecutively like membranes 80 and 81. Membrane 78 begins a fresh presentment.

It is to be inferred from the series xlvj–lix that the arrangement of the membranes now adopted is correct, though the modern numeration is sadly defective. This is explicable on the ground that some kind of provisional numeration must necessarily have been made prior to the transcription of the membranes, and considerable pains were expended to attain such results as we have.

The alphabetical notation refers generally to inclosures by the Abbot of Abingdon, and was no doubt adopted for the purpose of collecting the cases against him.

The second series of Roman numerations is very imperfect. It repeats iiij and supplies no notation until xiiij. This coincides both with the modern arrangement and the first series of Roman numerations in recognising membrane 71 as the last of those now preserved.

Obviously none of the series tells us anything as to the number of membranes missing at the end. See Introduction, p. 91.

It must be remembered in this, as in all the other counties, that the margins are particularly faded and damaged, and the marginal notes in consequence very difficult to decipher. It is highly probable that some of the numerations have ceased to be visible.

I. GENERAL ANALYSIS OF THE CHANCERY RETURNS

Reference [1]	Ingrossing of Farms				Parishes	Total areas presented as inclosed	Inclosures						
							Objects of inclosure			Condition of inclos			
	No. of farms ingrossed	No. of cases of ingrossing	Area ingrossed	Areas consolidated with farms			Park	Inclosure of arable	Pasture	Lay lords of manors	Lay freeholders	Ecclesiastical lords of manors	Other ecclesiastics
P. 159	3 {	1 {	acres 160	acres —	Asshendon . . .	acres 40	acr. —	acres —	acr. 40	—	—	—	1)
				—	Asshendon . . .	20	—	—	20	—	—	—	1 }
	—	—	—	—	Asshendon . . .	100	—	—	100	—	—	—	1)
					Eddeslbrough . .	30	—	—	30	—	1	—	—
					Byrdyston . . .	60	—	—	60	1)	—	—	—
					Byrdyston . . .	10	—	—	10	1	—	—	—
					Byrdyston . . .	12	—	—	12	1	—	—	—
	7	1	400	— {	Byrdyston . . .	80	—	—	80	1 }	—	—	—
					Byrdyston . . .	(80)	—	—	(80)	1	—	—	—
					Byrdyston . . .	(79)	—	—	(79)	1	—	—	—
					Byrdyston . . .	(79)	—	—	(79)	1 /	—	—	—
162	{ —			(	Dodershill . . .	960	—	—	960	1)	—	—	—
		—			Grendon . . .	100	—	—	100	1)	—	—	—
	29 [a]	—	} 1,261	— {	Litilcote . . .	120	—	—	120	1	—	—	—
		1			Litilcote . . .	21	—	—	21	1)	—	—	—
					Litilcote . . .	20	—	—	20	1	—	—	—
		—			Litilcote . . .	40	—	—	40	1 /	—	—	—
165	—	—	—	—	Stutley	40	—	—	40	—	1	—	—
	—	—	—	—	Litilcote . . .	100	—	—	100	—	1	—	—
	—	—	—	30	Donnyngton . .	30	—	—	30	—	1	—	—
	—	—	—	30	Donnyngton . .	30	—	—	30	—	1	—	—
	—	—	—	30	Donnyngton . .	30	—	—	30	—	1	—	—
	—	—	—	—	Donnyngton . .	90	—	—	90	—	—	—	—
	5	1	120	—	Ludgarshale . .	120	—	—	120	—	1	—	—
	—	—	—	—	Ludgarshale . .	30	—	—	30	—	1	—	—
				(	Lyscome . .	80	—	—	80	—	1)	—	—
169	5	1	132	— {	Lyscombeholynden and Brakynham . }	40	—	—	40	—	1 }	—	—
				(	Lyscombeholynden and Brakynham	12	—	—	12	—	1)	—	—
	—	—	—	—	Lyscome Holynden and Brakynham	30	—	—	30	—	1	—	—
				(	Flete Merston . .	140	—	—	140	) 1	2	—	—
	5	2	[324]	— {	Flete Merston . .	[184]	—	—	[184]	} (1)	—	—	—
				(	Waddesdon . . .	30	—	10	20	—	1)	—	—
	2	1	110	— {	Waddesdon . . .	80	—	40	40	—	1 }	—	—
				(	Cublyngton . . .	20	—	—	20	—	1)	—	—
	3	1	[104]	— {	Cublyngton and Bredyncote . . . }	[84]	—	—	[84]	—	1 }	—	—

[1] Each page to which reference is made is coincident with the beginning of a membrane.
[a] Same incloser as at Dodershill and Grendon. At time of Inquisition he also held Litilcote.

BUCKINGHAMSHIRE

THE INQUISITION OF 1517 FOR BUCKINGHAMSHIRE

	Inclosures				
	Consequences of inclosure				
Displacement of population [a]	No. of houses decayed	No. of churches decayed	Annual rental value	Date of inclosure	Memorabilia
persons			£ s. d.		
(13)	1 messuagium	—	(1 7 0)	1508 (6 Oct.)	The number of persons evicted given together as 20, and the total rental value as 40s.
(7)	1 ,,	—	(0 13 0)	1508 (6 Oct.)	
16	1 ,,	—	5 0 0	1500 (6 Nov.)	Incloser a farming abbot
—	—	—	1 0 0	1506 (10 Oct.)	—
(9)	1 ,,	—	1 10 0 ⎫	1489 (2 Mar.)	Eight ploughs put down and 60 persons evicted through the entire clearance of 400 acres. 'Predicte ville hamelettum et manerium de Byrdeston totaliter et integre in pasturam' &c. Total rental value of £13 1s. 8d. increased to £40 by inclosure &c.
(1)	1 ,,	—	0 8 4 ⎬ £13 1s. 8d. raised to £40	1489 (2 Mar.)	
(2)	1 ,,	—	0 10 0 ⎪	1489 (2 Mar.)	
(12)	1 ,,	—	2 13 4 ⎪	1489 (2 Mar.)	
(12)	1 ,,	—	(2 13 4) ⎪	1489 (2 Mar.)	
(12)	1 ,,	—	(2 13 4) ⎪	1489 (2 Mar.)	
(12)	1 ,,	—	(2 13 4) ⎭	1489 (2 Mar.)	
120	24 messuagia	—	40 0 0	1495 (11 Aug.)	This incloser also the incloser of the three bracketed areas at Litilcote, *infra*
5	1 orreum	—	7 0 0	1491 (8 Mar.)	—
(14)	1 messuagium	—	3 6 8	1494 (2 Oct.)	'In Litilcote quatuor aratra deponuntur .. et viginti et quatuor persone . . . recesserunt . . . Totum hamelettum de litilcote devastatur'
(3)	1 ,,	—	0 12 0	1499 (12 Feb.)	
(3)	1 ,,	—	0 10 0	1498 (21 Dec.)	
(4)	1 ,,	—	1 10 0	1507 (8 Nov.)	
—	—	—	1 0 0	1505 (10 July)	—
8	1 ,,	—	3 6 8	1507 (10 Dec.)	
(4)	1 ,,	—	1 13 4	1515 (7 Mar.)	The number of persons evicted in these three cases given as 12 in all. 'Terras predictas cum aliis mesuagiis locari et ocupari fecerunt'
(4)	1 ,,	—	1 13 4	1515 (7 Mar.)	
(4)	1 ,,	—	1 13 4	1515 (7 Mar.)	
—	—	—	3 0 0	1515 (10 Feb.)	'Tres virgatas .. continentes in se quateruiginti et decem acras'
20	5 messuagia	—	4 0 0	1514 (6 Nov.)	'Sex virgatis .. qualibet inde virgata viginti acras .. continente'
4	1 messuagium	—	1 6 8	1514 (6 Nov.)	—
30	4 messuagia	—	5 0 0	1506 (6 Mar.)	
5	—	—	(1 0 0)	1505 (6 Mar.)	Inclosures of 40 acres on first date and 10 acres on second. Total rental, £1 6s.
—	—	—	(0 6 0)	1509 (7 April)	
[4]	1 messuagium	—	1 0 0	1515 (10 Feb.)	—
20	4 messuagia	—	20 0 0	1511 (16 Jan.)	—
(25)	(1 manerium)	—	—	[1507]	
8	1 messuagium	—	0 13 0	1507 (7 Jan.)	Rental value of 30 acres
8	1 ,,	—	7 6 8	1501 (6 Mar.)	Rental value of 80 acres
—	—	—	0 10 0	1509 (20 Jan.)	—
6	1 ,,	—	3 6 8	1513 (2 Mar.)	The rental value includes that of lands in Bredyncote, of which the area is inferred, being illegible

[a] The numbers of actual persons are in round brackets where they represent an apportionment of totals given in the text; in square brackets where they are conjectural. Displacements for employment, not being evictions, are indicated by italic numerals.

572   THE DOMESDAY OF INCLOSURES, 1517

I. GENERAL ANALYSIS OF THE CHANCERY RETURNS

Reference	Ingrossing of Farms				Parishes	Total areas presented as inclosed	Inclosures						
								Objects of inclosure		Condition of inclos			
	No. of farms ingrossed	No. of cases of ingrossing	Area ingrossed	Areas consolidated with farms			Park	Inclosure of arable	Pasture	Lay lords of manors	Lay freeholders	Ecclesiastical lords of manors	Other ecclesiastics
			acres	acres		acres	acr.	acres	acr.				
174	—	—	—	—	Middelclaydon	120	—	—	120	—	—	—	—
	3	1	60	—	Cranwell	60	—	60	—	1	—	—	—
	—	—	—	—	Cranwell	120	—	60	60	—	1	—	—
				30	Overwynchendon	30	—	—	30	—	—	—	—
	2 {	1	171 {										
				—	Overwynchendon	131	—	—	131	—	—	—	—
	—	—	—	—	Overwynchendon	10	—	—	10	—	1	—	—
	—	—	—	—	Ramston	24	—	24	—	—	1	—	—
	3	1	[96]	48	Ramston	48	—	48	—	—	—	1	—
	2	1	80	—	Wyllyn	80	—	—	80	—	—	—	—
					Blecheley	40	—	—	40	1)			
178	2	1	180	—	Blecheley	120	—	—	120	1 }	—	—	—
					Blecheley	20	—	—	20	1)			
	—	—	—	—	Moulsowe	20	—	—	20	—	1	—	—
	—	—	—	—	Moulsowe	20	—	—	20	—	—	—	1
	—	—	—	—	Woughton	20	—	—	20	—	1	—	—
	—	—	—	—	Stokehamond	30	—	30	—	—	1	—	—
	—	—	—	—	Stokehamond	30	—	30	—	—	1	—	—
	—	—	—	—	Walton	30	—	—	30	1	—	—	—
	—	—	—	—	Loughton	20	—	—	20	—	1	—	—
	—	—	—	—	Bradwell and Wuluerton	300	—	—	300	—	—	1	—
	—	—	—	—	Wuluerton and Bradwell	40	—	—	40	—	1	—	—
	—	—	—	—	Wuluerton and Bradwell	25	25	—	—	1	—	—	—
	—	—	—	—	Aston and Hardwyke	100	—	100	—	—	—	—	—
183	—	—	—	—	Stoke Pewges	200	—	—	200	1	—	—	—
	—	—	—	—	Dytton	100	—	—	100	—	—	—	—
	—	—	—	—	Dytton	30	—	—	30	—	—	—	—
	—	—	—	—	Burnham	20	—	20	—	—	1	—	—
	3	1	100	66	Burnham	100	—	100	—	—	—	—	—
	2	1	48	—	Woburne	40	—	40	—	—	1 }	—	—
					Wobourn	8	—	—	8	—	1 }	—	—
	—	—	—	—	Stone	40	—	40	—	—	—	—	—
	—	—	—	—	Stone	20	—	20	—	—	—	—	—
	—	—	—	—	Denham	24	—	—	24	1	—	—	—
187	—	—	—	—	Denham	20	—	20	—	1	—	—	—
	2	1 {	—	—	(Denham)	40	—	—	40	1	—	—	—
			[1040]	—	Denham	[44]	—	—	[44]	—	—	—	—

INQUISITION OF 1517 FOR BUCKINGHAMSHIRE—(continued)

Displacement of population	No. of houses decayed	No. of churches decayed	Annual rental value (£ s. d.)	Date of inclosure	Memorabilia
5 persons	—	—	3 0 0	1495 (7 March)	Incloser a leaseholder
6	3 cotagia	—	1 10 0	1490 (10 Feb.)	—
[15]	1 messuagium	—	1 10 0	1493 (6 March)	'sex virgatis . . . qualibet . . . viginti acras continente'
(3)	1 ,,	—	1 0 0	1514 (6 Jan.)	Incloser a copyholder of St. Frideswide's, Oxford, of 161 acres and house. These two inclosures involved the putting down of 3 ploughs and eviction of 10 persons
(7)	—	—	3 0 0	1514 (6 Jan.)	
—	—	—	0 4 0	1514 (6 Jan.)	—
[3]	1 ,,	—	1 0 0	1497 (24 Jan.)	—
4	2 messuagia	—	1 6 8	1507 (6 July)	'terrasque predictas cum alio mesuagio ocupari fecit'
10	2 ,,	—	2 13 4	1511 (16 Jan.)	'tenet et a diu tenuit in feodi firma'
8	2 ,,	—	1 4 0	illegible	—
10	—	—	7 0 0	1490 (16 Dec.) / 1487 (23 Oct.)	Two inclosures of 100 acres and 20 acres respectively. No mention of a messuage. The ploughs put down, &c., apparently refer to the whole area
6	1 messuagium	—	0 15 0	1509 (6 July)	
2	1 ,,	—	0 15 0	1506 (17 April)	Incloser the Abbess of Elstowe, a freeholder
4	1 ,,	—	0 15 0	1491 (7 March)	—
2	1 ,,	—	1 0 0	1491 (16 Jan.)	—
2	1 ,,	—	1 0 0	1496 (6 Dec.)	—
4	1 ,,	—	1 6 8	1516 (2 March)	—
[3]	1 ,,	—	0 10 0	1497 (10 June)	—
20	—	—	10 0 0	1507 (7 March)	No mention of a messuage
[5]	1 ,	—	1 13 8	1496 (19 Nov.)	—
—	—	—	0 13 0	1501 (10 July)	
—	—	—.	5 0 0	1495 (20 Jan.)	—
12	1 ,,	—	8 0 0	1511 (12 Sept.)	'in pasturam cuniculorum et ouium conuertit'
2	—	—	3 0 0	1513 (8 Feb.)	Incloser a leaseholder of the Crown. Conversion of 70 acres arable
3	—	—	1 10 0	1516 (4 Oct.)	Incloser a leaseholder
2	1 ,,	—	1 6 8	1506 (11 July)	—
12	2 messuagia	—	3 6 8	1506 (6 March)	Incloser a leaseholder. Two out of three messuages destroyed
6	1 messuagium	—	2 6 8	illegible (12 Mar.)	—
—	—	—	0 5 0	1507 (20 March)	
6	1 messuagium	—	2 0 0	1496 (12 Nov.)	Incloser a leaseholder
4	1 ,,	—	1 0 0	1511 (5 Feb.)	Incloser a leaseholder
8	1 ,,	—	2 13 4	1509 (7 July)	Incloser a widow
4	1 ,,	—.	1 6 0	1514 (14 June)	Incloser a widow
6	1 ,,	—	3 0 0	1501 (1 June)	—
12	—	—	44 0 0	1517	Incloser an ingrosser of one farm of £20, and of another of £24

I. General Analysis of the Chancery Returns

Reference	Ingrossing of Farms				Parishes	Total areas presented as inclosed	Inclosures						
							Park	Objects of inclosure		Condition of inclos[ures]			
	No. of farms ingrossed	No. of cases of ingrossing	Area ingrossed	Areas consolidated with farms				Inclosure of arable	Pasture	Lay lords of manors	Lay freeholders	Ecclesiastical lords of manors	Other ecclesiastics
P. 188	—	—	acres —	acres —	Weston Turfild	acres 160	acr. —	acres —	acr. 160	—	—	—	—
	—	—	—	—	Vpton	27	—	27	—	—	—	—	1
	—	—	—	—	Vpton	30	—	30	—	—	1	—	—
	—	—	—	—	Vpton	80	—	80	—	—	1	—	—
	—	—	—	—	Iver	50	—	—	50	—	1	—	—
	—	—	—	—	Iver	50	—	50	—	—	1 ⎫	—	—
190	3	1	140	—	Iver	50	—	50	—	—	1 ⎬	—	—
	—	—	—	—	Iver	40	—	40	—	—	1 ⎭	—	—
	2	1	140	30	Dynton	30	—	—	30	—	—	—	—
	—	959[1]	—		Hoggeshawe and Fulbroke	—	—	—	—	—	—	—	—
	—	—	—		Hoggeshawe	60	—	—	60	—	—	—	—
	—	—	—		Hoggeshawe	16	—	—	16	—	—	—	—
	11 ⎰ 1	—	—		Hoggeshawe	17½	—	—	17½	—	—	—	—
	—	—	—		Hoggeshawe	30	—	—	30	—	—	—	—
	—	—	—		Hoggeshawe	20	—	—	20	—	—	—	—
	—	—	—		Fulbroke	30	—	—	30	—	—	—	—
	—	—	—		Fulbroke	20	—	—	20	—	—	—	—
	—	—	—		Fulbroke	20	—	—	20	—	—	—	—
	—	—	—		Fulbroke	100	—	—	100	—	—	—	—
	—	—	—		Fulbroke	21	—	—	21	—	—	—	—
	—	—	—		Fulbroke	30	—	—	30	—	—	—	—
193	—	—	—		Fulbroke	16	—	—	16	—	1	—	—
	2	1	77	—	Tyrryngham	30	—	—	30	1	—	—	—
					Tyrryngham and Philgrav	47	—	—	47	1	—	—	—
	2	1	—	160	Gayhurst	100	—	—	100	1	—	—	—
					Lathbere	60	—	—	60	—	1	—	—
	—	—	—	—	Hanslap	26	—	—	26	—	1	—	—
	7	1	140	—	Wuluierston	32	32	—	—	—	1	—	—
					Wuluierston	140	—	140	—	—	1	—	—
197	8	1	164	143½	Lyllyngton Darell	164	—	—	164	1	—	—	—

[1] This total includes the subsequent conversions in this place together
[2] The slight difference between the sum total of £15 given in the Retur[n]
[3] Illegible.

BUCKINGHAMSHIRE 575

The Inquisition of 1517 for Buckinghamshire—(continued)

Inclosures					
Consequences of inclosure				Date of inclosure	Memorabilia
Displacement of population	No. of houses decayed	No. of churches decayed	Annual rental value		
persons			£ s. d.		
8	1 messuagium	—	6 0 0	1517	Incloser a leaseholder
3	1 ,,	—	1 0 0	1514 (11 Dec.)	Incloser the Abbot of Osney, a freeholder. (27 acres : see Exch. Roll)
3	1 ,,	—	2 0 0	1506 (6 Sept.)	—
4	1 ,,	—	4 6 8	1501 (3 ")	'de . . quatuor virgatis . . quelibet virgata continet in se viginti acras'
2	1 ,,	—	2 0 0	1492 (12 March)	—
8	1 ,,	—	3 0 0	1507 (9 March)	—
8	1 ,,	—	3 0 0	1506 (10 Nov.)	—
8	1 ,,	—	3 0 0	1507 (5 July)	—
7	1 ,,	—	2 0 0	1499 (6 Oct.)	The rental value is of 30 acres only. There was a second holding of 110 acres, and a messuage attached to each holding
—	—	—	—	1498 (6 March)	'villam et hamelettum predicta sepibus incluserunt'
(10)	1 principale messuagium manerii	—	(4 4 6)	1498 (6 March)	'et occasione illa in hoggeshaw et fulbroke predictis nouem aratra deponuntur et sexaginta persone mansionibus et occupacionibus suis carent'
(3)	1 messuagium	—	(1 2 6)	1493 (6 March)	
(3) 60	1 ,,	—	(1 3 8) }	1498 (6 March)	—
(5)	1 ,,	—	(2 2 3)	1498 (6 March)	—
(3)	1 ,,	—	(1 8 2)	1498 (6 March)	—
(5)	1 ,,	—	(2 2 3) $\}\pounds 15$	1498 (6 March)	—
(3)	1 ,,	—	(1 8 2)	1498 (6 March)	—
(3)	1 ,,	—	(1 8 2)	1498 (6 March)	—
(17)	1 ,,	—	(10 0 0)	1498 (6 March)	—
(3)	1 ,,	—	(3 0 0) $\}\pounds 15$	1498 (6 March)	—
(5)	1 ,,	—	(2 0 0)	1498 (6 March)	—
—	—	—	0 6 8	1498 (6 March)	—
[4]	1 messuagium	—	0 18 0	1509 (6 April)	—
[7]	1 ,,	—	1 10 0	1509 (6 April)	—
[14]	1 ,,	—	5 0 0	1516 (2 Feb.)	—
—	—	—	2 0 0	1516 10 Jan.)	—
3/3	1 messuagium	—	0 13 4	1502 (18 Jan.)	—
—	—	—	0 16 0	1500 (20 Nov.)	—
20	7 messuagia	—	6 8 0	1501 (6 Feb.)	—
40	{ 7 ,,. 4 cotagia }	—	40 0 0	1491 (4 Feb.)	Eight carucates of 20½ acres each. No land to cottages. 'Tota villa . . . prosternitur et totaliter devastata existit

acres of pasture over and above the sum total of the twelve following items.
sum total of these items calculated therefrom arises from the rejection of fractions.

I. GENERAL ANALYSIS OF THE CHANCERY RETURNS

| Reference | Ingrossing of Farms |||| Parishes | Inclosures ||||||||
| | No. of farms ingrossed | No. of cases of ingrossing | Area ingrossed | Areas consolidated with farms | | Total areas presented as inclosed | Park | Objects of inclosure || Condition of inclosure ||||
								Inclosure of arable	Pasture	Lay lords of manors	Lay freeholders	Ecclesiastical lords of manors	Other ecclesiastics
P. 198	—	—	acres —	acres —	Thornborugh	acres 40	acr. —	acres 40	acr. —	—	—	—	1
	—	—	—	—	Shipden Lye	18	—	18	—	—	—	—	—
	—	—	—	—	Buorton and Buertonhold	21	—	—	21	—	1	—	—
	—	—	—	—	Stepyll Cleydon	90	—	90	—	—	—	—	1
	—	—	—	—	Cleydon	36	—	—	36	—	—	—	—
	2	1	[51]	15	[Adyngton]	15	—	15	—	—	—	—	—
	—	—	—	—	Adyngdon	15	—	15	—	—	—	—	—
	3	1	48	—	Whitwode	48	—	48	—	—	1	—	—
202					Bechampton	40	—	—	40	1	—	—	—
	6	1	66	—	Bechampton	10	—	—	10	1	—	—	—
					Bechampton	16	—	—	16	1	—	—	—
	—	—	—	15	Preston	15	—	15	—	—	1	—	—
	—	—	—	—	Hyllysden	4	4	—	—	—	1	—	—
	—	—	—	—	Shalweston	24	—	—	24	1	—	—	—
	—	—	—	—	Lekehamstede	16	—	—	16	1	—	—	—
	—	—	—	—	Lykehamstede	20	—	—	20	—	1	—	—
	—	—	—	—	Lekhamstede	30	—	—	30	1	—	—	—
	—	—	—	—	Galcotte	30	—	—	30	—	—	—	1
	—	—	—	—	Lechynburgh in Galcotte	60	—	—	60	—	1	—	—
	2	1	[98][1]	—	Magna Kembill	40	—	—	40	—	—	—	—
				[16]	Walton	—	—	—	—	—	—	—	—
206					(Walton)	—	—	—	—	—	—	—	—
					Chalfount St. Peter	80	—	—	80	1	—	—	—
	3	1	90	—									
					Chalfount St. Peter	10	—	—	10	1	—	—	—
	—	—	—	—	Ilmer	60	—	—	60	—	—	—	—
	2	1	246	—	Kyngyshey	100	—	—	100	—	1	—	—
					Kyngyshey	146	—	—	146	—	1	—	—
	2	1	100	—	Aston Molent	40	—	—	40	—	—	—	—
					Aston Molent	60	—	—	60	—	—	—	—
					Chesham	60	—	60	—	—	1	—	—
	3	1	220	—	Chesham	80	—	80	—	—	1	—	—
					Chesham	80	—	80	—	—	1	—	—

This represents [82] acres and

BUCKINGHAMSHIRE

THE INQUISITION OF 1517 FOR BUCKINGHAMSHIRE—(continued)

Displacement of population	Inclosures				Date of inclosure	Memorabilia
	Consequences of inclosure					
	No. of houses decayed	No. of churches decayed	Annual rental value			
			£ s. d.			
persons 4	1 messuagium	—	4 6 8		1496 (5 Nov.)	Incloser Abbot of Byttelsden, a freeholder
3	1 ,,	—	0 18 0		1505 (10 Mar.)	—
4	1 ,,	—	0 18 0		1486 (10 Nov.)	—
4	1 ,,	—	2 0 0		1507 (9 Oct.)	'de tribus virgatis ... qualibet virgata continente ... triginta acras.' Incloser Abbot of Osney, a freeholder
5	—	—	2 0 0		1507 (4 July)	No mention of a messuage
6	1 messuagium	—	0 10 0		1501 (not given)	Rental value of 15 acres only, being one of two hold:ngs
3	1 ,,	—	0 10 8		1512 (6 March)	—
12	3 messuagia	—	0 13 4		1509 (16 Feb.)	—
(12)	2 ,,	—	1 0 0		1509 (5 Jan.)	—
(3)	1 messuagium	—	(0 10 0)		1509 (6 Jan.)	This and the following rental grouped as 26s., and total evictions of the six inclosures as 20.
(5)	3 cotagia	—	(0 16 0)		1509 (6 Jan.)	
[2]	1 messuagium	—	1 0 0		1505 (10 June)	'de vna virgata ... continente in se quindecim acras'
—	—	—	0 2 0		1499 (6 Feb.)	'terre ille cum alio mesuagio ... demittuntur'
—	—	—	0 12 0		1513 (10 Jan.)	—
(3)	—	—	0 6 8		1508 (6 June)	The three inclosures here involved the putting down of four ploughs and the displacement from employment of twelve persons
(4)	—	—	1 0 0		1492 (19 Jan.)	
(5)	—	—	2 5 0		1508 (16 Mar)	
2	—	—	0 11 0		1496 (12 Dec.)	Inclosure of ecclesiastical glebe by the Rector
2	—	—	2 0 0		1500 (6 Nov.)	—
[6]	1 messuagium	—	2 0 0		1497 (10 Feb.)	—
—	—	—	4 0 0		1517	'tenet duas tenuras ad firmam'
(18)	(1 manerium)	—	0 16 0		1517	—
20	2 messuagia	—	6 13 6		1507 (14 Mar)	'de duabus carucatis ... qualibet carucata inde quadraginta acras ... continente'
—	—	—	0 5 0		1511 (6 Oct.)	—
6	—	—	1 0 0		1496 (6 Oct)	Incloser a leaseholder. No mention of a messuage
9	—	—	4 0 0		1496 (4 Nov.)	No mention of a messuage
9	1 messuagium	—	5 0 0		1490 (22 Feb.)	—
(4)	1 ,,	—	1 13 4		1505 (10 Mar.)	In the two inclosures ta' en together two ploughs put down and ten persons evicted
(6)	1 ,,	—	1 13 4		1505 (10 Mar.)	
(4)	1 ,,	—	2 0 0		1497 (20 Jan.)	In the three inclosures taken together fourteen persons evicted
(5)	1 ,,	—	2 6 8		1497 (20 Jan.)	
(5)	1 ,,	—	2 0 0		1491 (6 Mar.)	

llowing [16] acres consolidated with it.

II.

THE DOMESDAY OF INCLOSURES, 1517

I. GENERAL ANALYSIS OF THE CHANCER

Reference	Ingrossing of Farms				Parishes	Total areas presented as inclosed	Inclosures						
								Objects of inclosure		Condition of incloser			
	No. of farms ingrossed	No. of cases of ingrossing	Area ingrossed	Areas consolidated with farms			Park	Inclosure of arable	Pasture	Lay lords of manors	Lay free-holders	Ecclesiastical lords of manors	Other ecclesiastics
209	7 {	1	acres 280	acres —	Castelthorp . . .	acres 160	acr. —	acres —	acr. 160	1	—	—	—
				—	Castelthorp . . .	120	—	—	120	1	—	—	—
	6	1	360	300	Stanton Barey . .	360	—	—	360	1	—	—	—
	—	—	—	—	Stonystratford . .	40	—	40	—	—	1	—	—
	—	—	—	—	Wuluerton . . .	60	—	42	18	1	—	—	—
	2	1	60	—	Chessham . . .	60	—	—	60	—	1	—	—
	—	—	—	—	Prynces Rysborough .	20	—	—	20	—	1	—	—
	—	—	—	—	Magna Myssynden .	80	—	—	80	—	—	—	1
212	3 {	1	120	—	Broughton (Mentmore)	60	—	—	60	— —	—	—	—
				60	Broughton (Mentmore)	60	—	—	60	—	—	—	—
	—	—	—	—	Morsley . . .	20	—	—	20	—	—	—	—
	154	36	7905	813½	Totals	8985½	61	1662	7262½	21	47	2	7

BUCKINGHAMSHIRE

RETURNS OF THE INQUISITION OF 1517—(continued)

	Inclosures				
	Consequences of inclosure			Date of inclosure	Memorabilia
Displacement of population	No. of houses decayed	No. of churches decayed	Annual rental value		
persons (50)	1 principale messuagium manerii	—	£ s. d. (21 0 0)	1502 (16 Nov.)	'quatuor carucate . . . qualibet carucata inde quadraginta acras'
(38)	6 messuagia	—	(17 0 0)	1502 (16 Nov.)	In the two inclosures taken together ten ploughs put down and eighty-eight persons evicted, and total annual value 38*l*.
40	5 ,,	—	£20 increased to £30	1490 (7 Nov.)	The rental value includes *six* messuages, to which the area of 360 acres belongs
4	1 messuagium	—	not given	1501 (19 Mar.)	—
[8]	1 ,,	—	2 13 4	1507 (7 April)	Part of the land converted to pasture, part arable
[7]	2 messuagia	—	1 9 0	1497 (7 Jan.)	'cum quolibet eorundem mesuagiorum triginta acre'
—	—	—	0 10 0	1514 (7 March)	—
12	1 messuagium	—	2 10 0	1515 (4 March)	Incloser a farming Abbot of Myssynden
8	—	—	4 0 0	1511 (20 Oct.)	Inclosers of this and the next leaseholders for a term of forty years. These two inclosures caused the putting down of two ploughs and the evictions of eight persons. Sixty acres were attached to one messuage and 30 acres to each of two others
	2 messuagia	—		1511 (20 Oct.)	'duo mesuagia . . . in cotagia conuerterunt.' A cottage without land also held by inclosers
—	—	—	0 6 0	1514 (6 Nov.)	Incloser a leaseholder
1067+64 / 1131	164 mess. 4 maneria 10 cotagia 1 orreum	—	—	—	—

II

TABLE SHOWING THE HUNDREDS[1] FROM WHICH INCLOSURES ARE RETURNED

	LAY OWNERSHIP				ECCLESIASTICAL OWNERSHIP				
			Inclosures					Inclosures	
Hundred	Parish	Total area	Inclosures of arable	Conversions to pasture	Hundred	Parish	Total area	Inclosures of arable	Conversions to pasture
		acres	acres	acres			acres	acres	acres
Ashendon	Asshendon	60	—	60					
,,	Asshendon	100	—	100					
,,	{ Dodershill	960	—	960					
,,	{ Grendon	100	—	100					
,,	Ludgarshale	120	—	120					
,,	Ludgarshale	30	—	30					
,,	Flete Merston	140	—	140					
,,	Flete Merston	[184]	—	[184]					
,,	Waddesdon	30	10	20					
,,	Waddesdon	80	40	40					
,,	Middelclaydon	120	—	120					
,,	Cranwell	60	60	—					
,,	Cranwell	120	60	60	Ashendon	Overwynchendon	161	—	161
,,	Overwynchendon	10	—	10					
,,	Hoggeshawe and Fulbroke	213½	—	213½	,,	Fulbroke	151	—	151
,,	Fulbroke	16	—	16	,,	Shipden Lye	18	18	—
,,	Ilmer	60	—	60					
,,	Kyngyshey	100	—	100					
,,	Kyngyshey	146	—	146					
—	—	2649½	170	2479½	—	—	330	18	312
Cottesloe	Eddeslbrough	30	—	30					
,,	Byrdyston	400	—	400					
,,	Litilcote	201	—	201					
,,	Stutley	40	—	40					
,,	Litilcote	100	—	100					
,,	Donnyngton	90	—	'90					
,,	Donnyngton	90	—	90					
,,	Lyscome	80	—	80					
,,	Lyscombeholynden and Brakynham	40	—	40					
,,	Lyscombe Holynden and Brakynham	12	—	12					
,,	Lyscombe Holynden and Brakynham	30	—	30					

[1] As is shown by the Returns for Cheshire, and also by the Lansdowne MS., the original presentments were made by Hundreds.

BUCKINGHAMSHIRE

II. TABLE SHOWING THE HUNDREDS FROM WHICH INCLOSURES ARE RETURNED—(continued)

Lay Ownership					Ecclesiastical Ownership				
Hundred	Parish	Total area	Inclosures of arable	Conversions to pasture	Hundred	Parish	Total area	Inclosures of arable	Conversions to pasture
		acres	acres	acres			acres	acres	acres
Cottesloe .	Cublyngton and Bredyncote	20 [84]	—	20 [84]					
,, .	Aston and Hardwyke	100	100	—					
,, .	Broughton (Mentmore)	120	—	120					
					Cottesloe .	Morsley . .	20	—	20
—	—	1,437	100	1,337	—	—	20	—	20
Newport .	Ramston .	24	24	—					
,, .	Wyllyn . .	80	—	80	Newport .	Ramston .	48	48	—
,, .	Blecheley .	40	—	40					
,, .	Blecheley .	140	—	140					
,, .	Moulsowe .	20	—	20					
,, .	Woughton .	20	—	20	,, .	Moulsowe .	20	—	20
,, .	Stokehamond .	30	30	—					
,, .	Stokehamond .	30	30	—					
,, .	Walton . .	30	—	30					
,, .	Loughton .	20	—	20					
					,, .	Bradwell and Wuluerton	300	—	300
,, .	Wuluerton and Bradwell	40	—	40					
,, .	Wuluerton and Bradwell	25	—	25					
,, .	Tyrryngham .	30	—	30					
,, .	Tyrryngham and Philgrav.	47	—	47					
,, .	Gayhurst .	100	—	100					
,, .	Lathbere .	60	—	60					
,, .	Hanslap . .	26	—	26					
,, .	Wuluierston .	32	—	32					
,, .	Wuluierston .	140	140	—					
,, .	Castelthorp .	280	—	280					
,, .	Stanton Barey	360	—	360					
,, .	Stonystratford	40	40	—					
,, .	Wuluerton .	60	42	18					
—	—	1,674	306	1,368	—	—	368	48	320
Stoke .	Stoke Pewges	200	—	200					
,, .	Dytton . .	100	—	100					
,, .	Dytton . -	30	—	30					
,, .	Denham . .	24	—	24					
, .	Denham . .	20	20	—					

II. TABLE SHOWING THE HUNDREDS FROM WHICH INCLOSURES ARE RETURNED—(*continued*)

Lay Ownership					Ecclesiastical Ownership				
Hundred	Parish	Total area	Inclosures of arable	Conversions to pasture	Hundred	Parish	Total area	Inclosures of arable	Conversions to pasture
Stoke	(Denham)	acres 40	acres —	acres 40			acres	acres	acres
					Stoke	Denham[1]	[44]	—	[44]
,,	Vpton	30	30	—	,,	Vpton	27	27	—
,,	Vpton	80	80	—					
,,	Iver	50	—	50					
,,	Iver	50	50	—					
,,	Iver	50	50	—					
,,	Iver	40	40	—					
—	—	714	270	444	—	—	71	27	44
Burnham	Burnham	20	20	—					
,,	Burnham	100	100	—					
,,	Chalfount St. Peter	90	—	90					
,,	Chesham	220	220	—					
,,	Chessham	60	60	—					
—	—	490	400	90					
Desborough	Woburne	40	40	—					
,,	Wobourn	8	—	8					
—	—	48	40	8					
Aylesbury	Stone	40	40	—					
,,	Stone	20	20	—					
,,	Weston Turfild	160	—	160					
,,	Dynton	30	—	30					
,,	Magna Kembill	40	—	40					
,,	Aston Molent	40	—	40					
,,	Aston Molent	60	—	60					
,,	Prynces Rysborough	20	—	20					
,,	Magna Myssynden	80	—	80					
—	—	490	60	430					

[1] The incloser was an ingrosser of lay as well as of ecclesiastical land, but the inclosure appears to have been of part of the latter.

II. TABLE SHOWING THE HUNDREDS FROM WHICH INCLOSURES ARE RETURNED—(*continued*)

Lay Ownership					Ecclesiastical Ownership				
Hundred	Parish	Total area	Inclosures		Hundred	Parish	Total area	Inclosures	
			Inclosures of arable	Conversions to pasture				Inclosures of arable	Conversions to pasture
		acres	acres	acres			acres	acres	acres
Buckingham	Lyllyngton Darell	164	—	164					
,,	Buorton and Buertonhold	21	—	21	Buckingham	Thornborugh .	40	40	—
,,	Cleydon . .	36	—	36	,,	Stepyll Cleydon	90	90	—
,,	[Adyngton] .	15	15	—					
,,	Adyngdon .	15	15	—					
,,	Whitwode .	48	48	—					
,,	Bechampton .	66	—	66					
,,	Preston . .	15	15	—					
,,	Hyllysden .	4	—	4					
,,	Shalweston .	24	—	24					
,,	Lekehamstede	16	—	16					
,,	Lykehamstede	20	—	20					
,,	Lekhamstede .	30	—	30	,,	Galcotte . .	30	—	30
,,	Lechynburgh in Galcotte	60	—	60					
—	—	534	93	441	—	—	160	130	30

III

Analysis of the preceding Table, showing (1) the Areas of the Hundreds of the County and the Areas inclosed in each Hundred; (2) the Proportions of the Total Areas returned as Inclosed to the Total Areas of the Hundreds; (3) the Proportions of the Total Areas returned as Inclosed in each Hundred to the Total Areas of the several Hundreds; and (4) the Proportions of the Total Areas remaining Arable and Inclosed to Pasture in each Hundred

Hundred	Area of Hundred	Total area inclosed	Inclosures remaining arable	Conversions and inclosures to pasture	Proportion per cent. of total area inclosed to area of Hundred	Proportion per cent. of inclosures remaining arable to area of Hundred	Proportion per cent. of conversions and inclosures to pasture to area of Hundred
	acres	acres	acres	acres			
Ashendon	66,670	2,979½	188	2,791½	4·46	·28	4·18
Aylesbury (including borough)	63,650	490	60	430	·76	·09	·67
Buckingham (including borough)	56,230	694	223	471	1·23	·39	·83
Burnham	50,980	490	400	90	·95	·78	·17
Cottesloe	70,010	1,457	100	1,357	2·08	·14	1·93+
Desborough	52,370	48	40	8	·09	·07	·01+
Newport	75,770	2,042	354	1,688	2·69	·46	2·23+
Stoke	28,140	785	297	488	2·78	1·05	1·73
Totals	463,820 [1]	8,985½	1,662	7,323½	1·93	·35	1·57+

[1] Figures from the Census of 1831.

The Census appends the following note: 'The area of the county of Buckingham is 738 square miles, and consequently 472,320 acres, while the area herein assigned to the several parishes [sic] amounts to no more than 463,820 acres; but no attempt to reconcile the apparent discrepancy has been deemed allowable.' I have thought it best to assume the total of the areas of the Hundreds as correct. It may be that some parts included in the general limits of the county were not included in the Hundreds, but belonged to another county; which would account for the difference.

BUCKINGHAMSHIRE

IV

YEARLY PROGRESS OF INCLOSURES CLASSIFIED ACCORDING TO THE STATUS OF THE LANDLORDS RESPONSIBLE FOR THEM, AND SHOWING WHETHER LAND HELD IN HAND OF OWNER AT TIME OF INCLOSURE OR UPON WHAT TENANCY DEMISED.[1] INFERRED FIGURES INCLUDED

Year	Tenure or tenancy	Lay Ownership						Tenure or tenancy	Ecclesiastical Ownership					
		Parish	Hundred	Lords of manors		Freeholders			Parish	Hundred	Lords of manors		Freeholders	
				Arable	Pasture	Arable	Pasture				Arable	Pasture	Arable	Pasture
				acres	acres	acr.	acr.				acr.	acr.	acr.	acr.
1485		Nil												
1486	H.F.	Buorton & Buertonhold	Buckingham	—	—	—	21							
1487	H.M.	Blecheley	Newport	—	20	—	—							
1488		Nil												
1489	H.M.	Byrdyston	Cottesloe	—	60	—	—							
,,	H.M.	Byrdyston	,,	—	10	—	—							
,,	H.M.	Byrdyston	,,	—	12	—	—							
,,	H.M.	Byrdyston	,,	—	80	—	—							
,,	H.M.	Byrdyston	,,	—	(80)	—	—							
,,	H.M.	Byrdyston	,,	—	(79)	—	—							
,,	H.M.	Byrdyston	,,	—	(9)	—	—							
1490	H.M.	Blecheley	Newport	—	120	—	—							
,,	H.F.	Kyngyshey	Ashendon	—	—	—	146							
,,	H.M.	Stanton Barey	Newport	—	360	—	—							
1491	H.M.	Grendon	Ashendon	—	100	—	—							
,,	H.F.	Woughton	Newport	—	—	—	20							
,,	H.F.	Stokehamond	,,	—	—	30	—							
,,	H.M.	Lyllyngton Darell	Buckingham	—	164	—	—							
,,	H.F.	Chesham	Burnham	—	—	80	—							
1492	H.F.	Iver ..	Stoke .	—	—	—	50							
,,	H.F.	Lykehamstede	Buckingham	—	—	—	20							
1493		Nil												
1494	H.M.	Litilcote	Cottesloe	—	120	—	—							
1495	H.M.	Dodershill	Ashendon	—	960	—	—							
,,	L.	Middelclaydon	,,	—	120	—	—							
,,	H F.	Cranwell	,,	—	—	60	60							
,,	L.	Aston & Hardwyke	Cottesloe	—	—	100	—							
1496	H.M.	Cranwell	Ashendon	60	—	—	—							
,,	H.F.	Stokehamond	Newport	—	—	30	—							
,,	H.F.	Wuluerton and Bradwell	,,	—	—	—	40							
,,	L.	Stone .	Aylesbury	—	—	40	—							
,,								H.F.	Thornborugh	Buckingham	—	—	40	—

[1] H.M. = In hand of lord of manor; H.F. = In hand of freeholder; C. = Copyhold; L. = Leasehold; F.T. = Farm tenancy.

IV. YEARLY PROGRESS OF INCLOSURES CLASSIFIED—(*continued*)

Year	Tenure or tenancy	Lay Ownership			Lords of manors		Free-holders		Tenure or tenancy	Ecclesiastical Ownership			Lords of manors		Free-holders	
		Parish	Hundred	Arable	Pasture	Arable	Pasture		Parish	Hundred	Arable	Pasture	Arable	Pasture
				acres	acres	acr.	acr.				acr.	acr.	acr.	acr.
1496	L.	Ilmer	Ashendon	—	60	—	—	H.F.	Galcotte	Puckingham	—	—	—	30
,,	H.F.	Kyngyshey	,,	—	—	—	100							
1497	H.F.	Ramston	Newport	—	—	24	—							
,,	H.F.	Loughton	,,	—	—	—	20							
,,	F.T.	Magna Kembill	Aylesbury	—	—	—	40							
,,	H.F.	⎧Chesham	Burnham	—	—	60	—							
,,	H.F.	⎨Chesham	,,	—	—	80	—							
,,	H.F.	Chessham	,,	—	—	60	—							
1498	H.M.	Litilcote	Cottesloe	—	20	—	—							
,,	F.T.	Hoggeshawe	Ashendon	—	60	—	—							
,,	F.T.	Hoggeshawe	,,	—	16	—	—							
,,	F.T.	Hoggeshawe	,,	—	17½	—	—							
,,	F.T.	Hoggeshawe	,,	—	30	—	—							
,,	F.T.	Hoggeshawe	,,	—	20	—	—							
,,	F.T.	Fulbroke	,,	—	30	—	—							
,,	F.T.	Fulbroke	,,	—	20	—	—							
,,	F.T.	Fulbroke	,,	—	20	—	—							
,,								F.T.	Fulbroke	Ashendon	—	—	—	100
,,								F.T.	Fulbroke	,,	—	—	—	21
,,								F.T.	Fulbroke	,,	—	—	—	30
,,	H.F.	Fulbroke	Ashendon	—	—	—	16							
1499	H.M.	Litilcote	Cottesloe	—	21	—	—							
,,	F.T.	Dynton	Aylesb'y	—	—	—	30							
,,	H.F.	Hyllysden	Buckingham	—	—	—	4							
1500	F.T.	Asshendon	Ashendon	—	—	—	100							
,,	H.F.	Wuluierston	Newport	—	—	—	32							
,,	H.F.	Lechynburgh in Galcotte	Buckingham	—	—	—	60							
1501	H.F.	Waddesdon	Ashendon	—	—	40	40							
,,	H.M.	Wuluerton & Bradwell	Newport	—	25	—	—							
,,	H.F.	(Denham)	Stoke	—	—	—	40							
,,	H.F.	Vpton	,,	—	—	80	—							
,,	H.F.	Wuluierston	Newport	—	—	140	—							
,,	F.T	[Adyngton]	Buckingham	—	—	15	—							
,,	H.F.	Stonystratford	Newport	—	—	40	—							
1502	H.F.	Hanslap	,,	—	—	—	26							

BUCKINGHAMSHIRE

IV. Yearly Progress of Inclosures Classified—(continued)

| Year | Tenure or tenancy | Lay Ownership | | Lords of manors | | Free-holders | | Tenure or tenancy | Ecclesiastical Ownership | | Lords of manors | | Free-holders | |
		Parish	Hundred	Arable	Pasture	Arable	Pasture		Parish	Hundred	Arable	Pasture	Arable	Pasture
				acres	acres	acr.	acr.				acr.	acr.	acr.	acr.
1502	H.M.	Castelthorp	Newport	—	160	—	—							
,,	H.M.	Castelthorp	,,	—	120	—	—							
1503		Nil												
1504		Nil												
1505	H.F.	Stutley	Cottesloe	—	—	—	40							
,,	H.F.	Lyscombeholynden and Brakynham	,,	—	—	—	40							
,,								F.T.	Shipden Lye	Ashendon	18	—	—	—
,,	H.F.	Preston	Buckingham	—	—	15	—							
,,	F.T.	Aston Molent	Aylesbury	—	40	—	—	}						
,,	F.T.	Aston Molent	,,	—	—	—	60	}						
1506	H.F.	Eddesbrough	Cottesloe	—	—	—	30							
,,	H.F.	Lyscome	,,	—	—	—	80							
,,								H.F.	Moulsowe	Newport	—	—	—	20
,,	H.F.	Burnham	Burnham	—	—	20	—							
,,	L.	Burnham	,,	—	—	100	—							
,,	H.F.	Vpton	Stoke	—	—	30	—							
,,	H.F.	Iver	,,	—	—	50	—							
1507	H.M.	Litilcote	Cottesloe	—	40	—	—							
,,	H.F.	Litilcote	,,	—	—	—	100							
,,	H.M.	Flete Merston	Ashendon	—	[184]	—	—							
,,	H.F.	Waddesdon	,,	—	—	10	20							
,,								H.M.	Ramston	Newport	48	—	—	—
,,								H.M.	Bradwell and Wuluerton	,,	—	300	—	—
,,	H.F.	Wobourn	Desborough	—	—	—	8							
,,	H.F.	Iver	Stoke	—	—	50	—							
,,	H.F.	Iver	,,	—	—	40	—							
,,								H.F.	Stepyll Cleydon	Buckingham	—	—	90	—
,,	F.T.	Cleydon	Buckingham	—	36	—	—							
,,	H.M.	Chalfount St. Peter	Burnham	—	80	—	—							
,,	H.M.	Wuluerton	Newport	42	18	—	—							
1508	F.T.	Asshendon	Ashendon	—	—	—	40	}						
,,	F.T.	Asshendon	,,	—	—	—	20	}						

IV. YEARLY PROGRESS OF INCLOSURES CLASSIFIED—(*continued*)

Year	Tenure or tenancy	Lay Ownership					Tenure or tenancy	Ecclesiastical Ownership				
		Parish	Hundred	Lords of manors		Freeholders			Parish	Hundred	Lords of manors		Freeholders	
				Arable	Pasture	Arable	Pasture				Arable	Pasture	Arable	Pasture
				acres	acres	acr.	acr.				acr.	acr.	acr.	acr.
1508	H.M.	Lekehamstede	Buckingham	—	16	—	—							
,,	H.M.	Lekehamstede	,,	—	30	—	—							
1509	H.F.	Lyscombeholynden and Brakynham	Cottesloe	—	—	—	12							
,,	H.F.	Cublyngton	,,	—	—	—	20							
,,	H.F.	Moulsowe	Newport	—	—	—	20							
,,	H.F.	Denham	Stoke	—	—	—	24							
,,	H.M.	Tyrryngham	Newport	—	30	—	—							
,,	H.M.	Tyrryngham and Philgrav	,,	—	47	—	—							
,,	H.F.	Whitwode	Buckingham	—	—	48	—							
,,	H.M.	Bechampton	,,	—	40	—	—							
,,	H.M.	Bechampton	,,	—	10	—	—							
,,	H.M.	Bechampton	,,	—	16	—	—							
1510		Nil												
1511	H.M.	Flete Merston	Ashendon	—	140	—	—							
,,	L.[1]	Wyllyn	Newport	—	—	—	80							
,,	H.M.	Stoke Pewges	Stoke	—	200	—	—							
,,	L.	Stone	Aylesbury	20	—	—	—							
,,	H.M.	Chafount St. Peter	Burnham	—	10	—	—							
,,	L.	Broughton (Mentmore)	Cottesloe	—	60	—	—							
,,	L.	Broughton (Mentmore)	,,	—	60	—	—							
1512	F.T.	Adyngdon	Buckingham	—	—	15	—							
1513	H.F.	Cublyngton and Bredyncote	Cottesloe	—	—	—	[84]							
,,	L.	Dytton	Stoke	—	100	—	—							
,,	H.M.	Shalweston	Buckingham	—	24	—	—							
1514	H.F.	Ludgarshale	Ashendon	—	—	—	120							
,,	H.F.	Ludgarshale	,,	—	—	—	30							

[1] A fee farm.

BUCKINGHAMSHIRE

IV. YEARLY PROGRESS OF INCLOSURES CLASSIFIED—(continued)

Year	Tenure or tenancy	Lay Ownership		Lords of manors		Freeholders		Tenure or tenancy	Ecclesiastical Ownership		Lords of manors		Freeholders	
		Parish	Hundred	Arable	Pasture	Arable	Pasture		Parish	Hundred	Arable	Pasture	Arable	Pasture
				acres	acres	acr.	acr.				acr.	acr.	acr.	acr.
1514								C.	Overwynchendon	Ashendon	—	30	⎫ —	—
,,								C.	Overwynchendon	Ashendon	—	131	⎬ —	—
,,	H.F.	Overwynchendon	Ashendon	—	—	—	10						⎭	
,,	H.F.	Denham	Stoke	—	—	20	—	H.F.	Vpton	Stoke	—	—	27	—
,,	H.F.	Prynces Rysborough	Aylesbury	—	—	—	20							
,,								L.	Morsley	Cottesloe	—	—	—	20
1515	H.F.	Donnyngton	Cottesloe	—	—	—	30							
,,	H.F.	Donnyngton	,,	—	—	—	30							
,,	H.F.	Donnyngton	,,	—	—	—	30							
,,	F.T.	Donnyngton	,,	—	90	—	—							
,,	H.F.	Lyscome Holynden and Brakynham	,,	—	—	—	30							
,,	F.T.	Magna Myssynden	Aylesbury	—	—	—	80							
1516	H.M.	Walton	Newport	—	30	—	—							
,,	L.	Dytton	Stoke	—	—	—	30							
,,	H.M.	Gayhurst	Newport	—	100	—	—							
,,	H.F.	Lathbere	,,	—	—	—	60	F.T.	Denham[1]	Stoke	—	—	—	[44]
1517														
,,	L.	Weston Turfild	Aylesbury[2]	—	—	—	160							
—	—	—	—	122	4384½[3]	1277[3]	2173	—	—	—	66	461	157	265

[1] The incloser was an ingrosser as well of lay as of ecclesiastical land, but the inclosure appears to have been of part of the latter.
[2] The above entries number 140. The total entries in Table I. = 142. From these last must be deducted an inclosure of 40 acres at Blecheley and one of 40 acres at Woburne, the dates of which are illegible.
[3] 40 less than corresponding total in Table V., owing to 40 acres inclosed of date not ascertained.

	acres		acres
Total lay arable	1,399	Total ecclesiastical arable	223
Total lay pasture	6,557½	Total ecclesiastical pasture	726
	7,956½		949

	acres
Total arable	1,622
Total pasture	7,283½
	8,905½

IV. YEARLY PROGRESS OF INCLOSURES CLASSIFIED ACCORDING TO THE STATUS OF THE LANDLORDS ULTIMATELY RESPONSIBLE FOR THEM. ALL INFERRED AND DOUBTFUL CASES INCLUDED

Year	Lay ownership		Ecclesiastical ownership		Totals	
	Arable	Pasture	Arable	Pasture	Arable	Pasture
	acres	acres	acres	acres	acres	acres
1485	—	—	—	—	—	—
1486	—	21	—	—	—	21
1487	—	20	—	—	—	20
1488	—	—	—	—	—	—
1489	—	400	—	—	—	400
1490	—	626	—	—	—	626
1491	110	284	—	—	110	284
1492	—	70	—	—	—	70
1493	—	—	—	—	—	—
1494	—	120	—	—	—	120
1495	160	1,140	—	—	160	1,140
1496	130	200	40	30	170	230
1497	224	60	—	—	224	60
1498	—	249½	—	151	—	400½
1499	—	55	—	—	—	55
1500	—	192	—	—	—	192
1501	315	105	—	—	315	105
1502	—	306	—	—	—	306
1503	—	—	—	—	—	—
1504	—	—	—	—	—	—
1505	15	180	18	—	33	180
1506	200	110	—	20	200	130
1507	142	486	138	300	280	786
1508	—	106	—	—	—	106
1509	48	219	—	—	48	219
1510	—	—	—	—	—	—
1511	20	550	—	—	20	550
1512	15	—	—	—	15	—
1513	—	208	—	—	—	208
1514	20	180	27	181	47	361
1515	—	290	—	—	—	290
1516	—	220	—	—	—	220
1517	—	160	—	44	—	204
	1,399	6,557½	223	726	1,622	7,283½

BUCKINGHAMSHIRE

Decennial Progress of Inclosures classified according to the Status of the Landlords ultimately responsible for them. All Inferred and Doubtful Cases included

Years	Lay ownership		Ecclesiastical ownership		Totals	
	Arable	Pasture	Arable	Pasture	Arable	Pasture
	acres	acres	acres	acres	acres	acres
1485–1490	—	1,067	—	—	—	1,067
1491–1500	624	2,370½	40	181	664	2,551½
1501–1510	720	1,512	156	320	876	1,832
1511–1517	55	1,608	27	225	82	1,833
	1,399	6,557½	223	726	1,622	7,283½

Percentage of Increase and Decrease of Inclosure

Years	Lay ownership		Ecclesiastical ownership		Totals	
	Arable	Pasture	Arable	Pasture	Arable	Pasture
1485–1490	—	—	—	—	—	—
1491–1500	—	+122·16	—	—	—	+139·12
1501–1510	+15·38	−34·01	+290	+76·79	+31·92	−28·19
1511–1517	−92·36	+6·34	−82·69	−29·68	−90·63	+·05

Percentage of Total Increase and Decrease of Inclosure

Years	Per cent.
1485–1490	—
1491–1500	+201·35
1501–1510	−15·47
1511–1517	−28·87

V

NUMBER OF INCLOSURES AND DISTRIBUTION OF AREAS INCLOSED ACCORDING TO TENURES AND TENANCIES. INFERRED FIGURES INCLUDED

I. Land in hands of lords of manors

	LAY OWNERSHIP					ECCLESIASTICAL OWNERSHIP			
No. of inclosures[1]	Parish	Total	Arable	Pasture	No. of inclosures	Parish	Total	Arable	Pasture
		acres	acres	acres			acres	acres	acres
8	Byrdyston	400	—	400					
16	Dodershill	960	—	960					
1	Grendon	100	—	100					
(3)	Litilcote	120	—	120					
1	Litilcote	21	—	21					
1	Litilcote	20	—	20					
1	Litilcote	40	—	40					
4	Flete Merston	140	—	140					
4	Flete Merston	[184]	—	[184]					
3	Cranwell	60	60	—					
					2	Ramston	48	48	—
2	Blecheley	40	—	40					
2	Blecheley	120	—	120					
	Blecheley	20	—	20					
1	Walton	30	—	30					
					4	Bradwell and Wuluerton	300	—	300
1	Wuluerton and Bradwell	25	—	25					
2	Stoke Pewges	200	—	200					
1	Tyrryngham	30	—	30					
1	Tyrryngham and Philgrav	47	—	47					
1	Gayhurst	100	—	100					
8	Lyllyngton Darell	164	—	164					
2	Bechampton	40	—	40					
1	Bechampton	10	—	10					
3	Bechampton	16	—	16					
1	Shalweston	24	—	24					
1	Lekehamstede	16	—	16					
1	Lekehamstede	30	—	30					

[1] The principle adopted has been to reckon inclosures by the number of ploughs put down, a half plough being reckoned as one inclosure; but where no ploughs are mentioned, the number is supplied from that of the houses destroyed; where neither is returned, the inclosure is reckoned as one, unless otherwise specified in the text.

V. Number of Inclosures, &c.—(continued)

I. Land in hands of lords of manors—(continued)

No. of inclosures	Parish	Lay Ownership			No. of inclosures	Parish	Ecclesiastical Ownership		
		Total acres	Arable acres	Pasture acres			Total acres	Arable acres	Pasture acres
2	Chalfount St. Peter	80	—	80					
1	Chafount St. Peter	10	—	10					
1	Castelthorp .	160	—	160					
6	Castelthorp .	120	—	120					
5	Stanton Barey .	360	—	360					
1	Wuluerton ,	60	42	18					
88	Totals .	3747	102	3645	6		348	48	300

II. Land in hands of freeholders

No. of inclosures	Parish	Lay Ownership			No. of inclosures	Parish	Ecclesiastical Ownership		
		Total acres	Arable acres	Pasture acres			Total acres	Arable acres	Pasture acres
1	Eddeslbrough .	30	—	30					
1	Stutley . .	40	—	40					
1	Litilcote . .	100	—	100					
1	Donnyngton .	30	—	30					
1	Donnyngton .	30	—	30					
1	Donnyngton .	30	—	30					
3	Ludgarshale ,	120	—	120					
1	Ludgarshale .	30	—	30					
4	Lyscome . .	80	—	80					
1	Lyscombeholynden and Brakynham	40	—	40					
1	Lyscombeholynden and Brakynham	12	—	12					
1	Lyscome Holynden and Brakynham	30	—	30					
1	Waddesdon .	30	10	20					
2	Waddesdon .	80	40	40					
1	Cublyngton .	20	—	20					
2	Cublyngton and Bredyncote	[84]	—	[84]					

II.

P

V. Number of Inclosures, &c.—(continued)

II. Land in hands of freeholders—(continued)

	Lay Ownership					Ecclesiastical Ownership			
No. of inclosures	Parish	Total	Arable	Pasture	No. of inclosures	Parish	Total	Arable	Pasture
		acres	acres	acres			acres	acres	acres
1	Cranwell . .	120	60	60					
1	Overwynchendon	10	—	10					
1	Ramston . .	24	24	—					
1	Moulsowe .	20	—	20					
					1	Moulsowe .	20	—	20
1	Woughton .	20	—	20					
1	Stokehamond .	30	30	—					
1	Stokehamond .	30	30	—					
1	Loughton .	20	—	20					
1	Wuluerton and Bradwell	40	—	40					
1	Burnham . .	20	20	—					
1	Woburne . .	40	40	—					
1	Wobourn . .	8	—	8					
1	Denham . .	24	—	24					
1	Denham . .	20	20	—					
1	(Denham) .	40	—	40					
					1	Vpton . .	27	27	—
1	Vpton . .	30	30	—					
1	Vpton . .	80	80	—					
1	Iver . .	50	—	50					
1	Iver . .	50	50	—					
1	Iver . .	50	50	—					
1	Iver . .	40	40	—					
1	Fulbroke . .	16	—	16					
1	Lathbere . .	60	—	60					
1	Hanslap . .	26	—	26					
1	Wuluierston .	32	—	32					
7	Wuluierston .	140	140	—					
					1	Thornborugh .	40	40	—
1	Buorton and Buertonhold	21	—	21					
					1	Stepyll Cleydon	90	90	—
3	Whitwode .	48	48	—					
1	Preston . .	15	15	—					
1	Hyllysden .	4	—	4					
1	Lykehamstede .	20	—	20					
					1	Galcotte .	30	—	30
1	Lechyngburgh in Galcotte	60	—	60					

BUCKINGHAMSHIRE

V. NUMBER OF INCLOSURES, &C.—(*continued*)

II. Land in hands of freeholders—(*continued*)

	LAY OWNERSHIP				ECCLESIASTICAL OWNERSHIP			
No. of inclosures	Parish	Total	Arable	Pasture	No. of inclosures	Parish	Total	Arable	Pasture
		acres	acres	acres			acres	acres	acres
1	Kyngyshey	100	—	100					
1	Kyngyshey	146	—	146					
1	Chesham	60	60	—					
1	Chesham	80	80	—					
1	Chesham	80	80	—					
1	Stonystratford	40	40	—					
1	Chessham	60	60	—					
1	Prynces Rysborough	20	—	20					
72	Totals	2580	1047	1533	5		207	157	50

III. Copyholds

	LAY OWNERSHIP				ECCLESIASTICAL OWNERSHIP			
No. of inclosures	Parish	Total	Arable	Pasture	No. of inclosures	Parish	Total	Arable	Pasture
		acres	acres	acres			acres	acres	acres
					2	Overwynchendon	161	—	161
					2		161	0	161

IV. Leaseholds

	LAY OWNERSHIP				ECCLESIASTICAL OWNERSHIP			
No. of inclosures	Parish	Total	Arable	Pasture	No. of inclosures	Parish	Total	Arable	Pasture
		acres	acres	acres			acres	acres	acres
2	Middelclaydon	120	—	120					
2	Wyllyn [1]	80	—	80					
1	Aston and Hardwyke	100	100	—					
1	Dytton	100	—	100					
1	Dytton	30	—	30					
3	Burnham	100	100	—					
1	Stone	40	40	—					
1	Stone	20	20	—					
1	Weston Turfild	160	—	160					

[1] A fee farm.

V. NUMBER OF INCLOSURES, &C.—(continued)

IV. Leaseholds—(continued)

	LAY OWNERSHIP				ECCLESIASTICAL OWNERSHIP				
No. of inclosures	Parish	Total acres	Arable acres	Pasture acres	No. of inclosures	Parish	Total acres	Arable acres	Pasture acres
1	Ilmer	60	—	60					
1	Broughton (Mentmore)	60	—	60					
1	Broughton (Mentmore)	60	—	60					
					1	Morsley	20	—	20
16		930	260	670	1		20	0	20

V. Farm tenancies

	LAY OWNERSHIP				ECCLESIASTICAL OWNERSHIP				
No. of inclosures	Parish	Total acres	Arable acres	Pasture acres	No. of inclosures	Parish	Total acres	Arable acres	Pasture acres
1	Asshendon[1]	40	—	40					
1	Asshendon[1]	20	—	20					
2	Asshendon[1]	100	—	100					
3	Donnyngton	90	—	90					
					1	Denham[2]	[44]	—	[44]
1	Dynton	30	—	30					
8	Hoggeshawe and Fulbroke[3]	213½	—	213½					
					3	Fulbroke	151	—	151
					1	Shipden Lye	18	18	—
1	Cleydon	36	—	36					
1	[Adyngton]	15	15	—					
1	[Adyngdon]	15	15	—					
1	Magna Kembill	40	—	40					
1	Aston Molent	40	—	40					
1	Aston Molent	60	—	60					
1	Magna Myssynden[4]	80	—	80					
23		779½	30	749½	5		213	18	195

[1] Lay freehold farmed and inclosed by an ecclesiastic, Abbot of Notley.
[2] The incloser is an ingrosser of lay as well as of ecclesiastical land, but the inclosure appears to belong to the latter.
[3] On the total 363½ acres, 9 ploughs are put down. As the plough is taken as the primary index of the area of inclosure, I have reckoned the whole as 9 inclosures, proportionately distributed.
[4] Lay freehold farmed by the Abbot of Myssynden.

V. Number of Inclosures, &c.—(*continued*)
General Total

	Lay Ownership				Ecclesiastical Ownership			
No. of inclosures	Parish	Total acres	Arable acres	Pasture acres	No. of inclosures	Parish	Total acres	Arable acres	Pasture acres
199		8036½	1439	6597½	19		949	223	726

Total arable 1,652
Total pasture 7,323½

Summary of the Distribution of Areas according to Tenures and Tenancies. Inferred Areas included

A. TENURES
I. Land in owners' hands

	Lay			Ecclesiastical		
	Total area acres	Percentage of total area in lay owners' hands		Total area acres	Percentage of total area in ecclesiastical owners' hands
1. In hands of lay lords of manors .	3,747	59·22	1. In hands of ecclesiastical lords of manors	348	62·70
2. In hands of lay freeholders .	2,580	40·77	2. In hands of ecclesiastical freeholders .	207	37·29
	6,327	99·99		555	99·99

II. Total areas held in hand by both lay and ecclesiastical owners, and proportions per cent. of total areas so held in hand by lay and ecclesiastical owners respectively

	Total area acres	In hands of lay lords of manors acres	In hands of ecclesiastical lords of manors acres	Proportion per cent. in hands of lay lords of manors	Proportion per cent. in hands of ecclesiastical lords of manors
1. In hands of lords of manors . .	4,095	3,747	348	91·50	8·49

	Total area acres	In hands of lay freeholders acres	In hands of ecclesiastical freeholders acres	Proportion per cent. in hands of lay freeholders	Proportion per cent. in hands of ecclesiastical freeholders
2. In hands of freeholders . .	2,787	2,580	207	92·57	7·42

598   THE DOMESDAY OF INCLOSURES, 1517

V. NUMBER OF INCLOSURES, &C.—(continued)

	Total area	In hands of lay owners	In hands of ecclesiastical owners	Proportion per cent. in hands of lay owners	Proportion per cent. in hands of ecclesiastical owners
	acres	acres	acres		
3. Totals in hands of lords of manors and freeholders	6,882	6,327	555	91·93	8·06

B. TENANCIES
III. Lands let in hands of tenants

LAY			ECCLESIASTICAL		
	Total area	Proportion of total area of lay land let		Total area	Proportion of total area of ecclesiastical land let
	acres			acres	
1. Copyholds	—	—		161	40·86
2. Leaseholds	930	54·40		20	5·07
3. Farm tenancies	779½	45·59		213	54·06
Total area of lay land let	1,709½	99·99	Total area of ecclesiastical land let	394	99·99

IV. Proportion per cent. of total areas of land in hands of owners and land let to tenants respectively

LAY			ECCLESIASTICAL		
	Total area	Proportion per cent.		Total area	Proportion per cent.
	acres			acres	
1. Land in owners' hands	6,327	78·72		555	58·48
2. Land let to tenants	1,709½	21·27		394	41·51
	8,036½	99·99		949	99·99

V. Total areas and relative proportion per cent. of lay and ecclesiastical lands

Total area	LAY		ECCLESIASTICAL	
	Total area	Proportion per cent.	Total area	Proportion per cent.
acres	acres		acres	
8,985½	8,036½	89·43	949	10·56

V. Number of Inclosures, &c.—(*continued*)

Summary of Numbers and Areas of Inclosures of Arable and Pasture according to Tenures and Tenancies

	Lay									Ecclesiastical								
	Arable			Pasture			Total arable and pasture			Arable			Pasture			Total arable and pasture		
	No. of inclosures	Area	Average area of inclosures	No. of inclosures	Area	Average area of inclosures	No. of inclosures	Area	Average area of inclosures	No. of inclosures	Area	Average area of inclosures	No. of inclosures	Area	Average area of inclosures	No. of inclosures	Area	Average area of inclosures
I. Land in owners' hands																		
1. Lords of manors	4	acres 102	acres 25·5	84	acres 3,645	acres 43·55	88	acres 3,747	acres 42·57	2	acres 48	acres 24	4	acres 300	acres 75	6	acres 348	acres 58
2. Freeholders	32	1,047	32·71	44	1,533	34·84	76[1]	2,580	33·94	3	157	52·3	2	50	25	5	207	41·4
II. Land let																		
1. Copyholds	—	—	—	—	—	—	—	—	—	—	—	—	2	161	80·5	2	161	80·5
2. Leaseholds	6	260	43·3	10	670	67	16	930	58·1	—	—	—	1	20	20	1	20	20
3. Farm tenancies	2	30	15	21	749½	35·69	23	779½	33·89	1	18	18	4	195	48·75	5	213	42·6
III. Totals and Total Averages							203[1]	8,036½	39·58							19	949	49·94

IV. Totals of lay and ecclesiastical land together • • • No. of inclosures 222 • • Area acres 8,985½ • Average area of inclosures acres 40·47

[1] Inclosures by lay freeholders here appear as 76 *vice* 72, the total arrived at above, by reason of 4 inclosures to both arable *and* pasture together.

VI.

Status of Landlords responsible for Inclosure, Objects
from Labour.[1]

		Lay Ownership					
Parish	Hundred	Total	Inclosures of arable	Parks and inclosures to pasture	No. of persons evicted	No. of persons displaced from labour	Lord of manor
		acres	acres	acres			
Asshendon	Ashendon	60	—	60	20	—	—
Asshendon	,,	100	—	100	16	—	—
Eddeslbrough	Cottesloe	30	—	30	—	—	—
Byrdyston	,,	400	—	400	60	—	1
{ Dodershill	Ashendon	960	—	960	120 }	—	1
{ Grendon	,,	100	—	100	5 }	—	
Litilcote	Cottesloe	201	—	201	24	—	2
Stutley	,,	40	—	40	—	—	—
Litilcote	,,	100	—	100	¦ 8	—	—
Donnyngton	,,	90	—	90	12	—	—
Donnyngton	,,	90	—	90	—	—	1
Ludgarshale	Ashendon	120	—	120	20	—	—
Ludgarshale	,,	30	—	30	4	—	—
Lyscome	Cottesloe	80	—	80	30	—	—
Lyscombeholynden and Brakynham	,,	40	—	40	—	5	—
Lyscombe Holynden and Brakynham	,,	12	—	12	—	—	—
Lyscombe Holynden and Brakynham	,,	30	—	30	[4]	—	—
{ Flete Merston [2]	Ashendon	140	—	140	20	—	1 [3]
{ Flete Merston	,,	[184]	—	[184]	(25)	—	(1)
Waddesdon	,,	30	10	20	8	—	—
Waddesdon	,,	80	40	40	8	—	—
Cublyngton	Cottesloe	20	—	20	—	—	—
Cublyngton and Bredyncote	,,	[84]	—	[84]	6	—	—
Middelclaydon	Ashendon	120	—	120	—	5	1
Cranwell	,,	60	60	—	6	—	1
Cranwell	,,	120	60	60	[15]	—	—
Overwynchendon	,,	10	—	10	—	—	—
Ramston	Newport	24	24	—	[3]	—	—
Wyllyn	,,	80	—	80	10	—	
Blecheley	,,	40	—	40	8	—	} 1
Blecheley	,,	140	—	140	10	—	

[1] The total evictions &c. on all accounts appear in Table I., but in order to arrive at acc
consolidation and ingrossing (as at Walton, *infra*) are excluded from
[2] Two lords of the manor engaged in successive inclosures, but the evi
[3] For statistical purposes I treat these inclosures as by the lord of the m

BUCKINGHAMSHIRE

VI.

CLOSURE, AND NUMBER OF PERSONS EVICTED AND DISPLACED
*ERRED FIGURES INCLUDED

Parish	Hundred	Total	Inclosures of arable	Parks and inclosures to pasture	No. of persons evicted	No. of persons displaced from labour	Landlord responsible	
							Lord of manor	Freeholder
		acres	acres	acres				
wynchendon	Ashendon	161	—	161	10	—	1	—
ston	Newport	48	48	—	4	—	1	—

ges of evictions specifically associated with inclosure, such as belong to cases returned for
. These two latter classes do not comprise many cases.
ouped together in the Returns. Similarly with Donnyngton.
gh two freeholders acted with him—it is not clear in what capacity.

THE DOMESDAY OF INCLOSURES, 1517

VI. STATUS OF LANDLORDS RESPONSI[BLE]

	Lay Ownership						
Parish	Hundred	Total	Inclosures of arable	Parks and inclosures to pasture	No. of persons evicted	No. of persons displaced from labour	Lord of manor
Moulsowe	Newport	acres 20	acres —	acres 20	6	—	—
Woughton	,,	20	—	20	4	—	—
Stokehamond	,,	30	30	—	2	—	—
Stokehamond	,,	30	30	—	2	—	—
Walton	,,	30	—	30	4	—	I
Loughton	,,	20	—	20	[3]	—	—
Wuluerton and Bradwell	,,	40	—	40	[5]	—	—
Wuluerton and Bradwell	,,	25	—	25	—	—	I
Aston and Hardwyke	Cottesloe	100	100	—	—	—	—
Stoke Pewges	Stoke	200	—	200	12	—	I
Dytton	,,	100	—	100	2	—	I
Dytton	,,	30	—	30	3	—	—
Burnham	Burnham	20	20	—	2	—	—
Burnham	,,	100	100	—	12	—	—
Woburne	Desborough	40	40	—	6	—	—
Wobourn	,,	8	—	8	—	—	—
Stone	Aylesbury	40	40	—	6	—	—
Stone	,,	20	20	—	4	—	I
Denham	Stoke	24	—	24	8	—	—
Denham	,,	20	20	—	4	—	—
(Denham)	,,	40	—	40	6	—	—
Weston Turfild	Aylesbury	160	—	160	8	—	—
Vpton	Stoke	30	30	—	3	—	—
Vpton	,,	80	80	—	4	—	—
Iver	,,	50	—	50	2	—	—
Iver	,,	50	50	—	8	—	—
Iver	,,	50	50	—	8	—	—
Iver	,,	40	40	—	8	—	—
Dynton	Aylesbury	30	—	30	7	—	—
Hoggeshawe and Fulbroke	Ashendon	213½	—	213½	(35)	—	I
Fulbroke	,,	16	—	16	—	—	—
Tyrryngham	Newport	30	—	30	[4]	—	I
Tyrryngham and Philgrav	,,	47	—	47	[7]	—	

[1] The incloser was an ingrosser of lay as well as of ecclesia[stical]

BUCKINGHAMSHIRE

R INCLOSURE, &C.—(*continued*)

Parish	Hundred	Ecclesiastical Ownership					Landlord responsible	
		Total	Inclosures of arable	Parks and inclosures to pasture	No. of persons evicted	No. of persons displaced from labour	Lord of manor	Freeholder
ulsowe	Newport	acres 20	acres —	acres 20	2	—	—	1
dwell and Wulerton	Newport	300	—	300	—	20	1	—
ham [1]	Stoke	[44]	—	[44]	(12)	—	—	1
on	,,	27	27	—	3	—	—	1
roke	Ashendon	151	—	151	(25)	—	—	1

but the inclosure appears to have been of part of the latter.

VI. Status of Landlords Responsi[ble]

		Lay Ownership					
Parish	Hundred	Total	Inclosures of arable	Parks and inclosures to pasture	No. of persons evicted	No. of persons displaced from labour	Lord of manor
		acres	acres	acres			
Gayhurst	Newport	100	—	100	[14]	—	1
Lathbere	,,	60	—	60	—	—	—
Hanslap	,,	26	—	26	3	—	—
Wuluierston	,,	32	—	32	—	3	—
Wuluierston	,,	140	140	—	20	—	—
Lyllyngton Darell	Buckingham	164	—	164	40	—	1
Buorton and Buertonhold	,,	21	—	21	4	—	—
Cleydon	,,	36	—	36	5	—	1
[Adyngton]	,,	15	15	—	6	—	—
Adyngdon	,,	15	15	—	3	—	—
Whitwode	,,	48	48	—	12	—	—
Bechampton	,,	66	—	66	20	—	1
Preston	,,	15	15	—	[2]	—	—
Hyllysden	,,	4	—	4	—	—	—
Shalweston	,,	24	—	24	—	—	1
Lekehamstede	,,	16	—	16	—	(3)	1
Lykehamstede	,,	20	—	20	—	(4)	—
Lekhamstede	,,	30	—	30	—	(5)	1
Lechynburgh in Galcotte	,,	60	—	60	—	2	—
Magna Kembill	Aylesbury	40	—	40	[6]	—	—
Chalfount St. Peter	Burnham	90	—	90	20	—	1
Ilmer	Ashendon	60	—	60	—	6	1
Kyngyshey	,,	100	—	100	—	9	—
Kyngyshey	,,	146	—	146	9	—	—
Aston Molent	Aylesbury	40	—	40	(4)	—	1
Aston Molent	,,	60	—	60	(6)	—	—
Chesham	Burnham	220	220	—	14	—	—
Castelthorp	Newport	280	—	280	88	—	1
Stanton Barey	,,	360	—	360	40	—	1
Stonystratford	,,	40	40	—	4	—	—
Wuluerton	,,	60	42	18	[8]	—	1
Chessham	Burnham	60	60	—	[7]	—	—
Prynces Rysborough	Aylesbury	20	—	20	—	—	—
Magna Myssynden	,,	80	—	80	12	—	—
Broughton (Mentmore)	Cottesloe	120	—	120	8	—	1
Totals		8,036½	1,439	6,597½	982	42	30

BUCKINGHAMSHIRE

R INCLOSURE, &C.—(*continued*)

| Parish | Hundred | ECCLESIASTICAL OWNERSHIP ||||| Landlord responsible ||
		Total	Inclosures of arable	Parks and inclosures to pasture	No. of persons evicted	No. of persons displaced from labour	Lord of manor	Freeholder
		acres	acres	acres				
rnborough . .	Buckingham .	40	40	—	4	—	—	1
oden Lye . .	Ashendon .	18	18	—	3	—	1	—
oyll Cleydon .	Buckingham .	90	90	—	4	—	—	1
cotte . . .	Buckingham .	30	—	30	—	2	—	1
sley . . .	Cottesloe . .	20	—	20	—	—	—	1
tals . . .		949	223	726	67	22	4	8

VI. STATUS OF LANDLORDS RESPONSIBLE

LAY OWNERSHIP				ECCLESIASTICAL OWNERSHIP			
Arable inclosed		Pasture inclosed		Arable inclosed		Pasture inclosed	
Total arable inclosed on land of lords of manors	Total arable inclosed on land of freeholders	Total pasture inclosed on land of lords of manors	Total pasture inclosed on land of freeholders	Total arable inclosed on land of lords of manors	Total arable inclosed on land of freeholders	Total pasture inclosed on land of lords of manors	Total pasture inclosed on land of freeholders
acres 122	acres 1,317	acres 4,424½	acres 2,173	acres 66	acres 157	acres 461	acres 265
1,439		6,597½		223		726	

PROPORTIONATE ANALYSIS OF THE ABOVE

Proportion per cent. of total arable inclosed on lay land		Proportion per cent. of total pasture inclosed on lay land		Proportion per cent. of total arable inclosed on ecclesiastical land		Proportion per cent. of total pasture inclosed on ecclesiastical land	
8·47	91·52	67·06	32·93	29·59	70·40	63·49	36·50

Total arable inclosed	Proportion per cent. of arable inclosed to total area inclosed	Total pasture inclosed	Proportion per cent. of pasture inclosed to total area inclosed
acres 1,662	18·4	acres 7,323½	81·5

Proportion per cent. of lay arable inclosed to total arable inclosed	Proportion per cent. of lay pasture inclosed to total pasture inclosed	Proportion per cent. of ecclesiastical arable inclosed to total arable inclosed	Proportion per cent. of ecclesiastical pasture inclosed to total pasture inclosed
86·58	90·08	13·41	9·91

Total inclosures	Total lay land inclosed	Total ecclesiastical land inclosed
acres 8,985½	acres 8,036½	acres 949

BUCKINGHAMSHIRE

FOR INCLOSURE, &C.—(continued)

Proportion per cent. of lay land inclosed to total inclosures	Proportion per cent. of ecclesiastical land inclosed to total inclosures
89·43	10·56

EVICTIONS AND DISPLACEMENTS FROM LABOUR

LAY OWNERSHIP				ECCLESIASTICAL OWNERSHIP			
Land of lords of manors		Land of freeholders		Land of lords of manors		Land of freeholders	
Total evictions	Total displacements from labour	Total evictions	Total displacements from labour	Total evictions	Total displacements from labour	Total evictions	Total displacements from labour
persons	persons	persons	persons	persons	persons	persons	persons
593	13	389	29	17	20	50	2

Total evictions on lay land	Total displacements from labour on lay land	Total evictions on ecclesiastical land	Total displacements from labour on ecclesiastical land
persons	persons	persons	persons
982	42	67	22

PROPORTIONATE ANALYSIS OF THE ABOVE

LAY OWNERSHIP				ECCLESIASTICAL OWNERSHIP			
Land of lords of manors		Land of freeholders		Land of lords of manors		Land of freeholders	
Proportion per cent. of evictions to total evictions on lay land	Proportion per cent. of displacements from labour to total displacements from labour on lay land	Proportion per cent. of evictions to total evictions on lay land	Proportion per cent. of displacements from labour to total displacements from labour on lay land	Proportion per cent. of evictions to total evictions on ecclesiastical land	Proportion per cent. of displacements from labour to total displacements from labour on ecclesiastical land	Proportion per cent. of evictions to total evictions on ecclesiastical land	Proportion per cent. of displacements from labour to total displacements from labour on ecclesiastical land
60·38	30·95	39·61	69·04	25·37	90·90	74·62	9·09

VI. STATUS OF LANDLORDS RESPONSIBLE FOR INCLOSURE, &C.—(*continuea*)

Total evictions	Total displacements from labour
persons 1,049	persons 64
1,113	

PROPORTIONATE ANALYSIS OF THE ABOVE

Proportion per cent. of evictions on lay land to total evictions	Proportion per cent. of displacements from labour on lay land to total displacements from labour	Proportion per cent. of evictions on ecclesiastical land to total evictions	Proportion per cent. of displacements from labour on ecclesiastical land to total displacements from labour
93·61	65·62	6·38	34·37

Proportion per cent. of evictions and displacements from labour on lay land to total ditto	Proportion per cent. of evictions and displacements from labour on ecclesiastical land to total ditto
92·00	7·99

VII

STATUS OF ACTUAL INCLOSERS, TOGETHER WITH THE EVICTIONS AND DISPLACE-
MENTS FROM LABOUR ON INCLOSED ARABLE AND ON PASTURE RESPECTIVELY.[1]
INFERRED FIGURES EXCLUDED

1. Lords of manors holding land in hand

Parish	Lay Ownership					Parish	Ecclesiastical Ownership				
	Total	Inclosure of arable	Evictions and displacements from labour	Parks and inclosures to pasture	Evictions and displacements from labour		Total	Inclosure of arable	Evictions and displacements from labour	Parks and inclosures to pasture	Evictions and displacements from labour
	acr.	acr.	persons	acres	persons		acr.	acr.	persons	acres	persons
1. Byrdyston	400	—	—	400	60						
2. Dodershill	960	—	—	960	120						
3. Grendon	100	—	—	100	5						
4. Litilcote	201	—	—	201	24						
5. Flete Merston[2]	140	—	—	140	20						
6. Cranwell	60	60	6	—	—						
						1. Ramston	48	48	4	—	—
7. Blecheley	40	—	—	40	8						
8. Blecheley	140	—	—	140	10						
9. Walton	30	—	—	30	4						
10. Wuluerton & Bradwell	25	—	—	25	—						
						2. Bradwell & Wuluerton	300			300	20
11. Stoke Pewges	200	—	—	200	12						
12. Lyllyngton Darell	164	—	—	164	40						
13. Bechampton[3]	66	—	—	66	20						
14. Shalweston	24	—	—	24	—						
15. { Chalfount St. Peter	80	—	—	80	20						
{ Chafount St. Peter	10	—	—	10	—						
16. Castelthorp	280	—	—	280	88						
17. StantonBarey	360	—	—	360	40						
Totals	3280	60	E. 6 | D. 0 — 6	3220	E. 471 | D. 0 — 471	Totals	348	48	E. 4 | D. 0 — 4	300	E. 0 | D. 20 — 20

[1] Where an area is returned as inclosed, but the inclosure is unaccompanied by evictions, it is entered in this Table.
[2] Two freeholders, perhaps joint feoffees to uses, joined the lord of the manor in this inclosure.
[3] Lekehamstede (where the inclosure of 66 acres involved the displacement of twelve persons from employment) excluded, because one of the inclosures was made by a freeholder, and there are no data for distributing the total displaced.

II.   Q

VII. STATUS OF ACTUAL INCLOSERS, &C.—(continued)

2. Freeholders holding land in hand.

Parish	Lay Ownership					Parish	Ecclesiastical Ownership				
	Total	Inclosure of arable	Evictions and displacements from labour	Parks and inclosures to pasture	Evictions and displacements from labour		Total	Inclosure of arable	Evictions and displacements from labour	Parks and inclosures to pasture	Evictions and displacements from labour
	acr.	acr.	persons	acres	persons		acr.	acr.	persons	acres	persons
1. Eddeslbrough	30	—	—	30	—						
2. Litilcote	100	—	—	100	8						
3. Stutley	40	—	—	40	—						
4. Donnyngton	90	—	—	90	12						
5. Ludgarshale	120	—	—	120	20						
6. Ludgarshale	30	—	—	30	4						
7. Lyscome	80	—	—	80	30						
8. Lyscombeholynden & Brakynham[1]	40	—	—	40	5						
9. Cublyngton	20	—	—	20	—						
10. Overwynehendon	10	—	—	10	—						
11. Moulsowe	20	—	—	20	6	1. Moulsowe	20	—	—	20	2
12. Woughton	20	—	—	20	4						
13. Stokehamond	30	30	2	—	—						
14. Stokehamond	30	30	2	—	—						
15. Burnham	20	20	2	—	—						
16. { Woburne	40	40	6	—	—						
{ Wobourn	8	—	—	8	—						
17. Denham	24	—	—	24	8						
18. Denham	20	20	4	—	—						
19. (Denham)	40	—	—	40	6	2. Vpton	27	27	3	—	—
20. Vpton	30	30	3	—	—						
21. Vpton	80	80	4	—	—						
22. Iver	50	—	—	50	2						
23. Iver	50	50	8	—	—						
24. Iver	50	50	8	—	—						
25. Iver	40	40	8	—	—						
26. Fulbroke	16	—	—	16	—						
27. Lathbere	60	—	—	60	—						
28. Hanslap	26	—	—	26	—						
29. Wuluierston	32	—	—	32	3						
30. Wuluierston	140	140	20	—	—	3. Thornborough	40	40	4	—	—
31. Buorton and Buertonhold	21	—	—	.21	4	4. Stepyll Cleydon	90	90	4	—	—
32. Whitwode	48	48	12	—	—						
33. Hyllysden	4	—	—	4	—	5. Galcotte	30	—	—	30	2
34. Lechynburgh in Galcotte	60	—	—	60	2						
35. Kyngyshey	100	—	—	100	9						
36. Kyngyshey	146	—	—	146	9						
37. Chesham	220	220	14	—	—						
38. Stonystratford	40	40	4	—	—						
39. Prynces Rysborough	20	20	—	—	—						
Totals	2045	858	E. 97 / D. 0 → 97	1187	E. 116 / D. 19 → 135	Totals	207	157	E. 11 / D. 0 → 11	50	E. 2 / D. 2 → 4

[1] The inclosures at Waddesdon are omitted, because it is not clear how many of the evictions were due to the inclosures of 50 acres to arable and how many to those of 60 acres to pasture.]

BUCKINGHAMSHIRE

VII. Status of actual Inclosers &c.—(*continued*)

3. Copyholders

Parish	Lay Ownership					Parish	Ecclesiastical Ownership				
	Total	Inclosure of arable	Evictions and displacements from labour	Parks and inclosures to pasture	Evictions and displacements from labour		Total	Inclosure of arable	Evictions and displacements from labour	Parks and inclosures to pasture	Evictions and displacements from labour
	acr	acr.	persons	acres	persons		acr.	acr.	persons	acres	persons
						1. Overwynchendon	161	—	—	161	10
							161	—	—	161	E. 10 | D. 0 — 10

4. Leaseholders

Parish	Total	Incl. arable	Evict.	Parks	Evict.
1 Middelcleydon	120	—	—	120	5
2. Wyllyn	80	—	—	80	10
3 Aston and Hardwyke	100	100	—	—	—
4. Dytton	100	—	—	100	2
5. Dytton	30	—	—	30	3
6. Burnham	100	100	12	—	—
7. Stone	40	40	6	—	—
8. Stone	20	20	4	—	—
9. Weston Turfild	160	—	—	160	8
10. Ilmer	60	—	—	60	6
11. Broughton (Mentmore)	120	—	—	120	8
	930	260	E. 22 | D. 0 — 22	670	E. 31 | D. 11 — 42

Parish	Total	Incl. arable	Evict.	Parks	Evict.
Morsley	20	—	—	20	—
	20	—	—	20	—

5. Farm tenants

Parish	Total	Incl. arable	Evict.	Parks	Evict.
1. Asshendon	160	—	—	160	36
2. Donnyngton	90	—	—	90	—
3. Dynton[1]	30	—	—	30	7
4. Cleydon	36	—	—	36	5
5. (Anyngton)	15	15	6	—	—
6. Adyngdon	15	15	3	—	—
7. Aston Molent	100	—	—	100	10
8. Magna Myssynden[2]	80	—	—	80	12
	526	30	E. 9 | D. 0 — 9	496	E. 70 | D. 0 — 70

Parish	Total	Incl. arable	Evict.	Parks	Evict.
1. Shipden Lye	18	18	3	—	—
	18	18	E. 3 | D. 0 — 3	—	—

[1] The apportionment of evictions being uncertain, the Hoggeshawe and Fulbroke inclosures are omitted.
[2] Lay freeholder's property farmed by the Abbot of M.

VII. Status of actual Inclosers, together with the Evictions and Displacements from Labour on Inclosed Arable and Pasture respectively

Summary.

	Lay Ownership										Ecclesiastical Ownership								
	1. Total area per person evicted and displaced	2. Total area per person evicted	3. Total area per person displaced	4. Total area of inclosed arable per person evicted and displaced	5. Total area of inclosed arable per person evicted[1]	6. Total area of inclosed arable per person displaced[2]	7. Total area of inclosed pasture per person evicted and displaced	8. Total area of inclosed pasture per person evicted[1]	9. Total area of inclosed pasture per person displaced[2]		1. Total area per person evicted and displaced	2. Total area per person evicted	3. Total area per person displaced	4. Total area of inclosed arable per person evicted and displaced	5. Total area of inclosed arable per person evicted[1]	6. Total area of inclosed arable per person displaced[2]	7. Total area of inclosed pasture per person evicted and displaced	8. Total area of inclosed pasture per person evicted[1]	9. Total area of inclosed pasture per person displaced[2]
	acres	acres	acres	acres	acres	acres	acres	acres	acres		acres	acres	acres	acres	acres	acres	acres	acres	acres
1 Lords of manors holding land in hand	6·87	6·87	—	10	10	—	6·83	6·71	—		14·5	8·7	17·4	12	12	—	15	—	15
2 Freeholders holding land in hand	8·81	9·6	107·63	8·84	8·6	—	8·79	6·6	12·2		13·8	15·9	103·5	14·27	14·2	—	12·5	10	15
3 Copyholders	14·53	17·54	84·54	11·81	7·27	—	15·9	21·5	—		16·1	16·1	—	—	—	—	16·1	16·1	—
4 Leaseholders	6·65	6·65	—	3·3	3·3	—	70·8	5·8	60·9		6	6	—	6	6	—	—	—	—
5 Farm tenants																			

[1] Taking the areas only from which evictions took place.   [2] Taking the areas only from which displacements took place.

VIII

EVICTIONS AND DISPLACEMENTS FROM LABOUR, AREA OF EVICTED LANDS, AND STATUS OF LANDLORDS RESPONSIBLE. INFERRED AND DOUBTFUL FIGURES EXCLUDED

	Lay Ownership						Ecclesiastical Ownership						
	Lords of manors			Freeholders			Lords of manors			Freeholders		
Place	Area	Population displaced [1]		Place	Area	Population displaced	Place	Area	Population displaced	Place	Area	Population displaced
	acres	persons			acres	persons		acres	persons		acres	persons
1. Byrdyston .	400	60	1.	Asshendon	60	20						
2. Dodershill .	960	120	2.	Asshendon	100	16						
3. Grendon .	100	5										
4. Litilcote .	201	24	3.	Litilcote .	100	8						
			4.	Donnyngton	90	12						
			5.	Ludgarshale	120	20						
			6.	Ludgarshale	30	4						
			7.	Lyscombe .	80	30						
			8.	Lyscombe-holynden and Brakynham	40	5						
5. Flete Merston [2]	140	20	9.	Waddesdon	30	8						
			10.	Waddesdon	80	8						

[1] This term includes both evictions and displacements from employment.
[2] Two freeholders joined with the lord of the manor in this inclosure.

VIII. Evictions and Displacements from Labour, &c.—(continued)

	Lay Ownership				Freeholders				Ecclesiastical Ownership				Freeholders		
	Lords of manors								Lords of manors						
	Place	Area acres	Population displaced persons		Place	Area acres	Population displaced persons		Place	Area acres	Population displaced persons		Place	Area acres	Population displaced persons
6.	Middelcley-don	120	5					1.	Overwynch-endon	161	10				
7.	Cranwell	60	6					2.	Ramston	48	4				
				11.	Wyllyn	80	10								
				12.	Moulsowe	20	6					1.	Moulsowe	20	2
8.	Blecheley	40	8	13.	Woughton	20	4								
9.	Blecheley	140	10	14.	Stoke-hamond	30	2								
				15.	Stoke-hamond	30	2								
10.	Walton	30	4					3.	Bradwell and Wulueton	300	20				
11.	Stoke Pewges	200	12	16.	Dytton	30	3								
12.	Dytton	100	2	17.	Burnham	20	2								
				18.	Burnham	100	12								
				19.	Woburne	40	6								
				20.	Stone	40	6								

BUCKINGHAMSHIRE

13. Stone.	20	4		
			2. Vpton	27	3
	21. Denham	24	8	
	22. Denham	20	4	
	23. (Denham)	40	6	
	24. Weston Turfild	160	8	
	25. Vpton	30	3	
	26. Vpton	80	4	
	27. Iver	50	2	
	28. Iver	50	8	
	29. Iver	50	8	
	30. Iver	40	8	
	31. Dynton	30	7	
	32. Hanslap	26	3	
	33. Wuluierston	32	3	
	34. Wuluierston	140	20	
			3. Thornborugh	40	4
14. Lyllyngton Darell	164	40		
	35. Buorton and Buerton-hold	21	4	
			4. Shipden Lye		
			4. Stepyll Cleydon	90	4
15. Cleydon	36	5		
	36. (Adyngton	15		
	37. Adyngdon	15	3	
	38. Whitwode.	48	12	
			5. Galcotte	30	2
16. Bechampton	66	20		

VIII. EVICTIONS AND DISPLACEMENTS FROM LABOUR, &C.—(*continued*)

	LAY OWNERSHIP						ECCLESIASTICAL OWNERSHIP					
	Lords of manors			Freeholders			Lords of manors			Freeholders		
Place	Place	Area acres	Population displaced persons	Place	Area acres	Population displaced persons	Place	Area acres	Population displaced persons	Place	Area acres	Population displaced persons
17. Chalfount St. Peter		80	20	39. Lechynburgh in Galcotte	60	2						
18. Ilmer		60	6									
				40. Kyngysley	100	?						
				41. Kyngysley	146	9[1]						
19. Castelthorp		280	88	42. Chesham	220	14						
20. Stanton Barey		360	40	43. Stoneystratford	40	4						
				44. Magna Mys-synden	80	12						
21. Broughton (Mentmore)		120	8									
		$3497^2 + 186^2$	E. D. $496 + 11$		$2425^2 + 232^2$	E. D $332 + 19$		$227^2 + 300^2$	E. D. $17 + 20$		$177^2 + 30^2$	E. D. $13 + 2$
		3677	507		2657	351		527	37		207	15

[1] In the next entry, Aston Molent, there was an inclosure on the land of the lay lord of the manor of 40 acres, and another on the land of a lay freeholder of 60 acres. The evictions for the two numbered in all 10; but as there are no data for precisely apportioning them, they are excluded. Similarly at Lekehamstede, *supra*.

[2] The first of these totals is that of the areas from which evictions took place, the second of those on which only displacements from employment are returned, and they correspond respectively with the totals E. and D. of the following bracket. See Summary Tables on next page.

VIII. Evictions and Displacements, &c.—(continued)
Summary

1

	Lay Ownership								Ecclesiastical Ownership							
	Lords of manors				Freeholders				Lords of manors				Freeholders			
	Areas from which evictions took place	Persons evicted	Areas of displacement from employment	Persons displaced from employment	Areas from which evictions took place	Persons evicted	Areas of displacement from employment	Persons displaced from employment	Areas from which evictions took place	Persons evicted	Areas of displacement from employment	Persons displaced from employment	Areas from which evictions took place	Persons evicted	Areas of displacement from employment	Persons displaced from employment
	acres 3,497	496	acres 180	11	acres 2,425	332	acres 232	19	acres 227	17	acres 300	20	acres 177	13	acres 30	2

2

No. of acres per person evicted	No. of acres per person displaced from employment	No. of acres per person evicted	No. of acres per person displaced from employment	No. of acres per person evicted	No. of acres per person displaced from employment	No. of acres per person evicted	No. of acres per person displaced from employment
7·05	16·36	7·3	12·2	13·3	15	13·6	15

3

Total acres	Persons evicted and displaced from employment	Total acres	Persons evicted and displaced from employment	Total acres	Persons evicted and displaced from employment	Total acres	Persons evicted and displaced from employment
3,677	507	2,657	351	527	37	207	15

VIII. Evictions and Displacements from Labour, &c.
Summary (continued)

Total number of acres per person evicted and displaced from employment	Total number of acres per person evicted and displaced from employment	Total number of acres per person evicted and displaced from employment
7·2	7·56	13·8
Total number of acres from which evictions took place (lay and ecclesiastical land together)	Total number of persons evicted (lay and ecclesiastical together)	Total number of persons displaced from employment
6,326	858	52
Total number of acres per person evicted (lay and ecclesiastical land together)	Total number of acres per person evicted and displaced from employment	Total number of acres per person displaced from employment
7·37	14·2	14·26
Total number of acres from which evictions and displacements took place (lay and ecclesiastical land together)	Total number of acres from which displacements of labour took place	Total number of persons evicted and displaced from employment
7,068	742	910
Total number of acres per person evicted and displaced from employment (lay and ecclesiastical land together)		
7·76		

IX

NUMBER OF ACRES TO A MESSUAGIUM (MANOR HOUSES AND INFERRED CASES EXCLUDED) CLASSIFIED ACCORDING TO TENURES AND TENANCIES

I. Land in hands of lords of manors

LAY OWNERSHIP

Parish	Number of messuages	Acres
1. Byrdyston	7	400
2. Dodershill	24	960
3. Litilcote	1	120
4. Litilcote	1	21
5. Litilcote	1	20
6. Litilcote	1	40
7. Flete Merston[1]	4	140
8. Blecheley	2	40
9. Walton	1	30
10. Stoke Pewges	1	200
11. Tyrryngham	1	30
12. Tyrryngham and Philgrav	1	47
13. Gayhurst	1	100
14. Lyllyngton Darell	8	164
15. Bechampton	2	40
16. Bechampton	1	10
17. Chalfount St. Peter	2	80
18. Castelthorp	6	120
19. Stanton Barey	5	360
20. Wuluerton	1	60
	71	2,982

Average number of acres to a messuagium . . . 42

ECCLESIASTICAL OWNERSHIP

Parish	Number of messuages	Acres
1. Ramston	2	48
	2	48

Average number of acres to a messuagium . . . 24

[1] Two freeholders, perhaps joint feoffees to uses, joined the lord of the manor in this inclosure

II. Land in hands of freeholders

LAY OWNERSHIP

Parish	Number of messuages	Acres
1. Litilcote	1	100
2. Donnyngton	1	30
3. Donnyngton	1	30
4. Donnyngton	1	30
5. Ludgarshale	5	120
6. Ludgarshale	1	30
7. Lyscome	4	80

ECCLESIASTICAL OWNERSHIP

Parish	Number of messuages	Acres

IX. NUMBER OF ACRES TO A MESSUAGIUM (MANOR HOUSES AND INFERRED CASES EXCLUDED) CLASSIFIED ACCORDING TO TENURES AND TENANCIES

II. Land in hands of freeholders—(*continued*)

	LAY OWNERSHIP			ECCLESIASTICAL OWNERSHIP		
	Parish	Number of messuages	Acres	Parish	Number of messuages	Acres
8.	Lyscome Holynden and Brakynham	1	30			
9.	Waddesdon	1	30			
10.	Waddesdon	1	80			
11.	Cranwell	1	120			
12.	Ramston	1	24			
13.	Moulsowe	1	20	1. Moulsowe	1	20
14.	Woughton	1	20			
15.	Stokehamond	1	30			
16.	Stokehamond	1	30			
17.	Loughton	1	20			
18.	Wuluerton and Bradwell	1	40			
19.	Burnham	1	20			
20.	Woburne	1	40			
21.	Denham	1	24			
22.	Denham	1	20			
23.	(Denham)	1	40	2. Vpton	1	27
24.	Vpton	1	30			
25.	Vpton	1	80			
26.	Iver	1	50			
27.	Iver	1	50			
28.	Iver	1	50			
29.	Iver	1	40			
30.	Hanslap	1	26			
31.	Wuluierston	7	140	3. Thornborugh	1	40
32.	Buorton and Buertonhold	1	21	4. Stepyll Cleydon	1	90
33.	Whitwode	3	48			
34.	Preston	1	15			
35.	Kyngyshey	1	146			
36.	Chesham	1	60			
37.	Chesham	1	80			
38.	Chesham	1	80			
39.	Stonystratford	1	40			
40.	Chessham	2	60			
		56	2,024		4	177

Average number of acres to a messuagium . . 36·14

Average number of acres to a messuagium . . 44·25

BUCKINGHAMSHIRE

IX. NUMBER OF ACRES TO A MESSUAGIUM (MANOR HOUSES AND INFERRED CASES EXCLUDED) CLASSIFIED ACCORDING TO TENURES AND TENANCIES

III. Copyholds

LAY OWNERSHIP			ECCLESIASTICAL OWNERSHIP		
Parish	Number of messuages	Acres	Parish	Number of messuages	Acres
			1. Overwynchendon	1	30
				1	30
			Average number of acres to a messuagium	. .	30

IV. Leaseholds

LAY OWNERSHIP			ECCLESIASTICAL OWNERSHIP		
Parish	Number of messuages	Acres	Parish	Number of messuages	Acres
1. Wyllyn . .	2	80			
2. Burnham .	3	100			
3. Stone . .	1	40			
4. Stone . .	1	20			
5. Weston Turfild	1	160			
6. Broughton (Mentmore)[1]	1	60			
7. Broughton (Mentmore)	2	60			
	11	520			

Average number of acres to a messuagium . 47·27

V. Farm tenancies

LAY OWNERSHIP			ECCLESIASTICAL OWNERSHIP		
Parish	Number of messuages	Acres	Parish	Number of messuages	Acres
1. Asshendon .	1	40			
2. Asshendon . [2]	1	20			
3. Asshendon .	1	100			
4. Dynton . . [3]	1	110			
5. Dynton . .	1	30	1. Shipden Lye .	1	18
6. (Adyngton) .	1	15			
7. Adyngdon .	1	15			
8. Magna Kembill	1	40			
9. Aston Molent	1	40			
10. Aston Molent	1	60			
11. Magna Myssynden[4]	1	80			
	11	550		1	18

Average number of acres to a messuagium . 50

Average number of acres to a messuagium . . 18

[1] In this case there were three messuages, one cottage, and 120 acres in all. To one messuage 60 acres were attached, and 30 acres to each of the other two.
[2] Lay freeholder's property farmed by an ecclesiastic, Abbot of Notley.
[3] It was this second holding that was consolidated with the first.
[4] Lay freeholder's property farmed by the Abbot of Myssynden.

NUMBER OF ACRES TO A 'COTAGIUM.' INFERRED AND DOUBTFUL
FIGURES EXCLUDED

I. Land in hands of lords of manors

LAY OWNERSHIP

	Number of cottages	Number of acres
1. Cranwell	3	60
2. Lyllyngton Darell	4	0
3. Bechampton	3	16
	10	76

Average number of acres to a cotagium . . 7·6

ECCLESIASTICAL OWNERSHIP

Number of cottages   Number of acres

II. Land in hand of freeholders

III. Copyholds

IV. Leaseholds

LAY OWNERSHIP

	Number of cottages	Number of acres
Broughton (Mentmore)	1 [1]	0

ECCLESIASTICAL OWNERSHIP

Number of cottages   Number of acres

V. Farm tenancies

Number of acres to a manor house

LAY OWNERSHIP

	Number of manor houses	Acres
Hoggeshawe	1 [2]	60
Castelthorp	1 [2]	160
	2	220

Average number of acres to a manor house . 110

ECCLESIASTICAL OWNERSHIP

Number of manor houses   Acres

---

[1] This cottage does not appear in Table I., because it was not destroyed.
[2] 'Principale messuagium manerii.'

BUCKINGHAMSHIRE

Total

Lay Ownership		Ecclesiastical Ownership	
messuagia	acres	messuagia	acres
149	6,076	8	273

Average number of acres to a messuagium

acres	acres
40·77	34·12

Total average number of acres to a messuagium

acres
40·4

cotagia	acres	cotagia	acres
11	76	0	0

Total average number of acres to a cotagium

acres
6·9

X

NUMBER OF INHABITANTS OF A MESSUAGE (COTTAGES, MANOR HOUSES, AND DOUBTFUL CASES EXCLUDED) CLASSIFIED ACCORDING TO TENURES AND TENANCIES. INFERRED AND DOUBTFUL FIGURES EXCLUDED

I. Land in hands of lords of manors

LAY OWNERSHIP			ECCLESIASTICAL OWNERSHIP		
Parish	No. of messuages	No. of inhabitants	Parish	No. of messuages	No. of inhabitants
1. Byrdyston	7	60			
2. Dodershill	24	120			
3. Litilcote	4	24			
4. Flete Merston [1]	4	20			
			1. Ramston	2	4
5. Blecheley	2	8			
6. Walton	1	4			
7. Stoke Pewges [2]	1	12			
8. Chalfount St. Peter	2	20			
9. Stanton Barey	5	40			
	50	308		2	4
Average number of inhabitants of a messuagium		6	Average number of inhabitants of a messuagium		2

II. Land in hands of freeholders

LAY OWNERSHIP			ECCLESIASTICAL OWNERSHIP		
Parish	No. of messuages	No. of inhabitants	Parish	No. of messuages	No. of inhabitants
1. Litilcote	1	8			
2. Donnyngton	3	12			
3. Ludgarshale	5	20			
4. Ludgarshale	1	4			
5. Lyscome	4	30			
6. Waddesdon	1	8			
7. Waddesdon	1	8			
8. Cublyngton and Bredyncote	1	6			
9. Moulsowe	1	6			
			1. Moulsowe	1	2
10. Woughton	1	4			
11. Stokehamond	1	2			
12. Stokehamond	1	2			
Carried forward	21	110	Carried forward	1	2

[1] Two freeholders, perhaps feoffees to uses, joined the lord of the manor in this inclosure.
[2] Lyllyngton Darell, which is the next entry, is necessarily excluded because the inhabitants of the cotagia confuse the average. So in the case of Bechampton. So in Castelthorp, the evictions from a ' principale mesuagium manerii ' and 6 mesuagia are summarised.

BUCKINGHAMSHIRE

X. NUMBER OF INHABITANTS OF A MESSUAGE, &C.—(*continued*)

II. Land in hands of freeholders—(*continued*)

	Lay Ownership			Ecclesiastical Ownership		
	Parish	No. of messuages	No. of inhabitants	Parish	No. of messuages	No. of inhabitants
	Brought forward	21	110	Brought forward	1	2
13.	Burnham	1	2			
14.	Woburne	1	6			
15.	Denham	1	8			
16.	Denham	1	4			
17.	(Denham)	1	6			
				2. Vpton	1	3
18.	Vpton	1	3			
19.	Vpton	1	4			
20.	Iver	1	2			
21.	Iver	1	8			
22.	Iver	1	8			
23.	Iver	1	8			
24.	Hanslap	1	3			
25.	Wuluierston	7	20			
				3. Thornborough	1	4
26.	Buorton and Buertonhold	1	4			
				4. Stepyll Cleydon	1	4
27.	Whitwode	3	12			
28.	Kyngyshey	1	9			
29.	Chesham	3	14			
30.	Stonystratford	1	4			
		49	235		4	13
	Average number of inhabitants of a messuagium		5 (4·79)	Average number of inhabitants of a messuagium		3

III. Copyholds[1]

IV. Leaseholds

	Lay Ownership			Ecclesiastical Ownership		
	Parish	No. of messuages	No. of inhabitants	Parish	No. of messuages	No. of inhabitants
1.	Burnham	2	12			
2.	Stone	1	6			
3.	Stone	1	4			
4.	Weston Turfild	1	8			
5.	Broughton (Mentmore)	2	8			
		7	38			
	Average number of inhabitants of a messuagium		5			

[1] The only cases of copyhold tenure, the two at Overwynchendon, leave it doubtful whether the 10 persons evicted represent the house destroyed on the 30 acres, or whether some of them are to be assigned to the putting down of ploughs on the 131 acres. They are therefore excluded.

X. NUMBER OF INHABITANTS OF A MESSUAGE, &c.—(*continued*)

V. Farm tenancies

LAY OWNERSHIP			ECCLESIASTICAL OWNERSHIP		
Parish	No. of messuages	No. of inhabitants	Parish	No of messuages	No. of inhabitants
1. Asshendon [1]	2	20			
2. Asshendon [1]	1	16			
3. Wyllyn	2	10			
4. Dynton	1	7	1. Shipden Lye	1	3
5. (Adyngton)	1	6			
6. Adyngdon	1	3			
7. Aston Molent	2	10			
8. Magna Myssynden [2]	1	12			
	11	84		1	3

Average number of inhabitants of a messuagium . 8

Average number of inhabitants of a messuagium . 3

NUMBER OF INHABITANTS OF A 'COTAGIUM' (INFERRED AND DOUBTFUL FIGURES EXCLUDED) CLASSIFIED ACCORDING TO TENURES AND TENANCIES

I. Land in hands of lords of manors

LAY OWNERSHIP			ECCLESIASTICAL OWNERSHIP		
Parish	No. of cottages	No. of inhabitants	Parish	No. of cottages	No. of inhabitants
1. Cranwell [3]	3	6			
	3	6			

Average number of inhabitants of a cotagium . 2

NUMBER OF INHABITANTS OF MANOR HOUSES

A 'manerium' is decayed at Flete Merston and Walton; a 'principale mesuagium manerii' at Hoggeshawe and Castelthorp; but in all four cases the number of inhabitants is matter of inference, other messuages being grouped with them.

---

[1] Evictions by a farming Abbot of Notley.
[2] Lay freeholder's property farmed by the Abbot of Myssynden.
[3] The other examples of cottages are at Lyllyngton Darell (4), and at Bechampton (3). In both instances they are grouped with messuages so far as the number of inhabitants is concerned.

BUCKINGHAMSHIRE

Average Number of Inhabitants to a Messuagium (Manor Houses excluded) classified according to Tenures and Tenancies

I

	Lay Ownership Average number of inhabitants to a messuagium	Ecclesiastical Ownership Average number of inhabitants to a messuagium
1. Land in hands of lords of manors	6	2
2. Land in hands of freeholders	5	3
3. Copyholds	—	—
4. Leaseholds	5	—
5. Farm tenancies	8	3

II. Total messuages and inhabitants [1]

Lay Ownership		Ecclesiastical Ownership	
Messuages	Inhabitants	Messuages	Inhabitants
117	665	7	20
Average number of inhabitants of a messuagium 6 (5·68)		Average number of inhabitants of a messuagium	3

III. Total messuages and inhabitants [1] on lay and ecclesiastical properties taken together

Messuages	Inhabitants
124	685

Average number of inhabitants of a messuagium, 6 (5·52)

[1] *I.e.* excluding manor houses, houses from which only a partial displacement took place, and houses the number of inhabitants of which is not specified.

XI

NUMBER OF ACRES AND PERSONS TO AN ARATRUM CLASSIFIED ACCORDING TO TENURES AND TENANCIES. INFERRED FIGURES EXCLUDED.

LAY OWNERSHIP.

Parish	Aratra	Land in hands of lords of manor		Land in hands of freeholders		Copyholds		Leaseholds		Farm tenancies	
		acr.	per.	acr.	per.	acr.	per.	acr.	per.	acr.	per.
1. Asshendon	2	—		—		—		—		—	
2. Byrdyston	8	400	60	—		—		—		100	16
3. Dodershill	16	960	120	—		—		—		—	
4. Grendon	1	100	5	—		—		—		—	
5. Litilcote	4	201	24	—		—		—		—	
6. Litilcote	1	—		100	8	—		—		—	
7. Ludgarshale	3	—		120	20	—		—		—	
8. Ludgarshale	1	—		30	4	—		—		—	
9. Lyscome	4	—		80	30	—		—		—	
10. Lyscombeholynden and Brakynham	1	—		40	5	—		—		—	
11. Flete Merston	4	140	20	—		—		—		—	
12. Waddesdon[1]	1	—		20	8	—		—		—	
13. Waddesdon[1]	2	—		40	8	—		—		120	5
14. Middelclaydon	2	—		—		—		—		—	
15. Wyllyn	2	—		—		—		—		80	10
16. Blecheley	2	140	10	—		—		—		—	
17. Moulsowe	1	—		20	6	—		—		—	
18. Woughton	1	—		20	4	—		—		—	

ECCLESIASTICAL OWNERSHIP.

Parish	Aratra	Land in hands of lords of manor		Land in hands of freeholders		Copyholds		Leaseholds		Farm tenancies	
		acr.	per.	acr.	per.	acr.	per.	acr.	per.	acr.	per.
1. Overwynchendon	3	—		—		161	10	—		—	
2. Moulsowe	1	—		20	2	—		—		—	
3. Bradwell and	4	300	20	—		—		—		—	

BUCKINGHAMSHIRE

				E.[4]	E. D.[4]		E. D.	E. D.	E. D.	E.
					120 19		18 11			
20. Denham	.	1	—	—	24 8	—	—	—	—	—	—
21. (Denham)	.	1	—	—	40 6	—	—	—	—	—	—
22. Iver	.	1	—	—	50 2	—	—	—	—	—	—
23. Dynton[2]	.	1	½	—	—	—	—	—	30 7	—	—
24. Hanslap	.	—	—	—	26 3	—	—	—	—	—	—
25. Wuluierston	.	—	—	—	32 3	—	—	—	—	—	—
26. Lyllyngton Darell	.	8	164 40	—	—	—	—	—	—	—	—
27. Buorton and Buertonhold	.	1	—	—	21 4	—	—	—	—	—	—
28. Cleydon	.	1	—	—	—	—	—	—	36 5	—	—
29. Lechynburgh in Galcotte	.	1	—	—	60 2	—	—	—	—	—	—
30. Chalfount St. Peter	.	2	80 20	—	—	—	—	—	—	—	—
31. Ilmer	.	1	—	—	—	—	60 6	—	—	—	—
32. Kyngyshey	.	1	—	—	100 9	—	—	—	—	—	—
33. Kyngyshey	.	1	—	—	146 9	—	—	—	—	—	—
34. Aston Molent	.	2	—	—	—	—	—	—	—	—	100 10
35. Castelthorp	.	10	280 88	—	—	—	—	—	—	—	—
36. Stanton Barey	.	5	360 40	—	—	—	—	—	—	—	—
37. Broughton (Mentmore)	.	2	—	—	—	—	—	—	120 8	—	—
		98	3025 439	969 139	—			380 29	266 38		

4. Galcotte[3] . ½ 8½ 300 20 50 4 161 10 —

E. D. E. D.
0+20 2+2

[1] The two holdings were 30 acres and 80 acres respectively; but the Return states that it was due to the conversion to pasture of 20 acres that the plough was put down, &c., and the conversion of 40 acres in the second holding has been taken as the cause of the evictions there also.

[2] It is not possible to apportion exactly between the land held of the Hospitallers and that held of the Abbot of Eynesham in Hoggeshawe and Fulbroke the 9 ploughs put down and the 60 persons evicted. It has been thought better, therefore, to exclude these entries.

[3] Three inclosures of 16, 20, and 30 acres at Lekehamstede involved the putting down of 4 ploughs and the displacement from employment of 12 persons; but as they were made by a lord of a manor and a freeholder, and there are no data for precisely apportioning the distribution of ploughs and persons evicted, it has been thought better to exclude them.
E. = evictions; D. = displacement from employment.

Number of Persons and Acres &c. to Aratra

Total number of aratra put down, acres assigned thereto, and persons evicted or displaced thereby.

Lay Ownership				Ecclesiastical Ownership			
Aratra	Acres	Persons		Aratra	Acres	Persons	
		E.	D.			E.	D.
98	4,640	615 + 30		8½	511	12	22
		645				34	

	Land in hands of lords of manors	Land in hands of freeholders	Copyholds	Leaseholds	Farm tenancies		Land in hands of lords of manors	Land in hands of freeholders	Copyholds	Leaseholds	Farm tenancies
Number of aratra	62	23	0	7	6	Number of aratra	4	1½	3	0	0
Average number of persons to an aratrum	7	6	0	4	6·3	Average number of persons to an aratrum	5	3	3	0	0
Average number of acres to an aratrum	48·79	42·1	0	54·2	44·3	Average number of acres to an aratrum	75	33·3	53·6	0	0

General average

Average number of persons to an aratrum . . . . . 6·58
Average number of acres to an aratrum . . . . . 47·34

Average number of persons to an aratrum . . ; . . 4
Average number of acres to an aratrum . . . . . 60·1

Total general average (lay and ecclesiastical property together)

Average number of persons to an aratrum . . . . 6·37
Average number of acres to an aratrum . . . . 48·36

XII

RENTAL VALUES OF INCLOSED ARABLE AND PASTURE. LAND CLASSIFIED ACCORDING TO TENURES AND TENANCIES. INFERRED FIGURES EXCLUDED

I. Land in hands of lords of manors

LAY OWNERSHIP

Parish	Total area inclosed	Arable	Parks and inclosures to pasture	Total rental value	Rental value per acre
	acr.	acr.	acr.	£ s. d.	s. d.
Byrdyston	400	—	400	40 0 0	2 0
{ Dodershill	960	—	960	40 0 0	0 10
{ Grendon	100	—	100	7 0 0	1 4¾
Litilcote	120	—	120	3 6 8	0 6¾
Litilcote	21	—	21	0 12 0	0 6¾
Litilcote	20	—	20	0 10 0	0 6
Litilcote	40	—	40	1 10 0	0 9
Flete Merston[1]	140	—	140	20 0 0	2 10¼
Cranwell	60	60	—	1 10 0	0 6
{ Blecheley	40	—	40	1 4 0	0 7¼
{ Blecheley	140	—	140	7 0 0	1 0
Walton	30	—	30	1 6 8	0 10¾
Wuluerton and Bradwell	25	—	25	0 13 0	0 6¼
Stoke Pewges	200	—	200	8 0 0	0 9¾
{ Tyrryngham	30	—	30	0 18 0	0 7¼
{ Tyrryngham and Philgrav	47	—	47	1 10 0	0 7¾
Gayhurst	100	—	100	5 0 0	1 0
Lyllyngton Darell	164	—	164	40 0 0	4 10½
{ Bechampton	40	—	40	1 0 0	0 6
{ Bechampton	26	—	26	1 6 0	1 0
Shalweston	24	—	24	0 12 0	0 6
Lekehamstede	16	—	16	0 6 8	0 5
Lekhamstede	30	—	30	2 5 0	1 6
{ Chalfount St. Peter	80	—	80	6 13 6	1 8
{ Chalfount St. Peter	10	—	10	0 5 0	0 6
Castelthorp	280	—	280	38 0 0	2 8½
Stanton Barey[2]	360	—	360	30 0 0	1 8
	3503	60	3443	260 8 6	—

Average rental value per acre = 1s. 5¾d.

ECCLESIASTICAL OWNERSHIP

Parish	Total area inclosed	Arable	Parks and inclosures to pasture	Total rental value	Rental value per acre
	acr.	acr.	acr.	£ s. d.	d.
Ramston	48	48	—	1 6 8	6¾
Bradwell and Wuluerton	300	—	300	10 0 0	8
	348	48	300	11 6 8	—

Average rental value per acre = 7¾d.

[1] Two freeholders, perhaps joint-feoffees to uses, joined the lord of the manor in this inclosure.
[2] In the next entry, Wuluerton, the total of 60 acres is 42 acres arable and 18 acres inclosed to pasture the total rental value being 53s. 4d. ; but as there are no data by which to apportion this, it is excluded.

XII. Rental Values of Inclosed Arable and Pasture, &c.—(*continued*)

II. Land in hands of freeholders

Lay Ownership						Ecclesiastical Ownership					
Parish	Total area inclosed	Arable	Parks and inclosures to pasture	Total rental value	Rental value per acre	Parish	Total area inclosed	Arable	Parks and inclosures to pasture	Total rental value	Rental value per acre
	acr.	acr.	acr.	£ *s.* *d.*	*s.* *d.*		acr.	acr.	acr.	£ *s.* *d.*	*s.* *d.*
Eddeslbrough .	30	—	30	1 0 0	0 8						
Stutley . .	40	—	40	1 0 0	0 6						
Litilcote . .	100	—	100	3 6 8	0 8						
Donnyngton .	30	—	30	1 13 4	1 1¼						
Donnyngton .	30	—	30	1 13 4	1 1¼						
Donnyngton .	30	—	30	1 13 4	1 1¼						
Ludgarshale .	120	—	120	4 0 0	0 8						
Ludgarshale .	30	—	30	1 6 8	0 10½						
Lyscome . .	80	—	80	5 0 0	1 3						
Lyscombeholynden and Brakynham[1]	52	—	52	1 6 0	0 6						
Lyscome Holynden and Brakynham	30	—	30	1 0 0	0 8						
Cublyngton[2] .	20	—	20	0 10 0	0 6						
Overwynchendon	10	—	10	0 4 0	0 4¾						
Ramston . .	24	24	—	1 0 0	0 10						
Moulsowe . .	20	—	20	0 15 0	0 9						
						Moulsowe .	20	—	20	0 15 0	9
Woughton . .	20	—	20	0 15 0	0 9						
Stokehamond .	30	30	—	1 0 0	0 8						
Stokehamond .	30	30	—	1 0 0	0 8						
Loughton . .	20	—	20	0 10 0	0 6						
Wuluerton and Bradwell	40	—	40	1 13 8	0 10						
Burnham . .	20	20	—	1 6 8	1 4						
Woburne . .	40	40	—	2 6 8	1 2						
Wobourn . .	8	—	8	0 5 0	0 7½						
Denham . .	24	—	24	2 13 4	2 2½						
Denham . .	20	20	—	1 6 0	1 3½						
Denham . .	40	—	40	3 0 0	1 6						
						Vpton . .	27	27	—	1 0 0	0 9
Vpton . . .	30	30	—	2 0 0	1 4						
Vpton . . .	80	80	—	4 6 8	1 1						
Iver . . .	50	—	50	2 0 0	0 9½						
Iver . . .	50	50	—	3 0 0	1 2½						
Iver . . .	50	50	—	3 0 0	1 2½						
Iver . . .	40	40	—	3 0 0	1 6						
Fulbroke . .	16	—	16	0 6 8	0 5						
Lathbere . .	60	—	60	2 0 0	0 8						
Hanslap . .	26	—	26	0 13 4	0 6¼						
Wuluierston .	32	—	32	0 16 0	0 6						
Wuluierston .	140	140	—	6 8 0	0 11						
						Thornborugh .	40	40	—	4 6 8	2 2
Buorton and Buertonhold	21	—	21	0 18 0	0 10¼						
						Stepyll Cleydon	90	90	—	2 0 0	0 5¼
Whitwode . .	48	48	—	0 13 4	0 3¼						
Preston .	15	15	—	1 0 0	1 4						
Hyllysden . .	4	—	4	0 2 0	0 6						
Lykehamstede .	20	—	20	1 0 0	1 0						
						Galcotte . .	30	—	30	0 11 0	0 4½
Lechynburgh in Galcotte	60	—	60	2 0 0	0 8						
Kyngyshey . .	100	—	100	4 0 0	0 9½						
Kyngyshey . .	146	—	146	5 0 0	0 8¼						

[1] In the next two entries, Waddesdon, the totals of 30 acres and 80 acres are made up of 10 acres and 20 acres pasture in the one case, and 40 acres arable and 40 acres pasture in the other. The rentals are 13*s.* and £7 6*s.* 8*d.* respectively; but as there are no data by which to apportion these, they are excluded.

[2] In the next entry, Cranwell, the total is made up of 60 acres arable and 60 acres pasture at a rental value of 30*s.* Excluded for the same reason.

XII. Rental Values of Inclosed Arable and Pasture, &c.—(continued)

II. Land in hand of freeholders—(continued)

Lay Ownership

Parish	Total area inclosed	Arable	Parks and inclosures to pasture	Total rental value	Rental value per acre
	acr.	acr.	acr.	£ s. d.	s. d.
Chesham	60	60	—	2 0 0	0 8
Chesham	80	80	—	2 6 8	0 7
Chesham [1]	80	80	—	2 0 0	0 6
Chessham	60	60	—	1 9 0	0 5¾
Prynces borough	Rys 20	—	20	0 10 0	0 6
	2226	897	1329	91 14 4	—

Average rental value per acre = 10d.

Ecclesiastical Ownership

Parish	Total area inclosed	Arable	Parks and inclosures to pasture	Total rental value	Rental value per acre
	acr.	acr.	acr.	£ s. d.	s. d.
	207	157	50	8 12 8	—

Average rental value per acre = 10d.

III. Copyholds

Lay Ownership

Number of holdings	Parish	Total area inclosed	Arable	Parks and inclosures to pasture	Total rental value	Rental value per acre
		acr.	acr.	acr.	£ s. d.	s. d.

Ecclesiastical Ownership

Number of holdings	Parish	Total area inclosed	Arable	Parks and inclosures to pasture	Total rental value	Rental value per acre
		acr.	acr.	acr.	£ s. d.	d.
1	Overwynchendon	30	—	30	1 0 0	8
2	Overwynchendon	131	—	131	3 0 0	5½
		161	—	161	4 0 0	—

Average rental value per acre = 6d.
Average area of holding = 53·6 acres

IV. Leaseholds

Lay Ownership

Number of holdings	Parish	Total area inclosed	Arable	Parks and inclosures to pasture	Total rental value	Rental value per acre
		acr.	acr.	acr.	£ s. d.	s. d.
1	Middelclaydon	120	—	120	3 0 0	0 6
2	Wyllyn [2]	80	—	80	2 13 4	0 8
1	Aston and Hardwyke	100	100	—	5 0 0	1 0
1	Dytton	100	—	100	3 0 0	0 7¼
1	Dytton	30	—	30	1 10 0	1 0
2	Burnham	100	100	—	3 6 8	0 8
1	Stone	40	40	—	2 0 0	1 0
1	Stone	20	20	—	1 0 0	1 0
1	Weston Turfild	160	—	160	6 0 0	0 9
1	Ilmer	60	—	60	1 0 0	0 4
3	Broughton (Mentmore)	120	—	120	4 0 0	0 8
15		930	260	670	32 10 0	—

Average rental value per acre = 8½d.
Average area of holding = 62 acres

Ecclesiastical Ownership

Number of holdings	Parish	Total area inclosed	Arable	Parks and inclosures to pasture	Total rental value	Rental value per acre
		acr.	acr.	acr.	£ s. d.	d.
1	Morsley	20	—	20	0 6 0	3½
		20	—	20	—	—

Average rental value per acre = 3½d.
Average area of holding = 20 acres

[1] The rental value of the next entry of 40 acres arable at Stonystratford is not returned.
[2] A fee farm.

XII. Rental Values of Inclosed Arable and Pasture, &c.—(continued)

V. Farm tenancies

Number of holdings	Parish	Total area inclosed	Arable	Parks and inclosures to pasture	Total rental value	Rental value per acre
		acr.	acr.	acr.	£ s. d.	s. d.
{2	Asshendon[1]	60	—	60	2 0 0	0 8
{1	Asshendon	100	—	100	5 0 0	1 0
3	Donnyngton	90	—	90	3 0 0	0 8
2	Dynton	30	—	30	2 0 0	1 4
8	Hoggeshawe and Fulbroke	213½	—	213½	15 0 0	1 4¾
1	Cleydon	36	—	36	2 0 0	1 1¼
1	Adyngton[2]	15	15	—	0 10 0	0 8
1	Adyngdon	15	15	—	0 10 8	0 8½
1	Magna Kembill	40	—	40	2 0 0	1 0
1	{Aston Molent	40	—	40	1 13 4	0 10
1	{Aston Molent	60	—	60	1 13 4	0 6¾
1	Magna Myssynden[3]	80	—	80	2 10 0	0 7½
23		779½	30	749½	37 17 4	—

Average rental value per acre = 11¾d.
Average area of holding = 33·89

Number of holdings	Parish	Total area inclosed	Arable	Parks and inclosures to pasture	Total rental value	Rental value per acre
		acr.	acr.	acr.	£ s. d.	s. d.
3	Fulbroke	151	—	151	15 0 0	2 0
1	Shipden Lye	18	18	—	0 18 0	1 0
4		169	18	151	15 18 0	—

Average rental value per acre = 1s. 10¾d.
Average area of holding = 42·25

Rental Values of Inclosed Arable and Pasture. Land classified according to Tenures and Tenancies. Inferred Figures excluded

I. Land in owners' hands

	Lay Ownership						Ecclesiastical Ownership					
	Arable	Parks and inclosure to pasture	Total rental value of arable	Total rental value of pasture	Average rental value of arable per acre	Average rental value of pasture per acre	Arable	Parks and inclosure to pasture	Total rental value of arable	Total rental value of pasture	Average rental value of arable per acre	Average rental value of pasture per acre
	acr.	acr.	£ s. d.	£ s. d.	d.	s. d.	acr.	acr.	£ s. d.	£ s. d.	d.	d.
1. In hands of lords of manors	60	3,443	1 10 0	258 18 6	6	1 6	48	300	1 6 8	10 0 0	6¾	8
2. In hands of freeholders	897	1,329	39 9 8	52 4 8	10½	0 9½	157	50	7 6 8	1 6 0	11¾	6¼
Totals	957	4,772	40 19 8	311 3 2	—	—	205	350	8 13 4	11 6 0	—	—

	Total arable	Total pasture		Total arable	Total pasture
	d.	s. d.		d.	d.
Average rental value	10¾	1 3¾		10¼	7¾

[1] Lay freehold farmed and inclosed by an ecclesiastic, Abbot of Notley.
[2] There were two holdings, one of 15 acres, the area of the other not distinctly stated. It has therefore been thought better to take only the one of which the details are given.
[3] Lay freeholder's property farmed by the Abbot of Myssynden.

Rental Values of Inclosed Arable and Pasture. Land Classified according to Tenures and Tenancies. Inferred Figures Excluded

II. Land let, and in hands of tenants

—	Lay Ownership: Arable	Lay: Parks and inclosure to pasture	Lay: Total rental value of arable	Lay: Total rental value of pasture	Lay: Average rental value of arable per acre	Lay: Average rental value of pasture per acre	Ecclesiastical Ownership: Arable	Eccl.: Parks and inclosure to pasture	Eccl.: Total rental value of arable	Eccl.: Total rental value of pasture	Eccl.: Average rental value of arable per acre	Eccl.: Average rental value of pasture per acre
	acr.	acr.	£ s. d.	£ s. d.	d.	d.	acr.	acr.	s. d.	£ s. d.	s. d.	s. d.
1. Copyholds .	—	—	—	—	—	—	—	161	—	4 0 0	—	0 6
2. Leaseholds .	260	670	11 6 8	21 3 4	10½	7½	—	20	—	0 6 0	—	0 3½
3. Farm tenancy .	30	749½	1 0 8	36 16 8	8¼	11¾	18	151	18 0	15 0 0	1 0	2 0
Totals . .	290	1,419½	12 7 4	58 0 0	—	—	18	332	18 0	19 6 0	—	—

	Lay: Total arable	Lay: Total pasture	Eccl.: Total arable	Eccl.: Total pasture
	d.	d.	s. d.	s. d.
Average rental value . .	10¼	9¾	1 0	1 1¾

Total average value of pasture let (lay and ecclesiastical together) . . Per acre 10½

III. Total areas and rental values

—	Lay Ownership: Arable	Lay: Parks and inclosure to pasture	Lay: Total rental value of arable	Lay: Total rental value of pasture	Lay: Average rental value per acre	Ecclesiastical Ownership: Arable	Eccl.: Parks and inclosure to pasture	Eccl.: Total rental value of arable	Eccl.: Total rental value of pasture	Eccl.: Average rental value per acre
	acr.	acr.	£ s. d.	£ s. d.	s. d.	acr.	acr.	£ s. d.	£ s. d.	d.
(I. and II.) . .	1,247	6,191½	53 7 0	369 3 2	1 1¾	223	682	9 11 4	30 12 0	10¾

IV. Total areas and rental values of arable and pasture in owners' hands (lay and ecclesiastical together)

—	Total arable	Total rental value of arable	Average rental value of arable per acre	Total pasture	Total rental value of pasture	Average rental value of pasture per acre	Total arable and pasture	Total rental value of arable and pasture	Average rental value of arable and pasture together per acre
	acr.	£ s. d.	d.	acr.	£ s. d.	s. d.	acr.	£ s. d.	s. d.
(I.)	1,162	49 13 0	10¼	5,122	322 9 2	1 3	6,284	372 2 2	1 2¼

RENTAL VALUES OF INCLOSED ARABLE AND PASTURE. LAND CLASSIFIED ACCORDING TO TENURES AND TENANCIES. INFERRED FIGURES EXCLUDED

V. Total areas and rental values of land let, both arable and pasture (lay and ecclesiastical together)

	Total arable	Total rental value of arable	Average rental value of arable per acre	Total pasture	Total rental value of pasture	Average rental value of pasture let per acre	Total arable and pasture	Total rental value of arable and pasture	Average rental value of arable and pasture let together per acre
(II.)	acr. 308	£ s. d. 13 5 4	d. 10¼	acr. 1,751½	£ s. d. 77 6 0	d. 10½	acr. 2,059½	£ s. d. 90 11 4	d. 10½

VI. Total areas and rental values of land, both arable and pasture (lay and ecclesiastical together)

	Total arable	Total rental value of arable	Average rental value of arable per acre	Total pasture	Total rental value of pasture	Average rental value of pasture per acre	Total arable and pasture	Total rental value of arable and pasture	Average rental value of arable and pasture let together per acre
(IV and V.)	acr. 1,470	£ s. d. 62 18 4	d. 10¼	acr. 6,873½	£ s. d. 409 15 2	s. d. 1 2¼	acr. 8,343½	£ s. d. 462 13 6	s. d. 1 1¼

XIII

Selected Inclosures exceeding an Area of 300 Acres in one Place or Parish, showing the Proportion per cent. of the Inclosures to the Total Area of the Place or Parish in which such Inclosures were made.

No. of inclosures	Place or Parish	Area of parish, &c.	Total area inclosed	Proportion of total area inclosed to area of parish &c.	Area inclosed. Arable	Proportion of arable inclosed to total area of parish &c.	Area inclosed. Pasture	Proportion of pasture inclosed to total area of parish &c.
		acres	acres	acres	acres		acres	
8	Byrdyston . .	2,180[1]	400	·18	—	—	400	·18
16	Dodershill . .	5,150[2]	960	·18	—	—	960	·18
8	Stutley[3] . .	4,330	341	·07	—	—	341	·07
8	Flete Merston .	930	324	·34	—	—	324	·34
7	Bradwell and Wuluerton	3,700[4]	425	·11	42	·01	383	·10
12	Hoggeshawe and Fulbroke	1,030[5]	380½	·77	—	—	380½	·77

[1] This is the area of the parish of Aston Abbots, in which B. is situate. But the MS. says expressly: 'Predicte villa, hamellettum et manerium de Byrdeston totaliter et integre in pasturam,' &c.

[2] This is the area of Quainton, in which parish D. is situate.

[3] This includes the inclosures at Litilcote, in the parish of Stutley (Stewkley).

[4] This includes Bradwell Parish, 790 acres; Bradwell Abbey, 650 acres; Wolverton Parish 2,260 acres.

[5] Area of the parish of Hogshaw with Fulbrook.

XIV

The Area of the Virgate in Buckinghamshire

Place	Virgates	Acres	Acres to a virgate
Dodershill	24	—	40
Donnyngton	3	90	30
Ludgarshale	6	—	20
Cranwell	6	—	20
Vpton	4	—	30
Stepyll Cleydon	3	—	30
Preston	1	—	15
	47	1,515	185

Taking each entry as a unit, the average area to a virgate in Bucks is 26·42 acres. Taking the average by dividing the virgates into the sum of the acres returned (1,515), the result is 32·2 acres. Since in Bucks, as in Northants and Warwickshire, the virgate is always defined—a sign that its use is going out of date—there is no need to decide between the two methods.

The Area of the Carucate in Buckinghamshire

Place	Carucates	Acres	Acres to a carucate
Lyllyngton Darell	8	—	20½
Chalfount St. Peter	2	—	40
Castelthorpp	4	—	40
	14	404	120½

Taking each entry as a unit, the average area to a carucate in Bucks is 40·16 acres. Taking the average by dividing the carucates into the sum of acres returned, the result is 28·8 acres. Since in Bucks, as in Northants, Oxon, and Warwickshire, the carucate is always defined—a sign that its use is going out of date—there is no need to decide between the two methods.

XV

COMPARATIVE TABLE OF NUMERATIONS OF MS.

Page	Modern numeration. Membrane	Marginal numeration (1)	Marginal numeration	
			(2)	(3)
158	25	xxj	—	—
162	26	xxij	2	—
165	27	—	—	—
166	—	xxiij	—	—
169	—	—	—	c iij
169	28	xxiiij	—	—
174	—	—	—	d iiij
174	29	xxv	—	—
178	30	—	—	s
179	—	xxvj	—	—
182	31	—	—	xxx [1]
183	—	xxvij [1]	xj [1]	vij [1]
187	32	xxviij	iiij	—
190	—	—	—	h viij
190	33	xxix	—	—
193	—	—	—	I ix
193	34	—	—	—
194	—	xxx	—	—
197	35	xxxj	—	xj
202	36	xxxij	—	xij
205	—	—	—	xij
206	37	xxxiij	—	xiij
209	38	xxxiiij	—	xiiij
209	—	—	—	xiiij
212	39	—	—	xv [2]
213	—	xxxv [2]	—	—

[1] It is perfectly possible that there is a loss of three membranes here, as xxx might seem to ndicate. If so, series (1), which gives xxvij as the numeration of membrane 31, must be of later date. The series which gives vij, however, corroborates series (1). Series (2), which gives xj, is altogether puzzling ; for, if this numeration began, as is presumable, at j, and three membranes were lost, then it should be x, and not xj. Series (1) is consecutive ; and, though incomplete, series (3) is, excluding xxx, also consecutive, vij being the correct numeration beginning from j. On the other hand, xxx is isolated. The balance of evidence, therefore, is in favour of the document as being, so far, consecutive and complete. The mystery of xxx fo. is not solved by supposing that the numerator began with the first membrane of Berks as j, for this membrane of Bucks would in that case be xx, unless we are to suppose as many as ten membranes lost.

[2] The coincident consecutiveness of two sets of numerations from title to colophon, both of them of ancient date, is strong testimony in favour of the completeness of the Buckinghamshire Returns.

CHESHIRE

INTRODUCTION

THIS Return was discovered in the Record Office after the others were already in type. It has not, therefore, been possible to print it in its alphabetical place among the other Returns of 1517, to which year it belongs, nor has any attempt been made, for reasons stated above,[1] to analyse and tabulate it. Its importance is twofold. Firstly, like the Returns for Essex and Lincolnshire, and the Return in the Lansdowne MS. for Norfolk, it shows that the presentments were taken by Hundreds; secondly, the preservation of this original form in the final Returns to Chancery, by its exclusion of the possibility of lost entries within the defined areas, establishes the conclusion derived from other sources that the inclosing movement had made practically no way in the North of England. The names of families which are flourishing down to the present day will be of interest to the genealogist and local historian.

[1] P. 5, n. 1.

INQUISITION OF 1517

CHESHIRE

CHANCERY MISCELL. $\frac{13}{4}$

SESSIO tenta apud Cestriam infra comitatum palatinum
^{a scilicet} Cestrie die Jouis proximo post festum sancti Petri quod
dicitur ad vincula anno regni Regis Henrici octaui post
conquestum Anglie nono coram Reverendo in Christo presule Galfrido permissione divina Coventriensi & Lichfeldensi episcopo & Thoma Cornwell milite Commissionariis
dicti domini Regis in comitatu predicto assignatis ad
inquirendum virtute commissionis eis directe per sacramentum proborum & legalium hominum de comitatu predicto
tam infra libertates quam extra ac aliis viis modis & mediis
quibus eis melius scitum fuerit seu videbitur que & quot
ville domus & edificia a festo sancti Michaelis archangeli
anno regni Regis henrici septimi quarto prosternuntur Et
quot & quante terre que tunc in cultura erant & iam in
pasturam conuertuntur Necnon quot & quanti parci pro
[f]eris [1] nutriendis citra idem festum includuntur ac de aliis
articulis & circumstanciis in predicta commissione specificatis
secundum tenorem & effectum eiusdem

Inquisicio capta scilicet eisdem die anno & loco coram
prefatis commissionariis per sacramentum Ed[ward]i faryngton hamonis Johnson Roberti Colbourne Ricardi Lowe
Ed[ward]i Smyth Ricardi Walton henrici Radford Thome
Smyth Ricardi Grosuenour hamonis Goodman Ricardi
ffleccher hugonis Clerk Thome hoghton Roberti Wright
Roberti Aldersey Ricardi Grymsdich Ricardi Classh Roberti

[1] MS. mutilated.

Wright coruesour Roberti mercer Ranulphi Wirehall Roberti Gile Thome Colbourne Willelmi Shawe Stephani Crosse Radulphi Middelton Roberti Hatton Jacobi Busshell Ricardi forbe Henrici Chaluer Johannis Molyners Alexandri Stuard & Galfridi Tarlton juratorum ad inquirendum pro domino Rege infra comitatum ciuitatis Cestrie super premissa

Qui dicunt super sacramentum suum quod Ranulphus Wirehall & Ricardus Lyme de ciuitate Cestrie Bakers incluserunt siue imparcauerunt vnam clausuram terre per spacium viginti iiij^{or} annorum iacentis in le houbrigfildes infra libertatem comitatus ciuitatis Cestrie que quidem clausura continet in se iiij^{or} acras & fuit in cultura ante datum commissionis predicte Et ex quo dicta clausura sic fuit occupata per prefatos Ranulphum & Ricardum in pasturam & Petrus Dutton & Jacobus Hurlston habent statum & hereditatem dicte claus[ure][1]

Item dicunt quod Johannes monkesfeld inclusit siue imparcauit aliam paruam clausuram per spacium sex annorum iacentem in le houbrigfildes predicto que quidem clausura continet in se duas acras & diversis temporibus fuit in cultura & aliis temporibus in pastura & nunc occupata est in pastura per predictum Johannem & heredes Willelmi Enlowe habent statum & hereditatem clausure predicte

Item dicunt quod Johannes harper de ciuitate predicta mercator inclusit siue imparcauit aliam paruam clausuram iacentem in Chester feldes infra libertatem comitatus ciuitatis Cestrie per spacium octo annorum que quidem clausura continet in se vnam acram & dimidiam & nunc occupata est in pastura per predictum Johannem & quod dictus Johannes habet statum & hereditatem clausure predicte

Item dicunt quod Johannes Molyners de ciuitate predicta Bocher imparcauit aliam paruam clausuram per spacium vnius anni iacentem in le houbrig feldes predictum infra libertatem predictam que quidem clausura continet in se vnam acram terre & fuit antea in pastura & nunc occupata est in cultura per predictum Johannem & quod Jacobus

[1] MS. mutilated.

CHESHIRE

hurlton habet statum & hereditatem clausure predicte Et vlterius dicunt jurati predicti quod nulle ville hameletta domus edificia neque cotagia prosternantur[1] siue in ruina eiicientur[1] nec alique persone minime sunt inhabitantes infra libertates comitatus ciuitatis Cestrie Racione alicuius inclausure siue imparcacionis

Alias scilicet eisdem die anno & loco presentatum fuit coram prefatis commissionariis per sacramentum Roberti Radishe Jacobi Domvile Johannis mere Thome Hulse Radulphi Leycestre Petri Danyell hugonis Cokkes hugonis Venables Willelmi Wilne Petri Grymsdych Roberti Venables Petri hatton Petri Colsonsok Gilberti Cleve Ricardi Merbury & Johannis dutton quod Johannes Legh miles imparcauit siue cum quadam pala inclusit vnum parcum apud Baggeley in comitatu predicto & in eodem duodecim acras terre que in cultura erant in anno v^{to} domini Regis nunc & iam in eodem feras custodit

Et quod Philippus legh armiger in anno iiij^{to} domini Regis nunc imparcauit & cum quadam pala inclusit vnum parcum & in eodem parco duas acras que in cultura erant inclusit & in eodem feras custodit

Et quod Johannes assheley in anno iiij^{to} Domini Regis nunc imparcauit siue cum quadam pala inclusit iiij^{or} acras terre arabilis apud   [2]   in comitatu predicto & easdem in pasturam conuertit

Et quod Robertus Chantrell imparcauit siue cum quadam pala inclusit in anno xx^{mo} henrici septimi sex acras terre arabilis apud   [2]   in Comitatu predicto & easdem in pasturam conuertit

Et quod nulle ville hameletta domus edificia neque cotagia prosternuntur siue in ruina eiicientur[1] nec alique persone minime sunt inhabitantes infra hundredum de Buklowe in Comitatu predicto racione alicuius inclausure siue imparcacionis

Alias scilicet eisdem die anno & loco presentatum fuit coram prefatis commissionariis per sacramentum Willelmi

---

[1] Sic.   [2] Blank in MS.

Stanley Willelmi Pole Thome Massy Johannis Clegge Johannis Whetmore Johannis Cleyve Johannis Clyff Ricardi Bunbury Roberti Bille Ricardi Wilbram Johannis Doo & Ricardi Bunbury juratorum infra hundredum. de Wirehall quod Willelmus Troutebeke inclusit in quodam parco apud Brimstach in comitatu xx^{ti} acras terre arabilis in anno xxiij^{cio} henrici vij^{mi} & easdem in pasturam conuertit & quod Johannes Talbot miles habet statum & hereditatem acrarum predictarum

Et quod Thomas massy imparcauit siue in quodam parco inclusit sex acras terre arabilis apud Podyngton in comitatu predicto & easdem in pasturam conuertit in anno iiij^{to} domini Regis nunc & quod dictus Thomas habet statum & hereditatem in terris predictis Et quod nulle ville hameletta domus edificia neque cotagia prosternantur [1] siue in ruina eiicientur [1] infra hundredum predictum racione alicuius inclausure siue imparcacionis predicte

Alias scilicet eisdem die anno & loco presentatum fuit coram prefatis Justiciariis per sacramentum Jacobi Stanley Philippi Eggerton Thome Trafford Johannis Bryn Radulphi Donne Johannis Aldersey Johannis Brassy hameletti Trauerse Ricardi Ayce hugonis Walker Ricardi lightfote & Radulphi Page Juratorum infra hundredum de Eddesbury quod Radulphus Eggerton miles in anno sexto domini Regis nunc imparcauit siue in quodam parco inclusit apud Ridley in comitatu predicto sex acras terre arabilis & vnam acram terre communis & easdem in pasturam animalium conuertit & vnum cotagium prosternitur racione inclausure predicte

Et quod nulle plures domus edificia neque cotagia prosternantur [1] siue in ruina eiicientur [1] racione alicuius inclausure siue imparcacionis.

Alias scilicet eisdem die anno & loco presentatum fuit coram prefatis commissionariis per sacramentum [2]

[1] Sic.
[2] The MS. here abruptly terminates, leaving about five inches of space blank at the foot of the single sheet of parchment on which the above presentments are contained.

THE INQUISITIONS OF 1517, 1518, AND 1549, FROM THE DUGDALE MSS.

LIST OF TABLES

		PAGE
I.	Dugdale's Notes of the Inquisition of 1517 . . .	647
II.	Dugdale's Notes of the Inquisition of 1518 . . .	651
III.	Dugdale's Notes of the Inquisition of 1549 . . .	656
IV.	Concordance of Dugdale's Notes with the Chancery Returns of 1517	666
V.	Differences between Dugdale's Notes of the Inquisition of 1517 and the Chancery Returns . . .	668
	Synoptic Comparison of the Differences between Dugdale's Notes of the Inquisition of 1517 and the Chancery Returns	673
VI.	Tabulation of Dugdale's Notes of the Inquisition of 1518	674
VII.	Tabulation of Dugdale's Notes of the Inquisition of 1549	676
VIII.	Tabulation of Dugdale's Notes of the Inquisition of 1518, showing Returns additional to the Chancery Returns of 1517	678
IX.	Tabulation of Dugdale's Notes of the Inquisitions of 1518 and 1549, showing the Restitution of Inclosures &c. mentioned in the Inquisitions . . .	680
X.	Tabulation of Dugdale's Notes of the Inquisition of 1518, showing Status of Actual Inclosers in the Additional Returns	682
XI.	Tabulation of Dugdale's Notes of the Inquisition of 1518. Additional Returns. Number of Acres to a Messuagium, &c.	683

		PAGE
XII.	TABULATION OF DUGDALE'S NOTES OF THE INQUISITION OF 1549, SHOWING RETURNS ADDITIONAL TO THE CHANCERY RETURNS OF 1517 AND TO DUGDALE'S NOTES OF THE INQUISITION OF 1518	684
XIII.	TABULATION OF DUGDALE'S NOTES OF THE INQUISITION OF 1549, SHOWING STATUS OF ACTUAL INCLOSERS IN THE ADDITIONAL RETURNS	686
XIV.	DUGDALE'S NOTES OF THE INQUISITION OF 1549. ADDITIONAL RETURNS. NUMBER OF ACRES TO A MESSUAGE . . .	687

WARWICKSHIRE

Dugdale's Notes of the Inquisition of 1517 and 1518

Dugdale MSS., Bodl. Library, D. 1. 7.

fo. 543

'In officio Rotulorum in quodam bundello.'[a]
E quodam bundello in capella
Rotulorum excerpta per me
W. D. A° 1641.

Inquisicio capta apud Allesley ii^{do} die Sept. ix° Henr viij. Regis Anglie coram Johanne Veysy clerico Decano Capelle Regis, Johanne Port armigero, Rogero Wigston et Johanne Hales ad inquirendum super depopulacionibus &c in comitatu predicto per sacramentum Henrici Squyer gentilman, Nich. Rugeley gent., Ricc. Mountford gent., Johannis Lisley gent., Rob. Redell de Coleshull &c et aliis. Ad inquirendum scilicet quot ville quot domus et edificia a festo S. Mich. anno quarto regis H. 7 prosternuntur, et quot et quante terre que tunc in cultura erant, et iam in pasturam convertuntur ; necnon quot et quanti parci pro feris nutriendis citra idem festum includuntur, et que terre aliquibus parcis, qui tunc fuerant, pro elargatione huiusmodi parcorum includuntur, et per quos &c. Qui dicunt quod

ix° H. Warr.' ss.

[a] This line in pencil in Dugdale's handwriting.

Prior de Maluerne .	vj messuag'. ii cottag' xl acr. tre. arabil.	Shuttington parcell. Priorat' de Alcote
Tho. nuper Marchio Dorset	x mess. & ccc acr. tre. 7 H. 7	Wedington
Iacobus at Holt armiger .	l acr. tre. arabil. . .	Manceter
Riccus. Caue . . .	l acr. tre. arabil. . .	ibidem
Willms. Rowley nuper de Coventre Humfridus Alablaster de eadem Tho. Harper de Merevale	l acr. tre. arabil. . .	ibidem
Iohes. Bonde de Coventre draper	xxx acr. tre. palis inclusit pro feris nutriendis, et in eadem feras posuit. 6º H. 8	Bromwich parua
Tho. Cokeyn miles . .	cxl acr. tre et bosci in H. 7 fossis sepibus et palis imparcauit et parcum novum inde fecit pro feris ibidem nutriendis, et feras in eodem parco posuit et adhuc habet :	Poley 6º Nov. 22º
Iohes. Arden armiger .	ii croft' vocat' Ladycroftes cxl acr. pasture et bosci et x acr. terre arab. 2º H. 8 imparcauit, et feras in eodem parco posuit ᵃ	Castle-Bromwich
Tho. Massy gentilman . Cornelius Wirley & Ricus. Caue	l mess. xxiiij acr. tre. . l mess. xx acr. tre. . .	Mereden Birmingham
Willms. Chetewyn . .	l mess. vocat. Meredenhall & c acr. tre	Mereden
Iohes. Brerely. . .	l mess. & x acr. tre. .	Fillongley
Heres Willi. Spencer .	l mess. xx acr. tre. . .	ibidem
Willm Coope gentylman .	xij mess. iii cottag'. & ccxl acr. tre. ; 14º H. 7 devastavit et inclusit	Wormleighton
Willms. Gascoigne miles .	l mess. xxx acr. tre. .	Grafton
Henr. Smyth nuper de Coventr'.	l mess. & lx acr. tre. .	Grafton
Radus. nuper Abb. de Kenelworth	medietat. m. de Tachbrok-Malory et mediet. viij mess. j cottag. cccx acr. tre.	Tachbroke Malory
Willms. Medley . .	de altera medietate eiusdem manerii	
Edw. Raleigh miles .	l mess. xxij acr. tre. .	Darset
Abb. de Kenelworth .	ii mess. & j cottag. . .	Salford
Pr. de Wroxall . .	xxx acr. tre. . . .	Shuckbrough
Tho. Catesby . . .	l mess. xx acr. tre. . .	Nether Shuckbrough
Edw. Raleigh miles .	l mess. & j carucat' tre. .	Vpton
Ioh. Warner . . .	l mess. & j car. tre & dim.	ibidem
Willms. Dauers miles .	iij mess. & cxx acr. tre. 14 H. 7	Vpton
Edw. Raleigh. . .	l mess. xl acr. . . .	Farnborough
Dauid Owen miles . .	l mess. xl acr. tre. . .	Oxshulfe

ᵃ In a smaller script—apparently an interpolation. Not in the Chancery returns.

Agnes Walshe vidua .	l mess. vocat. Booston house	Warwick
Matilda Rouse vidua .	v mess. & cc. acr. tre. .	Darsington
Kebull nuper Aldermannus London	vij mess. i cottag. cc acr. tre	Weston iuxta Cheriton in parochia - de Longa Compton
Willms. Willington. 24° H. 7.	Maner. de Barcheston iiij[or] mess. j cottag. D xxx acr. tre. ; & cum vno mess. vocat. Frances mese et diuersis aliis, Ita quod dictus Willms. tantum vnum principale messuag. viz. scitum m[i] predicti & lxiiij[or] acr. tre. parcell. &c predict cum vno aratro ibidem in vsum culture et [a]	
Willms. Compton miles .	ij mess. & c acr. tre. arab. a° 4° Regis nunc inclusit parcum pro feris ibidem nutriendis &c.	Compton
fo. 545 Idem Willms Compton .	l mess. xxx acr. tre. .	ibidem
Willm. Browne . .	l mess. xij virgat' tre. .	Brayles
Henr. Grenefeild gentylman	iij mess. j cottag' & cxx acr. tre.	Chelmescote
Magr. & fres. gilde scte Trinit. & scti Georgii in Warwico.	j mess. & j carucat. tre. & dim. contin'. in se lx acr. tre.	Chelmescote
Willms. Browne clericus perpetuus capellan' Cantarie de Chelmescote	j mess. & l acr. tre.	ibm.
Pr. scti. Sepulcri Warr. .	cccc [b] acr. tre.	Warwick.
Rob. le Straunge . . Iohes le Straunge modo habet statum in premissis	vij mess. j cottag. & clx acr. tre.	Walton Deuile
Iohes Rouse . . .	xxiiij acr. tre.. . .	Harborough
Tho. Hall . . .	j mess. xx. acr. tre. .	ibm.
Edw. Belknap miles .	xij mess. ccclx acr. tre. 14 H. 7	Derset & Birton

Et dicunt quod Henr. Rex Angl. vij diu post inclusionem predict. &c. sc. xiiij Apr. 24° Regni literas suas Patentes iuratoribus ostens. Et de pardonacione &c pro eodem.

Willm. Clerke . . Rob. Greene . . .	j mess. xxx acr. tre.. } j mess. x acr. tre . }	Bishops-Hampton
Minister domus de Thelesford & vicar. perpetuus de Newbold	l mess. & xl acr. tre. ibm. permisit deuastari. .	Rector de Snyterfeild m. de Bishops-Hampton
Pri. hospit. scti Iohis. Ihrlm. in Angl.	ccc acr. tre. . . .	Ruyton ita quod ecclesia parochialis nisi remedium prouideatur in desolationem &c.

Henr. Smyth vj[to] Dec. ix° Regis H. 7 inclusit &c. xij mess. iiij cottag. & dcxl acr. tre. in Stretton super streete, ita quod lxxx persone qui ibm. circa culturam eorum solebant occupari ab inde recedere coacti fuerunt & sic ociosi ac miseram vitam duxerunt & sic misere obierunt & quod magis dolendum est ecclesia parochialis ea occasione de Stretton predict. in ruinam &c existit. Ita quod con-

[a] Sic.
[b] Probably a misreading of quadringent[as] for quateruigint[i]. See p. 655, *n*. 6, *infra*.

gregacio Xpianorum qui ibidem pro diuinis officiis audiendis venire solebant, vlterius ibm. non habetur & cultus Dei ibidem penitus cassatur, animalia in ecclesia illa ab tempestatibus aeris protegantur, Ac animalia bruta super sepulturas corporum Xpianorum in cimiterio ecclesie illius sepult' pascuntur & ecclesia & cemiterium illa in omnibus prophanantur in malum exemplum aliorum in tali casu se habere disponentium.

fo. 546	Geo. Co. Salop	ij mess. & lx acr. tre.[1]	Willey
	Nich. Mallory	j mess. & xxx acr. tre.	Esenhull
	Edw. Caue iure dorothea[1] uxoris eius fil. & hered. dicti Nichi. Mallory modo seisitus existit de eodem		
	Haruy	j mess. xxiiij^{or} acr. tre.	Bulkinton
	Johes. Quincy	j mess. & xl acr. tre.	Wolvehamcote
	Johes. Ferrers miles	j mess. xxx acr. tre.	ibm.
	Willms. Pereson	j mess. xxviij acr. tre.	Alseley
	Willms. Smyth	j mess. xx acr. tre.	ibm.
	Johes. Hugford	ij mess. l acr. tre.	Princethorpe
	Tho. Shuckborough ar	j capital' mess. & lxx acr. tre.	Napton
	Tho. Catesby ar.	j mess. xxx acr. tre.	Wollescote
	Idem Thomas	j mess. xxx acr. tre.	Greneborough
	Wills. Medley	ij mess. xl acr. tre.	Whitnashe
	Johes. Rodburne	j mess. xxx acr. tre.	Wollescote
	Will. Banwell de Couentre	j mess. xx acr. tre.	Bobenhull
	Tho. Draper	ij mess. xl acr. tre.	ibm.
	Johe. Turner	lxx acr. tre.	Eythorpe
	Nich. Mallory	j mess. xx. acr. tre.	Paylton
	Johes. Smyth	c acr. pastur.	Fletchamsted
	Henr. Smyth fil. & heres	ij mess. j cottag'. xl acr. tre.	ibm.
	Ric. Hastings	j capital' mess. & cc acr. tre. arab.	Draknage
	Thomas Ashby	j mess. vocat'. Barnsplace & xxx acr. tre.	Lapworth
fo. 547	Jasper Leke	j mess. & xxx acr. tre.	Fillingley
	Decan. & capl. bte. M. Warr.	j mess. xxx acr. tre.	Woluerton
	Johes. Bewfo ar.	capit. mess. & lx acr. tre.	Kingswood
	Johes Bewfo fil. & heres infra æt. et in custod.		
	Edw. Ferrers milit. nunc habet statum in eodem		
	Willms. Huett	mess. lx acr. tre.	Wollescote Pr. de Ronton spect'
	Tho. Catesby	j mess. xl acr. tre.	Greneborough
	Edw. Odingsells	j mess. xxx acr. tre.	Itchington
	Johes. Buckmore	j mess. xxiiij acr. tre.	ibm.
	Johes. Whore	j mess. lxxx acr. tre.	ibm.
	Johes. dns. Clinton	{ capital' mess. vocat. & cc acr. tre. in = =	Boulhall Amyngton
	Tho. Vnderhill	ij mess. xl acr. tre.	Honyngham
	Ric. Hollier	j mess. xxx acr. tre.	Bentley
	Lawrence Robinson	j mess. xx acr. tre.	Solyhull
	Tho. Herthill	ij mess. & xl acr. tre.	Kingsbury
	Johe. Bracebridge ar.	iij mess. & lx acr. tre.	Kynnesbury

[1] Sic.

WARWICKSHIRE: THE DUGDALE MSS.

Abb. de Stonley . .	capital'. mess. & ccc acr. tre. in	Stonley
Radus. Abb. de Kenelworth	imparcauit Parcum de nouo vocat' a° 4° H. 7 & xl acr. tre. arab. in eodem conclusit & feras nunc in eodem habet.	Wrygfyn
Robtus. Throckmorton miles	de nouo imparcauit parcum apud a° 2° H. 7 & inclusit in eodem xx^D acr. tre. arab. & dim. pro feris nutriendis.	Coughton
Tho. nup. marchio Dorset	de nouo imparcauit & palis circumclusit xxx acr. bosci pasture &c de terris dominicalibus & elargiuit alium parcum cum xviij acr. tre. in Astley.	
Henr. Smyth . . .	xxx acr. tre. . . .	Thirford
Johe. Bracebruge . .	elargiuit parcum in cum x acr. tre.	Kynnesbury
Baldw. Hethe . .	imparcauit xxiiij acr. tre. .	Wotton
Willms. Woodward .	j mess. xxiiij acr. arab. tre.	Harborough

II.

In alio bundello [a]

Inq. capta apud Warr j° Sept. x H. viij [b]
Coram Johe. Veysy clerico &c.

Tho. Enyse [c] . . .	j mess. xxiiij acr. tre. .	Warwick
Ric. Grenefeild [d] . .	iij mess. & cxx acr. tre. .	Chelmescote
Custos cantarie de Chelmescote [e] [1]	j mess. lx acr. tre. . .	ibm. eidem cantari spect'.

[a] In Dugdale's hand, in pencil.   [b] 1518.
[c] Entry not in Chancery Returns of 1517.
[d] Qu. whether the same entry, the cottage being omitted, as on fo. 545, *supra*; see p. 419.

[1] The inclosure of 60 acres bears at first sight a suspicious resemblance to the inclosure here of 50 acres by 'William Browne clericus & perpetuus capellanus Cantarie de Chelmescote' as noted by Dugdale on fo. 545 from the Inquisition of 1517 (see p. 421, *supra*). On the whole, however, it is probable that this is another inclosure. In the first place, the description of the incloser in the two cases is not the same, and Dugdale's *Warwickshire*, p. 399, shows that by the constitution of the Chantry at Chelmescote two priests were there resident, one of whom may very well have had the title of warden and the other of chaplain. Secondly, in his *Warwickshire*, p. 398, Dugdale cites only the inclosure of 50 acres from the Inquisition of 1517, and does not, as is customary with him, refer to the Inquisition of 1518 at all, the inference being that he overlooked this entry, rather than that he identified it with the previous return. Thirdly, though Dugdale's accuracy is far from unimpeachable, the areas are different. Fourthly, a fresh inclosure by Ric. Browne, priest of the chantry of Chelmescote, occurs in this Inquisition on next page.

Johes. Bigge [a]	j mess. xl acr. tre. arab. .	Cheriton [1]
Mgr. & fres. gilde de Warwick . . . . [b]		Chelmescote
Edw. Raleigh . .	j mess. xx acr. tre.[a] .	Farnborough
Tho. Gebons . . .	j mess. xx acr. tre.[a] .	Morton Morell [2]
Johes. Bery . . .	j mess. xlv acr. tre.[a] .	Barton [3]
Ric. Browne pbr. Cantar. de Chelmescote	j mess. xx acr. tre.[a] .	Brayles dicte cantar. de Chelmescote pertin.
Tho. Lucy miles . .	j mess. xl acr. tre.[a]. .	Cherlecote
Rob. Straunge & Johes. Straunge	v mess. & cl acr. tre.[a] .	Walton Deuill [4]
Edw. Kniuet & Anna [v]x. eius nuper vx. predicti Rob. Straunge & M[a]rgareta relicta dicti Johis. Straunge modo tenent.		
Henr. Kebull . . .	vij mess. & cccl acr. tre.[c]	Weston in parochia de long Compton.[5] Tota deletur & desolatur preterquam capitale mess. cum quo lxxx acr. tre. occupat'.
Wills. Blount dns. Montioy modo tenet iure vx. filie et heredis dicti H. Kebull.		

[a] Entry not in Chancery Returns of 1517.   [b] Sic. *Cf.* fo. 545, *supra*.
[c] Entry varied from Chancery Returns of 1517.

[1] Now Cherington. A comparison of Dugdale's entries of the Inquisition of 1517 with the Chancery Returns shows that Dugdale's note of the land inclosed, sometimes as 'terre,' sometimes, as in this instance, as 'terre arabilis,' is purely arbitrary and does not necessarily point to any distinction between the transactions recorded. The Exchequer Memoranda also show that 'terra,' as distinguished from 'pratum' and 'pastura,' commonly meant arable.

[2] Morton Merhull, Dugdale. Now Morton Morrell. Dugdale cites Rous for his assertion that 'Depopulation since [Ed. I.'s time] hath shrunk the Inhabitants into a lesse number than twenty-one' (*Warwickshire*, p. 358).   [3] Barton on the Heath, Dugdale and modern.

[4] Walton Deuill. The transcripts from the Inquisition of 1549 throw a light upon this entry. It is, as they show, a new presentment of an inclosure made in 12 H. VII. (1497), the inclosure returned in the Inquisition of 1547 having taken place in January 1509. Robert Straunge died in 1511, *Warwickshire*, p. 411, Blomefield's *Norfolk*, x. 114.

[5] Weston juxta Chiriton, Dugdale. The Inquisition of 1517 recorded the destruction by Kebyll at this place of seven messuages and one cottage and the inclosure to pasture of 200 acres of land. As Dugdale in his *Warwickshire* cites the Inquisition of 1518 only, though we know from his transcripts that he had the evidence before him of the inclosures returned by that of 1517, it follows that he identified the two. I have followed his example and tabulated among the Additional Returns of 1518 the additional inclosures since those returned in 1517, viz. 150 acres, the difference between 200 acres and 350 acres. Note that Dugdale's transcript of 1518 fills up the blanks of the Returns of 1517 as to the succession of the property. For the Return in 1549 of 300 acres inclosed here see p. 658, *infra*.

WARWICKSHIRE: THE DUGDALE MSS. 653

Abbas de Kenelworth .	iiij mess. & cxx acr. tre.ᵃ .	Tachebrok vnde vj aratra deponuntur & xxiiij persone mancionibus carent.[1]
Willms. Medley . .	iiijᵒʳ mess. & cxx acr. tre.ᵃ	
Tho. Thomason . .	j mess. xl acr. tre.ᵇ . .	Stratford super auon
Minister domus de Thelesford	j mess. xx acr. tre.ᵇ	Woluardington [2]
Rob. Gybbs . . .	j mess. lx acr. tre.ᵇ . .	Honyngton
Henr. Smyth . . .	. . . . . (sic)ᶜ . .	Grafton
Tho. Marchio Dorset .	. . . . . (sic)ᵈ . .	Wedington
Willm. Chatwyn . .	. . . . . (sic)ᵈ . .	Mereden
Tho. Shugbrough . .	ij mess. xl acr. tre.ᵇ .	Shugbrough [3]
Tho. Herthill . . .	ij mess. xl acr. tre.ᵉ .	Cliffe in parochia de Kimesbury.
Johes. Hugford . .	ij mess. l acr. tre.ᶠ . .	Princethorpe
Tho. Shugbrough ar .	j capital'. mess. & lxx acr. tre. arab.ᶠ	Napton
Tho. Catesby ar . .	j mess. xxx acr. tre.ᶠ .	Wollescote
Idem Tho. . . .	j mess. xxx acr. tre.ᶠ .	Greneborough
Johes. Ferrers miles & Rob. Quincy	. . . . (sic)ᶠ . .	Wolfhamcote

ᵃ Entry varied from Chancery Returns of 1517.
ᵇ Entry not in Chancery Returns of 1517.
ᶜ *Cf.* fo. 544, *supra*.   ᵈ *Cf.* fo. 543, *supra*.
ᵉ *Cf.* fo. 547, *supra*.   ᶠ *Cf.* fo. 546, *supra*.

[1] Dugdale in his *Warwickshire*, p. 354 (cf. p. 648, *supra*), while only citing the Returns of 1517, gives six ploughs as put down here. This number is evidently taken from his notes of the Returns of 1518, the number given in the Chancery Returns of 1517 being ten, while no reference whatever to ploughs occurs in his notes for 1517. The inference, as before, is that Dugdale, probably on the explicit authority of the original presentments, regarded both these returns as relating to the same proceedings. The number of messuages destroyed in both is the same, though again, as before, the cottage mentioned in the former Return does not appear. In the Return for 1518, however, the number of acres inclosed to pasture is reduced to 240, implying a reconversion to arable since 1517 of 70 acres and the restitution of four ploughs. The 24 persons now presented as houseless indicate the replacement of 36 out of the 60 originally returned as evicted. These reversionary movements are collected in a separate table, p. 680, *infra*. If any further evidence be needed that such is the character of this Return, and that it is not a fresh set of inclosures, &c., it is to be found in Dugdale's addition to his citation of the Inquisition of 1517, 'So that now there is not above 4 houses left in all the village' (*Warwickshire*, l.c.).

[2] Now Wolverton. This minister was no doubt John Brogden, returned both as an ingrosser of farms and an incloser in and near Bysshopshampton in 1517 (p. 428, *supra*).

[3] A comparison of Dugdale's notes of the Returns for 1517 with the original Inquisition will show that by Shugbrough Dugdale means Higher S., of which the incloser was lord of the manor.

Abb. de Kenelworth .	. . . . . (sic)^a . .	Beuyngton
Johe. Bracebridge ar .	iij mess. lx acr. tre.^b .	Kingsbury
Abb. de Stonley . .	j capit'. mess. ccc acr. tre.^c	Stonley
Johes. Hugford ar . .	capital'. mess. & ccxl acr. tre.^d	Brayles,[1] ita quod quinque aratra ibm. deponuntur.
Willm. Dauers miles .	j mess. xxviij acr. tre. cc acr. pastur.^e	Vpton [2]
Edw. Raleigh miles .	j mess. xxx acr. tre.^{e f} .	Vpton [3]

^a *Cf.* fo. 544, *supra, sub* Salford.   ^b *Cf.* fo. 548, *supra*.
^c *Cf.* fo. 547, *supra*.   ^d Entry not in Chancery Returns of 1517.
^e *Cf.* fo. 544, *supra*.   ^f Entry varied from Chancery Returns of 1517.

[1] Although a large inclosure of 192 acres by William Brown, accompanied by the putting down of four ploughs and two messuages and eviction of 16 persons, has already been returned in the Inquisition of 1517, this seems to have been an independent case. The manor was in the Crown and the incloser was probably a leaseholder, for in 1508 the manor was leased for 40 years to Richard Hungerford and John Hopper (*Warwickshire*, p. 397). This circumstance, coupled with the similarity of name, suggests that the families of Hungerford and Hugford were the same, though Dugdale does not appear to identify them.

[2] This is an entry not easy to interpret. The Returns of 1517, after recording the inclosure of 100 acres and destruction of two messuages by two freeholders, and the inclosure of 120 acres and destruction of three messuages by Sir W. Danvers, the lord of the manor, adds, 'et dicta hameletta de Vpton totaliter destruitur.' From this it is evident that the Return of 1518 cannot be the destruction of another house. Moreover, Dugdale having his notes of both Inquisitions before him, in his *Warwickshire* only cites this one (cf. note on Weston, p. 415, *supra*) 'which Will. [Danvers] depopulated i mess. and inclosed xxviij Acres of Land and cc Acres of Pasture in this Place' (*Warw.* p. 390). I take it, therefore, to be a return of the proceedings of Danvers up to that time, indicating on the one hand fresh inclosures by him of 108 acres, but, on the other, the restoration of two messuages. I have therefore entered the 108 acres in the table of Returns additional to those of 1517 and the restoration of the two messuages in the Table of Restitutions of Inclosures, &c. It is to be observed in support of this that his new inclosure was chiefly of pasture, and only of 28 acres arable. It may, of course, be that this was an altogether independent inclosure, prior to that of 1499 presented in 1517. Such an instance occurs, as has been seen, in Walton Deuill (p. 652, *n.* 2, *supra*). But the probabilities are greater in favour of the identity of the cases with those returned in the previous year.

[3] Adopting the reasoning with respect to the last inclosure I interpret this as implying the restoration to the plough of ten acres of arable land, the original inclosure having been of 40 acres, accompanied by the destruction of a messuage still, therefore, left in ruins.

Johes. Warner	j mess. xx acr. tre. arab. & lx ª ᵇ acr. prati & pasture	Ibm.¹
Et sicut in priori Inq. capt. ix° Henr. viij.		
Edw. Belknap miles	xij mess. ccclx acr. tre. 14° H. 7ᶜ	Derset & Birton cuilibet mess. xxiiij°ʳ acr. tre. solebant occupari.

But it appeareth by a second Inquisition² that this decay of tillage in Birton Dassett is noe preiudice, but benefitt to the publike viz. : wheras they were able to enterteine before the Inclosure xx strangers upon occasion now they can enterteyne lx aswell. That the church & ornamentes are in better sort than before hauinge cost the parish since cc li. That there are xxi ploughs mayntayned in the said parish. That before the Inclosure there was but one Preist mayntayned, now twoo Preistes and many clerkes doinge diuine seruice euerey holy day by note & many tymes with Prick-songe where none such seruice was kept before in regard of the disabilitye of the parishioners. Item that the benefice is better & more of yearly value to the Parson, then it was when the landes lay in Tillage by the somme of iij li. or theraboutes. Item that the children of the parish are better taught &c. Item that there be better housholds kept & yᵗ there are now inhabitant within the said parish seauen score houslings people & aboue, &c.

fo. 550

Decan' & canon' Colleg. de Warr.	j mess. xl acr. tre.ᵈ.	Woluardyngton³
Ric. Vernon	j mess. xx acr. tre.ᵈ.	Sekinton⁴
Pr. domus Carthus. de Axholme	j mess. xx acr. tre.ᵈ.	Harborough⁵
Pr. scti Sepulcri Warr	j mess. lxxx acr. tre.ᵉ	Warwick⁶
Dauid Owen miles	j mess. lxxx acr. tre.ᵈ	Oxshulfe

ª Entry varied from Chancery Returns of 1517.   ᵇ Cf. fo. 544, supra.
ᶜ Cf. fo. 545, supra.   ᵈ Entry not in Chancery Returns of 1517.
ᵉ Probably the same presentment as on fo. 545, where cccc is a mistaken reading of quateruiginti.

¹ This entry returns 20 acres inclosed in addition to the 60 recorded by the Inquisition of 1517. See note on Vpton, *supra*, p. 654, *n.* 2.

² This shows that despite the large language of the Letters Patent, a fresh inquiry was ordered at or immediately following upon the Inquisition of 1518 into these inclosures. See pp. 426, 478, *supra*.

³ Now Wolverton.

⁴ Sekindon, Dugdale. The manor was in the family of Burdet (*Warw.* p. 799). The incloser was therefore probably a freeholder. This is a fresh presentment.

⁵ As in the case of the messuage and 24 acres returned as owned by the Prior of Exholme in the Inquisition of 1517, this property would certainly have been let to farm. This entry accordingly shows that from among the names associated with inclosures Dugdale selected those ultimately responsible, whether as lords of manors or freeholders, the exception being the case of the lessee of the manor of Brayles, on preceding page.

⁶ It has been noticed (p. 649 b) that on fo. 545 of Dugdale's tables he evidently read 'quadringentas' (cccc) for 'quateruiginti.' This presentment confirms that view, and is doubtless the same as the former one, but with the right reading restored.

Willms. Cope ar. & Edw. Raleigh miles	vj messuag' &c in Wormleighton & quod postᵃ vastum & inclusum sic perpetrat' sc. 3° Sept. 22° H. 7 : predictus Wills. Cope barginizauit & vendidit m. predictum cuidam Johi Spencer ar. Qui quidem Johes. Spencer inde de eodem m. sesitus de nouo edificauit quoddam capitale messuag. & sufficiens in quo idem Johes. cum lx personis de familia sua iam moram trahit & inhabitat. Quod per ipsum Johem. ecclesia de Wormleighton tam in diuino seruicio quam in ornamentis melius sustentetur quam prius fuit &c. Et qd. m. de Wormleighton tenetur de dno. Rege vt de castro de Warwick etc.¹

III.

Dugdale MSS. Bodl. Library, D. 1. Fo. 535

INQUISITION SUPER DEPOP. 3 E. 6.

Certificates penes Joh. Hales de Coventre

fo. 535   'Extracted out of divers Certificates made vnto Sʳ Richard Catesby knᵗ, Sʳ Fouke Grevill kᵗ, John Hales Thomas Lucy and Roger Wigston esqʳˢ, comissioners assigned to enquire touching Inclosures and depopulations within this County of Warwick A° 3° E. 6 which certificates are now in the custody of John Hales of Coventre esqʳ scilicet 3° Julii A° 1653.

KINGTON HUNDRED

DASSET

Belknap   That Sʳ Edward Belknap² knᵗ depopulated xij houses and inclosed sixe hundred Acres of lande in Burton-Dasset 23° Oct.

     ᵃ Entry not in Chancery Returns of 1517.

     ¹ This entry must be interpreted by Dugdale's *Warwickshire*, p. 373, based upon the text of the original, from which it appears that the destruction of these 6 messuages was by Sir E. Raleigh, and over and above the twelve messuages returned as destroyed by W. Coope in the Inquisition of 1517. See p. 404, *supra*.

     ² The Chancery Returns for 1517 give 360 acres inclosed to pasture and twelve messuages destroyed by Sir E. Belknap in 1498 (p. 424, *supra*). Dugdale's *Transcript of the Inquisition of* 1518 shows that, no remedial measures having been taken, this presentment was then renewed. The

14° H. 7, for which he had a pardon from the Kinge, then exhibited to the Com^{rs}. And that at the time of the taking

Wotton
Cooke

this Inquisicion, scilt. 3° E. 6. Sir Edw. Wotton knt, Sr Anthony Cooke knt, and Mary Dannet widow were owners of the premises.

WORMLEIGHTON [1]

Wormleighton

Shirley
Cope

That in Wormleighton Sr Nicholas Shirley k^t and Sr Anthony Cope knt executors to Sr William Spensar did in 14° H. 7 depopulate xij houses, videlicet messuages,[2] three cottages and inclosed ccxl acres of arrable lande. John Letters Patent set out in the Chancery Returns (p. 426, *supra*), not only dispensed from penalties for inclosures effected, but for such as should be made here in future : 'nec [ullo] modo imposterum gravemus dictum Edwardum pro ruina aliquarum domorum vel inclusarum aliquarum terrarum per ipsum facta [*sic*] siue fienda [*sic*] infra manerium siue dominium de dorsett.' Apparently in reliance upon this dispensation, Sir E. Belknap had since inclosed an additional 240 acres here, though the recital gives the impression, which may be inferred from the Inquisitions of 1517 and 1518 to be erroneous, that the entire inclosure had been made as early as 1498. Cf. below sub Wood Bevinton and Little Dorsington, p. 661, *n*. 1, 2. Possibly it was this subsequent inclosure which gave rise to the inquiry at or following upon the presentment of 1518. See p. 655, *supra*.

[1] This repeats the recital of the Chancery Returns, but with the substitution for the names of the original incloser William Cope, who had died in 1513 (G. Baker's *Hist. of Northamptonshire*, i. 748), and of John Spencer, Esq., lord of the manor at the time of the Inquisition of 1517 (see p. 404, *supra*), those of Sir Anthony Cope, knighted 1547 (*Dict. of Nat. Biog.* s. v.) ; and Sir Nicholas Shirley (whom I have not been able to identify), co-executors to Sir William Spencer, who had died in 1532 (Lipscombe's *Hist. of Buckingham*, i. 564). Notwithstanding the substitution of names, the date 14 H. VIII. (1498) is left as in the Chancery Returns, showing that the object of this return was to ascertain the persons at the date of the return responsible in law for this inclosure of half a century preceding, which they are, by an anachronism, represented to have actually effected themselves. Apparently the reason of this presentment was that the land 'laid' to the twelve rebuilt houses was not, in the opinion of the Commissioners, a restitution of the whole area withdrawn from the plough. I have entered the restoration of the twelve houses in the table showing the restitutions of inclosures, &c., on p. 680.

[2] 'xij houses, videlicet, messuages.' 'Messuage, Messuagium is properly a dwelling-house, with some adjacent land assigned to the use thereof.' Cowel's *Interpreter*, s. v.

II.   T

Spensar — Spensar sonne and heire to the saide Sr William being then in warde to the kinge which John afterwards rebuilded xij houses laying land to them, as was certified to the com^{rs} in 3° E. 6.

WALTON D'EIUILL[1]

Mordant — That Robert Mordaunt Esqr in 23° H. 7, depopulated seaven messuages, and inclosed clx acres of lande in Walton-
Knevet D'eivill. And that Edw. Knevet esq^r and Anne his wife,
Strange late the wife to Robert Straunge, and Margaret Straunge widow late ye wife of John Strange, depopulated five messuages in the saide village of Walton D'civile in 12° H. 7.

UPTON

Warren — That Sr John Warren Knt. depopulated one messuage and ten acres of lande lying in Upton 12° H. 8.

WESTON

Keble — That Henry Kebull Esq. depopulated six houses, and inclosed ccc acres of errable lande lying in Weston (iuxta Barcheston[2]) 1° H. 8, and that William Sheldon esq. was possest thereof 3° E. 6.

[1] Inclosures of the same area, accompanied by the destruction of seven messuages, were made by Robert le Straunge in 24 H. VII. (see p. 422, *supra*). These similarities strongly point to identity with those here ascribed to Robert Mordant in 23 H. VII., the final unit of xxiiij having probably been overlooked by Dugdale. The inclosures were, as the Inquisition of 1517 shows, really the work of Robert le Straunge. Robert Mordaunt had acquired a moiety of the manor through his wife Barbara, daughter of John L'Estrange, and in 1540 purchased the other moiety of Sir Thomas Strange, son and heir of Sir Thomas le Straunge, so that in 1549 he was the legal representative in the manor of that incloser (*Warw.* p. 411 ; Blomefield's *Norfolk*, x. 114). For the other landowners here, see notes to the Inquisition of 1517, p. 423, *supra*. The fact that while the five messuages returned by the Inquisition of 1518 are still entered as destroyed, while nothing is said of the 150 acres of land then converted into pasture, may perhaps justify the inference that the land had been restored to the plough, and it has been so tabulated within brackets.

[2] This is the same place as that called in the Inquisition of 1517 'Weston iuxta Cheryton.' Kebull, or Kebyll, was presented in that year

Cotes That Anthony Cotes of Benifeild [1] in Com. Northton. esq^r. depopulated the capitall messuage of Whitchurch, and inclosed c acres of errable lande ; As alsoe one messuage more and two cottages, a° 25° H. 8. Whitchurch

as the incloser of 200 acres, and in the Inquisition of 1518 as of 350 acres (see pp. 415, 652, *supra*). As Dugdale tells us, citing this last Inquisition, that this included all the (arable) land of the village except eighty acres attached to the manor house, it may be inferred that the return of 1549 does not represent a new inclosure of arable. Nor, since the area is a hundred acres larger than that of the inclosure of 1509, does it correspond with the inclosure returned in 1517. Dugdale mentions that in 37 H. VIII. (1546), this William Sheldon, who had acquired the manor from Kebyll's representatives, 'obtained license from the king to impark ccc. Acres of Land, Meadow, Pasture, and Wood, to be called by the name of Weston Park for ever,' &c. (*Warw.* 417). It is true that previous entries have shown an anachronistic indifference to the real name of the incloser, but the object of this was to point to the person legally responsible in 1549, and they do not support the hypothesis that an inclosure really made by Sheldon may have been ascribed to Kebyll. We know, too, from the Lansdowne MS. returns for Gloucestershire, that inclosures made with licence were not returned (*Trans. R.H.S.*, 1894, p. 295). Moreover, Dugdale makes no mention of the destruction of houses for Sheldon's imparcation, and it may even be inferred from his language that there were no more houses left to destroy. On the whole, then, I incline to the view that this presentment implies that fifty acres and one house, possibly also the cottage, had been replaced in their former condition, leaving the incloser's representatives liable for the rest of the presentments of 1517 and 1518.

[1] 'This Mannour, inter alia, was in 13 H. 7 [a] allotted to him the said Edward [Belknap], who made much Depopulation and Inclosure here ; but being one of the Esquiers of the Body of Henry 7, in 24 of that kings Raign obtained a pardon for the same [b] (see pp. 426, 478). And afterwards, viz., in 4 H. 8 past [c] it away, with other Lands, in Exchange unto John Cotes of Honingham in this County ; from whom it came to Anthony Cotes of Benefeild in Com. Northampt. Esquier, which Anthony in 25 H. 8 depopulated the [d] Capitall Messuage and inclosed c. Acres of Land there' (*Warw.* p. 443). I have followed Dugdale, who does not mention the decay of the second messuage and the two cottages, so far as to assign the 100 acres, as the form of the entry seems to warrant, exclusively to the capital messuage. Cowel (*Interpr.*) notices s.v. that 'Messuagium in Scotland signifies the principal place or Dwelling-House within a Barony, which we call a Mannor-House.'

[a] Claus. 13. H. 7.   [b] Pat. 24, H. 7, P. 1, m. 17.   [c] Manwaring, q. 17.
                      [d] Inq. super depop. 3 E. 6.

660   THE DOMESDAY OF INCLOSURES, 1549

<small>Morton
Hunkes</small>   That John More fermour of the mannour of Aderston <small>Adderst</small>
and five yardland, inclosed the saide lande, being the lessee
of Thomas Mourton Esq. And that Thomas Hunkes in 3°
E. 6 was lord thereof.

<small>Grenefeild</small>   That Richard Grenefeild depopulated three messuages and
one cottage and inclosed cxx acres of lande lying in Chelmes- <small>Chelme</small>
cote a° 2° H. 8. William Walker being ye present possessor
3 E. 6.

<small>Willington
Walter</small>   That Willm Willington esq^r. being tenant by Indenture
to Willm Walter and . . . his wife,[3] in right of the saide . . . <small>(sic in</small>
holdinge foure messuages, and cccxxx acres of errable lande
in Chelmescote aforesaid, converted the saide messuages into
cottages, and cc acres of lande into pasture 1° E. 6. And
being seized in fee simple of one other messuage and lx
acres of lande, converted the messuage into a cottage and the
lande into pasture.

---

[1] Atherston super Stoure, Dugdale. Now Atherston on Stour.—'The mannour' appears here, like 'manerium,' &c., to stand for the Manor house. The average area of the virgate, or yardland, in Warwickshire is, in round numbers, 20 acres, upon which basis the area inclosed would be 100 acres. 'Thomas Morton Esquier, ... in 37 H. 8 past it to Thomas Hunks' (F. levat. T. Pasch. 37 H. VIII). *Warw.* p. 445. Among Dugdale's MSS. is a note : 'E primo libro cedularum de liberacionibus in Scaccario ex parte Rememoratoris Thesaurarii excerpta,' as follows : 'Hunckes. Thomas Huncks obiit anno 5° Phi. et M. ac Robertus est eius filius plene etatis (intr. al. in Glouc.). M. de Adderstone valet per annum xvj li.' (Bodl. MSS. D. 1. fo. 563.)

[2] R. Grenefeild's inclosures of 120 acres, &c., are now presented for the third time, having already appeared in the Inquisitions of 1517 and 1518 (pp. 419, 651, *supra*).

[3] 'Besides this [Grenefeild's] mannour . . . is there another here, at least in Reputation ; for in 30 H. 8 Will. Walter was possesst [a] thereof, in Right [b] of Isabel his wife : which Will. demised the same to Will. Willington Esq. . . . who in 1 E. 6 converted 4 Mess. here into Cottages, as also 200 Acres of Arable Land into Pasture ; and being seized in Fee Simple of one Mess. and lx Acres of Land more, did the like by it.' For the large inclosures by W. Wyllyngton, who was lord of the manor of Barcheston, at that place, see p. 416, *supra*. Barcheston and Chelmescote were adjacent.

[a] S. Mich. Rec. 30 H. 8, rot. 20.   [b] Inq. super depop. 3 E. 6.

BARLICHWAY HUNDRED

o. 536

Grey

That in Wood-Bevinton were six messuages and one cottage and to every messuage xxx acres of errable lande leased by the Canons of Kenilworth to William Gray the elder for a terme of yeares wch William, in Marche xxi⁰ H. 7 [1] inclosed the same and decayed the houses. To William Grey the'lder succeded William Grey his sonne and heire, who surrendring the saide lease purchased the inheritance thereof from the Cannons of Kenilworth for a fee ferme Rent of xiij^{li}. xiij^s. iiij^d. per annum. And that about 30 yeares before the taking of that Inquisition (sct. 3⁰ E. 6) the same William, the statute of Inclosures being then lookt into, reedifyed foure of the saide messuages. To him succeded Elizabeth his daughter and heire wife to Edw. Ferrers esq. (3 E. 6) who was then owner of those landes in her right.

Wood-Bevinton

errers

Rows

That Mawde Rows widow being seized of the capitall messuage and cc acres of lande lying in Little Dorsington in com. Warr. and in the parish of Welleford com. Glouc., inclosed the saide lande, and decayed three ploughs 4⁰ Martii

Little Dorsington [2]

---

[1] Here we have the date of the original inclosures by William Grey assigned to this fresh inclosure.

[2] This entry is remarkably like the inclosure by the same person of 200 acres, associated with the putting down of six ploughs and the decay of five messuages in the same place and at the same date returned in the Inquisition of 1517 (p. 414, *supra*). In that return, however, it is distinctly stated that to each of the messuages at least thirty acres were attached, whereas only the capital messuage is mentioned in this presentment. The inference is that this was a fresh inclosure, and as it is not mentioned in the Inquisition of 1518 it was probably made after that date, notwithstanding that the commissioners of 1549, as in the case of Wood Bevinton, have saved the trouble of more particular inquiry into a case at that time, perhaps, a generation old, by assigning to it the date of the original inclosures. These assignments of date show, at any rate, that the commissioners of 1549 worked with the returns of 1517 in their hands (see p. 6, *supra*), a circumstance to which the preservation of the returns of that Inquisition is perhaps due. The omission of the other inclosures both from the Inquisition of 1518 and from that of 1549 suggests the inference that they had been remedied. This inclosure would probably be of demesne land unaccompanied by evictions, and therefore less likely to afford cause of complaint. See *Trans. R.H.S.* 1893, p. 246.

Browne 17° H. 7. And that s¹ John Browne knt. was possessor thereof 3 E. 6.

Throgmorton That s¹ George Throgmorton knt. in 18° H. 8 inclosed within his parke¹ certeine landes lying in Samburne called Spyne'slyes, and another parcell of ground called Samburne- Samb hethe. And in 22° H. 8 inclosed within the same parke 18 acres of lande belonging to Alcestre.²

KNIGHTLOW HUNDRED

Twyforde That Thomas Twyford in 4° H. 7 depopulated foure messuages and three cottages in Stretton-Baskervill whervnto Strett clx acres of lande belonged; and soone after sold the whole Bask lordshipp to Henry Smyth gentleman, who in 9 H. 7 inclosed and depopulated yᵉ rest.³

¹ I have to thank Sir W. Throckmorton for having kindly communicated to me through Mr. John Throckmorton the information that Coughton Park is a wood of the area of about seventy acres, though in Mr. J. Throckmorton's opinion it was probably once of greater extent, for that much of the adjoining land appears to have been brought under cultivation within the last 150 or 200 years. Close to Coughton Park is Alcester Warren, part of the original area of which was doubtless inclosed. What is left of Wike, mentioned as inclosed in Dugdale's *Warwickshire*, p. 523 (cf. p. 693, *infra*), is 'scarcely an acre of ground surrounded by a moat, which was evidently in former days the position of some small manor house.' This lies outside, though 'close to Coughton Park,' and the 'common ground called Wike Wood' (*Warw.* l.c.) was probably once part of its waste. Upon these data I shall not be guilty of an excessive estimate if I take the additional inclosures made by Sir George Throckmorton in 18 H. VIII. (1527) as 32 acres, making up with the 20½ acres inclosed in 1487 and the 18 acres inclosed in 1531, the total of 70 acres. If any error is made it is in assigning an unduly large area to the inclosures of 1527 at the expense of that represented by the words 'cum aliis terris' &c. in the Inquisition of 1517.

² Alcestre, *i.e.* no doubt part of the manor of A.; at this time in the family of Grevill of Milcote (*Warw.* p. 538). The incloser was doubtless a freeholder of the manor.

³ This is remarkable as a presentment of an inclosure dating back to 1488-89, which had escaped presentment in 1517 and in 1518, notwithstanding that subsequent inclosures by Henry Smyth in 1493 are recorded in 1517 (p. 431, *supra*). The explanation may be that the commissioners did not record it in 1517 because anterior to the limit of retrospect fixed by their commission at Michaelmas 4 H. VII. (1488).

arch.   That Thomas Marquesse Dorset in 12° H. 7 impaled nynety acres of errable land, lying within the lordshipp of Arley, within his parke at Astley called the old parke.¹   Astley

myth   That Henry Smyth esq. imparked half of Fletchamsted   Fletchamsted ²
in 12° H. 7 and the rest turned into pasture, whereby foure of the fiue messuages therein went to decay : And that in his

(See p. 10, *supra*.) If this be so, the date of the inclosure must have been between 22 Aug., the first day of the regnal year of Henry VII., and 29 Sept. 1488. It has, however, already been observed that presentments were occasionally admitted prior to the date limited (see p. 364, n. 4). The instructions annexed to the commission of 1549 fixed the same limit of the fourth year of Henry VII., and the zeal of Hales, 'who acted very honestly in this commission and favourably to the commons,' may perhaps have stretched the interpretation of his commission so as to include this case. Strype, *Eccl. Mem.* vol. ii. Pt. i. p. 150 (ed. Oxford, 1822). The rest of the entry, the inclosures by Henry Smyth, evidently refer back to the Return of 1517, and have so been tabulated, though in brackets.

¹ This, as appears from Dugdale's *Warwickshire* (p. 775), is an inclosure additional to that presented in 1517, see p. 450, *supra*. The date of 12 H. VII. (1497) may be inferred to be the actual date, and not, as in some previous cases, an event antedated, because no date at all is given in the Inquisition for 1517, and the presentment was not repeated in 1518. 'Wedington, together with Astley, devolving to Grey, was inclosed and for the most part depopulated by Thomas Grey, Marquess of Dorset, in 7 H. VII., &c.' (*Warw.* l.c.). The two places are not contiguous.

² This entry appears to be, so far as the imparcations were concerned, a renewed presentment of the returns sub Flechamsted in the Inquisition of 1517, for Dugdale tells us that there were originally five messuages at this place, of which four were suffered to decay, precisely the number decayed by the imparcation of John Smyth the father and the inclosure of Henry Smyth the son. As a matter of fact the father died after 1500 (15 H. VII.), if Dugdale's statement in *Warw.* p. 184, be trustworthy, so that the inclosure attributed to his son and heir Henry Smyth in 1497 was probably in law the father's work. However, the inclosures of the two appear to have been presented together and to be repeated here. As they were not returned by the Inquisition of 1518, the inference is that fresh evidence, that as to the pool, was taken in 1549. The total imparcations returned in 1517 were 220 acres, so that if this return is expressed in figures 220 acres having been imparked, 220 acres remained which were converted into pasture ; but the figures are bracketed in the tables to indicate their inferential character. In the table of Additional Returns (p. 684), 60 acres having been returned in 1517, only 160 acres inclosed are scheduled.

said parke he made a poole of a peice of ground which had been formerly a meadow.

HEMLINGFORD HUNDRED

Dorset March. That the Marquesse Dorset in 12° H. 7 inclosed certeine errable lande within the compasse of his parke within the parish of Chilverscoton (in Griffe) called the new parke. Griffe

Bracebridge That John Bracebridge Esqr. depopulated three messuages and inclosed nynetie sixe acres of errable lande at Nether Holt in ye parish of Kingsbury, parcell of ye lordshipp of Kingsbury, 19° H. 7. And that Thomas Bracebridge in 3° E. 6 helde the same. Holt King.

Bonde That John Bonde of Coventre draper impaled xxx acres of lande pasture and wood at Little-Bromwich in 6° H. 8, and did put deere therein, which John dyed 30 H. 8, leaving Thomas Bonde his sonne and heire. Brom parva

fo. 537 That the yearely Rents to the kinge, of Sutton are in- Sutto

---

[1] A comparison of this entry with the Inquisition of 1517 on the one hand and with Dugdale's *Warwickshire*, p. 79, on the other suggests, though it is extremely doubtful, that this inclosure may be identical with that of 30 acres recorded at a place unnamed in the Inquisition of 1517, immediately preceding the inclosure of 18 acres at Astley. Dugdale, it must be borne in mind, had access to the original returns of both Inquisitions, and in his *Warwickshire* he mentions two inclosures only, one at Astley of 30 acres, for which he cites the Inquisition of 1517, and one in the lordship of Arley of 90 acres. It is clear that he overlooks the inclosure of 18 acres at Astley returned in the Inquisition of 1517. I have, therefore, though with much hesitation, tabulated in brackets, to show its inferential character, this inclosure at Griffe as of 30 acres.

[2] 'The village was in part depopulated by John Bracebrigge Esquire who in 19 H. 7 decayed three Messuages upon the Inclosure thereof; of which Lands Thomas Bracebrigge was possest in 3 E. 6.' (Esc. 3 E. VI.) *Warw.* p. 752. J. B. had previously inclosed 60 acres and imparked 10 acres, for the former of which he was a second time presented in 1518, pp. 449, 654, *supra*. The inclosure here recorded had, like that at Stretton Baskervill in 1488, escaped the researches of the two previous Inquisitions, or else was antedated.

[3] Now Sutton Coldfield. This anomalous entry is evidently the apologia of Bishop Harman or Veysy or Voysey, chairman of the commissioners of 1517 (see p. 73), and Bishop of Exeter 1519-51, and again in 1553-55 (Le Neve's *Fasti*, i. 377, 8). 'The later part of his days he spent here

creased from x^{li} per annum to 58^{li}, whereof 5^{li} for the herbage of the copices. That the late parke is now employed for pasturage of cattell belonging to ye Inhabitants ; viz. according to the old Rent xx^d by the yeare for a cow & xl^d by the yeare for a horse or mare : And for other young cattell from one yeare old to three yeare old xvi^d. That nyne acres inclosed out of part of the barren wast were soe taken in because much pennygrasse grew vpon them whereby sheepe often perished ; and partly for that the same place was noted for one of the most theevish corners in all those parts. Which nyne acres the Bpp. of Exeter not only inclosed, paying yerely to the kings fee ferme xviij^d ; but alsoe buit [*sic*] therevpon, and in other places adioyning, houses made of lyme and stone having inhabitants in them to the comfort of travailers. That the parish is much increased with people appeareth by the fullnesse of the Churche, notwithstanding

at Sutton' (*Warw.* p. 641), of which he was a native. He appears from this entry to have done something to reverse the inclosing movement at this place, although he began his operations as early as 1527, 'having obtained of the King in 19 H. 8 certain Parcells of Inclosure here, called More-Crofts, and Hethe-yards and more than xl Acres of Wast with license to inclose it.' (Pat. 19 H. VIII. p. 1. Cp. S. P. Dom. H. VIII. iv. 3747 [6].) 'The late parke' was the park of the Earls of Warwick mentioned by Leland (*Itin.* fo. 187, *a*) at this time in the hands of the Crown, upon which he erected 'divers pretty houses of stone and placed his poore kinsmen in them,' &c. (*ibid.*) The connexion of the inclosure of nine acres with theft is set out by Dugdale as follows : ' And for Prevention of Robberies which were in those days frequent upon the Road over Bassets-Heath (leading from Lichfeild towards London) he erected a House upon a Piece of Wast called Cotysmore, containing 9 Acres of ground, lying in a kind of desert Place, near to Canwell-Yate : which Place as by an Autograph I have seen, was deservedly called Latronum spelunca et receptaculum, wherein he placed one of his own domestique servants to reside' (*Warw.* pp. 640, 641). It is evident from these passages that the bishop's inclosure was not intended to be presented as an agricultural inclosure or conversion to pasture, and as it formed part of larger inclosures for similar objects which have not been returned, I have hesitated to admit it into the table of inclosures, in which, indeed, there is no strictly appropriate schedule. The bishop was probably acquainted with John Hales, the chairman of this commission, whose home was at Coventry, about fifteen miles distant. See *The Common Weal of this Realm of England*, edited by E. Lamond, Cambridge, 1893, p. xix.

the two new Iles added thereto, whereas within xx yeares before, the Churche without those Iles very well conteyned them.

IV.

Concordance of Dugdale's Notes with the Chancery Returns for 1517

Inclosures, &c., at [a]		
1. Poley		Chancery MS., membrane 45
2. ⎫		
3. ⎬ Manceter (3 entries)		
4. ⎭		
5. Bromwich parua		
6. Castle Bromwich (as two crofts = 10 ac.)	Dugd. fo. 543	Chancery MS., membrane 46
7. Mereden		
8. Birmingham		
9. Mereden		
10. ⎫ Fillongley (2 entries)		
11. ⎭		
12. Wormleighton		Chancery MS., membrane 47
13. ⎫ Grafton (2 entries)		
14. ⎭		
15. Tachbroke Malory [b]		
16. Highershukburgh		Chancery MS., membrane 48
17. Nethershukburgh [c]		
18. ⎫		
19. ⎬ Vpton (3 entries)	Dugd. fo. 544	
20. ⎭		
21. Farnborough		
22. Oxshulfe		Chancery MS., membrane 49
23. Weston iuxta Cheriton in parochia de Longa-Compton		
24. Bercheston		
25. ⎫ Compton (2 entries)		
26. ⎭		
27. Brayles		Chancery MS., membrane 51
28. Chelmescote		
29. Walton Deuile		
30. Harborough (Horborough MS.) (1st entry)	Dugd. fo. 545	
31. Darsett and Byrton		Chancery MS., membrane 52

[a] In Dugdale's spelling.
[b] Omission from *Warwickshire*, p. 606, of the destruction of one cottage here.
[c] But Dugdale omits from his tables the succeeding entry of an inclosure of fourteen acres.

WARWICKSHIRE: TABULATION OF THE DUGDALE MSS.

Inclosures, &c., at [a]	—	—
32. Bishops - Hampton (1st entry)		
33. Bishops - Hampton (4th entry)	Dugd. fo. 545	Chancery MS., membrane 53
34. Ruyton		
35. Stretton super Strecte .		
36. Willey		
37. Esenhull . . .		
38. Bulkinton . . .		
39. } Wolvehamcote . .		Chancery MS., membrane 54
40. }		
41. } Alseley . . .		
42. }		
43. Princethorpe . . .		
44. Napton		
45. Wollescote . . .		Chancery MS., membrane 55
46. Greneborough . .	Dugd. fo. 546	
47. Whitnashe (out of place)		Chancery MS., membrane 56
48. Wollescote . . .		Chancery MS., membrane 55
49. } Bobenhull . . .		
50. }		Chancery MS., membrane 55
51. Eythorp . . .		
52. Paylton . . .		
53. Fletchamsted (one entry only)		
54. Draknage . . .		Chancery MS., membrane 56
55. Fillingley . . .		
56. Woluerton . . .		
57. Kingswood . . .		
58. Wollescote . . .		
59. Ichyngton (1st entry) .		Chancery MS., membrane 57
60. ,, (3rd entry) .		
61. ,, (4th entry) .		
62. Amyngton . . .		
63. Honyngham . . .		
64. Bentley	Dugd. fo. 547	
65. Solyhull . . .		Chancery MS., membrane 58
66. Kingsbury . . .		
67. Kynnyry . . .		
68. Stonley		
69. Wrygfyn . . .		
70. Astley		
71. Kynnysbury . . .		Chancery MS., membrane 58
92. Wotton		
93. Harborough . . .	Dugd. fo. 548	

[a] In Dugdale's spelling.

V.

DIFFERENCES BETWEEN DUGDALE'S NOTES OF THE INQUISITION OF 1517 AND THE CHANCERY RETURNS

References	Inclosers	Messuages decayed and Areas inclosed	Places
1. Dugdale, fo. 543	Prior de Maluerne	vj messuag' ij cottag' xl acr. tre. arabil.	Shuttington parcella Priorat' de Alcote
Chancery MS., membrane 45	Prior monasterii de Malbourne	'de sex messuagiis, duobus cotagiis et centum et quateruiginti acris terre arrabilis'	'in Shyttyngton ... vt de parcella sui manerii siue Prioratus de alcote'
Chancery MS., membrane 45	Predictus Prior.	'de quadraginta et duabus acris terre arrabilis'	'in Shittyngton predicta'
Chancery MS., membrane 45	Idem Prior	'de triginta acris terre arrabilis'	'in Shyttyngton'
Chancery MS., membrane 45	Idem Prior	'de decem acris terre arrabilis vocate le Brache'	'in Shyttyngton'

It will be seen that none of these exactly corresponds with Dugdale's transcript. The conclusion seems that Dugdale intended to transcribe the first of these entries only but missed the words 'centum et' and erroneously read 'quadraginta' for 'quateruiginti.' Possibly because he was conscious of a mistake somewhere, he says nothing as to the area, but simply that 'the Monks of Aucote depopulated six messuages and two cottages therein, which I take to be a third part thereof (Inq. super depop. 9 H. VIII.),' 'Warw.' p. 801. The third part could scarcely have been only 40 acres.

WARWICKSHIRE: TABULATION OF THE DUGDALE MSS. 669

References	Inclosers	Messuages decayed and Areas inclosed	Places
2. Dugdale, fo. 543 Chancery MS., membrane 45	Johannes Arden, armiger Johannes Wardern, armiger	'ij croftes vocat' Lady croftes' 'de duobus croftis vocatis Ladye croftes continentibus decem acras terre arrabilis'	Castle Bromwich Castell Bromyche
Dugdale, fo. 543	Same . .	'cxl acr. pasture et bosci et x acr. terre arab. 2° H. 8. imparcavit et feras in eodem parco posuit'	Castle Bromwich

This last entry, bracketed with the first one by Dugdale, is evidently an interpolation, being in a smaller script. It therefore either belongs to a supplementary Return, or more probably has been inadvertently copied by Dugdale from his transcript of the preceding entry (Poley); for it does not appear in Dugdale's notes of the Inquisitions of 10 H. VIII. or 3 E. VI.

References	Inclosers	Messuages decayed and Areas inclosed	Places
3. Dugdale, fo. 544 Chancery MS., membrane 48	Edw. Raleigh miles Edwardus Raleigh miles	j mess. xxij acr. tre. 'de vno messuagio et viginti et duabus acris et dimidia acra terre arrabilis &c'	Dorset Dorsett
		Omission by Dugdale of half an acre	
4. Dugdale, fo. 544 Chancery MS., membrane 48	Abb. de Kenelworth Radulphus nuper Abbas de Kenelworth	ij mess. & j cottag.' 'de duobus mesuagiis et vno cotagio et sexdecim acris terre arrabilis . . . et cum vnoquoque mesuagio mesuagiorum predictorum viginti et quatuor acre ad minus de predictis terris arrabilibus.' . . . . 'Terram predictam arrabilem . . . in pasturam animalium conuertit.'	Salford Bevyngton Salford

Dugdale omits the whole area converted, which at the least must have been 16 ac. + 48 ac. or in all 64 acres.

The actual incloser in the Chancery Returns is not the Abbot, but the Abbot's lessee, William Grey. Dugdale selects the lessor as the person ultimately responsible.

References	Inclosers	Messuages decayed and Areas inclosed	Places
5. Dugdale, fo. 544	Omission		
Chancery MS., membrane 49	Thomas Shukborough	'de vno messuagio et quatuordecim acris.' (Messuage destroyed)	Nethershukburgh
6. Dugdale, fo. 544	Agnes Walshe vidua	j mess. vocat. Booston house	Warwick
Chancery MS., membrane 49	Agnes Walshe vidua	'de vno mesuagio vocato Booston house et viginti et quatuor acris terre arrabilis cum mesuagio illo' &c.	Warwick
	Omission by Dugdale of 24 acres		
7. Dugdale, fo. 545	Prior sancti Sepulcri Warr	cccc acr. tre. . .	Warwick
Chancery MS., membrane 51	'Prior Prioratus siue domus sancti sepulcri Warr'	'de quateruiginti acris terre'	Warwick
Dugdale (Warwickshire), fo. 330	'The Prior and Canons of St. Sepulchre inclosed 400 ac. here, and depopulated one mess. wherunto 80 acres belonged'		

In this case Dugdale evidently mistook 'quateruiginti' for 'quadringentis.' Cf. the case of Shuttington, *supra*, where he perhaps mistook it for 'quadraginta.' The MS. is clear, and the fact that only two ploughs were put down is in favour of the correctness of 'quateruiginti.' Dugdale does not enter the 'domus' as decayed.

WARWICKSHIRE: TABULATION OF THE DUGDALE MSS. 671

References	Inclosers	Messuages decayed and Areas inclosed	Places
8. Dugdale, fo. 545 Chancery MS., membrane 52	Tho. Hall. Thomas Hall	j mess. xx acr. tre.. 'de vno mesuagio et viginti quatuor acris'	Harborough Horborough
		Omission by Dugdale of 4 acres	
9. Dugdale, fo. 545 Chancery MS., membrane 53	Rob. Greene Robertus Hallesworth	j mess. x acr. tre.. 'de vno mesuagio et de decem acris'	Bishops-Hampton No place

This variation is inexplicable, save that the illegible space in the MS. is large enough to contain 'alias Greene' after Hallesworth. The entry is in all other respects the same, and though no place is mentioned in the Chancery Returns the place of the preceding and following inclosures is the same. [Halles]w[orth] is supplied from the following entry, the MS. here being illegible except the 'w,' but 'predictus' points to this entry.

References	Inclosers	Messuages decayed and Areas inclosed	Places
10. Dugdale, fo. 545 Chancery MS., membrane 53	Omission Simon Turnour clericus	'de vno mesuagio vocato the deyrye et de triginta acris'	Bysshopshampton
11. Dugdale, fo. 545 Chancery MS., membrane 53	Omission Predictus Frater Johannes Brogden	'de duobus aliis mesuagiis et de vno cotagio et quadraginta et quinque acris terre arrabilis'	Bysshopshamton

There are in all five entries respecting Byshopsshampton in the Chancery MS., the area comprised being 155 acres. Of these Dugdale only includes the first (30 ac.), presumably the second (10 ac.), the third (30 ac.) he omits. The fourth (40 ac.) he tabulates; the fifth (45 ac.) he omits; so that in all he tabulates 80 ac. only out of 155 ac., or not much more than one half.

References	Inclosers	Messuages decayed and Areas inclosed	Places
12. Dugdale, fo. 546 55	Joh. Turner	lxx acr. tre. . .	Eythorpe
Chancery MS., membrane 55	Johannes Turnour de Couentre Bocher	'de septuaginta acris' in Eythorp . . . 'et de triginta acris' in Eythorp	Eythorp
	Omission by Dugdale of 30 acres		
13. Dugdale, fo. 546	Henr. Smyth fil. & heres (Johis Smyth)	ij mess. j cottag'. xl acr. tre.	Fletchamsted
Chancery MS., membrane 56		'De duobus mesuagiis vno cotagio et quadraginta (*sic*) acris' &c. '. . . et cum vtroque eorundem mesuagiorum quadraginta [*sic*] acre' &c.	

Obviously this is a case in which it is not easy to interpret the MS. Twenty persons seems too large a number for 40 acres, and I have therefore interpreted it as meaning that each of the houses (including the cottage) had forty acres attached to it, though this is unusual in the case of the cottage, cottages being in this return either unaccompanied by land or by a less area. But cf. Stretton super Strete, p. 431, n. 2, *supra*.

References	Inclosers	Messuages decayed and Areas inclosed	Places
14. Dugdale, fo. 547	Omission		
Chancery MS., membrane 57	Johannes Nobull	'de vno mesuagio et viginti acris'	Ichyngton
	Omission by Dugdale of 20 acres		
15. Dugdale, fo. 547	Henr. Smyth	xxx acr. tre. . .	Thirford
Chancery MS., membrane 58	Henr. Smyth	'imparcauit et palis circumclusit triginta acras arabiles et centum acras terre boscis pasturis [*sic*]'	Shyrford
	Omission by Dugdale of 100 acres		

Synoptic Comparison of the Differences between Dugdale's Notes of the Inquisition of 1517 and the Chancery Returns

Place	Areas omitted by Dugdale. Acres	Place	Areas added by Dugdale Acres
Shyttyngton	100 [a]		
,,	42		
,,	30		
,,	10		
		Castell Bromwyche	140 [a]
Dorset	½		
Bevyngton (Salford)	64		
Nethershukburgh (1 messuage destroyed)	14		
Warwick	24		
		Warwick (1 domus decayed omitted by Dugd.)	320 [b]
Horborough	4		
Bysshopshampton	75		
Fletchamsted [c]	80		
Ichyngton	20		
Shyrford	100		
	563½		460

[a] Assuming that Dugdale intended xl for the 'centum et quateruiginti' (misread quadraginta) of the first entry, with which, in other respects, it is identical.
[b] 'Quateruiginti,' misread cccc.
[c] This is a question of the interpretation of the entry.

VI. TABULATION OF DUGDALE'S

Folio	No. of farms ingrossed	No. of inclosures to pasture	Parishes	Areas ingrossed	Areas consolidated with farms	Areas inclosed	Objects of inclosure			Condition of inclosers				
							Park	Inclosure	Pasture	Lay lords of manors	Lay freeholders	Ecclesiastical lords of manors	Other ecclesiastics	Lay
				acres	acres	acres	acres	acres	acres					
548	—	1	Warwick [b], [e]	—	—	24	—	—	24	—	1	—	—	—
	—	1	Chelmescote [c], [f]	—	—	120	—	—	120	1	—	—	—	—
	—	1	Chelmescote [b], [e]	—	—	60	—	—	60	—	—	—	1	—
	—	1	Cheriton [b], [e]	—	—	40	—	—	40	—	1	—	—	—
	—	1	Farnborough [b], [e]	—	—	20	—	—	20	1	—	—	—	—
	—	1	Morton Morell [b], [e]	—	—	20	—	—	20	—	1	—	—	—
	—	1	Barton [b], [e]	—	—	45	—	—	45	—	1	—	—	—
	—	1	Brayles [b], [e]	—	—	20	—	—	20	—	—	—	1	—
	—	1	Cherlecote [b], [e]	—	—	40	—	—	40	1	—	—	—	—
	—	5	Walton Deuill [b], [d]	—	—	150	—	—	150	2	—	—	—	—
	—	7	Weston (Long Compton) [e], [f]	—	—	350	—	—	350	1	—	—	—	—
	—	{3	Tachebrok [c], [e]	—	—	120	—	—	120	—	—	1	—	—
	—	{3	Tachebrok [c], [e]	—	—	120	—	—	120	1	—	—	—	—
	—	1	Stratford super Auon [b], [e]	—	—	40	—	—	40	—	1	—	—	—
	—	1	Woluardington [b], [e]	—	—	20	—	—	20	—	—	—	1	—
	—	1	Honyngton [b], [e]	—	—	60	—	—	60	—	1	—	—	—
549	—	2	Shugborough [b], [e]	—	—	40	—	—	40	1	—	—	—	—
	—	2	Cliffe (Kimesbury) [a], [e]	—	—	40	—	—	40	—	—	—	—	1
	—	2	Princethorpe [a], [e]	—	—	50	—	—	50	1	—	—	—	—
	—	1	Napton [a], [c], [g]	—	—	70	—	—	70	1	—	—	—	—
	—	1	Wollescote [a], [e], [g]	—	—	30	—	—	30	1 }	—	—	—	—
	—	1	Greneborough [a], [e], [g]	—	—	30	—	—	30	1 }	—	—	—	—
	—	3	Kingsbury [a], [e]	—	—	60	—	—	60	1	—	—	—	—
	—	1	Stonley [a], [e]	—	—	300	—	—	300	—	—	1	—	—
	—	1	Brayles [b], [e]	—	—	240	—	—	240	—	—	—	—	1
	—	2	Vpton [c], [e]	—	—	228	—	—	228	1	—	—	—	—
	—	1	Vpton [c], [e]	—	—	30	—	—	30	—	1	—	—	—
	—	2	Vpton [c], [e]	—	—	80	—	—	80	—	1	—	—	—
	—	12	Derset and Birton [a], [f]	—	—	360	—	—	360	1	—	—	—	—
550	—	1	Woluardyngton [b], [e]	—	—	40	—	—	40	—	—	1	—	—
	—	1	Sekinton [b], [e]	—	—	20	—	—	20	—	1	—	—	—
	—	1	Harborough [b], [e]	—	—	20	=	—	20	—	—	—	1	—
	—	1	Warwick [a], [e], [h]	—	—	80	—	—	80	—	—	—	1	—
	—	1	Oxshulfe [b], [e]	—	—	80	=	—	80	1	—	—	—	—
	—	6	Wormleighton [b], [e]	—	—	( )	—	—	( )	1	1	—	—	—

[a] In Chancery Returns for 1517.   [b] Not in Chancery Returns for 1517.   [e] Varying from Chancery Returns for 1517.   [d] In Inquisition of 1549.   [e] Not in Inquisition of 1549.   [f] Varying from Inquisition of 1549.   [g] Inclosures simply in the Chancery Returns for 1517.   [h] In his Transcript of the Chancery Returns for 1517, Dugdale has by mistake read 'quadringentis' (cccc) for 'quateruiginti' (lxxx).

WARWICKSHIRE: TABULATION OF THE DUGDALE MSS. 675

Notes of the Inquisition of 1518

No. of ploughs put down	Displacement of population	No. of houses decayed	No. of churches decayed	Annual rental value	Date of inclosure	Observations
—	persons —	1 messuagium	—	—	—	—
—	—	3 messuagia	—	—	—	—
—	—	1 messuagium	—	—	—	—
—	—	1 ,,	—	—	—	—
—	—	1 ,,	—	—	—	—
—	—	1 ,,	—	—	—	—
—	—	1 ,,	—	—	—	—
—	—	1 ,,	—	—	—	—
—	—	5 messuagia	—	—	—	—
—	—	7 ,,	—	—	—	'Toto deletur&desolatur preterquam capitale messuagium cum quo lxxx acre terre occupantur.'
(3)	(12)	2 ,,	—	—	— }	'vnde vj aratra deponuntur & xxiiij persone
(3)	(12)	2 ,,	—	—	— }	mancionibus carent.'
—	—	1 messuagium	—	—	—	—
—	—	1 ,,	—	—	—	—
—	—	1 ,,	—	—	—	—
—	—	2 messuagia	—	—	—	—
—	( )	2 ,,	—	—	—	—
—	( )	2 ,,	—	—	—	—
—	( )	1 capitale messuagium	—	—	—	—
—	( )	1 messuagium	—	—	—	—
—	( )	1 ,,	—	—	—	—
—	( )	3 messuagia	—	—	—	—
—	( )	1 capitale messuagium	—	—	—	—
5	( )	1 capitale messuagium	—	—	—	—
—	( )	1 messuagium	—	—	—	—
—	( )	1 ,,	—	—	—	—
—	( )	1 ,,	—	—	—	—
—	( )	12 messuagia	—	—	1498	—
—	( )	1 messuagium	—	—	—	—
—	( )	1 ,,	—	—	—	—
—	( )	1 ,,	—	—	—	—
—	( )	1 ,,	—	—	—	—
—	( )	1 ,,	—	—	—	—
—	( )	6 messuagia	—	—	Before Sept. 3, 1506	'Post vastum *et inclusum* sic perpetratum.'

VII. Tabulation of Dugdale's

Folio	No. of farms ingrossed	No. of inclosures to pasture	Parishes	Areas ingrossed	Areas consolidated with farms	Areas inclosed	Objects of inclosure			Condition of inclosers				
							Park	Inclosure	Pasture	Lay lords of manors	Lay freeholders	Ecclesiastical lords of manors	Other ecclesiastics	Lay
				acres	acres	acres	acres	acres	acres					
535	—	12	Dasset [e], [f]	—	—	600	—	—	600	1	—	—	—	—
	—	12	Wormleighton [a], [f]	—	—	240	—	—	240	1	—	—	—	—
	—	7	Walton D'eiuill [a], [e]	—	—	160	—	—	160	1	—	—	—	—
	—	5	Walton D'eiulle [b], [f]	—	—	—	—	—	—	2	—	—	—	—
	—	1	Vpton [b], [e]	—	—	10	—	—	10	—	1	—	—	—
	—	6	Weston iuxta Barcheston [e], [f]	—	—	300	—	—	300	1	—	—	—	—
	—	1	Whitchurch [b], [e]	—	—	100	—	—	100	1	—	—	—	—
	—	1	Whitchurch [b], [e]	—	—	—	—	—	—	1	—	—	—	—
	—	5	Adderston [b], [e]	—	—	(100)	—	—	(100)	—	—	—	—	×
	—	3	Chelmescote [a], [f]	—	—	120	—	—	120	1	—	—	—	—
	—	4	Chelmescote [b], [e]	330	130	200	—	130	200	—	—	—	—	—
	—	1	Chelmescote [b], [e]	—	—	60	—	—	60	—	1	—	—	—
536	—	6	Wood-Bevinton [b], [e]	—	—	180	—	—	180	—	—	—	—	—
	—	3	Little Dorsington [b], [e]	—	—	200	—	—	200	1	—	—	—	—
	—	1	Samburne [b], [e]	—	—	(32)	(32)	—	—	1	—	—	—	—
	—	1	Alcester [b], [e]	—	—	18	18	—	—	—	1	—	—	—
	—	4	Stretton-Baskervill [b], [e]	—	—	160	—	—	160	1	—	—	—	—
	—	12	Stretton-Baskervill [a], [e]	—	—	(640)	—	—	(640)	1	—	—	—	—
	—	1	Astley [b], [e]	—	—	90	90	—	—	1	—	—	—	—
	—	2	Fletchamsted [c], [e]	—	—	(220)	(220)	—	—	1	—	—	—	—
	—	2	Fletchamsted [c], [e]	—	—	(220)	—	—	(220)	1	—	—	—	—
	—	1	Griffe (Chilverscoton [b], [e]	—	—	(30)	(30)	—	—	1	—	—	—	—
	—	1	Holt iuxta Kingsbury [b], [e]	—	—	96	—	—	96	1	—	—	—	—
	—	1	Bromwich Parva [a], [e]	—	—	30	30	—	—	1	—	—	—	—
	—	1	Sutton [b], [e]	—	—	9	—	—	9	—	—	—	1	—

[a] In Chancery Returns for 1517. [b] Not in Chancery Returns for 1517. [e] Varying from
Chancery Returns for 1517. [d] In Inquisition of 1518. [e] Not in Inquisition of 1518.
Varying from Inquisition of 1518.

WARWICKSHIRE: TABULATION OF THE DUGDALE MSS.

NOTES OF THE INQUISITION OF 1549

No. of ploughs put down	Displacement of population	No. of houses decayed	No. of churches decayed	Annual rental value	Date of inclosure	Observations
—	persons ( )	12 houses	—	—	1498 (23 Oct.)	Inclosers the two executors of late lord of manor.
—	( )	12 messuages	} —	—	1498 {	Messuages afterwards rebuilt.
—	( )	3 cottages				—
—	( )	7 messuages	—	—	1508 ᶜ	—
—	( )	5 ,,	—	—	1497	—
—	( )	1 messuage	—	—	1521	—
—	( )	6 houses	—	—	1509	—
—	( )	1 capital messuage	—	—	1534	—
—	( )	1 messuage	} —	—	1534	—
—	( )	2 cottages				—
—	—	—	—	—	Not given	Incloser a leaseholder.
—	( )	3 messuages	} —	—	1510	—
		1 cottage				
—	( )	4 messuages	—	—	1547	'converted the saide messuages into cottages.'
—	( )	1 messuage	—	—	(1547)	—
—	( )	6 messuages	} —	—	1506 (March)	Incloser a leaseholder.
	( )	1 cottage				
3	—	—	—	—	1502 (4 March)	—
—	—	—	—	—	1527	—
—	—	—	—	—	1531	—
—	( )	4 messuages	} —	—	1489	—
	( )	3 cottages				
(12)	(80)	12 messuages	} 1	—	1493	—
		4 cottages				
—	—	—	—	—	1497	'The old parke.'
—	—	2 messuages	—	—	1497 {	'whereby foure of the five messuages therein went to decay.'
—	—	2 messuages	—	—	1497	
—	—	—	—	—	1497	'The new parke.'
—	—	3 messuages	—	—	1504	—
—	—	—	—	—	1515	—
—	—	—	—	18d.	(1527)	—

VIII. TABULATION OF DUGDALE'S NOTES OF THE TO THE CHANCERY

Folio	No. of farms ingrossed	No. of inclosures to pasture	Parishes	Areas ingrossed	Areas consolidated with farms	Areas inclosed	Objects of inclosure			Condition of inclosers				
							Park	Inclosure	Pasture	Lay lords of manors	Lay freeholders	Ecclesiastical lords of manors	Other ecclesiastics	Lay tenants
				acres	acres	acres	acres	acres	acres					
548	—	1	Warwick	—	—	2¼	—	—	24	—	1	—	—	—
	—	1	Chelmescote	—	—	60	—	—	60	—	—	—	1	—
	—	1	Cheriton	—	—	40	—	—	40	—	1	—	—	—
	—	1	Farnborough	—	—	20	—	—	20	1	—	—	—	—
	—	1	Morton-Morell	—	—	20	—	—	20	—	1	—	—	—
	—	1	Barton	—	—	45	—	—	45	—	1	—	—	—
	—	1	Brayles	—	—	20	—	—	20	—	—	—	1	—
	—	1	Cherlecote	—	—	40	—	—	40	1	—	—	—	—
	—	5	Walton Deuill	—	—	150	—	—	150	2	—	—	—	—
	—	1	Weston (Long Compton)	—	—	150	—	—	150	1	—	—	—	—
	—	1	Stratford super Avon	—	—	40	—	—	40	—	1	—	—	—
	—	1	Woluardington	—	—	20	—	—	20	—	—	—	1	—
	—	1	Honyngton	—	—	60	—	—	60	—	1	—	—	—
549	—	2	Shugbrough	—	—	40	—	—	40	1	—	—	—	—
	—	5	Brayles	—	—	240	—	—	240	—	—	—	—	1
	(1)		Vpton	—	—	108	—	—	108	1	—	—	—	—
	—	1	Vpton	—	—	20	—	—	20	—	1	—	—	—
550	—	1	Woluardington	—	—	40	—	—	40	—	—	1	—	—
	—	1	Sekinton	—	—	20	—	—	20	—	1	—	—	—
	—	1	Harborough	—	—	20	—	—	20	—	—	—	1	—
	—	1	Oxshulfe	—	—	80	—	—	80	1	—	—	—	—
	—	6	Wormleighton	—	—	( )[1]	—	—	( )[1]	1	1	—	—	—
			Total	—	—	1,257	—	—	1,257	9	9	1	4	1

[1] Area 240 acr. (see p. 403, *supra*), not given by Dugdale.

Inquisition of 1518, showing Returns additional Returns of 1517

No. of ploughs put down	Displacement of population	No. of houses decayed	No. of churches decayed	Annual rental value	Date of inclosure	Observations
—	persons —	1 messuagium	—	—	—	—
—	—	1 ,,	—	—.	—	Incloser the 'custos cantarie de Chelmescote'
—	—	1 ,,	—	—	—	—
—	—	1 ,,	—	—	—	—
—	—	1 ,,	—	—	—	—
—	—	1 ,,	—	—	—	—
—	—	1 ,,	—	—	—	—
—	—	1 ,,	—	—	—	—
—	—	5 messuagia	—	—	—	—
—	—	1 messuagium	—	—	—	—
—	—	1 ,,	—	—	—	—
—	—	1 ,,	—	—	—	—
—	—	2 messuagia	—	—	—	—
5	—	1 capitale / messuagium	—	—	—	Incloser probably lessee of manor from Crown
—	—	—	—	—	—	—
—	—	1 messuagium	—	—	—	—
—	—	1 ,,	—	—	—	—
—	—	1 ,,	—	—	—	—
—	—	1 ,,	—	—	—	—
—	—	6 messuagia	—	—	—	—
5	—	29 messuagia	—	—	—	—

[1] The returns of 1518 as noted by Dugdale, which appear to be a second presentment of the same inclosure, are excluded from this table. Dugdale's transcript is in full on pp. 651–6. Dugdale's transcript, it will be observed, does not distinguish between inclosures simply and inclosures accompanied by conversion to pasture. It is therefore necessary to class all these as cases of conversion. No dates or rental values are given by Dugdale.

IX. TABULATION OF DUGDALE'S NOTES OF THE INQUI-
TUTION OF INCLOSURES, &C., MENTIONED

Places	Reconversions to arable	Houses repaired	Ploughs restored	Inhabitants restored
Tāchebrok	acres 70	[ ]	4	36
Vpton	—	2 messuagia	—	—
Vpton	10	—	—	—
INQUISITION OF 1549				
Wormleighton . . .	Not given [150]	12	—	[ ]
Walton D'Eiuile. . .		—	—	—
Weston iuxta Barcheston .	50	{ 1 house { 1 cottage	—	[ ]
Wood Bevinton . .	—	4 messuages	←	[ ]

SITIONS OF 1518 AND 1549, SHOWING THE RESTI-
IN THE INQUISITIONS

Lay lords of manors	Lay free-holders	Ecclesiastical lords of manors	Ecclesiastical free-holders	Lay tenants	Observations
1	—	1	—	—	E. Medley and the Prior of Kenilworth joint owners of manor
1	—	—	—	—	—
—	1	—	—	—	—
INQUISITION OF 1549					
1	—	—	—	—	'laying land' to them (the houses)
1	—	—	—	—	—
—	—	—	—	1	About 1519

X

Tabulation of Dugdale's Notes of the Inquisition of 1518, showing Status of Actual Inclosers in the Additional Returns.

Status of Actual Inclosers. Inferred and Doubtful Figures Excluded

Lay ownership			*Ecclesiastical ownership*	
Lords of manors having and in hand.				
Parish	Total Acres		Parish	Total Acres
1. Farnborough	20			
2. Cherlecote	40			
3. Walton Deuill	150			
4. Weston (Long Compton)	150			
5. Shugbrough	40			
6. Vpton	108			
			1. Woluardington	40
7. Oxshulfe	80			
	588			40
II. Freeholders having land in hand.				
Parish	Total Acres		Parish	Total Acres
1. Warwick	24			
			1. Chelmescote	60
2. Cheriton	40			
3. Morton Morell	20			
4. Barton	45			
			2. Brayles	20
5. Stratford super Avon	40			
			3. Woluardington	20
6. Honyngton	60			
7. Vpton	20			
8. Sekinton	20			
			4. Harborough	20
	269			120
III. Copyholders.	—		—	—
IV. Leaseholders.	—		—	—
V. Farm tenants.	—		—	—

XI

Tabulation of Dugdale's Notes of the Inquisition of 1518. Additional Returns. Number of Acres to a Messuagium, &c.

(Inferred and Doubtful Figures excluded)

Lay ownership

I. Land in hand of lords of manors.

Parish	messuages	acres
1. Farnborough	1	20
2. Cherlecote	1	40
3. Walton Deuill	5	150
4. Shugbrough a	2	40
5. Oxshulfe	1	80
	10	330

Average no. of acres to a messuagium = 33.

II. Land in hand of freeholders.

Parish	messuages	acres
1. Warwick	1	24
2. Cheriton	1	40
3. Morton Morell	1	20
4. Barton	1	45
5. Stratford super Avon	1	40
6. Honyngton	1	60
7. Sekinton	1	20
	7	249

Average no. of acres to a messuagium = 35·57.

III. Copyholds — —

IV. Leaseholds. — —

V. Farm tenancies. — —

VI. Manor House ('capitale messuagium').

| Brayles | 1 | 240 |

Ecclesiastical ownership

Parish messuages acres

1. Woluardington . . 1 40

  1 40

No. of acres to a messuagium = 40.

Parish	messuages	acres
1. Chelmescote	1	60
2. Brayles	1	20
3. Woluardington	1	20
4. Harborough	1	20
	4	120

Average no. of acres to a messuagium = 30.

— —

— —

— —

a Weston (Longcompton), where the Return for 1517 was 7 messuages and 1 cottage to 200 acres, has been excluded, the area in Dugdale's Notes of the Inquisition of 1518 being given as 350 acres. See Table VI., p. 674, *supra*.

XII. Tabulation of Dugdale's Notes of the to the Chancery Returns of 1517 and to

Folio	No. of farms ingrossed	No. of inclosures to pasture	Parishes	Areas ingrossed	Areas consolidated with farms	Areas inclosed	Objects of inclosure			Condition of inclosers				
							Park	Inclosure of arable	Inclosure to pasture	Lay lords of manors	Lay freeholders	Ecclesiastical lords of manors	Other ecclesiastics	Lay
				acres	acres	acres	acres	acres	acres					
535	—	[5]	Dasset [cf]	—	—	240	—	—	240	1	—	—	—	—
	—	1	Upton [af]	—	—	10	—	—	10	—	1	—	—	—
	—	2	Whitchurch [be]	—	—	100	—	—	100	1	—	—	—	—
	—	5	Adderston [be]	—	—	[100]	—	—	[100]	—	—	—	—	1
			{ Chelmescote [be]	330	130	200	—	130	200	—	—	—	—	1
	—	5	{ Chelmescote [be]	—	—	60	—	—	60	—	1	—	—	—
536	—	6	Wood Bevinton [be]	—	—	180	—	—	180	—	—	—	—	1
	—	3	Little Dorsington [be]	—	—	200	—	—	200	1	—	—	—	—
	—	1	Samburne (Coughton) [be]	⊥	—	[32]	[32]	—	—	1	—	—	—	—
	—	1	Alcester [be]	—	—	18	18	—	—	—	1	—	—	—
	—	4	Stretton-Baskervill [be]	}—	—	160	—	—	160	1	—	—	—	—
	—	1	Astley [be]	—	—	90	90	—	—	1	—	—	—	—
	—	4	Fletchamsted [ee]	—	—	[160]	—	—	[160]	1	—	—	—	—
	—	1	Griffe (Chilverscoton) [be]	—	—	[30]	[30]	—	—	1	—	—	—	—
	—	3	Holt iuxta Kingsbury [be]	—	—	96	—	—	96	1	—	—	—	—
537	—	1	Sutton [be]	—	—	9	—	—	9	—	—	—	1	—
			Total	330	130	1,685	170	130	1,515	9	3	..	1	3

[a] In Chancery Returns for 1517. [b] Not in Chancery Returns for 1517. [c] Varying from Chancery Returns for 1517.
[d] In Inquisition of 1518. [e] Not in Inquisition of 1518.
[f] Varying from Inquisition of 1518.

Inquisition of 1549, showing Returns additional Dugdale's Notes of the Inquisition of 1518

No. of ploughs put down	Displacement of population	No. of houses decayed	No. of churches decayed	Annual rental value	Date of inclosure	Observations
—	persons — ( )	— 1 messuage	— —	— —	— 1521	— —
—	{ ( ) { ( )	1 capital messuage 1 messuage 2 cottages	—	—	1534	—
—	( )	4 messuages	—	—	1547	Incloser a leaseholder. 'Converted the said messuages into cottages'
—	( )	1 messuage	—	—	1547	Same incloser freeholder of this land. 'Converted the messuage into a cottage'
—	( )	6 messuages	—	—	1506 (March 1)	Incloser a leaseholder
3	—	—	—	—	1502 (March 4)	—
—	—	—	—	—	} 1531	—
—	{ ( ) { ( )	4 messuages 3 cottages	} —	—	1489	—
—	—	4 messuages	—	—	1497 1497	—
—	—	—	—	—	1497	—
—	—	3 messuages	—	—	1504	—
3	—	25 messuages 5 cottages	—	—	—	—

XIII

Dugdale's Notes of the Inquisition of 1549, Showing Status of Actual Inclosers in the Additional Returns

	Lay				Ecclesiastical		
Parish	Total Acres	Inclosure of arable Acres	Parks and inclosure to pasture Acres	Parish	Total Acres	Inclosure of arable Acres	Parks and inclosure to pasture Acres

I. Lords of manors having land in hand.

1. Dasset	240	—	240				
2. Whitchurch	100	—	100				
3. Little Dorsington	200	—	200				
4. Stretton Baskervill	160	—	160				
5. Astley	90	—	90				
6. Holt iuxta Kingsbury	96	—	96				
	886		886				

II. Freeholders having land in hand.

1. Upton	10	—	10				
2. Chelmescote	60	—	60				
3. Alcester	18	—	18				
	88		88				

III. Copyholders.

— — — —

IV. Leaseholders.

1. Chelmescote [a]	330	130	200				
				1. Wood Bevinton	180	—	180
				2. Sutton	9	—	9
	330	130	200		189		189

V. Farm tenancies.

— — · — —

[a] The incloser was lord of the manor in 1510, but in 1549 the property was let to a leaseholder and he is entered in Table VII. as the incloser responsible.

XIV

Dugdale's Notes of the Inquisition of 1549. Additional Returns. Number of Acres to a Messuage

(Inferred and Doubtful Figures excluded)

Lay ownership			Ecclesiastical ownership		
Parish	messuages	acres	Parish	messuages	acres
I. Land in hand of lords of manors.					
1. Holt juxta Kingsbury	3	96			
	3	96			
Average no. of acres to a messuage = 32.					
II. Land in hand of freeholders.					
1. Upton	1	10			
2. Chelmescote	1	60			
	2	70			
Average no. of acres to a messuage = 35.					
II. Copyholds.	—	—		—	—
IV. Leaseholds.					
1. Chelmescote	4	330			
			1. Wood Bevinton	6	180
	4	330		6	180
Average no. of acres to a messuage = 82·5.			Average no. of acres to a messuage = 30.		

XV

Observations on the Chancery Returns of 1517 compared with Dugdale's MS. Notes of the Inquisitions of 1517 and 1518, on his Notes of the Inquisition of 1549, and on the Entries of Inclosures in Dugdale's 'Warwickshire.'

The Chancery Returns state the whole of the presentments to have been made at Allesley on 22 September, 9 H. VIII. (1517). The notes made by Dugdale in D. I. 7 give the date of 2 September, 9 H. VIII. (1517), at Allesley, and 1 September, 10 H. VIII. (1518), at Warwick. This last return the Chancery MS. does not include. According to the Chancery Returns the Commissioners at Allesley on 22 September, 1517, were John Veysy and Roger Wygston. According to Dugdale, those present on 2 September, 1517, at Allesley were John Veysy, John Port, Roger Wigston, and John Hales, of whom Port and Hales do not appear to have been originally commissioned at all, while Sir Andrew Wyndesore, who was a commissioner, was absent. See the Commission, p. 81, *supra*. Singularly enough, the jury, so far as the five enumerated by Dugdale are concerned, were the same and occur in the same order in both Dugdale and the Chancery MS., which suggests the suspicion that September 2 may possibly have been a mistake on Dugdale's part for September 22. On the other hand, in Exch. Q. R. Mem. Roll 299, M.T. 11 H. VIII. (1519), m. 40 dorso, occurs a recital of the presentment in the Chancery MS. for inclosures at Litel Darsyngton, in which the date is given as 2 September, 9 H. VIII. (1517), at Allesley, John Veysy and Roger Wygston being stated to be the commissioners present. But this stands alone, while I have come across as many as ten cases of presentments before these two commissioners on 22 September, at Allesley. As for the commissioners, after examining over 70 cases in the Exchequer Rolls in which recitals of presentments from various counties in 1517 occur, I do not find one in which either Port or Hales appears as of their body. All the four enumerated by Dugdale sat at Kenilworth on September 1, 1518, as we know from the Exchequer Proceedings. They may very well have sat at Warwick on the same and at Allesley on the following day, though of this I find no trace in the Exchequer Rolls. In 1517 September 2 fell on a Wednesday and September 22 on a Tuesday, so that no light is thrown by the dates themselves. On the whole, the most probable conclusion seems to be that Dugdale has erroneously attached the names of the four commissioners of 1518 to the proceedings of 1517. As to his date,

2 September, 1517, it may be conjectured that the evidence was taken in certificates or slips containing one or more entries returned to the clerks on September 2, and that from these slips Dugdale transcribed; that on September 22, 1517, the certificates having been in the interval transcribed on to the membranes now preserved in the Record Office, the presentments were formally received as stated in the concluding declaration. The membranes were filed in Chancery and the original certificates remained in the possession of John Hales, where they were noted by Dugdale. This will account for omissions from Dugdale's tables which would scarcely have occurred had he worked from the Chancery Returns. It also explains the fact that while in the Chancery Returns an effort was evidently made to group the entries according to locality, some of them appear out of place, being separated from other inclosures in the same place. See the case of Grenborough, *infra*. There are other internal evidences pointing to the same conclusion as to Dugdale's sources. The omission of the entries from Shyttyngton is intelligible if those certificates, being at the top of the bundle, had become illegible through dirt. Two entries are dropped at Bysshopshamton, one at Nether-Shuckburgh. It is possible that the last had been withdrawn for evidence in legal proceedings, and that this was the object of the retention of the certificates in the hands of the commissioners. We happen to know from a wholly different source that such proceedings did take place with reference to inclosures by Shuckborough.

More decisive is the manner in which Dugdale has treated the inclosure at Whitnashe. On fo. 546 of his MS. is, apparently interpolated after an entry of the inclosure of 1 mess. and xxx acres at Grenborough, the inclosure, &c., of 2 mess. and xl acres at Whitnashe by William Medley. Now this entry appears on a different membrane of the Inquisition (membrane 56) from that on which the Grenborough entry is found (membrane 55); Whitnashe being at the foot of m. 56, Grenborough halfway down m. 55. Had the entry been overlooked by Dugdale, it would naturally have been inserted afterwards in its proper place in his MS., where there is as much space as in the place in which it appears, the entries being made with ample space below each. The conclusion seems to be that it was on a loose document and that it was inserted after Grenborough because it was in the same Hundred (Knightlow). Finally, on fo. 548 of Dugdale's MS. there is a pencilled note in the margin of the heading to the Inquisition of 1518 'in alio bundello,' which again points to bundles of certificates as the source of his notes.

The synoptical Table V. of the differences between the areas noted by Dugdale from the Inquisition of 1517 and those given in the Chancery Returns shows that Dugdale's additions to those Returns are 460 acres, his omissions 563½ acres. It must be borne in mind, however, that the added 460 acres are almost certainly due to two misreadings of the originals. These struck out, the omissions represent some 14 per cent. of the whole area of 7948 acres inclosed for improved tillage or converted to pasture. This probably represents more in proportion than the omissions from the Inquisitions of 1518 and 1549, because a comparison of Dugdale's notes of those Inquisitions with his notes of that of 1517 shows unquestionably that the number of the original certificates must have been smaller, and confusion would consequently be more easily avoided.

There are peculiarities in Dugdale's notes of the Inquisition of 1518 not easy of explanation. Such are the cases, as at Chelmscote, Grafton, &c., in which the name of the incloser is entered and that of the place, but the entries of areas inclosed, &c., are omitted. It may be that, in sorting the slips, Dugdale intended to collect together the inclosures in one place, and forgot that he had not done so. An obvious objection to this is that in his notes of the Inquisition of 1517 he does not aggregate inclosures by different inclosers. Moreover the omissions are not mere blanks. The space is asterisked, as though to signify that they were intended. An explanation may perhaps be found in the character of the Inquisition of 1518. The marginal notes upon the Chancery Returns show that subpœnas were issued perhaps early in 1518, for appearances to be entered within fifteen days after Michaelmas. Now the Inquisition of 1518, which took comparatively little fresh evidence (see Table VIII. Additional Returns, 1518), may have been in its main scope an inquiry into the steps which had been taken in the interval to remedy the cases presented in the previous year. Colour is lent to this view by the preface to the inclosures of Sir Edward Belknap at Derset and Birton; 'Et sicut in priori Inq. capta ix° Henr. viij,' of which the intention appears to be to point to them as of capital importance and also to emphasise the fact that this is a repeated presentment of them. It might be suggested that these blanks were not filled up because Dugdale found at the end of the entry a note that the presentment had been cancelled by the restoration of the messuages, &c. Against this is the presentment in 1549 of the destruction at Wood-Bevinton of six messuages and one cottage assigned to the year 1506, by an incloser already presented in 1517, a blank having been left against the name of the place in Dugdale's notes of the Inquisition of 1518. In the same way Sir R. Throckmorton was presented for the formation of Coughton Park by an inclosure of $20\frac{1}{2}$ acres 'cum aliis terris,' &c. This was in 1517. No presentment appears in 1518, but that of 1549 clearly shows the park to have been then in existence. Similarly with the Marquis of Dorset's inclosure of 90 acres at Astley. It is unsafe, therefore, to infer that the Returns of 1518 comprised all cases in which no remedy had been applied. The Exchequer Rolls afford no solution of the difficulty. The only explanation which seems to meet all the cases is that the places omitted from the Returns of 1518 or left blank by Dugdale were those in which an undertaking to conform to the requisitions of the commissioners was made, though abandoned at a later date. It is apparent from the decree of Chancery of July 12, 1518, as well as from the proclamation of 1526 (p. 489), that a temporising policy had been frequently adopted, while we know, as a matter of fact, both from the Inquisition of 1549 and from the language of the Statutes, as also of contemporary writers, that, notwithstanding the efforts of the Commission, the laws were largely left unenforced.

There are features in Dugdale's notes of the Inquisition of 1549 which likewise demand explanation. Inclosures are returned assigned to a date anterior to 1517, but not included in that Inquisition nor in that of 1518. Such are Wood-Bevinton, Little Dorsington, Stretton-Baskervill, Astley, Fletchamsted, Griffe, Holt, and Sutton. Now, although it is apparent that the commissioners of 1549 worked with the Returns of 1517 in their hands, it is also certain that fresh evidence was taken, an illustration of which is the mention for the first time in the Inquisition of 1549 of the formation of a pool in the meadow at Fletchamsted. Another peculiarity of the same Inquisition is the attribution to the legal owners of 1549 of the construction of inclosures made by their predecessors in title with the date attached of the year as given in the Returns of 1517. A case in point is to be found at Walton d'Euill on p. 658. Such a method was probably extended to the assignment to the date already returned in 1517 of inclosures really effected subsequently, but at a date from its remoteness difficult to ascertain. A suspicion of this sort attaches itself to the inclosures at Wood-Bevinton by William Grey first recorded in 1549, but assigned to 1506, the date of his inclosures as returned in 1517. Similarly in the case of the inclosures at Little Dorsington. Obviously if this be so, the returns of 1549 are an inadequate register of the inclosing movement since 1517, a probability enhanced by the other circumstances of the inquiry.

These Inquisitions throw some light upon the composition of Dugdale's 'Warwickshire,' so far as the inclosing movement is concerned. Were his notices of inclosure in that work taken from his notes of the Inquisitions or from the original certificates themselves? About this there cannot be much doubt, so far at least as the returns of 1549 are concerned. In the case of Chelmscote (Inq. 3 E. VI.) Dugdale omits from his notes the name of the wife of William Walker. In his

'Warwickshire' (p. 398) he gives it as Isabel, with a reference to this Inquisition. Again, in the case of Cougheton Dugdale ('Warw.' p. 523) represents Sir Robert Throkmorton to have inclosed, inter alia, 'a certain common ground called Wike Wood,' apparently citing the Inquisition of 3 E. VI. as his authority. Now though the inclosure for the formation of a park of $20\frac{1}{2}$ acres at Cougheton by Sir Robert Throkmorton is recorded in the Inquisition of 1517 (p. 450, *supra*), no mention of an inclosure by him occurs in Dugdale's notes of the Inquisitions of 1518 and of 1549, nor in Dugdale's notes of the Inquisition of 1549 is there any mention of Wike Wood. The inference is that, though the form is different, the Inquisition of 1549 as it appears in Dugdale's MSS. is not a transcript but notes, and that, unless Dugdale conformed its orthography to that of his day, it was probably translated from Latin. Further, his notices of inclosures in Warwickshire must have been based upon the original documents and not on his own notes preserved in the Bodleian Library and here first published.

INDEX

ABBENDON. *See* Abingdon
Abell, Jo., 219
——, Will., of Sheldon, 394
Abendon. *See* Abingdon
Abingdon, Abendon, Abbyndon, Abbot of, 103, 111, 115, 116, 121, 125, 126, 127, 128, 133, 140, 141, 341, 368
Abrahall, Tho., 209
Abthorpe, co. N'hamp., 283
Aby, Tho. of Tateshall, 248, 249
Abyndon, co. Berk. *See* Abingdon
Adderbury, Addersberry, co. Oxon., 333, 336
Addington, Adyngton, co. Buck., 200, 201
Aderston, co. Warw. *See* Atherstone
Aisshefeld, Jo., 383
Alablaster, Humph., 399, 648
Albery. *See* Aldbury
Alcester, Alcestre, co. Warw., 662
Alcot, Priory of, 395, 648
Aldbury, Albery, co. Oxon., 364
Aldersey, Jo., 644; Rob., 641
Aldeworth, Jo., 134
Aldworth, Aldeworth, co. Berk., 105; Beche in, 104
Ale, Will., 214
Alee, Jo., 206
——, Will., 158
Alexton, Alaxton, co. Leic., 238
Aleyn, Will., 367
Allesley, Alseley, co. Warw., 86, 394, 435 *bis*, 650; Inquisition made at, 647
Alnot, Ric., 368
Alworth, Tho., 115
Alyn, Jo., 110-1
Alyngton, Giles, Kt., 84
Ambresbury, Aumsbery, Prioress of, 136
Amington, Amynton, co. Warw., 447, 650; messuage called 'Bowlhall,' 'Boulhall,' 447, 650
Andelet, Jo., 364
Andrewes, Andrews, Androus, Thos., 358, 359, 361
Annesley, Tho., 121

Apethorpe, Apetrop, co. N'hamp., 306
Appleford, Appelford, co. Berk., 141
Apryce, Aprice, Lewis, 196, 209; Jo., 100
Arches, Ralph, 175; Will., 175
Archester. *See* Irchester
Arden, Jo., 349, 648. *See also* Wardern
Ardington, Ardynton, co. Berk., 115
Ardley, Ardeley, co. Oxon., 350
Arley, Lordship of, 663
Arundell, Jo., Kt., 337
Ascot, co. Oxon., 343
Ashby next Horncastle, 255-6. Lord St. John's ground in, 255; Watkinson tenure in, 256; 'Inhamfeld' in, 256
Ashby-by-Partney, Ashby juxta Partiney, co. Linc., 254
Ashby, Assheby, de la Zouche, Leic., 233
Ashby, Tho., 650. *See* Assheby
Asshby, Jo., 295
Asshebroke, Will., 344; Joan, wife of, 344
Assheby, Tho. 442. *See* Ashby
Assheby, ——, 187
Asshefeld, Jo., 335
Assheley, Jo., 643
Asshendon, co. Buck., 159, 160
Assheton. *See* Aston le Walles
Asshton, Hugh, clk., 85
Asterleigh, Asterley co., Oxon., 330, 371
Asthall and Asthall Leigh, Astall and Astall Lye, co. Oxon., 346
Astley, co. Warw., 451, 663
Aston [Abbots], co. Buck., 182
Aston le Walles, Assheton, co. N'hamp., 297
Aston Molent, co. Buck., 208
Aston Turrold, co. Berk., 145 *bis*, 146
Atherstone, Aderston, co. Warw., 660
Atkynson, Tho., 470, 473
Audeley. *See* Tuchet
Aumsbery. *See* Ambresbury
Aungell, Jo., 101
Aungewyne, Awngevyne, Margaret, 256
Austyn, Jo., of Stepyng, 259

Axholme, Carthusian priory in the Isle of, 424, 655
Ayce, Ric., 644
Aydon. *See* Eydon
Ayleston, Tho., 132

BABYNGTON, Will., 371
Bagrave, Bagraue, co. Leic., 229
Baguley, Baggeley, co. Chesh., 643
Baker, Jo., 142 *bis*
——, Jo., 497, 498
Baldons, co. Oxon., 380
Baldwyn, Jo., 205
Balle, Hen., 201
Banaster, Will., 101
Banwell, Will., of Coventry, 438, 650
Barantyne, Will., Kt., 384. *See* Baryngton
Barby, co. N'hamp., 299
Barcheston, hamlet of, co. Warw., 417, 649; several messuages named in, 416
Baret, Rob., 382
Barford, Berford, co. N'hamp., 317
Barfote, Nich., 100
Barkeby, Jo., 399
Barkeley, Maur., jun., Kt., 233
Barker, Tho., 301
Barklay, Maur, Kt., 84
Barmeston, Barneston, Jo., 467
Barowe, Maur, Kt., 351, 352
Barreclose, co. Buck., 182
Bartilmew, Rob., of Sturton, 252
Barton, co. Warw., 652
Barton, Walt., 146
Barton Sharshill. *See* Sesswell Barton
Baryngton, Will., Kt., 359. *See* Barantyne
Basildon, Bastelden, co. Berk., 105
Battlesden, Batlesden, co. Bed., 465
Baynham, Alex., Kt., 84
Beachampton, Bechampton, co. Buck., 202
Beanton, Beynton, co. Oxon., 331
Bedford, 86
——, inquisition held at, 459
——, doct. dated at, 476
Bedone. *See* Beedon, co. Berk.
Bedycote, Jo., 327
Bedyll, Will., of London, 362
Beedon, Bedone, co. Berk., 111
Beell, Nich., 380
Bekyngham, Ric., 384
Belamy, —, 274
Belcott, Jo., of Lyttyllyngton, 459
Belgrave, co. Leic., 236; 'Old Park' in, 236
Belknap, Edw., Kt. 424, 425, 426, 427, 438, 439, 478–80, 649, 655, 656
Bell, Ric., 369

Bell, Tho., of Buknall, 252
Bellyngham, Christopher, 121
Bemond, Jo., 232
Bendowe, Jo., 459
Benefield, Benifeild, co. N'hamp., 659
Benet, Tho., 144
Benett, Tho., 120
Bentley, co. Warw., 448, 650
Berden, Berdyn, co. Essex, 220; 'Barkers' in, 221
Berford. *See* Barford
Berkeham, co. Berk., 131
Berners, John Bowrgchyer lord Barnesse, 331
Bery, Jo., 652
Besellys, Will., 370
Betterton, Beaterton, co. Berk., 116
Bevington, Bevyngton, co. Warw., 409–10, 654. *See* Wood Bevington
Bewfo, Bewffo, Jo., 444, 650; John, son of, 444, 650
Beyford, Joan, 111
Beynton. *See* Beanton
Bicester. *See* Burcester?
Biddenham, Bydenham, co. Bed., 475; 'Message called Davys,' 475
Bigge, Jo., 652
Bille, Rob., 644
Billyng, Tho., 310
Binfield, Bynfeld, co. Berk., 119
Binsey, Byndeshey, co. Oxon., 387
Bird, Rog., 182
Birdstone, Byrdyston, co. Buck., 161, 162
Birmingham, Brymycham, co. Warw., 402, 648
Birton. *See* Burton-Dasset, co. Warw.
Bisham, Bustellesham, co. Berk., 121; Prior of, 121
Blackfordby, Blakerby, co. Linc., 233
Blacknowe, Ric. and Will., 213
Blandey, Tho., 118
Blatherwick, Blatherwyke, co. N'hamp., 312
Bletchley, Blecheley, co. Buck., 178 *bis*; 'Cotmanfeud' in, 178
Blount, Tho., Kt., 346
——, Walt., Knt., Lord Mountgey, 238
Bobenhill. *See* Bubenhall
Bocher, Will., 257, 327
——, Katherine, wife of Thomas (?), 257
Bolingbroke, Bullingbrok, Soke of, 255
Boller, Henr., 327–8
——, Tho., 207
Bollyngdon, co. Oxon. *See* Bullington
Bolok, Tho., 130
Bolt, Rob., 341

INDEX

Bonde, Jo., of Coventry, 400, 648, 664; Thomas, son and heir of, 664
Bones, Jo., of Buknall, 248; Jo., of Tateshall, 248
Bonham, Jo., 84
Bordene, Will., 141
Borowe, Rob., 242
Boughton, Will,, 342
Bourchier. *See* Berners
Bourchier de Fitzwaren, Jo., 85
Bourton, Buorton, Buerton, co. Buck., 199
—— Hold, 199
Boxford, Boxforth, co. Berk., 119
Boyvyle, Geo., 316
Bracebrige, Bracebrigge, Bracebrygge, Jo., 449, 451, 650, 651, 654, 664; Tho., 449, 664
Bradbury, Joan, 353
Braddon, Bradden, co. N'hamp., 293
Bradfield, co. Berk., 149
Bradgate, co. Leic., 234, 235, 236
Bradwell, co. Buck., 181, 182 *bis*; Rob. Buston, prior of, 181
Bragenham, Brakynham, co. Buck., 170 *bis*
Brailes, Braylys, co. Warw., 419, 649, 652, 654
Brascote, Briscott, co. Leic., 241
Brassy, Jo., 644
Bray, co. Berk., 121, 131
Bray, Edm., Kt., 303, 465
Braybroke, Jac., 125, 126
Brayton, co. Berk. *See* Drayton
Bredyncote, co. Buck., 173
Brereley, Jo., 402, 648
Bresenorton. *See* Norton Brize
Brice, Will., 346
Brightwell, co. Berk., 107
Brightwell, co. Oxon., 330
Brigstock, Brigstok, co. N'hamp., 311
Brimstage, Brimstach, co. Chesh., 644
Brington, Bryngton, co. N'hamp., 298; 'Guy Robyn's' messuage in, 298
Briscott. *See* Brascote
Broadwell, Brodewell, co. Oxon., 347, 348; vicar of, 348
Brogden, Brother John, 428, 429
Broke, Jo., Serjeant at Law, 85
——, Jo., Kt., Lord Cobham, 358
——, Tho., of Ewelme, 364
——, Tho., Kt., Lord Cobham, 358, 370, 371
Bromeham, co. Bed., 466
Bromham, Jo., 459
Bromwich, Castle, 'Ladye Croftes' in, 410, 648
Bromwich, Little, co. Warw., 400, 648, 664

Bronkelow, Ric., 159
Brooksby, Brokysby, co. Leic., 237
Brothers, Hen., 349–50
Broughton, co. Buck., 212
——, Jo., 212, 213, 473, 474
Broun, Humph., 277, 278
——, Jo., 277, 278, 357, 470, 471
——, Matt., Kt., 85
——, Nich., 385
Brown, Will., 419, 649
——, Will., clk., 421, 649, 652
Browne, Jo., Kt., 662
——, Tho., of Tumby, 250
Brudenell, Edm., 206, 207
——, Rob., 306
——, Rob., Kt., 281, 304 *bis*.
——, —, 190
Brudnell, Rob., 230
——, Rob., Kt., 229
Bruer, Monastery of, 385
Bruern, Abbot of, 372
Brydon, Hen., 240
Brymycham. *See* Birmingham
Bryn, Jo., 644
Bubenhall, Bobenhill, co. Warw., 438 *bis*, 650
Buckingham, Henry, duke of, 473
Buckland, Bukland, Bukeland, co. Berk., 129 *bis*, 141, 142; le Personagelande, 142; Newynton in, 142; John, rector of, 142
Bucklow, Buklow hundred, co. Chesh., 643
Bukmere, Jo., 446. *See* Buckmore
Buckmore, Jo., 650. *See* Bukmere
Bucknall, Buknall, co. Linc., 252
Buerton. *See* Bourton
Buk, Jo., 146
Bukeregge, Jo., 105
Buldry, Will., 340
Bulkington, co. Warw., 433, 650
Bullingbrok. *See* Bolingbroke
Bullington, Bollyngdon, hundred of, co. Oxon., 342, 354, 355, 356, 369 *bis*
Bullok, Jo., 257
Bullyng, Will., 350
Bulstrode, Tho., 84
Bulwick, Bulwyk, co. N'hamp., 313
Bunbury, Ric. (1), 644; (2), 644
Buorton. *See* Bourton
Burcester, co. Oxon., Wrecchewyke in, 340
Burcester, Richard, Prior of, 340; John, Prior of, 340
Burcote, co. N'hamp., 293
Burcott, co. Buck., 173
Burford, co. Oxon., 344, 345
Burghfield, Burghfeld, co. Berk., 148

Burgoyn, Jo., 460
Burnham, co. Buck., 184
Burstone. *See* Birdstone
Burton, co. Berk., messuage called 'Hoggys' in, 124
Burton, co. Warw., 478
Burton, Birton-Dassett, Dorsett, Byrton, co. Warw., 424, 425, 649, 655, 656
Burton Latimer, co. N'hamp., 303
Burton Overy, co. Leic., 227
Burton, Ric., of Dovewode, 258
Bushmead, Bisshmede, Prior of, 459
Bury, Edw., 348
——, Maur. a, 150
Bury St. Edmund's, Abbot of, 83
Busby, Rob., 328
Busshell, Jac., 642
Bustellesham. *See* Bisham
Butler, Ric., 300, 302
——, Rog., of Haveryngham, 250
——, Will., 144
Button, co. N'hamp., 303
Bydenham, co. Bed. *See* Biddenham
Bygott, Pet., 239
Bynfeld. *See* Binfield, co. Berk.
Byrd, Jo., 271 *bis*
Byrdystone. *See* Birdstone
Byrton. *See* Burton-Dassett, co. Warw.
Bysseter, Prior of, 334
Bysshop, Ric., 158
Bysshopshampton. *See* Hampton Lucy
Byttelsden, Abbot of, 198

Calcote, Tho., 145
Calverley, Geo., 238
Camby, Jo., 329
Candlesby, Candilsby, co. Linc., 253, 254
Canons Ashby, 291
Canons Ashby, Prior of, 292. *See* Grenewey
Carlisle, Bishop of, 209, 257
Carpenter, Ric., 336
Carswell, Carcewell, co. N'hamp., 292
Carter, Jo., 147
——, Ric., 173
Cartwright, —, 180
——, Will., 395
Castell, Jo., receiver of Henry VIII., 280
Castelman, Agnes, 138
Castle Thorpe, Castelthorp, co. Buck., 209
Castor, Castir, co. N'hamp., 268 ; severall messuages named in, 268-9, 270
Catesby, 315 ; Prioress of St. Edmund's, 315

Catesby, Ant., 287. *See* Catysby
——, Humph., 290; Francis, 290
——, Sir Ric., Kt., 656
——, Tho., 437 *bis*, 410-1, 445, 648, 650, 653
Catland, —, 351
Catmore, Catmar, co. Berk., 102
Catysby, Ant., 297. *See* Catesby
Cave, Edw., 433, 650
——, Ric., 399, 402, 648 *bis*.
——, Tho., 310
Cawston, Jo., 218
Chaddleworth, Chadlyngworth, Chaddelworth, co. Berk., 111, 112 ; Wolley in, 112
Chadlington, Chadyllyngton, co. Oxon., 359 *bis*, 360; 'The Field' in, 385 *bis*; hundred of, 385
Chaldecote, Walt., 148
Chalfont St. Peter, co. Buck., 206, 207 ; messuages called 'Butterfeld' and 'Leter' in, 206
Chalver, Hen., 642
Chamberleyn, Ric., 110, 111
——, Sibyl, 328-9
——, Tho., 108
Chambernoun, Champernoun, Ph., 333, 368
Chantrell, Rob., 643
Chapman, Jo., of Tateshall Thorpe, 250
Chariour, Rob., of Kenilworth, 395
Chastleton, co. Oxon., 329
Chatwen, Will. *See* Chetwyne
Chebunherst. *See* Chippinghurst
Chebunherst, Chebenherst, Tho., 344 ; Joan, wife of, 344
Chelmscote, Chelmyscote, co. Warw., 419, 420, 421, 649, 651, 652, 660 ; Chantry of, 651 ; Will. Brown, Chaplain, 421, 649, 652
Cherington, Cheriton, co. Warw., 652
Chesham, Chessham, co. Buck., 209 ; messuages called 'Spencers' and 'Huettes' in, 209 ; messuages called 'Sewellys' and 'Borden' in, 211
Chester, 642-3 ; 'le houbrigfildes,' 642 *ter*; 'Chesterfeldes,' 642 ; Inquisition made at, 641
Chetewyne, Chetwyne, Chatwen, Chatwyn, Will., 402, 648, 653
Cheuerell, Rog., 85
Cheumdye, —, 359
Cheyne, Jo., Kt., 123, 124
Cheyny, Tho., Kt., 278 ; Lady Ann, 278
Chichester, Abbot of, 347
Chichester, Bp. of, 85
Chieveley, Chyveley, co. Berk., 111
Childrey, Chilrey, co. Berk., 107

Chilton, co. Berk., 105
Chilvers Coton, co. Warw., 664
Chilworth, co. Oxon., 342
Chipping Dorset, Dorsett, Darset, co. Warw., 408, 478, 648
Chippinghurst, Chebunherst in Cuddesdon, co. Oxon., 344
Chipping Norton, Chepyng Norton, co. Oxon., 330; messuage called 'Walle' in, 330
Chipping Norton, Chantry of, 365
Chirchehill, co. Oxon. *See* Churchill
Chiselhampton, Chesilhampton *alias* Chessyllyngton, co. Oxon., 341; 'le pasture of,' 341
Chitwood. *See* Whitwode
Churchill, Churchehull, co. Oxon., 360, 384
Chyveley. *See* Chieveley, co. Berk.
Clare, Clayour, co. Oxon., 350, 377 *bis*.
Clark. *See* Hayward
Classh, Ric., 641
Clavering Hundred, co. Essex, 220
Clayour. *See* Clare, co. Oxon.
Clegge, Jo., 644
Clendon, Glendon, co. N'hamp., 309
Clere, Rob., Kt., 83
Clerk, —, one of Henry VII.'s auditors, 209
——, Hugh, 641
——, Tho., 358
Clerke, Ric., 483
——, Will., 427, 649
Cleve, Gilb., 643
Clewer, co. Berk., 120; Langford manor in, 120
Cleydon. *See* Steeple Claydon
Cleyve, Jo., 644
Cliffe, Clyff, co. Warw., 449, 653
Clifton Hampden, Clyfton, co. Oxon., 334; 'Glasehouse' and 'Hycokes' in, 334
Clinton, Clynton, John, lord, 447, 650
Clyff, Jo., 644
Clyfton, Gervase, Kt., 181
Cobham, lord. *See* Broke
Coffyn, Ric., 83
Coggs, Coggys, co. Oxon., 380
Cokayn, Cokeyn, Tho., Kt., 400, 648
Cokkes, Hugh, 643
Colbourne, Rob., 641
——, Tho., 642
Colchester. *See* Crestemas
Cold Higham, co. N'hamp., 283
Coldnorton, co. Oxon., 383; monastery of, 383
Cole, Will., 459

Cole Orton, Horton Catermersshe, Ouerton Quatermersh, co. Leic., 232
Coley, Jo., of Gloston, 230
Colsonsok, Pet., 643
Colt, Jo., 170, 171
——, Jo., 470, 471
Colton, Christopher, 109
Colyer, Hen., 205
Colyns, Jo., 116
Combe, co. Oxon., 342
Combe, Ric., 108
Compton, co. Berk., 104
—— (Beauchamp or Regis), co. Berk., 123
—— [-Wingate], co. Warw., 418 *bis*, 649. *See* Long Compton
——, Will., 185
——, Will., Kt., 337, 417–18, 649
Comyn, Ric., 345
Constable, Jo., Kt., 239
——, John, Dean of Lincoln, 255
Conwey, Hugh, Kt., 172 *bis*, 203
Conyers, Will., de Hornby, Kt., 85
Cooke, Ant., Kt., 657
——, Jo., of Newenton Longvyle, 213
——, Rob., of Marome, 258
Cookham, Cokeham, co. Berk., 130
Coope, Will., 287, 403-4, 485-6, 489, 648. *See* Cope
Cootes, co. Oxon., 370
Cope, Ant., Kt., 657; Will., 656. *See* Coope
Copley, Rog., 148
Corbet, quidam, 423
Cornwayle, Tho. a, Kt., 83
Cornwell, Tho., Kt., 641
Corson, Jo., 133
Costard, Tho., 129
Cosyn, Ric., 470, 473
Cote, co. Oxon. *See* Cootes
Cotes, Cotys, co. Leic., 233
Cotes, Ant., of Benifield, co. N'hamp., 659
Cotesmore, Will., 341 *bis*, 364, 373
Cotnour, co. Oxon, 351
Coton, Jo., 449
Cottesbatch, Cottysbeche, co. Leic., 241
Cottesmore, Jo., 136
Cotton, Rob., Kt., 84, 217
Coughton, co. Warw., 450, 651
Councer, Counser, Cowncer, Will., 366, 377 *bis*, 378
Couper, Hen., 200
——, Rog., 177
Courteney, William, Earl of Devon, 124
—— Henry, Earl of Devon, 124
Coventry, fratres Hospitalis Sancti Johannis, 434

Coventry, Monastery of St. Mary, 438
——, Prior of, 231
Coventry and Lichfield, Bp. of, 83
—— —— ——, Geoff., Bp. of, 641
Cowley, co. Oxon., 363
—— Littlemore, co. Oxon., 363
Coxhed, Jo., 116, 117
Cradok, Jo., Kt., 134
Cranwell, Cranewell, co. Buck., 174, 175
Craycroft, Rob., 248
Crestemas, Tho., of Colchester, 220
Crick, Kreke, co. N'hamp., 291
Cristede, Convent of. *See* Kirkstead
Crokam, Crokeham, co. Berk., 125, 146
Crosse, Steph., 642
Crotall, Jo., 100
Crowmarsh-Gifford, Crowmershe Gefford, co. Oxon., 376
Croyland, Crowland, Abbot of, 252
Croyland, writ for Abbot of, 480 *et seq*
Cublington, Cublyngton, co. Buck., 173
Cuddesdon, Cuttesdon, co. Oxon., 341, 364 ; 'Grove lese' in, 364
Culnam, co. Oxon., 86, 339
Curbridge, Curbrigge, co. Oxon., 347
Curson, Jo., 140
——, Walt., 207. *See* Curzon
Curtes, Jo., 299
Curzon, Walt., 353. *See* Curson

Dacre. *See* Fenys
Dagnall, Jo., 167 *bis*
Dalby, Steph., 239, 240
——, Tho., clk., 85
Dannet, Mary, 657
Dantre. *See* Daventry
Danvers, Joan, widow, 341
——, Tho., Knt., 342. *See* Davers
Danyell, Pet., 643
Darell, Edw., Kt., 84, 135
——, Tho., 197, 198
Darset. *See* Chipping Dorset
Darsyngton, Little Dorsington, in Welford, co. Warw., 415, 649
Daunce, Jo., 196
Daventry, Prior of, 296
Davers, Will., Kt., 413, 648, 654 ; Tho., 413
Dawson, Symon, 248
Deane, Edw. a, 113
——, Jac. a, 340, 377
Dene, co. N'hamp., 304
Dene, co. Oxon., 361
Dene, Ric., 346
Denham, co. Buck., 186, 187 ; messuage called 'Tylehouse' in, 186 ; rectory of, 187
Denham, Jo., Kt., late Lord Denham, 174 ; Tho., 174
Denton, co. Oxon., 357
Denton, Tho., 134
Denys, Tho., Kt., 83
Derby, Earl of, 106, 115
——, Tho., Earl of, 332
Derby, Will., 335
Derset. *See* Chipping Dorset
Devereux, Walt., Kt., Lord Ferrers of Chartley, 240, 241
Devon, Earl of. *See* Courteney
Dey, Will., 470, 472
Digby, Everard, 230
Dinton, Dynton, co. Buck., 191, 192
Ditton, Dytton, co. Buck., 183, 184
Doddershall, Dodershill, co. Buck., 162
Domvile, Jac., 643
Donne, Rad., 644
Donnyngton, 'le Almeshouse' of, 354
Donyng, Jo., 218
Doo, Alice, 116
——, Jo., 644
Dormer, Rob., 213, 343
Dorset, Thomas, Marquis of, 234, 235, 236, 240, 241, 286, 398, 408, 444, 648, 651, 653, 663, 664 ; Margaret, wife of, 408, 444
Dorset, *alias* Chipping Dorset, co. Warw. *See* Chipping Dorset
Dorsett, co. Warw. *See* Burton Dassett
Dostrop, co. N'hamp., 279
Doynysdon. *See* Dunsden
Drakenedge, co. Warw., 442, 650
Drane, Jo., 248
Draper, Tho., 438, 650
Drayton, Brayton, co. Berk., 130, 134, 140
Drayton, Dreyton, co. Leic., 228
Druell, Margaret, 310
Drury, Rob., Kt., 84
Dudcott, Dudcote, co. Berk., 144 *bis*
Dudley, Jo., 297
Duke, Ric., 327
Dunsden, Doynysdon, co. Oxon., 381
Dunthorp, co. Oxon., 384
Dunton, Donnyngton, co. Buck., 166, 167
Dutton, Jo., 643
——, Pet., 642
Dycons, Ric., 459, 476
Dymmok, Sir Lyon, 257, 258
——, Rob., Kt., 84, 248, 251, 255
Dynham, Lord. *See* Denham
Dyrdount, Tho., 187
Dytton. *See* Ditton

INDEX

EARLEY, Erley, co. Berk., 121
Easenhall, Eysenell, Esenhull, co. Warw., 433, 650
East Ginge, Estgynge, co. Berk., 116, 117
East Hanney, co. Berk., 114, 115
East Hendred, Esthenred, co. Berk., 108, 113
East Lockinge, Estlokhenges, co. Berk., 116
Easton, Eston, co. N'hamp., 284
Eastwell, Estwell, co. Leic., 238
Eathorp, Eythorp, co. Warw., 439, 650; 'Maretyns house' and 'Hyllys house,' 439
Eberall, Laur., of Knoll, 394
Ecton, Ekton, co. N'hamp., 290 bis.
Eddisbury, Eddesbury, hundred, co. Chesh., 644
Edgcott, Edgecote, co. N'hamp., 303
Edlesborough, Eddeslbrough, co. Buck., 160
Edlyngson, Tho., 257
Edyngill, rector of. 102, 103
Egecombe, Pet., Kt., 83
Egellyngton, Tho., 159
Egelynton, Geof., 188
Eggerton, Phil., 644
——, Rad., Kt., 644
Ekton. See Ecton
Eland, Jo., 248
——, Jo., of Stirton, 257
Elleson, Will., 85
Ellys, Jo., 470, 473
Elmes, Humph., 327. See Elmys
——, Jo., 315
Elminton, Elynton, co. N'hamp., 282
Elmyngton, co. N'hamp., lands and houses named in, 481 et seq.
Elmys, Eliz., 277; Humph., 339, 381; Jo., 277. See Elmes
Elsfield, Elsfeld, co. Oxon., 355
Elston, Tho., 112
Elstow, Elmestowe, co. Bed., nunnery of, 179, 464, 473, 476
Ely, N., Bp. of, 84
Elynton. See Elminton
Elyot, Elyott, Ric., Kt., 112, 370; his wife, 370
Elys, Will., 83
Emerton, Tho., 159
Emery, Will., 106
Empson, Emson, Ric., Kt., 204, 205, 284, 384; Tho., 204
Enderby, Jo., 470, 472
Enderby, co. Linc., 259
England, Queen of, 122, 131

England, Katherine of Aragon, Queen of, 199, 200
Enlowe, Will., heirs of, 642
Enyse, Tho., 651
Erley. See Earley, co. Berk.
Erneley, Jo., 85
Escott, ——, 240
Esenhull. See Easenhall, co. Warw.
Est Gynge. See East Ginge, co. Berk.
Esthenrede. See East Hendred
Eston. See Easton
Estwell. See Eastwell, co. Leic.
Eton, co. Buck., 86, 158
Eton, Will., 182
Everdon, Everton, co. N'hamp., 299
Eversholt, co. Bed., 461
Eueryngham, Edw., 346
Ewelme, co. Oxon., 364
Ewen, David, Kt., 291
Exeter, H., Bp. of, 83, 665
Eydon, Aydon, co. N'hamp., 297
Eyleston, Tho., 102
Eynesham, Abbot of, 192, 193, 194, 338, 372; Miles, 328
Eynstok, co. Oxon., 329
Eyre, Ric., of Leicester, 233
Eythorp. See Eathorp, co. Warw.

FALDE, Ric., 459
Falley, co. Buck., 86, 214
Farnborough, Ferneburghe, co. Berk., 103
Farnborough, Farnborowe, co. Warw., 413, 648
Farnham, Fernham, co. Berk., 122, 123
Faryngton, Edw., 641
Faukenor, Hen., 159, 160
Fels, Tho., of Kenilworth, 395
Fenys, Tho., de Dacre, Kt., 85
Fermer, Fermour, Ric., of London, 495-7
Fermerewe, Edw., 186
Fermore, Laurence, 360, 361
Fermour, Will., 348, 367
Ferneburghe, co. Berk. See Farnborough
Fernham. See Farnham
Ferrers, Lord. See Devereux
——, Edw., 661; his wife, 661
——, Lady Dorothy, 452
Ferres, Edw., Kt., 444, 650
——, Jo., Kt., 434, 650, 653; his son and heir, 434
Fetyplace, Ph., 108
——, Tho., Kt., 124 bis, 125
——, Will., 201
Fewcot, co. Oxon., 362

Feyremare, Tho., 380
Fifield, Fyfeld, co. Berk., 139
Filgrove, Philgrau, co. Buck., 195
Fillongley, Fyllongley, Phyllyngley, Fillingley, co. Warw., 402, 403, 443, 648, 650
Fineshede, Fynyshede, Prior of, 311
Fingringhoo, Vyngrengoo, co. Essex, 220; Darson, hamlet in, 220
Fitzherbert, Nich., 227; Jo., 227
Fitzjames, Jo., 85
Fitzwaren. *See* Bourchier
FitzWaren, Lord, 113, 114
Fitzwater. *See* Ratclyff, Rob.
FitzWilliam, Will., Kt., 268, 269
——. *See* William
Fleccher, Ric., 641
Fleet Marston, Fletemerston, co. Buck., 171
Fletchamstead, co. Warw., 440, 441, 650, 663
Flowy, —, 259
Folkes, Jo., 100
Forbe, Ric., 642
Ford, Ric., sen., 107
Forde, Jo., 143
Fortescue, Adrian, Kt., 143
Foster, —, 124
——, Edm., 353
——, Geo., Kt., 108, 109; his wife, 108, 109
Foston, Rob., 248
Fotheringhay, Fotheryngaye, co. N'hamp., 306
Fowler, Geo., 128
——, Will., 164
Foxcote, Foscote, co. N'hamp., 295; 'Dyggedfeld Lee' and 'Gretefeld' in, 295
Frilford, Frylford, co. Berk., 133, 140
Frogmarton, Geo., 176, 177
Froste, Will., 86
Fulbrook, Fulbroke, co. Buck., 192-4; several messuages in, 193; 'Hichemanyshouse,' 491
Fulscot, co. Berk., 101
Fultrop, Tho., 355
Fulwell, co. Oxon., 366
Furthe, —, 210
Fyfeld, co. Berk. *See* Fifield
Fyllongley. *See* Fillongley, co. Warw.
Fynche, Jo., 119
Fyneux, Jo., Kt., 84
Fynse, Jo., 362
Fyssher, Michael, 470, 471
——, Reg., 140
——, Ric., 306

GALCOTTE. *See* Gawcott
Gardyner, Tho., 329
Garford, co. Berk., 133, 140
Garradon, Abbot of, 231, 235
Garsington, Garsyngton, co. Oxon., 354, 356
Gascoigne, Will., Kt., 405, 648
Gate hampton (Hampton Gay?), co. Oxon., 337, 374; messuage called 'Stapnell' in, 337
Gawcott, Galcotte, co. Buck., 204, 205; field of 'Lechynburgh' in, 205
Gayhurst, co. Buck., 195
Gayton, Jo., 270
Gebons, Tho., 652
Geddington, Gedyngton, co. N'hamp., 310
Gednay, Jo., of Bagenderby, 259
Gifford, Jo., 83
Gilberd, Jo., 83
Gile, Rob., 642
Gilton, Gyldon, co. Oxon., 381
Glapthorn, co. N'hamp., 306
Glendon. *See* Clendon
Gloostone, Gloston, co. Leic., 230; John Coley of, 230
Glover, Jo., of Merivale, 394
Gode, Ric., 378
Godelake, Tho., 107
Goden, Ric., 378
Godewyn, Jo., 175, 176
Godfrey, Ric., 470
Godstowe, Prioress of, 375
Godwyn, Jo., 185 *bis*
——, Tho., 310
Goldington, Goldyngton, co. Bed., 466
Goldyng, Clement, 125
——, Jo., 134
Golston, Jo., 459
Gomeley. *See* Gumley, co. Leic.
Goode, Rob., 101
Goodman, Hamo, 641
Gordon, Lady Katherine, 139. *See* Gorgen (?)
Gorgen, Lady Katherine, 114
Goring, Goryng, co. Oxon., 332-3, 338, 352, 375; Abbot of, 332, 337, 379; Prioress of, 374; 'Squyars' cottage in, 332; 'Brayes' cottage in, 332; 'Fulbrokes' cottage in, 332; 'Lanys' cottage in, 332; the cottage called 'litilhouse' in, 332; 'Lady Grove' in, 352
Gostwyk, Will., 459, 476
Goylyn, Jo., 316, 493, 495 *bis*, 496, 497; Eleanor, widow of, 493, 494, 495
Grace, Tho., 357
Grafton, Graffton, co. Oxon., 370
Grafton, co. Warw., 405 *bis*, 648, 653

INDEX

Granborough, Grenborough, Grendborough, co. Warw., 437, 445, 650, 653
Gray, Will., 661. *See* Grey
Graynfeld, Rog., 83
Great Kimble, Kembill, co., Buck, 205; 'le Mersshe' in, 205
Great Missenden, co. Buck., 212
Great Oakley, Okle Magna, co. N'hamp., 305; 'Oldfald feld' in, 305
Great Wigborough, Moche Wiggborrow, co. Essex., 220; Messyng and Wybbarowe in, 220
Greene, Rob., 649
Greenham, Greneham, co. Berk., 117, 118
Grendon, co. Buck, 163
Grene, Tho., 255, 308; Kt., 283, 284, 286, 287, 293
Grenefeild, Hen., 650
Greneffeld, Ric., 419, 660
Grenewey, Tho., prior of Canons Ashby, 291
——, Tho., 189, 205
Greteham, Will., 206
Grevill, Sir Fouke, Kt., 656
Grey, Jo., Kt., Lord Wilton, 178 *bis*, 179; Lady, *see* Pratt
——, Henry, Lord, of Codnor, 300
——, Will., of Bevington, 409-10, 661; William, son and heir of, 661; Eliz., daughter of, 661
Grosvenour, Ric., 641
Grove, co. Oxon., 328-9; Busbyes House, 328
Grove, Ric., 100
Grubbe, Rob., 249
Gryffyth, Alice, 298
Grymesby, Ric., 340
Grymsdich, Ric., 641
Grymsdych, Pet., 643
Guarradon, Thomas, Abbot of. *See* Garradon
Gumley, Gomeley, co. Leic., 230
Gybbs, Rob., 653
Gyfford, Rob., 470, 473
——, Rog., 174, 192, 193, 194
——, Will., Kt., 85
Gyldon. *See* Gilton

HADDON, —, of London, 137
Hadlond, Simon, 334
Hailey, Hayley, co. Oxon., 345
Hales, Christopher, 495
——, Jo., 459, 479, 482, 647, 656
Hall, Tho., 423, 649
Halle, Tho., 136

Hallesworth, Rob., 427
Halton Holegate, next Spillesby, co. Linc., 259
Halyoke. *See* Holyoaks
Hamden, Will. *See* Hampden
Hamkyns (Hauekyns?), Jo., 140
Hampden, Jo., Kt., 160, 192, 208
——, Ric., 212
——, Hamden, Will., 167 *bis*, 168, 189
Hampstead Marshall, co. Berk., 135; park called 'Casleston' in, 136
Hampstead Norris, Norreys, co. Berk., 110, 137
Hampton, co. Oxon. *See* Gate Hampton
Hampton Lucy, Bysshopshampton, co. Warw., 427-9, 649; 'the Deyrye,' 428
Hampton Poyle, Poyley, co. Oxon., 329, 348
Hamswet, Will., clk., 278
Hankyns, Will., of Coggys, 346
Hanslape, co. Buck., 196
Harbard, Jo., 111
Harborough, Horborough, co. Warw., 423 *bis*, 451, 649, 651, 655
Hardwick, Hardwyk, co. Buck., 182
Hardwick, Hardwik, co. Oxon., 367
Hardyng, Nich., 471
Hardyngton, Will., 367
Harecourt, Margery, 126 *bis*
——, Rob., Kt., 381; Simon, Kt., 381
Harleston, co. N'hamp., 300
Harpenden. *See* Harpsden
Harper, Jo., 465-6, 642
——, Tho., of Merivale, 399, 648
Harpole, Horpoll, co. N'hamp., 300, 303
Harpsden, Harpenden, co. Oxon., 379; Gregory, rector of, 378
Harrowden, Harreudon, Magna, co. N'hamp., 309, 314
Harryngton, Will., 362
Harrynton, Ric., 302
Harrys, Jo., 344
Hartley, co. Berk., 148, 149
Harvy, Haruy, —, 433, 650
——, Geo., Kt., 473, 474
——, Tho., 228
Harwell, co. Berk., 122, 146; Vicar of, 146
Haryson, Ric., 259
Hasilden, Francis, 84
Hasilwode, Edm., 371
——, Tho., 303
Hastinges, Jo., 340
Hastings, Hastynges, Ric., 442, 650
——, Lord, 346
Hastynges, Geo., Lord, 233
—— Geo., 238; Joan, wife of, 238

Hastynges, Lady, 369
Hatte, Matilda, 109
——, Tho., 118
Hatton, Pet., 643
——, Rob., 642
Haward, Edm., Kt., 85
Hawekyns, Jo., 180. (*See* Hamkyns?)
Hawley, Jo., 276
——, Rob., 276; his daughter, Ann Kyrkeham, 276
Hawtre, Tho., 168
Haydocke, Tho., 361
Hayle, Rob., 185
Hayward, Jo., *alias* Clark, 100
Hegges, Will., 345
Helpstone, Helpeston, co. N'hamp., 271 *bis*, 283; messuages called 'Nelysferme' and 'Tyndallysferme' or 'Tyndalysmaner' in, 272, 283
Hely, Ric., 330
Henham, co. Essex, 221
Henley, 86
Henley-on-Thames, 327, 339
Henley, Inquisition dated at, 388
Henne, Tho., 333
Henton. *See* Hinton Waldridge
Henton, Geo., 462
Hereford, C., Bp. of, 84
Heron, Jo., 84
Hert, Geof., 159
Hertford, Monastery of, 290
Herthill, Tho., 448, 650, 653
Heselrige, Tho., 226
Hethe, Baldwin, 451, 651
Heyes, Jo., of Wytnasse, 394
Higham Ferrers, Ferys, co. N'hamp., 289
Hill, Tho., 118
Hillesden, Hyllysden, co. Buck., 203
Hinckley, Hynkeley, co. Leic., 228
Hinton Waldridge, Henton, co. Berk., 128
Hogge, Will., 219
Hoghton, Tho., 641
Hogshaw, Hoggeshawe, co. Buck., 192; several messuages named in, 192-3; houses, &c. in, named, 490-1
Holdynby, Jo., 298
Hollenden, Holynden, co. Buck., 170
Hollier, Holyer, Ric., 448, 650
Holt, Jac. at, 398
Holyoaks, Halyoke, co. Leic., 229
Honingham. *See* Hunningham
Honington, co. Warw., 653
Horborough. *See* Harborough, co. Warw.
Hornby. *See* Conyers, Will.
Horncastle, co. Linc., 256-7
Horncastle, St. Katherine's Guild, 258
Horncastle, Soke of, 255
Horne, Jo., 190; Isabella, wife of, 190-1
Horneby, Harry, Warden of Tateshall College, 248, 250, 255
Horpoll. *See* Harpole
Horsley, Ric., 255
Horspath, co. Oxon., 363
Horton Catermersshe. *See* Cole Orton
Hospital of St. John of Jerusalem in England, 362, 471
——, Thomas Docwra, prior of, 117 150, 192, 194, 200, 294, 295, 429
——, John Kendale, prior of, 492
——, Thomas Weyston, prior of, 492
——, Prior of, 649
Hubbletherne, Geo., 248
Huddon, co. Berk., 136
Huett, Will., 445, 650
Hugford, Jo., 436, 650, 653, 654
Hulcote, co. N'hamp., 284
Huls, Will., 144, 376
Hulse, Tho., 643
Hungerford, co. Berk., 136
Hungerford, Edw., Kt., 84
——, Jo., Kt., 335
——, Lady. *See* Sacheverell
Hunkes, Tho., 660
Hunne, Jo., 136
Hunningham, Honingham, co. Warw., 447, 650
Huntingdon, Earldom of, 238
Hurlston, Jac., 642
Hurlton, Jac., 643
Hurst, co. Berk., 121
Hychyn, Tho., 166, 167
Hyde, Oliver, 135
——, Will., 112, 135, 352, 353
Hyed, Rob., 132
Hyll, Will., 217
Hynde, Geo., 106
Hynkeley. *See* Hinckley, co. Leic.
Hynton, Tho., 124
——, Tho., of Northweston, 369

ICHINGTON, Ichyngton, co. Warw., 446 *ter*, 447
Iffley, Yeftley, co. Oxon., 354, 357, 369
Illmire, Ilmer, co. Buck., 207
Ingelsby, Jo., 199
Ingleton, —, 353
Irchester, Archester, co. N'hamp., 287, 288 *bis*
Irtlingborough, Irtlyngburgh, co. N'hamp., 278
Isam, Eusebius, 288

INDEX

Isbery, Jo., 114
Isham, co. N'hamp., 308
Iver, co. Buck., 190 *bis*, 191 *bis*; messuage called 'Garden Allys' in, 190; messuage called 'Galyhylle' in, 191

JENER, Will., 143
Jerusalem. *See* Hospital
Jesson, Will., 495
Jewetson, Jo., 260
Johnson, Christopher, 464-5
——, Hamo, 641
——, Jo., 248
——, Sir Will., parson of Low Toynton, 257
——, Will., 115
Jordon, Will., 459
Joye, Hen., 470, 473
Justice, Will., 332

KEBULL, Kebyll, L., Alderman of London, 415, 649
——, Kebyll, Henr., 652, 658; his daughter, 652
Kedynton. *See* Kiddington, co. Oxon.
Kelsay, Walt., 255
Kembill. *See* Great Kimble
Kenilworth, Rad., Abbot of, 406, 408-9, 648, 651
——, Will., Abbot of, 410
——, Abbot of, 648, 653, 654
—— -, Canons of, 661
Kennington, Kenyngton, co. Berk., 126
Kent, Earl of, 468, 469
Kentbury, co. Berk. *See* Kintbury
Keto, Edm., 146
Keyt, Will., 102
Keyte, Jo., 103
——, Nich., 144
Kiddington, Kedyngton, co. Oxon., 371
King, the, 464
Kingsbury, Kynngsbury, co. Warw., 449, 451, 650, 651, 653, 654; Nether Holt in, 664
Kingsey, Kyngyshey, co. Buck., 207, 208
Kingston Bagpuze, Kyngeston Bagpues, co. Berk., 134-5; Hygons messuage in, 134; Newbrigg in, 135
Kingswood, Kingeswod, co. Warw., 444, 650
Kintbury, Kentbury, co. Berk., 136
Kirby, Kyrkby, Kyrby, co. N'hamp., 294, 295, 304
Kirkeby Malery, co. Leic., 236
Kirksted, Kirkesteid, Kirkesteyd, Kirsted, Cristede, John, Abbot of, 250, 253, 258
Knapp, Ric., 105

Knighton, Knyghton, co. Berk., 125
Knivet, Knyvett, Knevet, Edw., 423, 652, 658; Ann, wife of, 652
Knoll, patent dated at, 427
Knollys, Rob., 382
Knoston, co. N'hamp., 287, 288 *bis*
Knyght, Jo., 173 *ter*, 183
Knyvett. *See* Knivet
Kovkfold, Jo., 105
Kreke. *See* Crick
Kydevelle, Mich., 107
Kyllyngworth, Rad., Abbot of, 450
Kyng, Will., 470, 472
Kyngeston, Susanna, 134
Kyngyshey. *See* Kingsey
Kynne, Nich., 300
Kyrby. *See* Kirby
Kyrkby. *See* Kirby
Kyrkeham, Ann, 276

LACHEBROKE, co. Oxon., 378
Lambourn, Joan, 162
Lancaster, Duchy of, 206, 207, 228, 257, 359, 405, 424, 461, 473
Lancaster, Edm., Earl of, 136
Lane, Ralph., 192, 193, 491
——, Will., 310
Langenoo, Longnoo, co. Essex, 219; 'Bleynedhall' in, 219
Langford. *See* Clewer
——, Jo., Kt., 149
Langston, Jo., 202, 203
Langton, Ric., 203
Lantowe, Ric., of Dunstable, 463
Lapworth, co. Warw., 442, 650; 'Barnys place,' 442
Latchford, Lacheford, co. Oxon., 380
Lathbury, Lathebere, co. Buck., 196
Launt, Lawnt, Ric., 470, 473
Lavender, Ric., clk., 204; Prebendary of Buckingham and Rector of Gawcott, 204
Lawrens, Will., 459
Layer Marney, Layardemarney, co. Essex, 218; the 'Degrry' [Dairy] in, 218
Lech, Tho., 248
Leckhampstead, Lekehamstede, co. Berk., messuage called Geffreys in, 109
Leckhampstead, Lekehamstede, Lykehamstede, co. Buck., 203, 204 *bis*; 'Ternacres' in, 203
Lee, Jo., 130, 330, 461-2
——, Rob., 162, 170, 171
——, Tho., of Solihull, 394
Leek, Ric., 301
Legh, Jo., Kt., 643
Legyngam, Hen., 159

II.   Y

Leicester, 86
——, Newark College, Collegium Novi Operis, 287, 288-9
——, Richard, Abbot of, 236, 237; John, Abbot of, 228, 236
——. See Wygeston, Rog. of
Leigh, Mr., 161
Leighton, Tho., Kt., 83
Leke, Jasper, 443, 650
Lekehamstede. See Leckhampstead, co. Berk.
Lenam, Hen., 143. See Leynam
Lenthall, Tho., 339, 380, 388
Leukenore, Rog., Kt., 341
Lewes, David, 327
Lewes, Lord, his heirs, 287
Lewse, Ric., 123
Lewsham, Rob., 372
Lewynden, Jo., 106
Leyard Bretyn. See Loyer-Breton
Leycestre, Rad., 643
Leynam, Will., 144 bis. See Lenam
Lidcote, Litilcote, co. Buck., 164, 165, 166
Lightfote, Ric., 644
Lincoln, 248
——, Bp. of, 471
——, Dean of, 84
Lipscombe, Lyscome, co. Buck., 169; messuage called Tornes in, 170
Lisley, Jo., 647. See Lysle
Litilcote. See Lidcote
Little Billing, Lytylbyllyng, co. N'hamp., 297
Little Rollright, Litill Rolleryght, co. Oxon., 328, 372
Little Wigborough, Wydeborrow, co. Essex, 217; 'Copedhall' in, 217
Loge, Geof., 339
Lokke, Jo., 468, 469
London, Bp. of, his servant. See Songer
London, Clerkenwell. See Tate
London, Minoresses at, 'le Menoresses,' 111, 112, 137
Long, Jo., 149; his wife, 149
Long Compton, co. Warw., 415, 649
Longnoo. See Langenhoo
Longthorpe, co. N'hamp., 279
——, Westwode in, 280
Longvile, Jo., Kt., 176, 180, 196, 197, 211
Long Wittenham, Wittnam Comitis, co. Berk., 134
Lookyn, Rob., 344
Lord, Will., 475; Alice, wife of, 475
Lorimer, Ric., 459
Lorkyn, Tho., 159
Louell, Tho., Kt., 84

Louett, Ric., 169
Loughton, co. Buck., 181
Lound, Jo., 260
——, Hugh, 260
Lowe, Ric., 641
Lowick, Luffweke, co. N'hamp., 278
Low Toynton, Tynton Inferior, co Linc., 257
Loyer-Breton, Leyard Bretyn, co. Essex, 219
Lucy, Tho., 656
——, Tho., Kt., 622
Ludgershall, Lutgarshale, co. Buck., 168 bis
Lufweke. See Lowick
Lullyngton. See Lyllyngton
Lussher, Will., 122, 123 bis
Lutterell, Hugh, Kt., 85
Lutterworth, co. Leic., 86
Lyford, co. Berk., 135
Lyford, Jo., 135
Lykehamstede. See Leckhampstead
Lyllyngton Darell, co. Buck., 197, 198
Lyme, Ric.
Lyne, Jo., 362
——, Will., 306
Lyneham, Lynam, co. Oxon., 384
Lyscome. See Lipscombe
Lysle, Jo., 394. See Lisley
——, Jo., Kt., 85
Lytell Rollryght, co. Oxon. See Little Rollright
Lytell Wydeborrowe. See Little Wigborough
Lytton, Rob., Kt., 304
——, Will., 304

MABLY, Jo., vicar of Brodewell, 348
Madynwell, Allen, 25
Magna Rolryght, co. Oxon. See Rollright
Malbourne. See Malvern
Malet, Baldw., 85
Mallett, Tho., 158
Malory, Mallory, Nich., 433, 439, 650; Dorothy, wife of, 650
——, Rob., 309, 310; Joan, widow of, 310
Malthouse, Jo., 100
Malvern, Great, Monastery of, 395-7
——, ——, Prior of, 648
Manceter, Manceter, co. Warw., 398, 399 bis, 648
Manfeld, Rob., 184
Marcham, co. Berk., 140
Marche, Jo., 331
Mareham le Fen. See Cooke, Rob.

INDEX

Mareham-on-the-Hill, Maring of the Hill, co. Linc., 258
Marshall, Will., 160
Marten, Tho., 337, 338
Martin, Ric., 345
Marton. *See* Morton
Martyn, Tho., 374
Mascall, Jo., 159
Mason, Edw., 327
Massy, Thos., 401, 644 *passim*, 648
Mathewe, —, 336
——, Reg., 378
——, Rob., 293, 327
Matson, Tho., 84
Maulden, Maldoun, co. Bed., 463
Mauntyll, Walt., 309
Medley, Will., 407–8, 443, 648, 650, 653
Meis, Rob., 337
Melton, co. Leic., 239 *bis*
Melton, Lady Eleanor, 472, 474
Mentmore, co. Buck., 213; Broughton in, 212
Merbury, Ric., 643
Mercer, Rob., 642
Mere, Jo., 643
Merelake, Marlak, co. Oxon., 363
Meriden, Mereden, co. Warw., 401, 648, 653; Hall, 402
Mernys, Sir Hen., Kt., 218
Merton, co. Oxon., 363
Merydale, Ric., 180
Mewson, Will., of Candilsby, 253
Middelton, Mary, 308
——, Rad., 642
Middle Claydon, Middelclaydon, co. Buck, 174
Mille, Tho., 119
Millett, Jo., 169 *bis*
Milman, Geof., 144
Milton, co. Berk., 132
Milton, Griffith, 330
Miningsby, Mynyngesby, co. Linc., 259, 260
Minster Lovel, Mynster Lovell, co. Oxon., 375
Minting, Myntyng, co. Linc., 253; 'Ravyns Weng' in, 253
Missenden. *See* Great Missenden; Abbot of, 212
Mixbury, Myxbery, co. Oxon., 349
Moche Wygborrow. *See* Great Wigborough
Modentgrace. *See* Mountgrace
Molyners, Jo., 642 *bis*
Monkesfeld, Jo., 642
Montjoye, Will. Blount, Lord, 652; his wife, 652. *See also* Blount

Mordaunt, Jo., 177, 179, 182, 277, 278
——, Rob., 658
——, Will., 85
More, Jo., 660
——, Tho., 86
Morecote, Will., of Leamington, 394
Morgan, Tho., 460–1, 470, 473
Morres, Jo., 306
Morsley. *See* Mursley
Morton, Marton, co. Linc., 251
Morton-Morrell, co. Warw., 652
Mortymer, Geoff., 377
Morys, Jo., 104
——, Walt., 357
Moulsford, co. Berk. *See* Mulford (?)
Moulsoe, Moulsowe, co. Buck., 179
Mountford, Ric., 394, 647
——, Simon, Kt., 485
——, Tho., 438
Mountgey. *See* Blount
Mountgomery, Tho., 290
Mountgrace, Modentgrace, Prior of, 253
Mountjoy, Mongoye, Will. Blunt, Lord, 307, 308. *See also* Blount
Mountney, Nich., 238; Margaret, wife of, 238
Mourton, Tho., 660
Mulford, co. Berk (Moulsford?), 145
Mursley, Morsley, co. Buck., 213
Muston, co. Leic., 240
Myklowe, Jo., 187 *bis*
Mylys, Will., 467, 470
Mynting, Jo., 257
Myntyng. *See* Minting, co. Linc.
Myntyng, Tho., 255
Mynyngsby. *See* Miningsby
Myssenden. *See* Missenden
—— Magna. *See* Great Missenden
Myxbery. *See* Mixbury, co. Oxon.

NANEBY, Navysby, co. Leic., 241
Nanson, Will., Chancery clerk, 426
Napton, co. Warw., 436, 650, 653
Navysby. *See* Naneby
Neuell, Tho., Kt., 84
Nevile, Mich., 125, 196
Nevill, Geo., Lord of Burgavenny, 435
Neuport, Jo., Sergeant at Law, 85
Newbold, co. Warw., vicar of, 428, 649
Newbottle, Newbotill, co. N'hamp., 300
Newenham, Will., Kt., 495
Newes, Edw., 333
Newman, Will., 380
Newnam, Prior of, 467
Newportes, Jo., 218
Newton, Great and Little, co. N'hamp., 305

Newunton, —, 130
Nobill, Alice, 239
Nobull, Jo., 446
Noke, co. Oxon., 335
Nores, Ric., 150
——, Will., 139
Noreys, Jo., 138
Norfolk, Duke of, 380
Norfolk, Thomas, Duke of, 467, 471, 473
Normanton on the Heath, Normanson de la Heth, co. Leic., 231
Norreys, Jo., 109, 110. *See also* Nores
——, Lionel, 101, 102
Northampton, 86
—— Castle, 318
——, Monastery of St. James', 283, 312
——, Sheriff of, writ directed to, 493
Northill, Northell, co. Bed., 467
Northweston, 369
Norton, co. N'hamp., Thorpe in, 296
Norton Brize, Bresenorton *alias* Norton Bruyn, co. Oxon., 365
Norton, Jo., Kt., 85
Norwich, Bp. of, 84
Norys, Ric., 106. *See also* Nores
Noseley, co. Leic., 227
Notley. *See* Nutley
Nuneham, Newnham, co. Oxon., 364
—— Courtenay, co. Oxon., 364. *See* Newnam (?)
Nutley, Notley, Peter Caversham, Abbot of, 159, 160

ODDINGTON, Odyngton, co. Oxon., 361, 367
Odeby, Ric., 230
Odell, Fulk, 201
——, Nich., 473, 474
Odingsells, Odyngelles, Edw., 445, 446 *bis*, 650
Odyngton, co. Oxon. *See* Oddington
Okle Magna. *See* Great Oakley
Okynham. *See* Wokingham
Oldeman, Tho., 378
Opkyns, Will., 132
Osney, Osseney, Abbot of, 356, 366, 376
——, ——, William Burton, Abbot of, 189, 199
Oundle, Owndell, co. N'hamp., 281; Byggyng in, 281; field names &c. in, 281-2; Rectory of, 282
Overwynchenden. *See* Winchendon, co. Buck.
Ovyr, Will., 355, 482
Owen, David, Kt., 414, 648, 655
Owndell. *See* Oundle, co. N'hamp.
Oxford, 'Barasenose' College, 384

Oxford, Lincoln College, 369
——, Magdalen, St. Mary Magdalen College, 122, 254
——, 'Orryale' College, 355, 361
——, St. Frithiswide's Priory, 136, 137, 175, 353, 387
——, Earl of, 198
Oxhill, Oxshelff, Oxshulfe, co. Warw., 414, 648, 655

PACKINGTON, Pakynton, co. Leic., 231
Page, Rad., 644
Pailton, Payleton, co. Warw., 439, 650
Palmer, Jo., 248
Pancost, Will., 459
Pangbourn, co. Berk., 147
Papley, co. N'hamp., 277
Park, Jo., 129, 248
Parker, Brian, 255
Parre, Will., Kt., 310
Parrys, Iennis, of Stobyngpellam, 221
Parsons, Hugh, 301
——, Jo., of Milton, 340
Paston, co. N'hamp., 282
Paton, Will., 459
Paty, Will., 112
Paulet, Will., 85
Paulyn, Will., 255
Payn, Will., 347
Payne, Rob., 340
Pedyngton. *See* Piddington, co. Oxon.
Pek, Silvester, 100
Peldon, co. Essex, 219; 'Newportes in, 219
Percyvale, Jo., 289
Pereson, Will., of Banbery, 435, 650
Perse, Tho., 123
Persons, Pet., *alias* Tanner, 384
Perton. *See* Pyrton
Peterborough, 272, 273, 274, 275; 'le Ferme,' 273; 'Coldam,' 273; 'Incleys,' 273; 'Newclose,' 273; Cemetery, 274; Meldesworth Park, 274
——, Abbot of, 267, 268, 270, 272, 273, 274, 275, 278, 279, 280, 281, 282
Petyte, Tho., 327
Peverel, Fee of, 174
Phelip, Tho., of Staunford, 305. *See* Phylyp
Phelyp, Hugh, 271
Philgrau. *See* Filgrove
Phyllyngley, co. Warw. *See* Fillongley
Phylyp, Tho., 312; Tho., clk., son and heir of, 312
Phylyp. *See* Phelip
Piddington, Pedyngton, co. Oxon., 353

INDEX 709

Pigott, Tho., 162, 163, 164, 165;
   Elizabeth, wife of, 165
Pilsgate, Pyllysgate, co. N'hamp., 279
Pipwell, Abbot of, 305, 308
Planner, Ric., 100
Podyngton. *See* Puddington, co. Chesh.
Pokesley, co. N'hamp., 286
Pole, Will., 644
Polebrook, Polbroke, co. N'hamp., 280
Poley. *See* Pooley, co. Warw.
Polkyn, Simon, 357
Pooley, Poley, co. Warw., 400, 648
Pope, Will., 334
Port, Jo., 647
Portman, Jo., 85
Potcote, co. N'hamp., 283
Poughley, Prior of, 112, 113, 116
Powre, Rob., 164
Powyn, Jo., 368
Poyntz, Rob., Kt., 84
——, Tho., 84
Pratt, Lady Grey, wife of, 178, 179
Preston Bisset, co. Buck., 203
Prichard, Tho., 373
Princes Risborough, Prynces Rysborough, co. Buck., 212
Prince Thorp, Pryncethorp, co. Warw., 436, 650, 653
Priour, Tho., of Ardeley, 350
Pryce, Rob. a, 470, 473. *See* Apryce
Puddington, Podyngton, co. Chesh., 644
Pullyn, Alice, 366
Punter, Hen., 470, 472
Purfrey, Nich., 203
——, Tho., 228
Purston, co. N'hamp., 301 ; several messuages &c. named in, 301-2
Puttvill, Ric., 255
Pygot, Tho., serjeant at law, 278
——, Tho., 212
Pygott, Jo., 202 *bis*
——, Tho., 472
Pyllygsate. *See* Pilsgate
Pyrton, Perton, co. Oxon., 375, 376

QUINCY, Jo., 650
——, Rob., 653
Quyney, Ric., 434

RADFORD, Hen., 641
Radishe, Rob. 643
Radysshe, Ric., 100
Ragesdale. *See* Rakedale
Rakedale, Ragesdale on the Willows, co. Leic., 234
Ralegh, Raulegh, Raughley, Anthony, 408 ; Edw., 648, 652 ; Edw., Kt., 412, 413, 648 *bis*, 654, 656 ; George, 412, 413
Ramston. *See* Ravenstone
Randall, Isabella, 143
Rasse, Rob., 366
Ratclyff, Rob., de Fitzwater, Kt., 84
Raughley. *See* Ralegh
Ravenstone, Ramston, co. Buck., 176
——, Prior of, 177
Rawcitur, Ric., 253
Ray, co. Berk., 120
Raynesford, Jo., Kt., 85
Reading, Abbot of, 149
Reading, Redyng, Jo., Abbot of, 125, 146, 147
Reckerey, Rob., of Tateshall, 249
Rede, Kenelm, 331
——, Rob., Kt., 84
Redegate, Will., 181, 182
Redell, Rob., of Colshill, 394, 647
Redley, Edw., 356
Redmayn, co. Leic., fee of, 240
Remenham, co. Berk., 86, 101
Retherfeld. *See* Rotherfield
Revesby, Abbot and Convent of, 259
Rewley, Rowle, Rugheley, Abbot of, 349, 386
Reydyng, Maria, 358
Reynoldes, Renoldes, Hen., 364, 365
Reyse, Jo., 335
Richerdson, Jo., 257
Richmond, fee of, 464
Ridley, co. Chesh., 644
Rissheby, Jo., 248
Robartes, Will., 288
Robinson, Laurence, 448, 650
Rodbourne, Jo., 437, 650
Roderbe. *See* Rotherby, co. Leic.
Rogers, Hen., 305
——, Jo., 85
Rollright, Great, Magna Rolryght, co. Oxon., 335 *bis*, 383. *See* Little
Ronton, Thomas, Prior of, 445, 650
Rooper, Jo., 84
Roose, Jo., 423. *See* Rouse (?)
Rotherby, Roderbe, co. Leic., 237
Rotherfield, Retherfeld, Greys, co. Oxon., 382
Rotherfield, Retherfield, Pypard, 382-3
Roughton, Rughton, co. Linc., 250, 258 ; Rawes, 251
Rouse, Matilda, 649. *See* Rowse
——, John, 649. *See* Roose (?)
Rowe, Tho., 118
Rowley, Will., of Coventry, 399, 648
Rows, Mawde, 661
Rowse, Matilda, 414-5. *See* Rouse.

Rowse, Tho., 415
Rowtours House, 280
Roxall. *See* Wroxhall
Roys, Jo., 306
Rudde, Jo., parson of Castor, 209
Rufford, Jo., 160, 161, 462-3, 470, 472
Rugeley, Nich., 394, 647
Rughton. *See* Roughton
Rushton, Russhton, co. N'hamp., 308
Russell, Jo., 100
——, Ric., 283
Rychemond, Nich., 378
Rydyng, Jo. at, 159
Ryley, Sim., of Brayleys, 394
Ryton, Ruyton, co. Warw., 430, 649

SACHEVERELL, Ric., Kt., 182, 188, 191, 207, 208; Mary, his wife, Lady Hungerford, 189, 191, 207, 208
St. Benet, Abbot of, 83
St. John. *See* Hospital
Salcot Virle, Salcote Fyrly, co. Essex, 218; the 'Merehowse' in, 218
Salford, co. Warw., 648
Salisbery, Hen., 432
Salisbury, Margaret, Countess of, 146
Salter, Hen., of Stikford, 260
Sambourn, Will., 122, 123
Samburne, co. Warw.; 'Spyne'slyes' in, 662; heath, 662
Samford. *See* Sandford
Sampson, Rob., 119
Samwell, Ric., 367
Sandford, Samford, co. Oxon., 362
Sandhurst, 139; messuages called 'Cokehurst' and 'Crishillys' in, 139
Sandon, Will., of Ashby, 254
Sandys, Will., Kt., 85, 119, 120, 129, 139
Sankey, Tho., 113
Sapcote, Ric., 337
Satwell, Sotwell, co. Berk., 137, 143 *bis*
Saunder, Tho., 255
Saunders, Jo., 108
Saundres, ——, 354
Sawer, Rob., of Tateshall, 249
Scalford, Skalford, co. Leic., 239
Scharpe, 'Esebell,' 219
Scott, Tho., 459
Scotte, Jo., 85
——, Will., Kt., 84
Scrivelby, Screvylby, co. Linc., 251
Scyle, Rob., 459
Sebroke, Rob., 158
Sekinton, co. Warw., 655
Semeon, Rob., 375
Senlowe, ——, 231

Senyor, Gregory, 219
Sesswell Barton, Barton Sharshill, co. Oxon., 337
Sewell, Hen., 211
——, Jo., 212
Sexten, Simon, 335
Seymour, Jo., Kt., 84
Shalston, Shalweston, co. Buck., 203
Shalyngford. *See* Shellingford, co. Berk.
Sharpenhoe, co. Bed.,' 468, 469
Shawe, Will., 642
Sheldon, Will., 658
Shellingford, Shalyngford, co. Berk., 127 *bis*, 128 *bis*; Rector of, 128
Shelswell, Shelleswell, co. Oxon., 349
Shene, Carthusians of, 115
Shepard, Elias, 327, 359
——, Jo., 470, 472
——, Will., 166
Sherp, Tho., 255
Sheymaker, Will., 330. *See* Slemaker
Shiplake, Shypelake, co. Oxon., 352, 378
Shipton Lee, Shibden Lye, co. Buck., 199, 200
Shirford, Shyrford, co. Warw., 451. *See* Thirford
Shirley, Nich., Kt., 657
Shrewsbury, Earl of, 181, 346
——, George, Earl of, 432, 472, 650
Shuckborough, Higher, co. Warw., 410, 648, 653
Shuckborough, Nether, 411, 648
Shugborough, Shukboroug, Tho., 411 *bis*, 436, 650, 653
Shurley, Ralph, Kt., 231, 234
Shuttington, Shyttyngton, co. Warw., 395, 397, 648; 'le Brache' in, 397
Shyfford, Ro., 148
Shypelake. *See* Shiplake
Shyttyngton. *See* Shuttington
Sibford, Sybford, co. Oxon., 363
Skalford. *See* Scalford, co. Leic
Skyllyng, Jo., 84
Slatter, Jo., 124
Slemaker, Will., 371. *See* Sheymaker
Smyth, Ed., 641
——, Hen., of Coventry, 405-6, 648
——, Hen. 431; Walt. son of, 432
——, Hen., 451, 649, 651, 653, 662, 663
——, Jo., of Fletchamstead, 440, 650; Henry, son of, 440, 441, 650; Walter, son of, 441
——, Jo., 104
——, Ric., 168, 169
——, Ric., of Nuneaton, 394
——, Rob., 255

Smyth, Rob., of Low Toynton, 257
——, Tho., 125
——, Tho., 641
——, Walt., 406
——, Will., late Prebendary of Buckingham, 204-5
——, Will., Chaplain of Chipping Norton Chantry, 365
——, Will., 435, 650
Snelsale, Prior of, 213
Snitterfield, Snytterfeld, co. Warw., Rectory of, 428, 649
Solihull, co. Warw., 448, 650
Somerton, co. Oxon., 349
Songer, Ric., 221
Sonning, Sunning, co. Berk., 139
Soolys, Jo., 139
Sotwell. *See* Satwell
Souche, Jo., Kt., 472. *See* Zouche, Sowthe (?)
Southampton, Earl of, 353
Southcot, Southcoote, co. Berk., 135
Southill, Southwell, co. Bed., 474
Southmorton, co. Berk., 143, 144
Southorpe, co. N'hamp.; 'Moche Bette' in, 270; 'litil Bette' in, 270; 'Sowbridge close' in, 270
Southorpe hall, 271
Sowthe, Jo., Kt., 337
Sparsholt, Spersholt, co. Berk., 108, 109; Brodefeldes in, 108
Sparsold Court, Manor of, 113
Speke, Jo., Kt., 85
Spencer, Jo., 285, 286 *bis*, 354, 404-5
——, Jo., of Wormeleighton, petitions of, 485 *et seq*
——, Will., heir of, 403, 648
Spensar, Will., Kt., 657; John son and heir of, 658
Spersholt. *See* Sparsholt
Spicer, Joan, 111
——, Tho., 131
Spore, Ric., rector of Aston Turrold, 145
Spryngold, Tho., 382
Squier, Squyer, Hen., 394, 453, 647
Stafford, Humph., 315
——, Will., 104
Stamford, co. N'hamp., 279
Standley, Jo., of Stikley, 260
Stanes, Tho., of Haltham, 258
Stanford, Staunford, co. N'hamp., 279, 305
Stanley, Jac., 644
——, Will., 644
Stanton, Staunton, St. John, 355
Stanton and Stanton Barey, co. Buck., 210

Stanton, Staunton, Harcourt, co. Oxon., 381
Staunford, co. N'hamp. *See* Stanford
Staunton Harold, co. Leic., 232
Staveley, ——, 259
Staverton, Ric., 138
Staynes, Tho., 255
Staynfeild, Prioress of, 251
Stedeman, Jac., 380
Steeple Aston, co. Oxon., 337
Steeple Claydon, Stepyll Claydon, co. Buck., 200 *bis*
Stevenson, Ph., of Horncastle, 256
Steventon, Stephyngton, co. Berk., 131, 132
Stewkley, Stutley, co. Buck., 166
Stileman, Ant., 84
Stobyngpellam. *See* Parrys
Stok, Hen., 165
Stoke, co. Oxon., 362
Stoke Hammond, co. Buck., 180 *bis*
Stokenchurch, Stokkyng Churche, co. Oxon., 333, 368; 'Sladys' messuage in, 333
Stoke Poges, Pewges, co. Buck., 113
Stoke Talmage, co. Oxon., 368
Stokynchurche. *See* Stokenchurch
Stone, co. Buck., 185, 186
Stone, Hen., 128
Stoneleigh, Stonley, Stanley, co. Warw., 440 *bis*, 441, 450, 651, 654
——, Abbot of, 449, 651, 654
Stoner, Tho., 144
Stannar, Walt., 183
Stonour, Tho., 382
Stony Stratford, co. Buck., 211; messuage called 'Capons' in, 211
Stourton, Will., de Stourton, Kt., 85
Strachen, Jo., 459
Stratford-on-Avon, co. Warw., 653
Stratton Audley, Stretton Awdeley, co. Oxon., 331
Straunge, Robert (le), 422, 649, 652, 658
——, Jo. (le), 423, 649, 652; Margaret, relict of, 652, 658
Strayn, Jo. 335
Streatley, Stretley, co. Bed., 468 *bis*
Streatley, Stretley, co. Berk., 106
Streatly, Stretley, Will. Yong of, 379
Stretly, Jo., 351, 352
Stretton Baskervill, co. Warw., 662
Stretton super Strete, co. Warw., 431-2, 650
Strynger, Matilda, 105
Stuard, Alex., 642
Sturton, co. Linc., 252
Stutley. *See* Stewkley

INDEX

Suffolk, Charles Brandon, Duke of, 129 bis, 141, 142, 145, 146
Sunning. See Sonning, co. Berk.
Sutton, co. Bed., 460 bis; messuage called 'Gibbis' in, 461
Sutton (Coldfield), co. Warw., 664
Sutton Courtney, co. Berk., 141
Sutton, Edw., of Dudley, Kt., 83
———, Jo., 167
Swafeld, Jo., 161
Swinbrook, Swynbroke, co. Oxon., 371
Swyft, Ric., 327
Sybford. See Sibford
Sylby, Will., 184
Symkynson, Tho., of Ashby next Horncastle, 255
———, Rob., 256
Symmes, Rob., 327

TACHBROOK MALLORY, Tachebrooke Malory, co. Warw., 406-8, 648, 653
Tackley, Takla, co. Oxon., 333 : 'Costowe,' 'Fyveten' and 'Gybbyshedacre' in, 333
Taillour, Tayllour, Jo., 385
———, Ric., 386
———, Will., 332
Takla. See Tackley
Talbot, Jo., Kt., 644
Talbott, Will., 332
Tanner, Pet. See Persons
Tape, Jo., 167
Tarlton, Geoff., 642
Tate, Jo., of Clerkenwell, 126
Tattershall. Tateshall, Tatersale, co. Linc., 249 ; 'Woodcroft' and 'Northcroft' in, 249
———, Dean of, 84
———, Warden of, 248, 249, 260, and see Hornby
Tattershall Thorp, co. Linc., 250
Tayllour, Jo., 294, 295
Taylour, Walt., 200
Teilby, Steph., 255
Tewkesbury, Abbot of, 358
Teye, Sir Hen., Kt., 220
———, Thomas, 220
Teyngley, co. Oxon., 372
Teynton, co. Oxon., 357 bis
Thaccher, Will., 123
Thame, Abbot of, 199, 200, 368
———, John, Abbot of, 361
Thellesford, Brethren of the Holy Trinity at, 428
———, Minister de, 649
Thirford, co. Warw., 651. See Shirford

Thirlebeck, Jo., of Tateshall, 249
Thomason, Tho., 653
Thomlyns, Rog., 227
Thorn, Nich., 147
Thornborough, co. Buck., 198
Thorne, Nich., 352
———, Tho., 352
Thorney, Monastery of, 289
Thornhaugh, Thornoo, co. N'hamp., 267
Thorp Underwod, co. N'hamp., 314
Thorpe, co. N'hamp., 296
Thorpe, Will., 120
Thrapston, Trapeston, co. N'hamp., 276
Throgmorton, Geo., Kt., 662
———, Rob., Kt., 450, 651
Tilehurst, Tyleherst, co. Berk., 147
Tillesley, Geof., of Mareham, 259
Tiltey, Tilty, Abbot of, 221
Tirwhit, Will., Kt., 84, 248, 255
Tomson, Will., 255
Tornes. See Lipscombe
Torpell, manor of, 272
Towcester, co. N'hamp., 295
Townsend, —, 468, 469
Towse, Humph., 340
Trafford, Tho., 644
Trapeston. See Thrapston
Traverse, Hamlet, 644
Trenchard, Tho., Kt., 85
Tressam, Ric., 305
Trevanyon, Will., Kt., 83
Trevethen, 81
Trewe, Will., 121
Troutebeke, Will., 644
Trychefeld, Will., 131
Tuchet, Jo., de Audeley, 85
Tumby, co. Linc., 250
Tupholme, Abbot of, 256
Turfrey, Ric., 340
Turges, Rob., 85
Turner, Turnour, Jo., of Coventry, 439, 650
Turney, Jac., 170
Turnour, Sim., clk., 428
Turvey, Tyrvey, co. Bed., 86
Tutbery, Honor of, 232
Twayt, —, 239
Twyford, Tho., 662
Tyches, —, 310
Tyle, Will., 101
Tylehest. See Tilehurst, co. Berk.
Tylley et Goryng, co. Oxon., 338; land called 'Child' in, 338
Tyndail, Ph., 249
Tynley, Jo., 204
Tynton. See Low Toynton
Tyringham, Tyrryngham, co. Buck., 195; messuage called Morton's in, 195

Tyringham, Tyrryngham, Tho., 195
Tythrop, co. Oxon., 369

ULVERSCROFT, Wolcroft, Geof., prior of, 235
Ulygeston, Rog., 459
Umfrey, Ric., 312
Umpton, Tho., 127
Underhill, Tho., 447, 650
Undesdoun, Undesdon, Pet., 346, 365
Upton, Vpton, co. Berk., 107
Upton, Vpton, co. Buck., 189 *bis*
Upton, Vpton, co. Leic., 227
Upton, co. Warw., 412 *bis*, 413, 648, 654, 658
Upton, Will., 107
Upton in Burford, co. Oxon., 344

VAKELYN, Nich., 296. *See* Wakelyn
Valentyne, Jo., 255
Varneham, Ric., 397
Varney. *See* Verney
Vaus, Nich., Kt., 210, 287, 292, 293, 314, 466; Anne, wife of, 287, 292, 293
Venables, Hugh, 643
——, Rob., 643
Verney, Leonard, 350; his wife, 350
——, Ralph, Kt., 174, 186
——, Ralph, junior, Kt., 170, 171
Vernon, Ric., 655
Veyr, Hen., 276, 277
Veysy, Jo., dean of the Chapel, 81, 86, 100, 158, 327, 339, 394, 459, 481, 482, 493, 647
Villars, Jo., Kt., 237
——, Jo., Esq., 237
Vuedale, Will., Kt., 84
Vyce, Ric., 470. *See* Vyse
Vyngrengoo. *See* Fingringhoo
Vyse, Ric., 474. *See* Vyce
Vyve, Will., 133

WADDESDON, co. Buck., 172 *bis*
Wadell, Nich., 470, 473
Wadham, Will., 85
Wakelyn, Nich., 318. *See* Vakelyn
Wales, Principality of, 239
Waleys, Jo., 350
Walker, Hugh, 644
——, Rob., 327
——, Will., 660
Walleron, Alex., 188
Wallingford, land held as of the Honor of, 102, 122, 144, 146, 148, 162, 171, 172, 182, 302, 340, 342, 346, 352, 354, 357, 362, 365, 373, 374, 375, 377, 378, 380, 383. 387
Wallingford, Prison of, 137, 143
Walshe, Agnes, 414, 649
Walter, Rob., 114
– – –, Rog., 208
——, Will., 660
Waltham, Jo., 239
Walton, co. Buck., 180, 206
Walton, co. N'hamp., 267, 268, 316
Walton, Ric., 641
Walton-d'Eivile, -Devyll, -Deivill, co. Warw., 422, 649, 652, 658
Wantage, co. Berk., 108; 'Crokkers in Grove,' 113; 'Dyngollys,' 114; 'Grove,' 114; 'Tulwyke,' 108
Wardern, Jo., 401. *See also* Arden
Wardon, Abbot of, 471, 474
Warfield, Warfild, co. Berk., 138
Wargrave, co. Berk., 138
Warmington, Wermyngton, Papley in, co. N'hamp., 277
Warnde, Rob., 248
Warner, Jo., 459, 469, 470, 648, 655. *See also* Waryner
Warr, De la. *See* West
Warren, Jo., Kt., 658
Warwick, 649, 651, 655
——, lands held 'ut de castro,' 656
——, lands held 'ut de comitatu,' 196, 360, 361 *bis*, 385, 386, 410, 411, 420, 422, 423, 443
——, Booston House, 414
——, College of St. Mary, 443
——, College of, Dean and Chapter of, 650, 655
——, 'Lynelles Feeldes,' 422
——, 'Seynt Mighelles Feldes,' 422
——, Priory of Holy Sepulchre, 649, 655; Robert the Prior, 421
——, Guild of The Holy Trinity and St. George, 420, 649
Waryner, Jo., 412-3. *See also* Warner
Water, Jo., 358, 359
——, Rog., 191, 192
Water Eaton, Water Eton, co. Oxon., 376
Waterpery, co. Oxon., 353
Wattes, Ric., 299
Waymman, Ric., of Witnam, 381. *See* Weynman
Waynflet, Will., 255
Weddington, Wedyngton, co. Warw., 398, 648, 653
Wedon, Rob., 208, 209
Wegeston. *See* Wygeston, Rog.
Welford, co. Warw. and Glouc., 415, 661

II.   Z

Wellys, Jo., 337
——, Lord, 313
Wentworth, Nich., 203, 287
——, Ric., Kt., 83
Wermyngton. *See* Warmington, co. N'hamp.
West, Rob., 333, 368
——, Will., 355
West de la Warr, Tho., Kt., 85
Westhagbourne, co. Berk., 147
Westhenrede, co. Berk., 113
Westminster, Jo., Abbot of, 84
——, Monastery of St. Peter's, 186
West Ilsley, Westyllysley, co. Berk., 102, 103, 122 ; Rector of, 122, 145
West Lockinges, Lokhenges, co. Berk., 115
Weston by Cheryton in parish of Compton, co. Warw., 415, 649, 652 ; (by Barcheston), co. Warw. 658
Weston Favell, co. N'hamp., 298
Westoning, Westnyng, co. Bed., 462
Weston Turville, Turfild, co. Buck., 188
Westsandford, co. Berk. ; messuage called 'Brewmans' in, 125 ; 'Hamys' in, 126
Westwell, co. Oxon., 344
Wetering, co. N'hamp. *See* Wittering
Weynman, Ric., of Wytney, 365. *See* Waymman
Wheatfield, Whytfeld, co. Oxon., 351
Whetmore, Jo., 644
Whitacre, Whitaker, co. Warw., 442
Whitchurch, Whitechurch, co. Warw., 373, 426, 659
Whitlok, Ric., 180
Whitnash, Whitnasshe, co. Warw., 443, 650
Whittyng, Tho., 248
Whitwode, Chitwood, co. Buck., 201
Whore, Jo., 447, 650
Whyte, Jo., 328
Whytfeld. *See* Wheatfield
Wicken, co. N'hamp. *See* Wykedyve and Wykhamond
Wigborough. *See* Little and Great Wigborough
Wigston, Rog. *See* Wygeston
Wigy, Tho., 159
Wilbram, Ric., 644
Wilde, co. Berk., 137, 138
Wilkynson, Ric., 282
Willason, Wylleston in Myxbery, co. Oxon., 349
Willen, Wyllyn, co. Buck., 177
Willey, Wylly, co. Warw., 432, 650
William, Macfitz, 470, 471
Williams, Tho., 279

Willington, Willyngton, Will., 417, 649. *See* Wyllington, Wyllyngton
Willoughby de Broke, Rob., Kt., 85
Willows, Willous, Rakedale et, 234
Wilmott, Jo., 341. *See* Wyllymott
Wilne, Will., 643
Wilton, Lord. *See* Grey
Winchendon, Overwynchenden, co. Buck., 175, 176 ; land called 'Cockstyle' in, 176
Winchester, Ric., Bp. of, 84, 85 *bis*, 107, 138, 345, 347
——, Dean and Chapter of, 380
Windsor family, 135
Windsor, New, 158
Winkfield, Wynkefeld, co. Berk., 130 *bis*
Winster Hundred, co. Essex, 217
Winterbourn, Wynterbourn, co. Berk., 118
Wirehall, Ran., 642 *bis*
Wirley, Cornelius, 648. *See* Wyrley
Wirrall, Wirehall, hundred, co. Chesh., 644
Witney, Wytney, co. Oxon., 365
Wittering, Weteryng, co. N'hamp., 276 *bis*
Wittnam Comitis. *See* Long Wittenham
Woburn, co. Buck., 185 *bis*
——, Abbot of, 473
Wode, Jo. a, 84
Wodebregge, Will., 340
Wodef . . . , Rob., 185
Wodeward, Will, 451. *See* Woodward
Woghton, Joan, 470, 473
Wokingham, Okynham, co. Berk., 139
Wolcroft. *See* Ulverscroft
Wollaston, Wolawston, co. N'hamp., 288
Wolscot, Wollescote, co. Warw., 437 *bis*, 445, 650, 653
Wolson, Wolston, Guy, Kt., 307 *bis*
Wolthamcote, Wolvehamcote, co. Warw., 434 *bis*, 650, 653
Wolverton, Wulverton, co. Buck, 181, 182 *bis*, 211 ; 'Bradwelbye Ferm' in, 210
Wolverton, co. Warw., 443, 650, 653, 655
Wood-Bevington, co. Warw., 661. *See* Bevington
Woodward, Will., 651. *See* Wodeward
Woolhampton, Wolhampton, co. Berk., 150
Woolston, Gt., Wuluierston, co. Buck., 196, 197
Wootton, Wotton, co. Warw., 451, 651
Worcester, Bishop of, 429
Wormleighton, co. Warw., 403-4, 485 *seq.*, 648, 656, 657
Worsley, Rob., 394

Worsley, Will., 402
Wortham, Ric., 103
Worthington, Wrotynton, co. Leic., 232
Wotton, co. Warw. *See* Wootton
Woughton, co. Buck., 180
Wrastlingworth, co. Bed., 464
Wright, Rob., 641, 642
——, Tho., 255
Wrokeston, Prior of, 314
Wrotynton. *See* Worthington
Wroxhall, Roxall, prioress of, 410, 648
Wrygfeyn, Park called, co. Warw., 450, 651
Wy, Tho., 470, 473
Wygeston, Wygston, Wigston, Wegeston, Rog., of Leicester, Kt., 81, 86, 100, 152, 318, 327, 339, 394, 476, 481, 482, 490, 491, 647, 656
Wyghthill, Edm., 141
Wykedyve, co. N'hamp., 285, 286
Wykeley, co. N'hamp., 312, 313
Wykhamond, co. N'hamp., 285, 286
Wyklelyn, Jo., 117
Wylleston. *See* Willason, co. Oxon.
Wyllington, Will., 419. *See* Willyngton
Wylly, co. Warw. *See* Willey
Wyllymott, Jo., 340-1. *See* Wilmott, Wylmott
Wyllyn. *See* Willen
Wyllyngton, Will., 416. *See* Willington
Wylmer, Ric., 430
Wylmot, Hen., 355
Wylmott, Jo., 343. *See* Wilmott
Wynchester, Will., 370

Wyndesore, Andr., Kt., 81, 86, 158, 318, 327, 339, 481, 482
Wyng, Rob., 183
Wyngfeld, Ant., Kt., 83
——, Humph., 83
Wynkefeld. *See* Winkfield, co. Berk.
Wynter, Ric., 354
Wynterbourn. *See* Winterbourn, Berk.
Wyrley, Cornelius, 402. *See* Wirley
Wyse, Jo., 343
Wyse, Tho., 122
Wythed, Hen., 459
Wytney. *See* Witney, co. Oxon.
Wyx, Will., 141

YARNTON, Yarneton, co. Oxon., 386
Yate, Will., 127
Yates, Will., 376
Yattys, Jo., 144
Yatynden, Yatendone, co. Berk., Grove house in, 109; Park in, 110
Yeftley. *See* Iffley, co. Oxon.
Ynkson, Will., 248
Yong, Will., 329
——, Will., of Wyttenham, 329
——, Will., of Stretley, 336, 352, 379
York, Thomas [Wolsey], Archbishop of, 477
Yowny, Will., 336
Yppysden. *See* Ipsden, co. Oxon.

ZOUCHE, Jo., Kt., 463. *See* Souche